STEPHEN F

private empire

PIER
9

To Valsa

CONTENTS

IN ORDER OF APPEARANCE

THE LEADING CHARACTERS

SIR WILLIAM MACPHERSON OF CLUNY AND BLAIRGOWRIE 1926– A retired judge of the High Court of England and Wales; the current Chief of Clan Macpherson

ALLAN MACPHERSON 1740–1816 An officer in the East India Company's army; later often referred to as Colonel Allan and 'the founder of the family'

WARREN HASTINGS 1732–1818 Governor-General of Bengal, later impeached on charges of corruption

JOHN MACINTYRE 1750–1825 Another East India Company officer and Allan Macpherson's best friend; he marries Allan and Eliza Macpherson's daughter, Harriot

JAMES MACPHERSON 1735–1799 A kinsman of Allan Macpherson and John Macintyre; famous as translator or inventor of *The Ancient Poems of Ossian*; often referred to at the time as 'Ossian'

ALEXANDER CHAMPION, DIED 1793 A colonel in the Bengal Army; Allan Macpherson's commanding officer during the first Rohilla War

ELIZA MACPHERSON 1762–1830 Born Eliza Dell Fraser; Colonel Allan's devout and devoted wife

THE MURRAY BROTHERS, JOHN, ALEXANDER AND PETER Good friends of Allan and Eliza Macpherson in Bengal

JOHN MACPHERSON C1745–1821 Member of the Supreme Council and, briefly, Governor-General of Bengal; 'friend' of Allan Macpherson

SHUJA AD-DAULA 1732–1775 Nawab Wazir of Oudh, a formidable warrior; the East India Company's ally in the first Rohilla War

HAFIZ RAHMAT KHAN 1708–1774 The most exalted chieftain of the Rohilla tribes

EDMUND BURKE 1729?–1797 Member of the House of Commons, orator, author, reformer, and the scourge of Warren Hastings

WILLIAM MACPHERSON 1784–1866 Elder son of Allan and Eliza Macpherson, who seeks his fortune in Berbice in the West Indies and later serves as Clerk of the Councils in New South Wales

HARRIOT MACPHERSON 1786–1874 William Macpherson's sister, who first marries Lieutenant-Colonel John Macintyre and later Lieutenant-Colonel Edmund Craigie

ALLAN MACPHERSON 1788–1864 William Macpherson's brother, who follows William to the West Indies and later becomes a clergyman; referred to later in this history as 'Uncle Allan'

ASAF AD-DAULA 1748–1797 Nawab Wazir of Oudh, who succeeded his father Shuja ad-Daula in 1775; famous for his 'dissipation and inattention to business'

HYDER BEG KHAN, DATES UNKNOWN Asaf ad-Daula's chief minister, referred to conspiratorially in Gaelic as *duinne dù*, 'the black man'

DUGALD STEWART 1753–1828 Professor of Moral Philosophy at the University of Edinburgh and a leader of the Scottish Enlightenment

EDWARD SATCHWELL FRASER OF REELIG 1786–1813 A contemporary of William Macpherson in Berbice

COUNTESS, DATES UNKNOWN A slave in Berbice, and William Macpherson's concubine; William renames her Harriot, after his sister

ELIZA WILLIAMS 1807–1837 AND MATILDA WILLIAMS 1809–? Daughters of William Macpherson and Countess

ALLAN WILLIAMS 1810–1896 Son of William Macpherson and Countess; colonial official, sheep farmer, gold digger and family man; always referred to by both his names

JESSY MACPHERSON 1789–1847 Born Janet Chalmers (although she was always known as Jessy); the beloved wife of William Macpherson

ALLAN MACPHERSON 1818–1891 Australian squatter, Scottish laird, politician and 'a man who is never happy without a grievance'

EDMUND CRAIGIE 1784–1850 A retired Lieutenant-Colonel in the East India Company; Harriot Macpherson's second husband

Sir George Gipps 1791–1847 Governor of New South Wales from 1838 to 1846; previously he had served as an army officer in Guiana

William Forster 1818–1882 Squatter, politician and man of letters, and Allan Macpherson's best friend

William Timothy Cape 1806–1863 A schoolmaster in Sydney; Allan Macpherson and William Forster attended his academy

Sir Thomas Mitchell 1792–1855 Surveyor-General of New South Wales, explorer, author and self-promoter; a friend of William Macpherson and his son Allan

Black Charley, died 1848 An Aboriginal Australian, faithful, said Allan Macpherson, 'to the death'

Emma Macpherson 1833–1915 Born Emma Blake; adventurer, writer, mother and always 'dearest Emma' to her husband Allan

Snodgrass Chalmers, dates unknown The late Jessy Macpherson's nephew; a young man with a big thirst

Ellen Egan, dates unknown William Macpherson's devoted housekeeper in Sydney; a widowed lady

William Charles Macpherson 1855–1936 Allan and Emma Macpherson's eldest son, known as Willie; a long-serving civil officer in British India

Allan Williams 1840–1931 Second son of the first Allan Williams, and the second to carry that name; Australian bushman and horseman

Charles Cowper 1807–1875 New South Wales landholder, politician and several times Premier; universally known as 'Slippery Charlie'

James Martin 1820–1886 New South Wales lawyer, politician and Premier; Allan Macpherson's 'bitterest enemy'

George Ridding 1828–1904 Head Master of Winchester College; regarded by many as the school's 'second founder'

Alan David Macpherson 1887–1969 Army officer and the Chief of Clan Macpherson; father of Sir William Macpherson of Cluny

Allan Crowther Williams 1889–1976 Second son of the second Allan Williams; cattleman and horse breeder in Queensland, always known as Crowther

THE MAIN PLACES

IN SCOTLAND

Badenoch 'Macpherson country'; once a county in Inverness-shire
in the Scottish Highlands, including the villages—now
towns—of Kingussie and Newtonmore

Blairgowrie A village and estate in Perthshire at the foot of the
Grampian Mountains, where the Highlands and Lowlands
meet; now the second largest town in Perthshire

IN INDIA

Calcutta The seat of the East India Company's activities in Bengal;
now known as Kolkata

Oudh A princely state north-west of Bengal; later known as
Awadh, and now part of the state of Uttar Pradesh

IN ENGLAND

London A staging post on the way to Scotland

Winchester A town, now a city, 100 kilometres south-west of London;
the location of Winchester College

IN THE WEST INDIES

Berbice A Dutch and then British colony on the northern coast
of South America; with Demerara and Essequibo, part of
Guiana, now known as Guyana

Stabroek The principal town in Demerara and main port for the three
colonies of Guiana; name changed to Georgetown in 1813

IN AUSTRALIA

Sydney The capital of the colony of New South Wales

Keera A squatting run about 550 kilometres north of Sydney, on
the western slopes of the Great Dividing Range

Mount Abundance Another squatting run, about the same distance
from Keera as Keera is from Sydney; now the site of the
town of Roma in Queensland

Nebo A small town in Queensland near properties owned by the
Williams family, about 1000 kilometres north of Brisbane

1

PORTRAITS

SIR WILLIAM MACPHERSON OF CLUNY, RECENTLY RETIRED AS A JUDGE of the High Court of England and Wales and now living permanently at his family home in Scotland, was looking forward to golf, fishing, playing with his grandchildren and performing congenial duties as Chief of his Clan, when his plans for a leisurely retirement were interrupted by a phone call.

'It's Derry Irvine', his wife Sheila called out.

Sir William came in from the garden, took the phone, and listened to a proposal that Lord Irvine, the Lord Chancellor, put to him. Hanging up the receiver, he looked at his wife blankly. 'He wants me to chair the inquiry into the Stephen Lawrence case.'

'What did you tell him?' asked Lady Macpherson.

'I said I'd think about it—but I could hardly pretend to be enthusiastic. You know what these sorts of inquiries are like—inevitably thankless, and they rarely achieve anything. This one's sure to be a poisoned chalice.'

'But you *must* do it', she responded. 'It's your duty.'

A week later Sir William was on the train from Perth to London for discussions with the Lord Chancellor and the Home Secretary, Jack Straw, reading various documents that Irvine's office had sent him and reflecting on why the Stephen Lawrence case was so widely perceived as an appalling miscarriage of justice.

The essence of the case was known to everyone in Britain who read the headlines. Late one evening in April 1993, Stephen Lawrence, an eighteen-year-old black man, born in London to Jamaican parents, was waiting at a bus stop in the south-eastern suburb of Eltham, peering towards an approaching bus and hoping its route number would tell him that it would take him home. His friend, standing several metres away, called out, 'Can you see it?' Suddenly, Stephen was set upon by half a dozen white youths shouting, 'What? What? Nigger!' One of the whites took something from his jacket and stabbed Stephen twice—once through the shoulder and once through the lung. Struggling to his feet, Stephen ran about 200 yards, bleeding profusely. The police and an ambulance arrived, but within twenty minutes of the stabbing he was dead.

Everyone who kept up with the news also knew what followed: the botched police investigation, the parents' courageous quest for justice, the failed prosecutions, the continued recriminations. Four years later, with no one behind bars and the press demanding action, Tony Blair's Labour Opposition promised if elected to pursue the matter. Labour won office in June 1997 and acted quickly, announcing an inquiry into the murder and its aftermath, with the object of learning how racially motivated crimes could be better handled. The inquiry would no doubt be demanding. Its Chair would have to be expert in criminal law, highly efficient and of unquestionable integrity. Sir William Macpherson, recently retired, was an obvious choice for the job.

The public hearings began in March 1998, gathering evidence from witnesses to the murder, police officers and the alleged perpetrators, much of it harrowing and sensational. The 11,000 pages of transcripts were soon condensed in a play, *The Colour of Justice*, that ran to appreciative reviews in the West End. Sir William, who was assisted by three distinguished advisers, eventually delivered his judgment in February 1999. That judgment, said the Police Federation of England and Wales, was 'the most searing indictment of policing ever published'. According to the BBC, many people regarded it as 'a defining moment in British race relations'.

Sir William was never one to seek publicity; yet here he was in the spotlight of public attention and marked for a place in popular histories. The intense press scrutiny was tolerable only as an unavoidable part of doing the job. But he saw nothing unusual in being caught up in events of long-term historical significance. His family had been doing it for centuries.

So, of course, had many families. What distinguished the Macpherson family is that they left a detailed record of their activities, so that each generation could look back on its predecessors and reflect on their collective past. Sometimes, as in the case of Sir William and the Stephen Lawrence case, a family member contributed to large and small episodes relating to the history of Britain and its empire. At other times, their lives provide a window on the times and places in which they lived.

Two and a half centuries before Sir William was asked to chair the Stephen Lawrence inquiry, his ancestors were caught up in another defining moment in British history. In 1745 the Young Pretender, Bonnie Prince Charlie, returned from exile in France, determined to overthrow the Hanoverian King of Great Britain and Ireland, George II, and restore the House of Stuart to the monarchy. He and his ardent followers, the Jacobites, made quick gains, taking Edinburgh and then marching into England. But their support was failing. Irresolute and divided among themselves, they withdrew to Scotland, losing men along the way, but still strong enough to defeat the King's forces at Falkirk Moor, west of Edinburgh.

The Battle of Falkirk was fought at dusk in mud and heavy rain, and lasted just twenty minutes. Neither side could claim much glory; and so great was the confusion that for a while neither was sure which had won. When the bodies were counted, it appeared that the Jacobites had lost some fifty men, the Hanoverians many more. Among the Jacobites' list of dead was one William Macpherson, Purser of his Clan, the great-great-great-great grandfather of the present Sir William.

The Jacobites moved north, struggling with internal dissensions and undecided about what to do next. In the meantime, the Hanoverian army gathered strength under the King's son, the Duke of Cumberland. The opposing forces met at Culloden Moor, a few miles east of the town of Inverness; and there, on 16 April 1746, Bonnie Prince Charlie's forces were put to rout, leaving at least a thousand clansmen dead on the battlefield and ending any real prospect of a Stuart restoration. Cumberland's men then went on a campaign of pillage and slaughter, bent on punishing all who had supported the uprising and rooting out any remaining resistance to the King's rule.

Several weeks later and 50 miles or so to the south, the rampaging troops set fire to a new mansion belonging to the Chief of the Macpherson Clan. As the redcoats moved on to their next object of vengeance, young Allan Macpherson, the elder son of William who died at Falkirk, and aged just five or six, hurled stones in their direction. Presumably his stones did not hit their target, or his descendants might not be around to tell the story.

Stories are part of what holds a family together. It does not much matter whether outsiders regard them as true or false, so long as family members believe in (rather than simply believe) the legend. Allan Macpherson is understood to have told the stone-throwing story himself and it survived through frequent retelling until 1896, when it was first recorded in a family document. It might be apocryphal. The Macpherson Clan were lucky or unlucky enough to miss the actual battle of Culloden, so the story might have been invented by Allan or one of his descendants to confirm the family's Jacobite credentials. Yet even if this were so (which I doubt), it is firmly welded into the family's tradition, a link between present and past, between one generation and the next.

There are other links that bind the Macpherson family across the generations—an amalgam of heritage and inheritance, tangible and intangible legacies, oral tradition and written records. They include, most obviously, the family name. This stood, and still stands, for respectability, solidity and continuity. It was, and is, something to be warmly defended (and not just by the men in the family). Personal names served a similar purpose. From the 1780s, Macpherson parents followed the tradition especially common in Scotland of naming their children after their own parents, so that the first-born boys (or only sons) of seven generations, from William Macpherson who died at Falkirk to the present Sir William, are all called either William or Allan (except that in 1857 Allan and Emma Macpherson, sweltering in the Australian bush, had a rush of blood to the head and decided that their second-born son should be Alan rather than the more familiar Scottish spelling of Allan, and later generations followed their lead). The tradition has lately been maintained into a ninth generation, with the birth and baptism of another William in 2004.

Then there is the family's association with the land, its sense of belonging to a particular place. The Macphersons had a dual allegiance: to Badenoch, the ancient Highland country of the Macpherson Clan, where young Allan took his stand for the Jacobite cause; but also to the Perthshire estate of Blairgowrie, at the foot of the Grampians, which he purchased in the 1780s and which remains the family home today. When Blairgowrie was transformed by cotton mills from village to town, the family was remembered in the street names: Allan Street, William Street and so on. Most deceased members of the family are buried in the family plot in the local parish churchyard.

The Macphersons, when they were in Scotland, lived sequentially in two houses. More precisely, they first occupied one, soon moved to a new one close by on the Blairgowrie estate, then returned three generations later to the original. Houses, especially big ones, are repositories of memories and memorabilia: a sofa brought from India, a painting struck by lightning in Sydney, a ceremonial spade and wheelbarrow used to open the railway line to Blairgowrie; and of course the photographs and portraits, each significant in its own right, but together confirming the strength of the family's associations with its past.

A house with room to store things also encourages holding on to written records. Allan Macpherson, the stone thrower, spent much of his career in India; and there, in the 1770s, he began to keep all his letters and papers, private and official, ranging from letters to governors and nawabs to an order for a saddle. Later generations followed his example. Many families can document their histories back a few generations, sometimes through records held by the family, sometimes through public collections. A few, including the Macphersons, retain such detailed records that many of the experiences and attitudes of one generation are communicated on paper to the next. The Macphersons did not just keep the family records—they read them, sometimes commenting on them, sometimes censoring them, and sometimes alluding to the similarity of events past and present.

Other links are harder to define. They include the values and attitudes that are passed by word or deed from parent to child, and which, like family heirlooms, might fade with age or be cast aside, or might be refurbished, passed on to the next generation, and accorded greater respect. More elusive still are the physical and mental attributes—patterns of behaviour and thought—that are handed down, often unknowingly, from parents to their children, the specific characteristics that are written into each family's DNA. Can we ever know how much we owe our forebears?

Sir William Macpherson relaxes in his sitting room with his customary aperitif, a Manhattan, described by those who know as a drinking man's cocktail—strong, urbane and simple—which seems quite appropriate, as Sir William is a forthright man, unfailingly courteous, with no nonsense about him. He is reading the later chapters of this book—not, of course,

Sir William Macpherson of Cluny and Blairgowrie, November 2009. KEATHBANK PHOTOGRAPHY

as you are reading it, elegantly designed and bound between firm covers, but as a draft, with wide margins so that he may scribble comments.

It is fitting that he read the book before you do, as it tells his family's story. Many years ago, when he was still a High Court judge, he thought he might write the story himself. During breaks from the bench he removed hundreds of bundles of letters and papers from the boxes where they had been stored, sometimes for several generations, and carefully unfolded and flattened each document, pausing to read many of them along the way. Then, on the advice of a professional archivist from the National Register of Archives in Edinburgh, he placed the bundles in acid-free envelopes and boxes, converted part of the barn into a records room, and looked forward to returning to them after retirement. But golf, fishing and other pleasures and responsibilities got in the way; and the all-consuming Stephen Lawrence inquiry eventually diverted him from what he knew would be a huge undertaking.

So I am the happy (and accidental) beneficiary of his frustrated enthusiasm. Which means that the story is different. Self-evidently, an outsider approaches a family's story from another direction and with other eyes, readier perhaps to look beyond the family portraits to what was happening in the background. For me, this is not so much the story of a family as a narrative of empire, centred on the lives of a single family.

The range of my vision is limited by their travels and experiences; but it is extended by the opportunity to place their lives in circumstances which they took for granted. Grand themes relating to family, race and empire compete with their individual lives—or rather, the themes and the lives complement one another, so that one throws light on the other. Were they mostly steered and buffeted by events and circumstances beyond their control? Or were they in positions to shape their own destinies and the lives of others, perhaps even to influence the broad course of history?

Sir William, as he turns the pages of my draft and offers an encouraging word to Treacle, the elderly Labrador at his feet, is surrounded by his ancestors, the people who are at the centre of his and my story. Here he is with his father, Brigadier Alan Macpherson, along with evidence of his youthful prowess as a shooter. (Seventy years or so later, Sir William still has no problem controlling the rabbits in the paddocks around his home.) As he was born in 1926, the photograph appears to have been taken in the mid-1930s, probably by his mother Catharine. We meet her and his other female ancestors too—but I will introduce them when each arrives in the story. For the moment, we concentrate on six men, each the first-born (or only) male in the family, who carried forward the Macpherson of Blairgowrie name and who give continuity to the family's story.

As Sir William is a most unpretentious man, I should introduce him to you as Bill. Admittedly, he lives in a castle—but it is a small castle, with narrow spiral staircases, living rooms that are better described as cosy than grand, and a labyrinthine arrangement of several modest bedrooms. There is nothing comparable to the vast ballrooms that we might associate with stately mansions; when the Clan descends for the occasional celebration, they dance in the barn, adjacent to the records room.

Bill in 2009 is eighty-three, but young for his age. The usual epithet applied to energetic people over seventy is 'sprightly'; but this does not seem right. He is as fit and healthy as most people twenty years younger, apart from a bout of back pain (which he claims to have cured by dancing an energetic Scottish reel) and a recent operation to remove a hernia. Longevity runs in the family: all five of his patrilineal ancestors lived beyond seventy, and three of them into their eighties. Several women in the family were also long livers, though not Sheila, his wife of over forty years, who died suddenly in 2003. Now he has a thoroughly modern relationship with Hilary, the widow of Lord Burnham, who was, before her marriage in

A young Bill (now Sir William) Macpherson with his father Brigadier Alan Macpherson (1887–1969) at Blairgowrie in the mid-1930s.

1955, a favourite reel-dancing partner of Bill's. They met again after half a century and now commute regularly between Blairgowrie and Beaconsfield in England, and sometimes travel together to Clan functions abroad.

While I introduced Sir William as Bill, Clan members know him as Cluny, the name traditionally given to the Chief of the Clan. The Clan means a lot to him, and he gives it much attention. As the twenty-seventh hereditary Chief, he presides over annual gatherings at Badenoch and visits enthusiastic branches in other parts of the world. He likes ritual and respects tradition, though with a touch of whimsy: as a member of the Royal Company of Archers, he stood near Her Majesty during ceremonial occasions in Scotland, always ready, he says, to defend her with his bow and arrow.

Like his father and grandfather before him, Bill Macpherson was educated in England, in his case at Wellington College in Berkshire. He joined the Second World War towards its end, as an officer in the Scots Guards, in time to acquire a fund of good stories. He might have pursued a military career in peacetime, but headed instead for Trinity College, Oxford, and then to the Inner Temple, where he was admitted as a barrister in 1952. He became a Queen's Counsel in 1971 and was a judge from 1983 until his retirement in 1996. Despite a busy life in the law, he retained a hankering for the military, serving as commanding officer of a Territorial Regiment of the Special Air Service during the 1960s and later as the Regiment's Honorary Colonel. He also retained, and still retains, a military bearing and efficiency, though without a hint of the superiority that some senior officers carry into retirement.

Bill's father, Alan David Macpherson, figures least in this story—not because his life was uneventful or unrevealing, or even because he wrote fewer letters, but rather because he was less careful than his forebears in keeping the record up to date. He was a military man, whose career was shaped by the two world wars. During the Great War he served with distinction on the Western Front, emerging unscathed except for what he dismissed as 'punctures in the legs'. Retiring from active service a Brigadier in his mid-fifties, he threw himself into service with the Home Guard and domestic life at Blairgowrie. In 1966, when two Chiefs of Clan Macpherson died within a year, leaving no direct successor, the lineage was traced back beyond Culloden and forwards to the retired Brigadier, who became twenty-sixth Chief of the Clan.

Pictured opposite is the future Brigadier with his own father, another William. Middle names might help remove any confusion, but only the three most recent have them. This William was William Charles—but he was rarely known as such, except in official documents; among family and close friends he was known as Willie—an endearing name for a gentle man, and one that we will use to distinguish him from his namesakes. He shares with his son Alan David and grandson Bill facial characteristics: broad forehead, well-defined eyebrows, strong nose and chin, thin lips (well disguised in this portrait), and clear complexion. They and their three male ancestors are all above medium height, upright (even in old age) and (with a single exception) trim.

William Charles (Willie) Macpherson gave most of his life to the Raj, spending nearly thirty years there during the heyday of empire. In retirement, he worked through the family papers, especially those of his own great-grandfather, who had spent over twenty years in India a century earlier, and eventually published a book which includes extracts from his ancestor's papers. He died in 1936, when Bill Macpherson was ten. Bill remembers him well as a kind old man, bookish and reserved. If we describe the current Sir William as 'the judge' and his father Alan as 'the Brigadier', we should then identify William Charles Macpherson as 'the scholar'.

William the scholar's father, Allan, was anything but reserved. He began life in 1818 in a tub of whisky—a story Bill likes to recount, but that I will hold for a later chapter. At the age of ten Allan accompanied his parents to New South Wales, acquired a colonial education, and in

Alan Macpherson (1887–1969) with his
father William Charles (Willie) Macpherson
(1855–1936), in about 1890.

'The scholar': William Charles
(Willie) Macpherson (1855–1936),
probably painted in the 1930s.

due course set out to become a 'squatter', grazing sheep and cattle on
the remote frontier. Abandoning squatting, he was elected to the colony's
new Legislative Assembly, where he once took to a fellow member with
a horsewhip. In later years, when the portrait on page 20 was painted, he
travelled restlessly between New South Wales and Scotland, where he
eventually settled, nurtured his several children, and applied his formidable
talents to growing strawberries and establishing his family's pedigree.

Allan 'the squatter', ambitious, rebellious and temperamental, was
a constant cause of worry to his father, William. This William was born
in India in 1784 during the time of Warren Hastings, accompanying his
parents to Scotland at the age of three. Forced into the world to seek
his fortune, he spent over a decade growing cotton in the West Indies,
just as the slave trade was abolished. Later he secured an appointment as
Collector of Internal Revenue in New South Wales, then as clerk of the
local legislature, which he served for twenty-four years. We might refer to
him as 'the planter'; but given that his experiences in the West Indies were
disastrous, he would probably prefer to be called 'the clerk'.

'The squatter': Allan Macpherson (1818–1891). Oil by an unknown artist, probably 1850s.

'The clerk': William Macpherson (1784–1866). Oil by James Anderson, 1860.

This portrait was presented to him by members of the Legislative Council at the time of his retirement: a Sydney reporter described it as 'a faithful likeness'. William was pleased with it, except that the artist had portrayed him without his wig, which was later restored to its rightful place at his request. Here again are the familiar Macpherson forehead, nose and chin. Aged seventy-six, William appears to have lost his teeth— but certainly not his faculties (except, said his son Allan, in relation to one infuriating particular). He died at his son's residence near Sydney in 1866, having lived in New South Wales for more than thirty-six years.

William the clerk's father, Allan, we have already met, as a young lad throwing stones at the redcoats after Culloden. His career took him first to the Americas during the Seven Years War, then to India, and back to Scotland, where he purchased the castle where we find his portrait now hanging. It was painted in Calcutta early in 1782 by John Thomas Seton at a cost of around £40. We can only guess how well the artist captured the man—a later critic suggests that all Seton's portraits were 'somewhat stolid and banal'. Allan in his early forties looks opulent and satisfied with himself, as well he might: he had been recently promoted to the rank of Lieutenant-Colonel in the service of the Honourable East India Company; and he had just married a young lady much admired for her beauty and accomplishments. Unlike his successors, he appears portly (a few years later a close friend described him as fat); but he shares with them the Macpherson forehead, nose and chin. Today his descendents know him as Colonel Allan, or simply as 'the Colonel'.

At the time his portrait was painted, Allan Macpherson was looking forward to a good year. Six months earlier, though, when we begin this imperial story, his future was much less promising.

'The Colonel': Lieutenant-Colonel Allan Macpherson (1740–1816).
Oil by John Thomas Seton, 1782.

2

....

PROSPECTS

CALCUTTA 1781. MAJOR ALLAN MACPHERSON STEPS INTO his palanquin, instructing the head bearer to convey him to Government House, forthwith. Several peons run ahead to clear the way—past the palatial two- and three-storey residences that stand as a vexing reminder that some of his fellow officers on the civil and military side have amassed vast fortunes in India; around the corner at the Council House, where the Supreme Council endeavours to regulate the affairs of Bengal and beyond; and into the expanse of Esplanade Row, where an assortment of carriages, carts and palanquins weave and lurch among pedestrians, cows, horses, camels and the occasional elephant. Changing their positions and adjusting their dhotis without missing their stride, his wiry bearers convey him in a comfort and style measured to his rank and dignity as an officer of the Honourable East India Company.

Yet his mind is not at ease. Several times—more than he likes to count—he has hinted to the Governor-General, Mr Hastings, that his long and faithful service to the Company merits some form of promotion; and that although he has lately been elevated (by virtue of seniority) to the rank of Major, this falls far short of what he and friends consider his due. Mr Hastings has acknowledged the justice of his claims and repeatedly professed his readiness to serve him. More than that, he has promised to promote him to this or that situation just as soon as it should become vacant.

Promises, fair promises ... Macpherson fears they are worth nothing. For four years now he has been dancing attendance on Mr Hastings 'to no earthly purpose, except fresh matter of vexation every five or six months, by seeing the places promised myself given away to others'. Yet he is obliged to be patient and appear grateful for promises that never materialise.

The old court-house and writer's building, Calcutta. Allan Macpherson lived about half a mile from here, and might well have passed the artist, Thomas Daniell, as he sketched one of his dozen images of life in Calcutta. Etching, coloured, with aquatint, 1786. BRITISH LIBRARY

....

So as he gently bounces along Calcutta's vast and muddy Esplanade in mid-1781, Allan Macpherson steels himself to confront Hastings in what might be a final chance to add to his modest fortune. There is a straw to clutch at in Assam, a province north-east of Bengal, and currently beyond the Company's sphere of influence. Macpherson's friend, Captain Macintyre, has heard a whisper that the young prince who has lately succeeded as Rajah of Assam had been pressing the Company to bolster his precarious rule, promising generous rewards in return. If the Governor-General determines that the Company should come to the

Rajah's aid, the officer who leads such an enterprise might well make a few lakhs of rupees—say £30,000—a sum sufficient to transform Macpherson's world. Trying hard not to sound querulous, he presents the idea to the great man—who responds that he is as much likely to send troops to China as he is to Assam. Undeterred, Macpherson remarks that the office of Quartermaster General has lately become vacant, and reminds Mr Hastings that he has already acknowledged his claim to this position. The Governor-General answers with further expressions of goodwill, but once again intimates that the time is not ripe.

Major Macpherson takes his leave of Mr Hastings, steps into his palanquin and resolves once and for all to quit India and retire to his native Scotland.

BADENOCH

In 1781 Allan Macpherson had been absent from home for twenty-four years, excepting a two or three month interlude in 1763 when he passed through Scotland on his way from one hemisphere to the next. The Highlands were still fresh in his memory, partly because he and his fellow Scots, who made up a fair proportion of the Company's servants in Calcutta, so often gathered around the supper table, recounting nostalgically the adventures of their childhood and youth. Macpherson well remembered his last stand for the Jacobite cause, when he had thrown stones at the Hanoverians after they had burned the Macpherson Chief's new mansion at Cluny. He remembered too his early years in Badenoch, the picturesque stretch of land in the central Highlands, extending for more than 30 miles along Strathspey, the broad valley of the Spey River, bordered by rugged mountain ranges on the west and east, and populated by numerous small settlements of tenant farmers. This was Macpherson country, many of whose inhabitants shared the same surname and called one another 'cousin'. Snow-covered in winter, and glowing with heather in the warmer months, this was the place Macphersons were most likely to mean when they talked among themselves about 'home'.

Long before Allan Macpherson's birth in 1740, the traditional clan system, characterised by obedience to the chiefs and rivalry among clans that often erupted into warfare, was fraying at the seams. This process was hastened after the Jacobite uprising of 1745, when the King's ministers in London decided that the best way of keeping potential rebels in line was by annihilating the clans entirely. This they endeavoured to do by banning the carrying of arms, playing of bagpipes and wearing of tartan. But these and even sterner measures failed to weaken the bonds of kinship and the shared sense of attachment to places and landscapes that had been passed down over many generations. So when Allan Macpherson was left an orphan at the age of five or six, there was no question that he would be well looked after within his extended family, and given the care and affection that were his due as a member of the Macpherson Clan and a relative of the Chief.

Allan, together with his brother John, who was a year or two his junior, appear to have enjoyed a happy childhood: first in the care of their maternal uncle and his wife who lived in Strathmashie, towards the upper reaches of the Spey; and then with their maternal aunt and her husband and their children near the settlement of Ruthven, two days' walk away. Ruthven was remarkable then, as it is now, for being dominated by the ruins of a military barracks, built over several years from 1718 to keep the locals in order, but burned down immediately after Culloden by the Jacobites in a final, futile act of defiance.

Travelling along Strathspey between the homes of their two uncles, the brothers passed the ruins of Cluny House and the rugged peak of Creag Dhubh, the black rock, where the Clan Chief, Ewan Macpherson of Cluny, had one of his hideouts. Cluny, as the Chief was known, had been in hiding ever since Bonnie Prince Charlie, after the rout at Culloden, had told his followers that the Jacobite cause was lost and had urged them to save their own skins. The government reckoned Cluny a formidable opponent, and put a bounty of 1000 guineas on his head—but such was the loyalty he commanded among his fellow clansmen and women that the money remained unclaimed. Evading capture for nine years, in 1755 he eventually escaped to France. In the meantime, the valley was infested with redcoats, with a detachment in almost every town, serving as an odious reminder of the weight of the Hanoverian yoke.

At Ruthven, Allan and John Macpherson attended the local school, along with other boys of their age, both rich and poor. Equal access to education for young men was a privilege and entitlement that gave young Scots a distinct advantage over the English when they went out into the world. All their teaching was in English—although they learned enough Gaelic in their homes and villages to speak and write with reasonable fluency, sufficient at least to be able to converse privately among themselves without fear of any English eavesdroppers taking

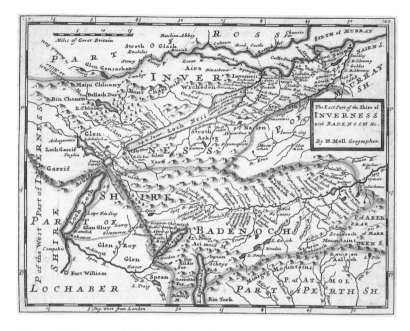

Herman Moll's map of 'The East Part of the Shire of Inverness with Badenoch &c.', published in London in 1745. Allan Macpherson as a child walked through the valley of the Spey, visiting many of the villages shown on the map. For a time he lived with his brother John and cousin James near the military barracks of Ruthven, which were torched by the Jacobites the year after this map was published. NATIONAL LIBRARY OF SCOTLAND. The map below locates the region in Scotland. PHOTOLIBRARY

their meaning. One of their cousins, the fair-haired James, took particular delight in Gaelic stories, and together the three boys listened to the local *seanachaidhs*, the storytellers, recite ancient ballads and recount tales of a heroic past. James, four years older than Allan, was a lively lad, convivial and sharp-witted, with a keen eye to his own prospects in life. He left Ruthven in 1752 to attend university in Aberdeen, returning a few years later to teach at the local charity school and then as a private tutor. Allan looked up to his older cousin, and rated him a particular friend.

Growing up in Badenoch uplifted the spirit and nourished the soul. But beyond that, its hills and valleys had little to offer young men looking to get ahead in the world. The earth, by the standards of the Highlands, was fertile—but even had their father been living, there would have been nothing for Allan to inherit, for supporters of the Jacobite cause had lost their lands when their rebellion failed. Fortuitously, just as he might have been contemplating how to gain his own livelihood, the wider world imposed itself on Badenoch; and all of a sudden, early in 1757, Allan found himself in military uniform in the service of the King.

How could this be? Just a decade earlier many Highlanders, including most of Badenoch, had regarded the English (along with most Lowland Scots) as bitter enemies; and since then they had been forced to endure sometimes savage repression by an army of occupation. Conversely, many Englishmen in positions of influence abhorred the Highland Scots as barbarians: untrustworthy, and potentially rebellious.

The puzzle is mostly explained by squabbles and skirmishes between Great Britain and France that erupted into war in 1756. This conflict, which later became known as part of the Seven Years War, is sometimes seen as laying the foundations of the second British empire. Certainly, it left Britain greatly strengthened in north America, the western Mediterranean and India, and on the high seas.

War needed soldiers. England, despite the diligence of its press gangs in scouring the public houses, was unable to meet the growing demand, especially after Prime Minister Pitt determined to bolster the King's forces in America by 8000 men. There were risks in relying too heavily, as in the past, on mercenaries from the Continent. Scotland, however, had potential troops in relative abundance. James Wolfe, who had fought against the Highlanders at the Battle of Falkirk (where Allan Macpherson had lost his father), thought they could be put to good use: 'they are hardy, intrepid, accustomed to a rough country, and no great mischief if they fall'. The King and his brother the Duke of Cumberland, who had led the government troops at Culloden, took some persuading. Yet there was no denying that Highlanders made formidable soldiers; and the threat of their rebelling was far less than it once had been.

If England stood to gain from recruiting Scottish soldiers, the great landowners of Scotland saw that they could serve themselves by supplying them. War offered a means—perhaps the only means—of regaining some of the influence they had lost after the fiasco of the '45. While they could offer little in the way of agriculture and commerce, they could certainly supply men as a means of winning concessions from Westminster. So Simon Fraser of Lovat, whose father had been executed by the Hanoverians after Culloden, was commissioned to raise a new battalion: within a few months he had recruited well over a thousand men (and awarded commissions to many relatives and friends).

The lairds went recruiting and the word got around. In Ruthven the local minister took up the cause, promising to pay a guinea to every young man in his congregation who was willing to serve. Did Allan Macpherson leap for joy at the prospect of bearing arms? Or was he, with nothing better to look forward to, won over by a guinea? However it might have been, we find him in 1757, aged sixteen or seventeen, wearing the sombre tartan of the 42nd Regiment—the Black Watch. He had enlisted as a mere Private, a fair indication of his humble status and lack of rich connections who might have purchased him an officer's commission. The following spring he was headed for Great Britain's American colonies to do battle with the French.

For five years or so after this first Atlantic crossing, Allan Macpherson's career followed that of his battalion: to Ticonderoga on Lake Champlain, strategically located between the French and British colonies, where the French inflicted a humiliating defeat on a British force four times its size and wiped out nearly two-thirds of his regiment; then to France's 'sugar colonies' of Martinique and Guadeloupe in the Caribbean; back to Ticonderoga and Montreal for a reversal of British fortunes; on to Martinique, and another encounter with the French; and then to the Spanish stronghold of Havana, where the British won a resounding victory, only to be overwhelmed by yellow fever and malaria. Back in New York in 1762, the feeble remnants of their forces learned that peace had been declared. Soon Allan Macpherson and his surviving colleagues were on their way back to Scotland.

The young soldier left no detailed account of his service during these years. The regimental records show that he was promoted to Corporal and Sergeant, then reduced to Private in line with adjustments to the establishments, and promoted again to Sergeant after disease ravaged his company in the Caribbean. Apart from staying alive, which was no small achievement, he distinguished himself among his fellow Highlanders as one of the few who could speak and read English as well as Gaelic.

At some stage during these campaigns, Allan Macpherson's qualities, whether as a soldier, interpreter or scribe, caught the attention of an officer, Lieutenant Thomas Fletcher, who offered him a word of advice: his future lay in the East. With the help of his brother, Sir Robert Fletcher, a rising officer in the service, Fletcher obtained for Allan a cadetship in the East India Company.

BENGAL

After a brief respite in Scotland, Allan Macpherson set out for India. Arriving in Calcutta in 1764, he received his commission as an Ensign in the East India Company and marched with Sir Robert Fletcher several hundred miles up the Ganges valley. There, he and his fellow recruits were to join the Bengal Army, made up chiefly of Indian sepoys led by British officers, against a formidable coalition that was challenging British control of the province. But they arrived too late: the battle had just been won. This was a momentous though narrow victory—the Battle of Buxar lasted just three hours—confirming Britain as the dominant power in Bengal and a force to be reckoned with across India. Allan Macpherson shared in the general rejoicing, with the added happiness of being reunited with his younger brother John, who had left Badenoch a few years after him to join the Bengal Army. When they met, they had not seen one another for eight years.

India around this time was in disarray. The Mughal empire was stumbling on like a wounded elephant, with each new laceration threatening to be its last. Individual nawabs, or princes, were asserting their independence from the imperial court at Delhi, squabbling with one another, or trying to suppress rebellions from within. Insurgents and invaders—Hindu Marathas, Sikhs and Afghans—were threatening any semblance of order and stability.

European companies—English, French, Portuguese and Dutch— stood ready to exploit whatever commercial opportunities arose, and to do whatever was necessary to stop their European rivals from getting the upper hand.

The mercantile arm of England, the Honourable East India Company, had been trading in India since the early seventeenth century. Protected by royal charter, it enjoyed a monopoly of Britain's commercial activity in the East. Its affairs in India were conducted by agencies, known as presidencies, located in the fortress towns of Madras, Calcutta and Bombay, each administered by a governor and council, or board, and each charged with defending the Company's interests in nearby provinces. Commerce ruled, supported as necessary by force of arms: at this stage there was little appetite for taking formal control of more territory than seemed essential for profit and security. Where possible, the Company made deals with nawabs, providing them with military support in return for tribute and commercial favours. But when local rulers became uppity, or a province dangerously unstable, decisive military action was sometimes called for.

So the Company's ambitions might as well be achieved by guile as by force of arms—which meant, for a young officer with intelligence and acumen, that opportunities for preferment were just as likely to exist off the battle field as on it. For Allan Macpherson, missing the Battle of Buxar was no great deprivation: there were other ways to get ahead.

Early in his Indian career, he realised that he could be of service to his employers by learning the local languages. Across the Atlantic, his knowledge of both English and Gaelic had served him well; and his ability to speak and write two languages, as well as a good basic Scottish education, made new linguistic adventures less forbidding. Nevertheless, setting himself this goal was no less remarkable than actually achieving it, for so far few British in India had made a serious effort to understand, in any sense of the word, the people they sought to control. There were exceptions, including young Warren Hastings who, about the time Allan Macpherson embarked on his Indian studies, was trying to persuade the University of Oxford to appoint a professor of Persian, who would teach the language to young men going to India and introduce them to a largely unknown civilisation. Hastings got nowhere with his proposal. His remarkable contribution to British understanding of India was yet to come.

Allan Macpherson was initially appointed as a staff officer; and although he sometimes commanded battalions of sepoys, most of his career was spent on administrative duties. This meant that he had much to do with Mughal potentates and their underlings, whose main language of communication was Persian. So, with the help of a *munshi*, or teacher (one of whom went on to serve him for fourteen years), Allan Macpherson learned to read and write Persian. Having achieved fluency in that language, he progressed naturally to Arabic, sometimes referred to as Moorish, which was spoken in some of the northern courts. Many years later he told a protégé (the natural son of his cousin James): 'A young man of interest and good sense with a proper knowledge of these languages can never miss being properly employed in this country'.

If the reason for learning languages was generally utilitarian, a side benefit was a broader appreciation of Indian civilisation. Allan Macpherson's collection of books and manuscripts in Persian—*ghazals* from the fifteenth century, astronomical commentaries, a history of the kings of India

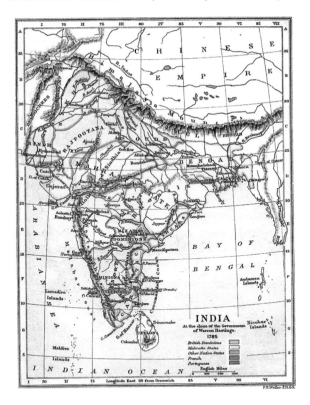

India in 1785, from Samuel Rawson Gardiner (ed.), *A School Atlas of English History*, London, Longmans, Green & Co., 1892.

composed at his instigation, and other works equally diverse—hints at an interest in learning something of the culture into which accident had thrown him. Towards the end of his Indian sojourn, a group of Calcutta gentlemen inaugurated the Asiatic Society of Bengal to encourage oriental studies. Allan Macpherson was one of its first members.

Less remarkably, he picked up Hindustani, the language of the market place and boudoir, and probably a smattering of Bengali. While there is no evidence that he made use of what was generally referred to as 'a sleeping dictionary', there are hints that he related well to the sepoys under his command, which might have had something to do with his fluency in their languages.

But usefulness to his employers was not enough. As he had learned in the Americas, the way for a soldier to get ahead (if he had no powerful friends to start with) was to catch the eye of an influential patron and impress him with his loyalty and dedication to duty. His first patron in India, Sir Robert Fletcher, served him well, retaining him as an aide-de-camp and promoting him to Lieutenant. Fletcher's career, however, provided him with a valuable, if ambiguous lesson in duty and obedience.

The occasion that gave rise to the lesson later became known as 'the *batta* mutiny'. As an officer in the field, Allan Macpherson received allowances, known as *batta*, which had no legitimacy beyond accepted convention. Sir Robert Fletcher's brigade, stationed far up the Ganges at the fort of Monghyr, received double *batta*, which multiplied officers' monthly salaries by five. When in 1766 the Governor of Bengal, Robert Clive, issued a summary order abolishing the system, the officers not surprisingly objected, complaining that their basic pay was not enough to live on. After a series of secret meetings, some 200 officers—Allan Macpherson and his brother John among them—resigned from the service, all on the one day. Clive's response was swift and sharp: he summoned loyal officers from elsewhere and arrested the malcontents. Fletcher, the most prominent of the ringleaders, was court-martialled and cashiered. The more junior officers were marched off to Calcutta and, having been given time to reflect on their folly, ultimately reinstated. After his court martial, Fletcher sent Allan Macpherson his sword, 'as a small token of my esteem'. Of the unhappy experience, Macpherson needed no tangible reminder.

Two of Allan Macpherson's Commanding Officers and patrons in Bengal. Left: Sir Robert Fletcher, mezzotint by William Dickinson, after Sir Joshua Reynolds, published 1774. NATIONAL PORTRAIT GALLERY, LONDON. Right: Colonel Alexander Champion, memorial sculpture by Joseph Nollekens. BATH ABBEY

Bengal, once its former rulers had been pulled into line, remained relatively calm. But there was trouble to the south. In 1767 Allan and John Macpherson were part of a force sent to help the Madras presidency resist a powerful army led by the self-appointed ruler of Mysore, Hyder Ali. A fierce warrior and astute strategist, Hyder pushed the Company's army back to within 5 miles of their fortress at Madras and imposed a peace on his own terms. Allan Macpherson, as a staff officer, was not at the front line—but he was close enough to smell the whiff of defeat and recognise that Indian resistance had to be taken seriously.

Back in Calcutta, with the *batta* mutiny long behind him, he was promoted to the rank of Captain and appointed an aide-de-camp to the brigade commander, Lieutenant-Colonel Alexander Champion. An aide-de-camp had to look the part, so he ordered a saddle, which 'must be Red & Gold, or Blue & Gold', preferably the former, with 'a little blue under the Lace', together with 'a pair of Handsome Spurrs'. His duties included conducting official correspondence and maintaining a journal of the brigade's activities. He also decided to keep a separate record of his own thoughts and movements, perhaps for his future interest and use, or perhaps because he recognised that the events he was observing at first hand might one day attract the interest of posterity. He remained an aide-de-camp for five years, during which Champion was promoted to Commander-in-Chief of the Bengal Army.

Much of the brigade's time during these years was spent marching from one location to another across Bengal, mostly along the broad flats of the Ganges and its tributaries, showing the Company's colours and keeping the peace, though the brigade did take part in one major campaign. This was an unsavoury war in 1774 against the Rohilla tribes north-west of Bengal, which resulted in a victory for the Company's forces but left Champion, Macpherson and many others wondering if right had been on their side.

The enemy was often the weather—torrential rains or intolerable heat—and the accompanying illnesses. 'A Sergeant of each Battn. of the Regiment', wrote Allan Macpherson on the road to Dinapore, 'dropped down dead this afternoon, who were not sick 5 minutes before their death.' European soldiers were ordered to keep out of the sun—but that did not stop many deaths from heatstroke and *pucka* (putrid) fever. Macpherson at least had the benefit of a horse and a palanquin; and often the brigade camped alongside a river, allowing the senior officers to seek relief aboard their budgerows, or houseboats, which followed them along the waterways. Famine sometimes added to the hardships of travel: 'This day's journey was very disagreeable', Colonel Champion recorded, 'from the great number of [human] carcases lying both sides of the road and by the river side'.

Allan Macpherson regarded Champion as a fine officer, a man of few words, and a valuable patron. Some other officers saw him as fastidious, censorious and indecisive, too ready to interfere in trivial matters, and too eager to extract the deference that he considered his due. Hard-faced, with a strong nose and jaw, a broad forehead and large wide-set eyes, he was a strict disciplinarian, for whom a breach of military etiquette by an officer, such as appearing at supper without a coat and gorget, was an offence no less grave than an assault and battery within the ranks. His temper was not improved by a susceptibility to gout.

Over the sepoys, he administered a rough and absolute justice. When three men were brought before him accused of stealing palm sugar from a local village, he ordered that one of them be hanged near the road where their fellow soldiers might see him. However, in the evening he changed his mind and ordered instead that all three should have both ears cut off and stand in public view while another man should proclaim the cause of their punishment.

On a later occasion, five deserters were sentenced to death, two to be shot, and three to be hanged. Champion ordered that they should each cast the dice, to determine who should suffer first. The prisoner who threw the lowest number was then shot; at which point the Colonel announced to the other prisoners that the Commander-in-Chief was pleased to pardon them. He then ordered all the troops to march past the dead soldier's body.

The Colonel had little time for local customs. After a pleasant day's fishing on the banks of the Ganges, he was kept awake by the sepoys incessantly beating their 'tom-toms'. So he ordered the local field commander to put a stop to it. The commander knew better, warning him that if he interfered with what was a solemn religious festival among the Muslim sepoys, they were likely to desert the service. A compromise was agreed to, by which the Muslims were allowed to beat their 'tom-toms' on holy days, so long as they remained a mile or so in the rear of the officers' camp.

Allan Macpherson recorded such events without comment, though his diary suggests that he sometimes questioned his commanding officer's judgment. The Colonel thought highly of his aide-de-camp, rewarding him with 'a present of a very Good Horse'. But he also regarded him as soft, accusing him on one occasion of watering down the oral reprimands that he was required to deliver to fellow officers. Macpherson took deep and instant offence: how could the Colonel suspect him of conveying anything other than the message he had been required to deliver? Remembering the *batta* mutiny, he reminded himself that soldiers were expected to obey orders without questioning them.

Champion returned to England in 1775, where he settled in Bath and indulged his passion for playing billiards. 'I owe him every advantage or success I have enjoyed in this country', Allan Macpherson told his cousin James—but the success was not great, for he was still a Captain. Soon he was presented with another opportunity to make himself useful, when he was asked to join an expedition to the other side of India to negotiate a treaty with the Marathas. Again he acquitted himself with distinction; but again promotion eluded him. Sir John Clavering, who succeeded Champion as Commander-in-Chief and looked likely for a moment to be appointed Governor-General, promised to serve him. But death intervened, leaving Macpherson to mourn the loss of another patron:

'Had he lived, my prospects were very flattering indeed. Now they are quite the opposite'.

So he was reduced to writing begging letters to the Governor-General, Warren Hastings, and to serving in situations that offered few opportunities for making an impression on those who mattered. In late 1780 we find him in charge of a battalion of seven to eight hundred sepoys encamped in 'a nasty, low, wet situation' south of Calcutta, protecting the road into Bengal against Maratha incursions. He is the oldest Captain in the army, grumbling about unkept promises, and waiting to receive his automatic promotion to Major and then return home to Scotland—yet clinging still to the faint hope that something might turn up.

THE FISHING FLEET

North of Badenoch, where the Highlands run down to the Moray Firth to meet the icy winds of the North Sea, Alexander Fraser lived with his wife and four children at Fairfield Cottage, near the ancient town of Inverness. Although Fraser was descended from a long line of Frasers of Fairfield, and although he was connected to the Frasers of Lovat—the most illustrious line of the Fraser Clan—his family's circumstances were modest. According to the Clan history, the decline had begun during the uprising of 1745, which Alexander Fraser's father had supported with patriotic enthusiasm, but much to his own cost. A generation later Alexander had shrunk into decrepitude, leaving his wife and children to fend for themselves.

Alexander's son could at least look forward to a military career, which might do something towards restoring the family's fortunes. His three daughters, however, shared the fate of most young ladies throughout the Highlands (and indeed throughout Britain), whose sole prospect of future happiness rested in making a good match. Although some of them had received an English education, which was considered a great advantage, they had no fortune to add to their attractions. This made the task of snaring a husband difficult, especially after 1776, when Britain's war with the rebellious Americans and their allies was again draining the Scottish countryside of its able-bodied men.

The eldest daughter, Eliza, was painfully aware of her own and her family's predicament, but bereft of a solution—until one day in summer 1779 she had the good fortune to meet the widow of a kinsman, Brigadier-General Fraser, and mentioned to her how uneasy she was about the future. The widow 'immediately asked me if I shd like to make a trip to India. I wd never have thought of such a thing. But her ladyship spoke of the service I might be able to render my dear family'. Without further ado, the matter was decided. Although her close family had no money to support the expedition, good friends came to the rescue; and the brother of General Fraser's widow, a Captain Vanas and his wife, who were soon to leave for India, agreed to act as her protectors.

So in mid-1780, Miss Eliza Dell Fraser joined what later became well known as 'the fishing fleet', equipped with the necessary bait and tackle. Although we are not privy to the exact contents of her sea chest, we can deduce much from the later advice she gave to her sister Susanna, who was contemplating a similar expedition. There was no purpose, Eliza wrote, in bringing out quilted silk petticoats, coloured pocket handkerchiefs or chemises, as no such things were to be seen in Calcutta. But certain items were essential: two full dresses (valued in total at £50); three dancing dresses (£30); one pair of handsome buckles (£3); twelve pairs of embroidered shoes (£15); two pairs of stays with very little bone (£4); 50 pounds of hair powder (£2/10s); six boxes of tooth powder (£1/10s); 10 shillings worth of lavender water; and so on, to a total of £172—to which it was necessary to add £120 for the passage money and £20 pocket money, leading to a grand total of £312. Eliza later reported with satisfaction that her things were thought genteel.

Eliza's friends were generous with their advice. There was scarcely need to mention that a young lady should follow the strictest rules of propriety and virtue; beyond that, she must acquire a refined language; she should read elegant books, and studiously avoid any cockney vulgarisms; she must be able to dance fashionably; and, once arrived in India, she must always wear gloves, taking particular care of the colour of her hands. There was some debate as to whether beauty mattered more than manners and gentility—but Eliza, if not glamorous, was generally reckoned sufficiently well endowed to attract attention. Her skin was smooth and white, her eyes gentle, her nose pert (and perhaps long, but not overly so), and her smile open and unassuming, accentuated by two distinctive dimples. Sometimes she allowed her flowing red-brown curls to fall over her shoulders, which invariably drew attention to her white and elegant neck.

However admirable her personal attributes, she had been warned not to set her expectations too high. Long before India had been suggested as a solution to her problem, a male relative had given her helpful advice about what she might reasonably look forward to:

> If the man is really disagreeable, cross and ill temper'd, don't take him while you have ten fingers. If he is good humour'd facetious and rich tho' he should neither be an Adonis or a Solomon, don't reject him till you have well consider'd the matter.

Furthermore, although the voyage to the East would open up opportunities, success could never be guaranteed, proof of which appeared in the passenger lists of ships returning from India with 'ladies that would not sell at the Bengal flesh market'.

In the event, however, of the outcome so much longed for, Eliza Fraser took with her on the voyage sound advice about what she might expect in a husband and how she should behave. The *Ladies Annual Journal* for 1780, Eliza's copy of which, over two centuries later, still falls open at the 'Rules and Maxims for Promoting Matrimonial Happiness', counselled her not to be over-sanguine about marriage, nor to promise herself 'felicity without alloy'. For the person she would marry was a man, not an angel; and if there was 'any thing in his humour or behaviour that is not altogether so agreeable as you expected, pass over it as a human frailty; smooth your brow; compose your temper; and try to amend it by cheerfulness and good nature'. She should avoid all thoughts of trying to manage him; and she should not dispute with him, but rather deny herself the trivial satisfaction of having her own will; for 'a woman's power as well as happiness, has no other foundation but her husband's esteem and love'.

Thus equipped, Eliza Fraser set sail from Portsmouth on a voyage that eventually took eight months. Long sea voyages were generally tedious and often dangerous. Many of the irritations and anxieties Eliza shared with her fellow passengers, including a long detour in the southern latitudes to escape French men of war. But other tribulations were peculiar to her sex. When the vessel was delayed for three weeks at Rio de Janeiro, she and the other ladies were allowed to disembark only twice, as the Portuguese Viceroy disliked the English, and English women in particular (and what purpose would it serve for Eliza to protest that she was a Scot?). Then there was an unfortunate misunderstanding with her chaperone, Mrs Vanas, who turned out to be exceedingly jealous: after Eliza unwittingly visited the captain's quarters without her, but presumably in company with Captain Vanas, she was viewed with deep distrust.

All in all, it was an uncomfortable voyage. But rather than complaining of the hardships young ladies were obliged to suffer, Eliza attributed her trials to the vicissitudes of fortune.

Bad luck pursued her when the ship arrived in Madras. The town was besieged on the land by the Mughal leader Hyder Ali, and at sea by the French, who were determined to regain some of the influence they had recently lost. The English were holed up in the local stronghold, Fort George, where Eliza observed 'distress and melancholy' on every countenance. Again she reflected on the wheel of fortune, and wondered if she would soon be coming home. But after a few months, she received an invitation from Captain Vanas' sister to visit her near Calcutta. As this was to have been her original destination, and as Calcutta was generally regarded as offering the brightest prospects to a person in her situation, she set out at the first opportunity, carrying with her a letter of introduction to Lieutenant John Murray, Secretary of the Board of Ordnance, and his vivacious wife Anne, who were reckoned among 'the first people' in Bengal.

LOVE ON A BUDGEROW

Just as the vessel carrying Miss Eliza Dell Fraser was sailing up the Bay of Bengal towards the River Hooghly, Major Allan Macpherson and his bachelor friends were discussing marriage. This was no remarkable coincidence, for scarcely a week went by when marriage did not enter into their conversation. On this occasion, as they sat languidly around the card table sipping their madeiras, there was a particular reason for the subject to capture their attention, as one of their number, John Murray's younger brother Peter, had announced his engagement. Allan Macpherson, whose views on marriage tended to waver, thought this a bad move; but his friend John Macintyre urged him to be more understanding: 'You must make allowances for young men—their passions are ungovernable, and often carry them headlong to destruction'.

If reason were to have its way, marriage was something best left until their return to Scotland, whenever that might be. Wives were notoriously expensive, requiring fashionable clothing, and jewellery, and carriages, and servants—all in all they were expected to cost at least £300 a year, well beyond the means of most officers in the service. Add another £300 for children and the prospect could lead to ruin. This readily explains why young ladies, although vastly outnumbered by men, often went home empty handed, and why only one in ten army officers in Bengal around this time took the fateful step.

A further consideration was that the officers' sexual appetites were well satisfied by an abundant supply of 'Hindostanee ladies', otherwise known as *bibis*. As another Scottish officer pointed out, it was easier to support 'a whole *zenana* of Indians than the extravagance of one English lady'. So Captain Macintyre, who kept a concubine and over the years had fathered several mixed-race children, was conducting himself in a fashion that, in local society, was scarcely worthy of comment.

Visitors to Calcutta, on the other hand, were inclined to be censorious. A Scottish traveller described a few years earlier the leisurely routines of a bachelor, attended by an army of servants waiting to do his bidding:

> The moment the master throws his legs out of bed, the whole posse in waiting rush into his room, each making three salams … He condescends, perhaps, to nod or cast an eye towards the solicitors of his favour and protection. In about half an hour after undoing and taking off his long drawers, a clean shirt, breeches, stockings and slippers are put upon his body, thighs, legs and feet, without any greater exertion on his part than if he was a statue.

The day proceeds effortlessly, with engagements, entertainments, and an afternoon nap, after which he and his friends take tea, followed at ten in the evening by supper.

> The company keep together between twelve and one in the morning, preserving great sobriety and decency; and when they depart, our hero is conducted to his bed room, where he finds a female companion to amuse him until the hour of seven or eight next morning. With no greater exertions than these, do the Company's servants amass the most splendid fortunes.

Macpherson, Macintyre and their friends dismissed such calumnies, especially the reference to 'splendid fortunes' which, although such things might have been acquired by a few officers in the service, certainly did not (so far) apply to them. Yet there was no denying that a bachelor's life did have its benefits, and that, accordingly, marriage was not something to be rushed into. So when Allan Macpherson, who appears not to have had a regular arrangement with a Hindostanee lady, and weakened perhaps by Peter Murray's star-struck condition, suggests that marriage might not be such a bad thing, Macintyre sets him straight: 'Go home now and you may marry to advantage and enjoy the state—stay a few years, and, if you do get married, it must be to an old Hag; or to a young woman who will marry you for your fortune'.

These exchanges are interrupted by the arrival of Eliza Fraser at the bungalow of Lieutenant and Mrs John Murray. Eliza probably follows the usual course of unmarried ladies recently landed in Calcutta, presenting herself at parties in a ritual known as 'sitting up'. This sometimes extended over several nights, and it gave ladies the opportunity to appear before prospective husbands to best advantage. Sometimes it yielded prompt results; but it was widely seen as 'disagreeable and foolish', not to mention degrading, and did not last much beyond the 1780s.

Macintyre is the first to set eyes on Eliza and promptly concludes that she is neither a fortune-hunter nor a hag. She is, in fact, exactly what his friend Macpherson needs. So he dashes off a letter:

> When you arrive at Calcutta, I think you will be apt to lose your heart—there is a young Lady just arrived at Mr Murray's who I think will meet your notice—although not a regular and striking beauty she is handsome, and her mental accomplishments are far beyond the generality of her sex in this Country—few excel her so far as [I can] Judge from a few days acquaintance, and she is in my opinion perfectly adapted for you—I could say a thousand things more to her advantage were I not afraid that you may feel the arrow before you see the object ... I had almost forgot to mention her name—Miss Frazer, Scotch descent, but educated in England—she has been at Inverness, but does not retain any of the *twang*. Come and see her as soon as you can.

She combines, in other words, the best of Scotland and the best of England—a formula calculated at the time to win any Scotsman's heart.

Macpherson, as he reads this letter in his dreary camp south of Calcutta, is feeling especially sorry for himself, partly because he is still bitter about Hastings' failure to promote him, but also because he is suffering from a violent attack of rheumatism. With the help of a sympathetic surgeon, who testifies that dropsy threatens unless he has prolonged exposure to a cold climate, he is planning his escape from India and has gone so far as to offer his resignation from his regiment. Macintyre's letter distracts him unexpectedly from thoughts of home.

The first encounter takes place at Lieutenant and Mrs John Murray's. Eliza appears to unleash in the Major unbounded passions, which suggests that he has held them in check for a long time. Happily, the Murrays propose to take Eliza on a journey 100 miles upstream to Cossimbazaar aboard their budgerow. Though sluggish, budgerows are often luxurious, with well-appointed cabins, sitting and dining rooms, a veranda, and a promenade deck, where travellers can exchange pleasantries or intimacies against a backdrop of picturesque sunsets, with the river gently lapping against the vessel's hull.

In such propitious circumstances Allan Macpherson confesses his love to Eliza Fraser and begs her to be his bride:

> Yes, my dearest Eliza I acknowledge with the most unfeigned pleasure, how truly I adore you and that my future happiness depends upon your determination. Oh my most lovely girl, endeavour, nay resolve to think favourably of a man whose life and fortune are entirely at your feet, and whose study and most earnest wishes will ever be to merit and reward the preference you have it in your power to give him.

Eliza is gratified, but alarmed. Having been tutored by her relatives and friends in the proprieties of courtship (and having probably been exposed to some ungenteel behaviour on the voyage out), she wonders if Major Macpherson has overstepped the mark. 'I have thought a great deal about the M—...', his downright honest open & undisguised sentiments', she tells Anne Murray. But there can be no further correspondence until there is an understanding between them (meaning that they agree to become engaged); and she declines to enter into such an understanding until she

Eliza Macpherson, 1762–1830. Oil by John Thomas Seton, 1782.
MACPHERSON COLLECTION

has had an opportunity to assess his intentions and character at further interviews. For the moment she is obliged to conclude that his behaviour is too forward to be entirely consistent with the principles of honour. She will regard him with indifference.

No hint of discouragement will quell the Major's ardour. He is in torment about the delay: what if another suitor should come between them? But Miss Fraser is a stickler for the unwritten rules that she has imbibed at home, and yields nothing to the warmer climate. Another of the Murray brothers, Alexander, takes this as an indication of her virtues, confirming her as 'a Girl of delicate sentiments, possessing just notions of propriety and … a disinterestedness which is seldom to be met with'. The only way forward is for Allan to come to Cossimbazaar and throw himself again at her feet.

But such a course, while obviously appealing, might undermine his other plans. Within the few weeks between his first meeting with Eliza and his proposal of marriage, a change in the Council House gives him reason to hope that advancement is at last within his reach. A fellow Clansman, Mr John Macpherson, well-known as a man of influence, returns to Calcutta after several years in England to take up an appointment as a member of the Governor-General's Supreme Council. John Macpherson has promised to do his best to assist Allan. Under such circumstances, it would be inexcusable for Allan not to inform him of his intention to marry—indeed, if he should fail to do so, Mr Macpherson might well withdraw his friendship. Allan's hands are tied: he cannot tell his friend of his intentions without the consent of his beloved; and he cannot visit his beloved in Cossimbazaar without signalling his intentions to everyone, and so offending his potential benefactor.

Too much coyness can be risky. When Anne Murray tells her of the Major's situation, Eliza confesses that her mind is in turmoil. She hastens back to Calcutta, where the two can meet without becoming the subject of conversation and innuendo. There Allan falls to his knees—and the conquest is complete. All their friends are delighted. 'Now Allan,' writes Captain Macintyre, 'you have got a Jewel, use it well and take care it does not lose its value: You are in my opinion uncommonly lucky—I thought you would be so from the first moment.' Allan makes sure that Mr John Macpherson is the among the first to know, so that there is no chance of his being offended.

Mr Macpherson, true to his word, has already written to the Governor-General reminding him that his kinsman is worthy of advancement and that any favour he cares to bestow on him would be warmly approved by their mutual friends in London. Hastings takes the hint and responds promptly, appointing Allan Macpherson to the office he has so long been seeking of Quartermaster General in Bengal, a position that carries with it an annual salary of £1500, a big advance on his current income, and sufficient to remove his anxieties about the financial burden of entering into married life.

As the day of their wedding approaches, Allan Macpherson—now, as a result of his appointment as Quartermaster General, promoted to the rank of Lieutenant-Colonel—and Miss Eliza Dell Fraser each reflect on their good fortune. Eliza has won the heart of a man of great talent and virtue, well placed to assist her own family back in Scotland. Allan reflects that he is about to marry a young lady who promises to make him truly happy; he has at last been promoted to an office worthy of his seniority and talents; and he has good friends in high places who have proven themselves ready to serve him. He dreams of 'a charming Villa in the Highlands', where he and his lady might reside in rural and domestic felicity, and entertain old friends from India. 'I pray to God we may live to See and enjoy this pleasing Scene.'

For the moment, though, this must wait. The office of Quartermaster General, as well as bestowing on its holder a handsome salary, has traditionally been associated with lucrative contracts that might well add substantially to his fortune. So by the time he and Eliza exchange rings at John and Anne Murray's garden house on the banks of the River Hooghly at the beginning of 1782, he has decided to remain in Bengal a few years longer. Suddenly, India does not seem such a bad place after all.

3

....

WAR AND PEACE

$\mathcal{A}$DECADE BEFORE THE HAPPY EVENTS JUST RECOUNTED, Captain Allan Macpherson, aide-de-camp to the brigade commander, Colonel Alexander Champion, had been camped near Benares, on the border between the Honourable East India Company's territories in Bengal and the Mughal province of Oudh, when news arrived that Warren Hastings had been appointed Governor of Bengal. Each division fired a salute: seventeen guns at sunrise and three volleys of small arms—though the small arms had to be restricted as there were not enough light cartridges to go around. Britain's administration of India was full of ironies, large and small.

The new Governor knew India well—its languages, landscapes and culture. He had joined the Company as a humble writer on £5 a year at the age of seventeen and risen slowly through the ranks. Now, in his fortieth year, he had been given the task of reforming the Bengal administration and restoring the Company's depleted revenues. A dedicated Company man, he nevertheless looked beyond the Company to assert the responsibility of the British nation for seeing that India was properly governed. He also wanted to rule with the support of the local population, which might well mean drawing on the forms of government that the Mughals had hitherto employed with such success. He was a man of grand vision. But opposition from others, and his own errors of judgment, both small and large, kept getting in the way. He had sought to govern 'with ease and moderation'; yet when he left India thirteen years later, an army of detractors would say that his regime had been characterised less by peace than by war.

THE ROHILLA BUSINESS
When Hastings took office in 1772, an immediate problem was pressing. The Marathas, the Hindu nation whose territories stretched across

A thoughtful Warren Hastings, painted about the time he was appointed Governor of Bengal. The artist, Tilly Kettle, had recently arrived in Calcutta after two years in Madras. He is generally known as the first British artist to make a career of painting in India. Oil on canvas, about 1772. NATIONAL PORTRAIT GALLERY, LONDON

India and who were the most formidable threat to Company interests, were bearing down on Oudh, a large inland province allied to the Company. Since Robert Clive's time in the 1760s, Oudh had served as a buffer, protecting the Company's frontiers against turbulence beyond. Its ruler had become, in turn, dependent on British protection, both to quell internal ructions and to secure the province against actual or suspected enemies.

The Nawab of Oudh was also known as the Vizier, or Wazir, a title conferred by the Mughal emperor, and which suggested high dignity as well as subservience—though in fact the province had long ceased to be subordinate to the imperial court at Delhi. In the early years of Hastings' administration, the Nawab Wazir was Shuja ad-Daula, who had ascended the *musnad*, or throne, in 1754. As a youth he had won a reputation for seducing young girls; later he was venerated and feared

Shuja ad-Daula, Nawab Wazir of Oudh, with four sons and British military officers, 1772.
The eldest son, standing behind the Nawab and to his right, succeeded him in 1775
as Asaf ad-Daula. The officer in the foreground is Sir Robert Barker, Commander-
in-Chief of the Bengal Army until 1773. Oil on canvas by Tilly Kettle, 1775.
VICTORIA MEMORIAL HALL, KOLKATA

as a formidable warrior, possessing remarkable physical strength. While
many saw him as 'an artful and able politician', he was also described
as treacherous and capricious, with a violent temper. His courage was
widely lauded—though, on close acquaintance, Allan Macpherson came
to regard him as an 'arrant coward'.

In 1772 the dreaded Marathas crossed the Ganges into Rohilkhand,
a territory north-west of Oudh at the foot of the Himalayas, populated
mainly by Hindus but governed by a confederacy of Afghan chieftains who
had imposed their rule over the country half a century earlier. Rohilkhand
was supposed to serve as a buffer to Oudh much as Oudh acted as a buffer
to Bengal; but, racked by instability, it was ill-suited to this purpose. The
Wazir, alarmed by the looming Marathas, begged Hastings to come to his
aid; and Hastings, fearing a Maratha conquest of all India, promised to
defend his dominions.

Accordingly, Colonel Champion's brigade marched into Oudh to show the Company's colours. The mood among the officers was buoyant, as it always was when there was the promise of action; for war was the way to win promotion and make money. As the brigade approached the court of Faizabad, Shuja ad-Daula came out to meet them, accompanied by what Champion described as a 'prodigious Retinue of Horse and Foot, with 3 or 4 Hundred Cammels', their riders firing into the air as fast as they could reload their guns. The Wazir alighted from his elephant and embraced the Colonel warmly. In the following weeks he cultivated his guests assiduously, meeting them often over breakfast (buttered toast and tea), and entertaining them with *nautches* (dances) and military displays, where he and two of his elder sons demonstrated their prowess at riding and shooting and throwing their lances which, said Champion, 'they are very expert at'. Captain Macpherson spent many hours with the Wazir, negotiating the details of how they might respond to the Maratha threat.

The combined forces advanced quickly through Oudh and into Rohilkhand, engaging the Marathas in several skirmishes. Suddenly the Marathas, intimidated by what appeared to be a fearsome coalition, pulled back across the Ganges and disappeared into the hills. But their retreat did not end the prospect of war: Shuja ad-Daula, having gained so much, was determined to seize the day. Strengthened by an agreement that he negotiated personally with Hastings, he proposed a war against the Rohillas, who up until now had been his allies (though they had always been deeply suspicious of one another, as the Rohillas were Sunni Muslims and the Wazir and his followers Shi'ites). When the Rohillas inadvertently gave the Wazir a pretext for invasion by not paying their tribute, Hastings agreed to support him with Company forces. In return for helping him expel (or was it extirpate?) the Rohillas, the Wazir would pay the Company 40 lakhs of rupees—about £400,000 (a vast sum of money)—followed by continuing payments to ensure that the job was properly done.

The outcome was a bloody war that gave Allan Macpherson much cause for reflection and, in the longer term, deeply damaged Hastings' reputation. Although the campaign lasted six months, its one significant battle was short and decisive. Colonel Champion's brigade of about 7000 men, notionally supported by the Wazir's massive army of 60,000, confronted a Rohilla force of around 30,000 to 40,000. Captain Macpherson had charge of intelligence, which meant supervising horseback patrols to identify enemy movements and gathering information from trusted *hircarahs*, or spies. He was therefore uniquely placed to follow the course of battle.

The opposing forces met on 23 April, St George's Day, 1774 at Mirrantpur Katra, about midway between Lucknow and Delhi, in sandy terrain furrowed by gullies and dotted with villages. Taking advantage of a moonless night, Champion's brigade was on the march soon after three o'clock in the morning. After dragging their heavy guns across a deep ravine, they encountered a good road which brought them to the enemy's camp around half past seven. The Colonel ordered Allan Macpherson to ride to the top of a nearby hill, where he saw the Rohilla army 'very plain in great confusion', and evidently taken entirely by surprise. Champion ordered his troops into formation; and at ten minutes to eight, when the enemy was about 600 yards distant, their guns opened fire. By now the enemy had pulled themselves into line and looked formidable, and they were pounding the Company's troops with artillery and rocket fire. As the infantry moved slowly forward, Macpherson noticed a large body of enemy troops taking cover in the gully. The Colonel ordered a detachment of 400 of the Wazir's cavalry to flush them out, but 'the Vagabonds' refused to do their duty. A Company battalion stepped into the breach, successfully dislodging the Rohillas and continuing in hot pursuit. Champion then ordered the line to move forward briskly, with the artillery supporting their advance, a tactic which 'struck the Enemy with so much Terror that they began to retreat in great Confusion'. According to Champion, the enemy 'made repeated attempts to charge, but our guns being so much better served than theirs, kept so constant and galling a fire that they could not advance, and when they were closest there was the greatest slaughter'.

Seeing how great was their peril, the most exalted Rohilla chieftain, Hafiz Rahmat Khan, who was in his mid-sixties, descended from his elephant and mounted a horse, the better to lead his followers into battle. But Macpherson's *hircarahs* had done their job well: a Company officer recognised the colour of the Hafiz's umbrella and aimed a 'six-pounder' in his direction. Hafiz, struck in the breast, slumped in his saddle—and within minutes the Rohilla army fell away, leaving their armaments and other possessions behind them.

In two and a half hours the Rohillas had been put to rout. Casualties numbered 132 of the Company's troops, at least 250 of the Wazir's and over 2000 Rohillas, including several of their chieftains. Champion reported the victory to Hastings and the Board with 'inexpressible satisfaction', praising his officers and men, and drawing out for particular attention 'the Gentlemen who showed such alertness and presence of mind in carrying my orders to the different bodies of the army during the course of the action', first among whom was Captain Allan Macpherson.

It seemed a good morning's work—except that the following day one of Allan's horses died, owing to the fatigue of battle. 'I think it but reasonable that the Company, or the Vizer, should reimburse me for this Loss, as has heretofore customed in this Service. I will therefore present a Bill for his Value ...'

But the immediate elation that accompanied victory having passed, Macpherson had second thoughts. No doubt the battle had gone well: the victory had been swift and their casualties few. The Colonel had led the Company's forces 'with great coolness and activity', while the sepoys, who made up the majority of the troops, had behaved with 'Steadiness, cheerfulness, and resolution'. 'In short, from the Commr. in Chief to the Private Soldier, every Man gave the greatest Satisfaction.'

Yet his own sense of achievement had been contaminated by the conduct of the Company's ally. During the preliminary skirmishes, as the brigade and the Wazir's forces had moved into Rohilkhand, the Wazir's troops were behaving 'like unmerciful villains', plundering villages and then setting fire to them, and putting innocent men, women and children to the sword. On the morning of battle, the Wazir remained with about two-thirds of his forces at a village some 7 miles from the main encounter, and did not stir from there until he heard news of victory, when he rode up 'like a brave fellow'. His cavalry remained in the rear during the action, but when the battle was won rushed forward to plunder the enemy, 'so that our Forces obtained the Glory and they the advantages'. Later, as the English army marched forward into lands previously occupied by the Rohillas, the Wazir's troops and followers hurried past them,

> which clearly proved to us that there was no Enemy of Consequence before—otherwise he and the Dastardly Cowards would have kept as far in the Rear as they did in the Day of Battle; but now their pursuit was plunder.

A week after the battle, around midday, he watched as forty-five covered *hackeries*, or bullock carts, ambled past the English camp, bearing as prisoners several hundred women of Hafiz's *zenana*, and four of his surviving sons.

They were supposedly being sent to Lucknow; 'but I am very much afraid', he wrote, 'their destiny is very uncertain'. Their rough treatment caused him to reflect:

> how little we ought to depend or trust to the Vain Pomp of this World, for this unfortunate family eight days ago were possessed of a fine Country, a Husband, and a father, with every Luxury that they could wish or think of, and in Two hours and a half lost their all with their liberty, and are now at the mercy of their most inveterate Enemy, who will most certainly destroy the Race of Haffies.

During the following weeks, he recorded in his journal how the families of the Rohilla chieftains were being made to suffer. *Hircarahs* brought him news that women and children were being deprived of food and water, and exposed day and night to the wind and rain. According to 'a Report Shocking to humanity', the Wazir (true to his reputation) had taken to his bed a daughter of one of the defeated chieftains, who was aged just ten or eleven. The story, he said, had 'some appearance of truth, tho' it cannot absolutely be confirmed'.

It was almost as though the ally had become the enemy and the enemy the ally. Where the Wazir and his followers had demonstrated their cowardice, the Rohillas had proven themselves valiant in battle, standing out as 'a steady, resolute, brave sett of Men'. When on the eve of battle the Rohillas murdered several of the Nawab's 'plundering rascals', Macpherson could not disguise his satisfaction. And after the battle, he repeatedly expressed compassion for the vanquished families, while according their persecutors nothing but disdain.

As the brigade moved deeper into Rohilkhand, stories of the Wazir's cruelty tended to dominate conversation in the Colonel's tent. Champion heard and read the intelligence reports gathered by *hircarahs* stationed in the Nawab's camp, saw with his own eyes the evidence of atrocities, and decided that he had had enough. Less than three weeks after the decisive battle, he submitted his resignation as Commander-in-Chief and made plans to return to England. The 'inexpressible satisfaction' of victory had quickly evaporated; now he wrote privately to Hastings that 'the nature of the service, and the terms on which I have been employed in this campaign, have been inexpressibly disagreeable'. His reports echoed and amplified the views of his aide-de-camp: he wrote of the Wazir's treachery, his 'shameful pusilanimity', his inhumanity, and the ravages wrought by his troops. Some of his words had already appeared in his aide-de-camp's journal, though who is to know who first uttered them? The whole army, he later wrote, were witnesses to 'scenes that cannot be described'.

Having determined to return to England, Champion evidently decided that he was at liberty to criticise the Board's (meaning, effectively, Hastings') policy. The Board, he told Hastings, could not have anticipated that their orders would have such dire consequences, including 'so sudden and so total an expulsion and downfal of a whole race of people'. While it was possible to argue that the Wazir, as 'the agent of oppression', was alone culpable, 'all Asia knows that the English gave him the rod'; and as they were unable to prevent its misuse, 'Will they not say, that every English chief is another Sujah?'

Champion was hardly one to feel squeamish. A decade earlier, when the Company was at war with Shuja ad-Daula, he had claimed responsibility for destroying 'upwards of a thousand villages'. And had he not ordered European soldiers to run the gauntlet, sepoys to have their ears cut off, and others to be summarily executed, their remains put on display as a warning to anyone who might contemplate a breach of military discipline? Not that there was anything remarkable about these or still more brutal penalties: many sepoys had ended their military careers being fired from the barrel of a cannon.

But the savagery of Shuja ad-Daula and his followers exceeded all that they had previously encountered. Before the battle, Champion had urged the Wazir to restrain his troops, arguing that cruelty towards innocent villagers reflected adversely on the English army, 'who were always reckoned remarkable for their Humanity and protection to a Conquered Enemy'. Afterwards, their shameless pursuit of plunder and callous treatment of women and children, especially the families of 'high birth', had flouted the conventions of war that the Company's officers had been taught to believe were sacrosanct. The campaign dragged on until there remained, said Champion, 'no more towns to plunder—no new discovered hoards of treasure to dig up—no unhappy man to rob of his wealth—no miserable woman of her raiment'. By the time it was over, perhaps some 20,000 Rohillas had been driven from their lands.

Several days after the battle, Champion had alerted Hastings to rumours that extensive treasure might be discovered, and asked for confirmation that the Company's forces should be entitled to a share of it. Under normal circumstances, the question would not need to have been asked— victorious armies looked to 'prize money' as part of their entitlement. But these circumstances were not normal: the army had provided paid services to the Wazir, whose appetite for riches was well known. Over the next fortnight, the rumours were confirmed—the Rohillas had indeed left a vast treasure, and the Wazir and his followers were getting down on it fast. Champion wrote to the Council more forcibly, even with a hint of menace, declaring that while the army had behaved admirably in resisting temptation,

> I am afraid that, if some mark of favour and gratification for their services is not manifested, it may be somewhat dangerous ever to try an experiment of this kind again, or to put the temper and patience of any part of your troops so much to the proof.

Hastings, however, was adamant: there was no place for plunder, unless it derived immediately from the assault of a place by storm. Any expectation of booty among the troops, he told Champion, must be 'avoided like poison'.

Having taken a moral stand on the Wazir's pursuit of plunder, how could Champion and his fellow officers then insist on receiving a share of it? By long established tradition, British soldiers, including sepoys wearing the Company's colours, expected to receive part of any treasure captured from the enemy. The exact entitlement was determined according to rank, and the proceeds precisely distributed after the battle. Like the *batta*, or field allowances, that Allan Macpherson and his fellow officers had so earnestly defended a decade earlier, plunder was as much a part of a soldier's perquisites as his regular pay. The promise of large rewards made fighting for the Company—and fighting to win—worthwhile.

So when Champion received a letter from the Board declaring that: 'We cannot Believe the Vizier found any Riches in proportion to what you write', and instructing him to tell his officers that 'we do not consider them in the smallest degree entitled to any share or proportion of Prize money, or donation, and they are not to expect it', the officers were, as Allan

Macpherson put it, 'equally astonished and affected' by 'this extraordinary letter'. Once they had recovered from the shock, they urged their Colonel to tell the Board that they would not 'upon any consideration' forego their rights, 'as Subjects of Great Britain', to their entitlements.

Before the campaign was over, the Wazir, who had no doubt calculated that too much disgruntlement among the English forces was not in his interest, presented the Company with seven lakhs of rupees—£70,000—for the troops, plus an additional three lakhs to Colonel Champion for the officers. This might have made the problem easier for Hastings, by converting 'plunder'—or what the sepoys called *lut*—into prize money or, still more respectably, a 'donation'. But Hastings held firm, referring the matter back to the Company's Directors in London for a decision. When Champion sailed from Calcutta early in 1775 he remained deeply indignant about having been obliged to participate in a war which, he said, had brought the national character of the English into 'the highest disrepute', while at the same time yielding him no personal profit.

The total amount of plunder was vast. It included forty elephants, 1000 horses, 400,000 rupees in gold *mohurs*, and great piles of jewellery, much of it stripped from captured women. Over a decade later the Court of Directors decided that the Wazir's ten lakhs could be distributed to the soldiers who had fought in the war, in the customary proportions. The task of distributing what was now called 'the Rohilla donation' fell to the Quartermaster General in Calcutta, Lieutenant-Colonel Allan Macpherson. By far the greatest share, totalling 105,000 rupees or more than £10,000, went to Colonel Champion, who was now living in Bath; Lieutenant-Colonels were awarded 10,960 rupees—about £1100; and Allan Macpherson, as a Captain during the war, received 5480 rupees—about £550. Not that he ever saw any of it—but that is another story.

Nor did Shuja ad-Daula derive much personal benefit from his plundering. He died early in 1775, less than three months after the war's end, from a boil in his thigh, the result of blood poisoning contracted during the campaign. A contemporary Persian historian remarked that 'the servants of the Nawáb struck their heads against stones in their grief, yet the subjects of Faizábád were very glad at the event'.

A SEVERED HEAD
Soon after the guns had fallen silent on St George's Day 1774, when the Company's forces had put the Rohillas to rout and opened the way for

A PRIVATE EMPIRE

Shuja ad-Daula to plunder the survivors, a mounted sepoy came across the body of the Rohilla chieftain, Hafiz Rahmat Khan, lying in the dust. Dismounting from his horse, the soldier severed the head from its body, and bore it exultantly to Shuja ad-Daula. Allan Macpherson viewed the proceedings that followed with disgust: 'The Vizier rejoiced at the sight of the Head of a Man who he had not Courage to face when living, and taking the head by the beard showed it in Triumph to the Spectators'. Then, according to Colonel Champion's Persian interpreter, the Wazir carried the head to the Colonel's tent, expressing 'a good deal of pleasure of having [it] in his possession'.

That story, along with other tales of cruelty and barbarity in which the Company's forces appeared to be implicated, tarnished Warren Hastings' reputation, not just at the time, but for many decades to come. The damage began as soon as the stories reached Calcutta, where Hastings' enemies were in the ascendant, owing in part to changes in the administration of India. During the previous year, Parliament had decided that the Governor of Bengal should now be given the new title of Governor-General, with limited and ill-defined powers extending to the other two presidencies in Bombay and Madras; but at the same time, it had created a five-member Council, headed by Hastings, and given it powers to overrule his decisions and question his past actions. This is precisely what some of the members proceeded to do. One of them, the ambitious and notoriously venomous Philip Francis, proved to be Hastings' implacable opponent. Looking for evidence of misgovernment and abuses of power, Francis and his colleagues found plenty of ammunition in what they now referred to as 'the Rohilla War'. They worked meticulously through the relevant correspondence, and questioned several participants, including an increasingly disgruntled Champion, and his aide-de-camp, Allan Macpherson.

Francis remained on the Council for the next six years, making life difficult for Hastings but failing in his ultimate aim to supplant him. In 1780 their antipathy culminated in a duel, in which Francis was slightly wounded. He promptly sailed for home, taking with him a thirst for revenge and an arsenal of information that he felt he could use to destroy Hastings' reputation. In England, reports from Bengal were already feeding a growing unease about Company misrule; and now Francis was on hand to provide Hastings' detractors with chapter and verse. He found an attentive listener in the great orator and parliamentarian Edmund Burke, who discovered in India a cause worthy of his extraordinary powers. Burke

56

concluded that the East India Company's administration was corrupt and oppressive; that abuses abroad threatened politics and society at home; and that the chief cause of corruption and source of misrule was the Governor-General of Bengal, Warren Hastings.

The Rohilla War was grist to Burke's mill. First there was a secret contract that Hastings had made with Shuja ad-Daula, which referred, in translation from the Persian, to the proposed 'extirpation' of the Rohillas. Then there were Champion's letters, including his vivid descriptions of atrocities and his suggestions that the war had stained 'the honor of the Empire'. Champion even drew a comparison between the British and the Romans: surely the British senate could not overlook 'the prostitution of the national honor in subjecting a British General [Champion had given himself a promotion] to the command of an Infidel Prince'. Thus inspired, Burke described to the House of Commons how the Company had sold the Rohilla people 'to utter *extirpation*, for the sum of four hundred thousand pounds', the whole nation 'slaughtered or banished', the country 'laid waste with fire and sword'; and their eminent chieftain, Hafiz Rahmat, who was as famous in the East for his literature and verse as he was for his courage, 'slain valiantly, fighting for his country'. The battle was between civilisation and barbarism—and the British nation had been on the wrong side.

Burke, as he admitted, was playing to the crowd. However much truth there might have been in his account, there were also significant distortions. The Rohillas were scarcely the innocents he described (Hastings called them 'freebooters'); their lands bore little resemblance to his depiction of an Arcadian paradise; and their leader was not a literary luminary (Burke having confused him with a bard from the fourteenth century). Similarly, he retailed the story of the severed head with a telling embellishment: that it had been delivered to the Wazir—'a barbarian'—for money.

In 1786, twelve years after the death of Hafiz, Burke presented the House of Commons with a list of twenty-two 'High Crimes and Misdemeanours' that constituted grounds for Hastings' impeachment. First among these, and as Francis put it, 'the first scene of the first act', was the Rohilla War. Burke castigated both the policy of the war and its execution, and above all the abuse of victory: the 'wanton Display of Violence and Oppression, of Inhumanity and Cruelty', and 'the sudden Expulsion and casting down of an whole Race of People, to whom the slightest Benevolence was denied'.

Burke put his Rohilla charges first in the list of crimes, thinking that they were most likely to succeed. In the event, the House of Commons voted against including them in the articles of impeachment, acknowledging perhaps that if Hastings had behaved so reprehensibly he should have been recalled long before. But the odium stuck in the public mind; and the long-term damage to Hastings' reputation was as deep as any of the other charges brought against him. Although he survived the most famous and spectacular political trial of eighteenth century England, and was eventually acquitted of the charges, his critics remained vocal through much of the next century.

The most eloquent of these was the Whig politician and historian Thomas Babington Macaulay, who devoted several pages to the Rohilla War in an essay on Hastings first published in 1841, and reprinted many times. Macaulay told how 'The finest population in India was subjected to a greedy, cowardly, cruel tyrant'; and how Hastings, having put down 'the brave struggles of innocent men fighting for their liberty ... had then only to look on, while their villages were burned, their children butchered, and their women violated'. And, varying the observation first recorded by Allan Macpherson and repeated by Champion, Burke and others, he reported that 'many voices were heard to exclaim, "We have all the fighting, and those rogues are to have all the profit"'.

Yet even as Macaulay wrote, the popular view of Hastings was changing. Half a century later it had turned full circle. In a volume published in 1892 Sir John Strachey, who had served many years in the Indian Civil Service, set out to prove that Burke and Macaulay had got it wrong. The Rohillas, he declared, were 'not a nation at all, but a cruel and rapacious body of Afghan adventurers'; the English army did not act as mercenaries; the campaign had been carried out with 'a degree of humanity altogether unusual in Indian warfare'. While it was true that the ladies of the Rohilla chieftains 'suffered much distress and inconvenience', the stories that they were subjected to personal outrage or gross insult were 'absolutely false, without any vestige of foundation'. And he showed how references to the 'extermination' or 'extirpation' of the Rohillas were founded on a mistranslation from the Persian, so that 'the story of their destruction is fictitious'.

These changing perspectives seem to have had less to do with what had actually happened during 1774 than with the transformation of Warren Hastings from villain to hero—which in turn reflected changing views

The Tomb of Hafiz Ramut. Bareilli. Rohilcund. The tomb, which still stands, was evidently erected within a decade of Hafiz Rahmat Khan's death at the 'Battle of St George' in 1774. According to the late nineteenth century historian Sir John Strachey, the tomb proved that the Rohillas had not been 'extirpated', adding to the evidence that Warren Hastings was innocent of monstrous crimes. Pencil and watercolour drawing by Thomas and William Daniell, 1789.
BRITISH LIBRARY

of the empire. Burke was no opponent of empire; but he believed that, having acquired one, Britain had a responsibility to govern it justly and honourably, for the benefit and happiness of its people. Hastings, who had betrayed this sacred trust, must be called to account. His impeachment would purge the empire of past misdeeds and proclaim to the world the principles of justice on which it would henceforth be governed. A century later, when the empire was at its most glorious and India the jewel in the imperial crown, historians had little patience with the alleged misdeeds of the past. Hastings was now lauded as the empire's saviour—in Strachey's words, he was wise, courageous and virtuous—and the calumnies against him could and should be met with a flat denial.

With each retelling, the truth about St George's Day, and events before and after, became harder to find. Strachey traced the slanders to Colonel Champion and asserted that his testimony was not to be trusted. Champion, he said, was peevish about being denied promotion to Brigadier-General (which was true); he was offended that Hastings' private arrangement with the Wazir had left him subservient and powerless to influence the course of events beyond the battle field (which was likewise true); and he was furious that he and his brigade were denied a share in the plunder (which was perhaps just half-true, for his complaints about the Wazir's conduct predated his protests about the prize money). But Champion was easy game. He would certainly not be the only soldier (or anyone else, for that matter) whose moral awakening coincided with having an axe to grind.

Strachey, well over a century after the war, was adept at bending the evidence to suit his own purpose. In his eagerness to play down the charges of cruelty against the Wazir, and by extension Hastings, he had drawn on two doubtful sources to present quite a different interpretation of the story of the severed head and to suggest that the Wazir's behaviour was entirely honourable. One source was the English Resident at the Wazir's court, who was as much beholden to Shuja ad-Daula as the Company's officers were resentful of him. The other was Hafiz Rahmat's son, who lovingly described in a book how the Wazir placed the head and the body in a palanquin, covered it with shawls and sent it to a nearby town for burial. 'The principal inhabitants of the town went out to meet the body, and after the proper forms had been observed, it was interred.' Strachey seems to have forgotten that he had already dismissed this book as having 'little historical value'. Its purpose, he wrote, was to eulogise Hafiz. Everything that reflected poorly on the late chieftain was suppressed, while certain events relating to the origins of the war were 'completely misrepresented'. Is it not possible, then, that Hafiz's son expunged evidence of the Wazir gloating over his father's severed head, presenting instead a scene where the Wazir treated the head with reverence rather than triumph?

Strachey was unaware of Allan Macpherson's private journal, which was then packed away in a large wooden box in Blairgowrie. This did not become publicly available until 1928, when Allan's great-grandson, William Charles Macpherson, published his book containing extensive extracts from his ancestor's papers. As a child of empire himself, and a respectful inheritor of Hastings' imperial legacy, he seems to have had difficulty coming to terms with his great-grandfather's comments on the Rohilla campaign: next to the relevant pages in the original manuscript he observed that the journal's account of the treatment of the Rohillas was 'of trivial importance'. In time, though, he decided that Strachey, by failing to take account of the views of officers who had served under

Champion, had got the story wrong, especially in regard to the justice of the campaign and the severities '(not to use the word "atrocities")' they had witnessed, and by their presence assisted.

In the 1920s historians of empire were still inclined to avert their eyes from the misdeeds of the past. William Charles Macpherson's eyes were opened in part by family loyalty, but also because the evidence presented by his great-grandfather was so compelling. Allan Macpherson, after all, had been there. As the officer responsible for gathering intelligence, he was in a better position than anyone else at the time to discover and report the truth of what was happening. And while he conceded that some of the information he received might well have been wrong, he had no obvious motive for exaggerating the reports he received from the field or the evidence before his own eyes. When interviewed by the truculent Council in Calcutta some months after the campaign and asked in effect whether he had tampered with the intelligence, he responded warmly that 'if I had gone by the common reports of the Camp, my minutes would appear much more extraordinary and the actions of the late Vizier in a much more horrid light than they already do'.

PEACE WITH THE MARATHAS

As Colonel Champion prepared to sail for England early in 1775, Allan Macpherson was trying to forget the uncomfortable experiences of the previous year and looking for other ways of moving ahead in the Company's service. Within a few months he was approached by Lieutenant-Colonel John Upton, with whom he had served before the Rohilla campaign. Upton had been appointed to lead a mission to the Maratha court near Poona, on the other side of India, about 100 miles from the English garrison at Bombay, and he wanted someone to accompany him as secretary and interpreter.

Since 1772 the Marathas, who might otherwise have constituted a larger threat to Company interests than the ill-fated Rohillas, had been engaged in an internecine struggle over who should succeed as their chief minister, or *peshwa*. Their conflict was of operatic complexity. A young and much admired *peshwa*, Madhava Rao, had died prematurely, and was succeeded by his ineffectual brother. An ambitious uncle, Raghunath Rao, conspired to have the new *peshwa* murdered and then installed himself as ruler. But there was resistance in court; and when Madhava Rao's widow gave birth to his child, opponents of Raghunath Rao placed the infant on the throne and established a regency in his name. Forced out of the court, Raghunath Rao appealed for help to the English at Bombay.

Affairs within the Company were equally complicated. The Bombay Council, which had traditionally conducted affairs with Poona, negotiated a treaty with Raghunath Rao which promised to help him regain the *musnad* in return for access to additional revenues and control over several islands near Bombay that the Company had long been coveting. But they had exceeded their authority, for Parliament had lately given the Calcutta Council supreme powers for all India in matters relating to war and peace. The Calcutta Council disavowed the treaty and decided to send Colonel Upton to Poona to negotiate with the regency a new treaty of lasting friendship.

Allan Macpherson set out with Colonel Upton and a retinue of elephants, horses, palanquins and about 1500 sepoys on a march across India, along roads blocked by 'rocks and jungles', and through unfamiliar territory where they might at any moment encounter hostile armies. After several months they arrived near the end of 1775 at Purandhar, several miles from Poona, where they camped beneath a hilltop fortress and prepared to meet the *peshwa's* ministers.

The astrologers fixed the following Saturday as a lucky day for the meeting—but in truth, the prospects for a successful outcome were far from propitious. The Maratha ministers, though eager to undo the Company's alliance with Raghunath Rao, were deeply suspicious of the English, wherever they might come from; the Company's representatives in Bombay were furious that Calcutta had usurped their role and questioned their strategies; Raghunath Rao, with significant forces behind him, had to be contained; the rulers of other princely states had to be appeased; and, most burdensome of all for the negotiators, the Supreme Council insisted that the Company should retain possession of the islands that Raghunath Rao had yielded under the former treaty.

Negotiations were conducted in accordance with Maratha customs, beginning with an elaborate ceremony in which the opposing dignitaries approached one another on their elephants until they were within a hundred paces of one another, then dismounted, walked towards one another, and embraced. This was a grand occasion, though somewhat asymmetrical, as the Maratha entourage comprised sixteen elephants and about 10,000 horse. Custom required that Colonel Upton should meet the *peshwa*. However, as all such meetings invariably involved an exchange of presents, the audience had to be delayed until appropriate toys and curiosities, suitable for a two-year-old, could be ordered from Bombay.

Meetings took place in a tent in a nearby village, beginning after noon and sometimes extending into the evenings. Although Allan Macpherson credited Colonel Upton with the substance of the eventual treaty, he was obviously as much concerned with negotiating as interpreting. He spent many hours in private discussion with the ministers' representative, Madanrao Sadashiv, who proved to be an able and litigious negotiator. The Marathas required that the timing of meetings be dictated by the astrologers—though Allan Macpherson suspected that 'their lucky days were suited to their conveniences'. Much of the talk was about honour and justice; but the substance was about the Company's claims to the islands of Salsette and Bassein. When Madanrao referred to the 'unjust and dishonorable' way the Bombay English, under their treaty with Raghunath Rao, had taken Salsette, Macpherson responded that they had done so only to forestall the Portuguese, who were based at Goa. 'A very Honorable excuse indeed', said Madanrao, 'for our friends to come and possess themselves of our Territories, because they knew an enemy was coming to attack us.' Macpherson hinted to Madanrao that the *peshwa*'s government had little choice: it was 'tottering from the very root' and desperately needed peace. Madanrao responded that, rather than give up Bassein, 'We will first set fire to our own Country and then to the Eastern World'.

Negotiations seemed to have reached an impasse. Then, just as Colonel Upton announced that he was about to abandon the mission, the Maratha negotiators relented, yielding to all of the Colonel's demands except one, which both parties agreed should be referred to the Supreme Council. The Company's negotiators were caught by surprise at this turnaround—though Macpherson thought he could guess at its cause. The *peshwa*'s mother, Ganga Bai, having heard that the prospects for peace were fading, and seeing more clearly than most how much her infant son and her people might lose from a war with the English, used her influence to persuade Madanrao and the ministers to give way. Then, to ensure that the men kept to their bargain, she and several other ladies concealed themselves in a small tent inside the *peshwa*'s durbar, listening intently to every word.

There was a more compelling reason for the ministers' change of heart. A pretender to the *musnad*, with plausible credentials, was fomenting unrest and attracting a strong following; and if he should form an alliance with Raghunath Rao, the infant *peshwa's* position would be imperilled. In this context, a treaty with the English seemed not just attractive but essential. So, as had happened with Shuja ad-Daula, Company forces became part of an alliance to shore up one provincial power against its rivals.

The Treaty of Purandhar, as drafted and redrafted by Allan Macpherson, was signed in March 1776, on what Madanrao had announced to be a lucky day for signing on the terms the Marathas had offered. Macpherson was pleased with the outcome, writing to his old patron Colonel Champion in Bath that while the agreement with the regency might not seem on the face of it as advantageous as the treaty the Bombay Council had negotiated with Raghunath Rao, it was in fact far preferable: for installing a usurper as *peshwa* could have been achieved, if at all, only at the cost of thousands of lives. 'On the whole,' he reflected,

> I think we are well rid of a war which too much resembled the Roheellah business, and might, had it been continued, involve all our settlements in war with the Mahrattas, who, I need not tell you, Sir, are the most formidable enemy we could have to do with in the eastern world, as well as the most destructive.

But there is more to maintaining a peace than merely signing a treaty. As Macpherson had feared, the Bombay Council denounced the new treaty as an affront to the Company's (meaning their) honour and interests, and proceeded to defy it. The Supreme Council in Calcutta insisted that they uphold it, but contrary orders from London strengthened Bombay's hand. Raghunath Rao continued to make trouble, protected by the English at Bombay in outright violation of the treaty. The situation was, in a word, a mess. In an effort to prevent hostilities, Upton remained at Purandhar for a full year after the treaty was signed, before setting out on the long march home.

Back in Calcutta, Macpherson watched as the treaty fell apart. Several years later, in 1779, war broke out between the English in Bombay and the Marathas, in which the English suffered an humiliating defeat. Warren Hastings reversed the losses by sending a strong army from Bengal, and in due course negotiated a new treaty which introduced a long period of peace with the Marathas and strengthened the Company's influence across northern India. But the actual gains were not much different from those provided for in the Treaty of Purandhar, and the financial losses were enormous.

Allan Macpherson, after the wheel had turned full circle, blamed the Bombay Council:

> After an expense of two millions what have they got?—why, a loss of reputation to the Nation, Revenues to the Company, and deprived themselves of the confidence of their neighbouring Powers … It is to be hoped the National faith is not in future to be played with at the pleasure of individuals.

Looking back twenty years later on the mission to Poona, Allan Macpherson prided himself that his 'unremitting exertions, day and night' to bring about an agreement had been of 'much public utility'. Certainly, his contribution was essential to ensuring the treaty was signed.

But was the treaty itself, so promptly ignored by both parties, of much benefit to the Company or the British public? Edmund Burke called it honourable, advantageous and 'the most useful Treaty that ever was in India'; but he was using it as a stick to beat Hastings, whom he accused of breaching it to conduct a war for resources. In truth, the Treaty of Purandhar was quickly forgotten, and appropriately dismissed by a later historian as 'a patchwork of compromises'. The best that could be said of it is that, given the constraints on the various parties, there had never been much chance of achieving any better.

If Allan Macpherson's year at Poona had no lasting impact on the shape of India, his earlier encounter with the Rohillas left a modest mark. His reports during that campaign influenced Champion (by how much, who could say?); Champion influenced Hastings' enemy, Philip Francis; Francis provided bloody detail of the encounter to Burke; and Burke fashioned what he learned into a story of national shame that profoundly influenced the way Britons viewed and sought to justify their emergent empire. Of course, Allan Macpherson was in no position at the time to see himself in the context of Britain's imperial expansion. In the short term, his comments on the Rohilla business suggest that this was an episode in his military career that he would be pleased to forget.

4

FRIENDS

ᴬLLAN MACPHERSON GREATLY VALUED HIS FRIENDS. LATE IN LIFE, back in Scotland, he proudly reflected that he had gone out into the world 'without Parents or friends to guide or help me, [yet] made myself many valuable friends, who promoted my interest to the first situations to which my rank in life could entitle me'. Ever since he had first set foot in India in 1764, without so much as a single letter of introduction to smooth his arrival, he had worked assiduously to merit the attention of his superiors. Two decades later, he could number among his friends men of the first rank and respectability, including senior officers in the civil and military line, and even members of the Supreme Council of the East India Company.

So much did his friends mean to him that he rarely wrote a letter of substance without identifying some person as a 'friend', or remarking on somebody's 'friendly' (or, occasionally, 'unfriendly') behaviour, or commending some particular aspect of 'friendship'. Indeed he used these terms so liberally that a casual reader of his letters might reasonably ask whether there was any common denominator among those he described as his friends, or whether the word had so many meanings in his lexicon that it threatened to become meaningless. Samuel Johnson in his celebrated dictionary, first published in 1755, defined a friend as 'One joined to another in mutual benevolence and intimacy: opposed to foe or enemy'; and while all Allan Macpherson's friends more or less fitted this description, the dictionary definition raises more questions than it answers. In Scotland there was the added complication that first and second cousins were counted in a special category of friends.

There could be no question, though, that Allan Macpherson, newly wed and recently appointed to the office of Quartermaster General in

Bengal, knew exactly who his friends were. First was his brother John, who had been in India even longer than he, though often in other parts of the country. John longed to return home. By 1780 he was desperately unhappy, seriously unwell, and above all most anxious to avoid 'leaving my bones in this vile country'. He achieved this wish, but only just, sailing from India in 1782, marrying in Scotland in 1783, and dying there in 1784, leaving a small estate, sixpence short of £3000.

Then there were the friends with whom he would play a round of cards and share a bottle of madeira: Captain John Macintyre, a young kinsman (the nephew of his cousin James) who had come to Bengal in 1771; the Murray brothers, John, Alexander and Peter, all of whom had fought alongside him during the Rohilla campaign; and two or three professional men such as his family doctor, William Dick, whom he regarded with affection and esteem.

His most *valuable* friend, though—the one to whom he was most firmly joined in 'mutual benevolence and intimacy'—was his cousin James, even though they had long lived far apart.

OSSIAN

Since leaving Badenoch in 1752, James Macpherson had gone on to become a great man in the separate worlds of literature and politics. After several years studying at Aberdeen, and a period of teaching and private tutoring back in Badenoch, he began to publish a series of poems based on ancient Gaelic ballads. In a country starved at that time of literary heritage and painfully aware of English dominance in all things, these were received with much enthusiasm, to the extent that a group of well-wishers raised money for him to tour the Highlands and Western Isles in search of further material. His efforts culminated in the appearance in 1762 of *Fingal, an ancient epic poem, in six books*, which had supposedly been composed by Ossian, the son of Fingal, a third century Scottish king, and was now translated by James Macpherson from the original Gaelic. Macpherson was then aged just twenty-five.

Fingal was instantly embraced among his countrymen as the great Scottish epic, reminiscent of the works of Homer, Virgil or Milton. Set among grand and wild landscapes, with noble heroes performing deeds of valour, the verses stirred the emotions and evoked the sublime. Here was evidence that Highlanders, far from being the barbarians they were often made out to be, had a literary culture predating that of the English.

Enthusiasm for Ossian spread to the Continent, where translations were published in several languages. Decades after their first publication, Napoleon was said to carry an Italian version into battle, while across the Atlantic Thomas Jefferson lauded Ossian as 'the greatest Poet that ever existed'. The Ossianic influence extended well into the nineteenth century, inspiring writers as diverse as Byron, Scott, Goethe and Poe, and many of the great romantic composers, including Schubert, Schumann, Brahms and, most famously, Mendelssohn, whose *Hebrides Overture* was initially titled 'Fingal's Cave'.

This enthusiasm was accompanied by a large dose of scepticism. Almost from the moment the verses appeared, there were some who concluded that they were more invention than translation and dismissed their self-styled translator as a charlatan. Dr Johnson, after his famous journey to the Western Isles, pronounced that no original manuscripts ever existed, prompting James Macpherson to challenge him to a duel. Johnson responded that he hoped he would not be deterred from detecting a cheat by 'the menaces of a ruffian'.

So James Macpherson won reputations as both a hero and a rogue. After the publication of *Fingal*, he continued to write, served briefly in Florida as a government official, and then settled in London, where he lived a life of much conviviality, with the help of a wide circle friends and a succession of mistresses. He was flamboyant, fair-haired, tall, well-built and generally well-satisfied with his own appearance, except for his thick legs, which he endeavoured to disguise by wearing unfashionably high boots. Strong in his own opinions, he was dismissive of those who disagreed with them. Affecting a disdain for pretence and excessive reserve, he made friends and enemies with equal ease—for, as he told John Macintyre, 'who is without enemies that deserves to have any friends'. In London he turned his writing skills to politics, publishing tracts in support of Lord North's government, and steadily adding to his influence and wealth so that in 1780 he was able to secure a seat in the House of Commons for a rotten borough in Cornwall. Although his Ossianic days were far behind him, some of his friends and acquaintances, when writing about him to one another, referred to him as 'Ossian', or sometimes 'Fingal' (though not Allan Macpherson, who was punctilious in calling his elder cousin 'Mr Macpherson'). For the sake of clarity, we will follow his more familiar friends and call him henceforth 'Ossian'.

Like his cousin Allan Macpherson, Ossian knew the value of friends. Occasionally he used the term 'political friends'—but with or without the adjective, he understood that the essential ingredient of friendship was reciprocity. As he told Allan, 'if my friends look after me I will look after my friends'. Ossian expressed this sentiment in Gaelic, much as he might have taken his listener aside and lowered his voice to impart some piece of confidential information. In letters to his Indian connections, including his cousins Allan and John Macpherson, and his nephew John Macintyre, he often included a phrase or paragraph of Gaelic, which served as a protection against prying eyes, as well as a reminder to his friends of the bonds of intimacy that existed between them, and the duty that one Highlander owed to another.

Ossian needed his Indian friends. He boasted to Allan Macpherson that he had almost depopulated the Highlands by sending fellow clansmen into the army. 'You will see Col. Macpherson of Cluny soon in India', he wrote. '*Smis a rain shin air a shon*'—I did that for him. Having found jobs for his friends, he expected them to repay the debt by looking after his other friends, supporting his own political ambitions and sharing with him some of the wealth that India was supposed to offer.

Ossian had additional interests in India as *vakeel*, or agent, for His Highness the Nawab of Arcot, who notionally presided over the Carnatic, a large province south of Bengal that included the British fort and settlement at Madras. The Nawab was chiefly famous for living extravagantly and acquiring immense debts, which were repayable to British bondholders at the expense of his own people. His concerns needed protecting and promoting in London, a task Ossian performed to the satisfaction of the Nawab and advantage to himself.

Allan Macpherson and his friends in India likewise needed Ossian. Officers in the civil and military service, if they were to advance their interests beyond the painfully slow promotion that came with seniority, were obliged to look to the higher echelons of the East India Company: to the Governor-General and Supreme Council in Calcutta, or to one of the Directors at the Company's headquarters at East India House in Leadenhall Street, within easy walking distance from Westminster. Ossian was well placed to represent their interests: as he told Macintyre, 'If my friends will take measures to support the influence acquired *here*, they themselves can not fail of being supported there—and *vice versa*'. There was always a hint of mystery about exactly how things might

James Macpherson, translator or inventor of the poems of Ossian. By the time this portrait was painted he was in his mid-forties, and busily engaged in Indian affairs. Oil on canvas by George Romney, 1779–80. NATIONAL PORTRAIT GALLERY, LONDON

happen, as certain matters 'should not be committed to paper'. Allan Macpherson considered himself especially privileged to have in Ossian a friend who was so well connected and so ready to act on his behalf.

The 'East Indians', as they often called themselves, also needed friends at home to receive the occasional remittances they sent from India, and to ensure that their money was safely invested in bonds or land. The task of getting money home was widely considered more difficult than making it. Apart from Company regulations that forbade its employees from engaging directly in trade with Britain, money could be lost through shipwreck and piracy, or the knavery or incompetence of merchants and bankers. Again, Allan Macpherson congratulated himself that Ossian was an intermediary he could absolutely trust.

Not everyone was so sure. John Murray, a level-headed friend with a sceptical view of the world, warned Allan against letting 'Mr James' have anything to do with money matters:

I have a great opinion of his merits as a Classic[ist] and an author but I am not informed that he is conversant in business of this nature nor do I understand that he is careful of his own affairs—I mention this to you because I wd not wish a friend for whom I have so sincere esteem to be disappointed on his return home.

But that was in 1776. Five years later any momentary doubt that might have crossed Allan's mind was completely erased when he was appointed to the office of Quartermaster General, an elevation that could only be attributed to his long support for Ossian and obedience to his directions. Ossian, now a member of parliament, was clearly an ascending star; and if further proof were needed, it could be found in the elongated form of John Macpherson, the new member of the Governor-General's Supreme Council, whom Ossian introduced to his East Indian supporters as 'my best and most intimate friend'. John Macpherson's arrival, he told Macintyre, 'will, I trust, complete the wishes and reasonable hopes of my friends in Bengal'.

Yet so determined was Ossian to promote his friends' welfare and happiness that he tended to neglect his own interests—a sad truth that he imparted reluctantly to Allan Macpherson and John Macintyre early in 1781. The cost of extending his influence had 'fallen too heavily on my resources', compelling him to drop a heavy hint that his friends might come to his aid.

And so they did, willingly. Allan wrote at once to Ossian authorising him to take £1000 from the money he had previously entrusted to his care, to be repaid only when convenient; and Macintyre, distressed 'beyond measure' to find Ossian in difficulties, but with none of his own money at home, asked Allan to lend him another thousand for Ossian to draw on. '[M]y dearest cousin', Allan wrote to Ossian:

> lay aside your reserve and improper delicacy. To whom in this world will you open yourself so properly as to your nephew and uncles son?—Are they not your nearest relations—have they ever appeared deficient in their affections or sincerity of friendship, or not having a due sense of your friendly attention to them?

That was in early September 1781, before the arrival in Calcutta of John Macpherson brought a sudden improvement to Allan's prospects. Two months later, happy in the knowledge that Eliza Fraser had agreed to be his bride and confident that his hopes of advancement would soon be realised, he wrote again to Ossian, declaring that the first 50,000 rupees he should realise from this day would be his; and that Macintyre had come to a similar resolution, making a promised total of £10,000—a very substantial sum. Ossian might use the money as he wished—but should he choose to purchase lands in Scotland, both he and Macintyre might in time add to them, ensuring for all an influential voice in Parliament and a comfortable retirement.

Allan insisted that his good friend Ossian was not to make any ceremony of this business. 'We wish nothing but that you will receive it with the same pleasure and ease, I declare to you, we give it; and that with real sincerity.'

Thus, in a mood of unbounded optimism, Allan Macpherson sowed the seeds of his undoing.

KEEPING UP APPEARANCES

Messrs Steuart & Company were the finest coachmakers in Calcutta. As well as manufacturing palanquins and other modes of conveyance, they imported from Europe a wide range of products, including mahogany panels and trimmings in the latest colours, which enabled them 'to fit up and repair Carriages in the most elegant and fashionable manner'. By the mid-1780s, their house and manufactory were flourishing, owing in part to the growing popularity of carriages. This might seem surprising, given that there were few places in and around Calcutta to drive to. The English town extended little more than a mile along the River Hooghly, and about half a mile inland, where it met 'the black town', into which Europeans were unlikely to venture unless on specific business. The streets were rutted and dusty in the dry season and boggy in the wet; beyond Calcutta, the only way to travel was on horseback or palanquin or, if time was no object, along the river by budgerow.

Yet for officers and successful merchants at least one carriage was essential, not so much as a means of conveyance, but rather to remind the world of their status and gentility. Mere writers in the Company's service were prohibited from owning a carriage, which made it even more necessary for their superiors to have one. During the cool season around

View of a House, Manufactory, and Bazar, in Calcutta. This is the house of Messrs Steuart & Company, manufacturers, suppliers and repairers of carriages, palanquins and other finely crafted products. The palanquin at the left appears to be conveying a European officer smoking a hookah, which is carried alongside by the pajama-clad bearer. Aquatint published by Francis Jukes, 1795, possibly based on an original drawing by François Balthazar Solvyns. BRITISH LIBRARY

sunrise and sunset, gentlemen and their ladies could be seen taking the air along the corse, a 2 mile circuit in the *Maidan* facing Government House, and congratulating one another, with appropriate degrees of gratification or envy, on the splendour of their equipage.

Lieutenant-Colonel Allan Macpherson, newly married and with a young one on the way, was the proud owner of two four-wheel vehicles: a closed chariot and an open phaeton, together with two pairs of carriage horses and 'a remarkable fine riding horse'. We can assume that he owned an array of palanquins, all elegantly decorated, including at least one of the type customarily used by European gentlemen, in which the passenger reclined on carpet and leaned against cushions; and for Mrs Macpherson a chair palanquin, which enabled ladies to sit upright with least disturbance to their finery. For leisurely conveyance along the river, the Colonel possessed a pinnace, an especially luxurious class of budgerow with masts and sails and a windowed cabin at the stern, as well as additional boats to carry a kitchen, furniture, servants and other travelling essentials. As one contemporary remarked, the handsomest nobleman's barge on the Thames was nothing to compare with the barges of Calcutta.

Keeping up appearances was what much of life in Calcutta was about, proof of which was evident in the mansions and bungalows built within the white town and along the river, competing in the grandeur of their porticos, colonnades and galleries. Here too Allan Macpherson was not found wanting, sharing a grand house in the centre of town with John Macintyre (a common arrangement between friends, known as 'chumming'). He also had a garden house just downstream from his friend John Murray's establishment on the banks of the Hooghly, in a row of mansions ideally situated to provide a fine view of new arrivals as they sailed upstream towards the town and repay the compliment by impressing the newcomers with their own magnificence. Murray remarked that Macpherson's garden house was 'a fine castle', and that the two properties took up a good lump of money which might have been better spent in Badenoch—but the Colonel's prospects were good, so there was no cause for concern.

The other requisite was an army of servants. Allan Macpherson employed a vast retinue—around sixty in the early years of his marriage, and increasing over the next few years to over one hundred—to match his growing family and rising status. These included eight *munshis* (secretaries or interpreters) and writers, five runners, sixteen bearers, six tailors, ten at the table, twenty in the stable, four in the garden, and thirteen in the pinnace and other boats. Such numbers, by no means unusual, were dictated in part by the religious and social strictures that prevented a member of one sect or caste doing the work of another. Eliza, moving comfortably into the role of memsahib, concluded that her servants were an indolent lot, and wanted to swap them all for a few good English ones. But what could you do? 'A man of rank in this service', she told her mother, 'is obliged to make an appearance equal to it.'

All this cost a lot of money: some thousands of rupees a year. Compared with officers on the civil side of the Company's service, and even more with successful merchants, soldiers were not well off; and Allan Macpherson encountered the specific problem that he was appointed to the office of Quartermaster General, 'a very genteel and respectable appointment', but without the generous perquisites to which his predecessors had been entitled. As a result, the family had to tread a path between ostentation and parsimony: 'money, money, money', bemoaned Eliza to Allan, 'is a sad plague'.

Allan's salary as a staff officer was scarcely sufficient to keep the claret flowing and the servants in the finest livery; and with each passing year, the opportunities seemed to diminish. In 1783, the Company came to terms with the Marathas, which was good news for the Company's revenues, but not for soldiers who expected to profit in one way or another from war. All that was left were opportunities on the civil side. What would suit him best, Allan told Ossian early in 1783, would be to succeed the late Colonel Alexander Hannay in the province of Oudh, where opportunities abounded for shaking the pagoda tree. Hannay had accumulated a vast fortune as the officer responsible for collecting moneys due to the Company from the *zamindars* or revenue farmers (an inapt term, as while they were expert at harvesting, they contributed nothing to sowing). If he were lucky enough to secure the appointment, Allan believed that he 'would be able to accomplish every reasonable wish without injuring my employer'.

A sense of duty to his employer had always been highest in Allan's list of obligations. He seemed not to have noticed that Hannay, who was famous (or infamous) for his diligence in collecting revenues, had caused misery among the people who were forced to pay. (Edmund Burke castigated him as 'a bloated leech'.) Over the next several months, as Oudh headed towards a disastrous famine, Allan observed that the country was in great distress, that 'cruel villains' were hoarding grain, and that people were selling their children for a pittance. But he, like most of his fellow officers, seems not to have made a link between his own prospects and the misery that was all around him.

Nothing came of the chance of succeeding Hannay. The other most likely way of getting rich, especially for a Quartermaster General, was through Company contracts. Several months after Allan and Eliza were married, he was awarded a contract for building cantonments, or barracks,

The nabob rumbled or a Lord Advocates amusement. The satirist expresses the popular disdain for nabobs. Sir Thomas Rumbold, the epitome of the upstart nabob, is currently being prosecuted by the House of Commons for corruption. He spews his ill-gotten gains into a pot held by Henry Dundas, Lord Advocate of Scotland. Etching by James Gillray, published 1783. BRITISH LIBRARY

at Barrackpore, 16 miles up the river. This involved the supervision of 500 workers and promised to make him 50,000 rupees, or £5000—but the money came at a cost. Eliza decided that she preferred to live at Barrackpore, to be near her beloved and away from the bustle of the town, so he had to build another house, equipped with all the necessary ornaments and comforts. Then a fierce storm caused havoc with the building of the cantonments, the cost of which Allan had to bear. Apart from the money he had sent home, he was now down to his last hundred rupees, and looking anxiously to an advance on his contract payments in order to get by.

More contracts were to come his way—paving roads around Calcutta, constructing an embankment along the Ganges and supplying boats to the army as and when required. But by the end of 1783 Allan had decided that the chances of adding to his fortune in India, let alone becoming a nabob, had well and truly passed.

NABOBS

Nabobs—there was the problem. The word, a corruption of the Persian term *nawab*, had been used since Clive's time to describe Company officers and private merchants who had made large fortunes in India. And now, in the 1780s, it had acquired at home a pungent odour which wafted back to India and made it hard for others to realise their dreams. Eliza told her mother that the country had been ruined by a few going home with large fortunes; but, 'For everyone who returns with £20,000, another 30 don't have more than 8 or 10 thousand, and some don't have enough to make their passage home'.

Robert Clive, who had asserted the East India Company's sovereignty over Bengal after the Battle of Plassey in 1757, had introduced an era of plunder that lasted for over a decade. Clive himself had accumulated a huge fortune, totalling more than £400,000. 'What is England now?' asked the diarist Horace Walpole: 'A sink of Indian wealth, filled by nabobs'. Warren Hastings, appointed Governor in 1772, managed over the next dozen or so years to send home more than £200,000, while still setting standards of opulence in India that few could aspire to. His wife Marian (a notorious divorcee, of whom the ladies were fond of saying that she would have been a great beauty, in her time) was famous for her extravagant attire: Alexander Murray told Eliza on one occasion about a spectacular dress the great lady was wearing, with a black satin riding jacket, a white waistcoat, and a magnificent hat, all studded with pearls and diamonds, and generally reckoned to be worth £25,000 to £30,000.

Back home, people were jealous and angry. When a low-born nabob, who owed his wealth to plunder and rapacity, could return from India and command a place alongside the great landed proprietors, it was obvious that something had to be done. The degeneracy of the nabobs became the focus of a public campaign, aimed simultaneously at the plunder of India and the misgovernment of the East India Company, and the impact of that plunder and misgovernment at home.

But Company interests were powerful; and for some years they effectively resisted demands for wholesale reform. All that changed in the early 1780s, following the loss of the American colonies and the beginnings of a period of parliamentary turmoil. Two committees probed the affairs of India: one public and one secret; one dominated by Edmund Burke, the other by the Scottish political broker Henry Dundas. Together they portrayed an administration in crisis, self-serving and corrupt, engaged in futile wars against the Marathas, humiliated by Hyder Ali's siege of Madras, and pursuing policies that they said were bringing the British nation into disrepute. Both committees looked for a scapegoat, and found one in Warren Hastings.

Ossian, from his vantage point in the House of Commons, watched these events intently, railing against the avarice and imbecility of his enemies (for in truth, he said, their objectives were no different from his own), and conspiring with men of influence in London to keep Hastings in power—or failing that, to ensure that he and his friends would be in favour with Hastings' successor. These were 'slippery times', he told his friends in India, 'disagreeable and uncertain'. At one moment he anticipated triumph, at the next ruin. 'My own affairs', he told Macintyre, 'have been totally neglected, and I am encountering daily vexations in supporting my absent friends.' Nevertheless, Macintyre and Allan Macpherson could rest assured that all their business in London had been carefully managed, and that no men absent from their homeland had been more faithfully served.

But just as Ossian was concluding that victory was within reach, Hastings, well aware that his enemies were in the ascendant, and weary of India, submitted his resignation and sailed for home. Ossian felt cheated. 'I own to you', he confided to Macintyre,

> that I am chagrined, angry and disappointed, after having played the game, to all its extent and brought it towards the certainty of a happy conclusion, to find the cards struck from my hand, by the awkwardness, to say no worse, of my partners ...

—meaning Hastings, as well as those other erstwhile supporters who had not shown sufficient resolution when put to the test. To make matters worse, Hastings and John Macpherson, who had hitherto been the closest of friends, had quarrelled over some policy matters. This extraordinary folly had deprived John Macpherson of any prospect of following Hastings as Governor-General, which Ossian, who fancied himself as a kingmaker, had rated a certainty. And what would they leave behind? Rather than looking after their own interests and those of their friends, they had spent too much time worrying about the 'committees of farts'. Smarting from their ingratitude, Ossian felt that all his plans were ruined. In Calcutta, several months away, Allan Macpherson and John Macintyre read his gloomy letters and counted their misfortunes.

PLANNING FOR RETIREMENT

Allan Macpherson was now a family man. In 1782 his wife Eliza had given
birth to their first child, a daughter, whom they named after her mother.
But infancy in India was always precarious, even with the constant
ministrations of Dr Dick: little Eliza survived smallpox, but succumbed
within two years of her birth to a bowel complaint. By that time, another
child was well on the way, this time a boy, whom they named William,
in memory of the father Allan had scarcely known. Long before he
had uttered his first word, little William was admitted to the East India
Company's establishment as a minor cadet, with token remuneration.
Ossian in London and Macintyre and Peter Murray in Bengal consented
to be the child's godfathers, ensuring that he began life with valuable
connections and favourable prospects. Two years later Eliza presented
William with a sister, whom they called Harriot.

'I am a constant slave to my children', said Eliza. When not tending
them during their illnesses or supervising their amusements, she passed
the time socialising with other ladies, discussing with them the latest
arrivals from home, the iniquities of the Marathas, or problems with
obstinate servants. An occasional concert or play at the Assembly Rooms,
or a ball at Government House (which might extend to the early hours),
broke the daily routines. Then, when Calcutta became impossibly hot,
it was time to retreat to Barrackpore, where Allan continued to supervise
his various projects.

Allan dined often with the 'great men' of Bengal (the Directors of the
Company) and their wives, and occasionally he attended, in an official
capacity, Mrs Hastings—a task that he did not relish. As one of the ladies
remarked, she had been raised to a 'giddy height', and therefore expected
to be treated 'with the most profound respect and deference'. When he
had a quiet moment with the Governor-General, he reminded Hastings
that he had promised to serve him, but to no avail. 'This world seems to be
made up of nothing but promises & forgetfulness,' he told Ossian, 'without
a spark of sincerity.'

Within their private circle, all their talk was of home—where they
should live, and how much it would cost. The choice was between
England and Scotland, and within Scotland, the Highlands or Lowlands.
Allan and Eliza favoured Scotland, perhaps Stirlingshire or Perthshire.
These counties reached into the Highlands while having the advantage
of being within a day's ride of Edinburgh, where the children might have

access to the finest masters, as well as the best physicians. But they were also keen to be near their friends, especially Ossian and Macintyre, both of whom were eager to become neighbours, but had their own ideas as to where. For Ossian the choice was clear: either the rustic elegance of the English countryside or the rugged wildness of the Scottish Highlands. In 1783 he travelled north as far as Perthshire to look at an estate and came back decided: the low country had nothing to offer. Leaving aside the poor climate, the cost of living and the lack of the most basic comforts, there was an 'incorrigible want of cleanliness in the people'. Macintyre fancied England, until he returned there temporarily in 1786 and decided that the customs and manners of the people were so disgusting that anyone returning would wish themselves immediately back in Bengal. (Had England changed so much since he had left? Were Macintyre and his ilk, with the double burden of being 'East Indians' and Scots, dismissed as upstarts? Or had the 'East Indians' become so used to their own society that they had no time for the old?) As England was out, he suggested that Allan buy an estate in Badenoch, where the name Macpherson would carry more weight than anywhere else in the country; and to be near his friend, Macintyre was ready to purchase land adjacent.

But what could they afford? Everyone reported that the cost of living in England and Scotland had increased alarmingly in recent years. Eliza asked her mother to tell her:

> as near as you can what one may spend a year, to keep a Genteel table with Giving a dinner to a few friends Once a fortnight or three weeks and to have wine Constantly at table & to keep a Carriage which will require Coach man footman & foot boy.

And then she remembered that Allan would need a man servant and a horse, and that she would need a good female servant who could dress her hair and work with the needle, and who knew something of millinery and mantua making. Some said that genteel families needed at least £2000 a year to live, which was far beyond Allan and Eliza's means. Allan calculated and recalculated their modest fortune, but each time came up with no more than £700 per annum. They would have to trim their sails and abandon, for example, any idea of living in Stirlingshire, where the gentry were understood to be immensely rich. Society would be very unpleasant, Eliza predicted, if they were 'taking their boiled egg' while those around them were 'feasting with French dishes and swimming in liquerers'.

Regardless of how they might live, there was no doubt about the immediate imperative: they must have land. Land was the only secure investment, the only means of allowing a comfortable retirement and providing for their children's future. So Allan urged Ossian, as his friend and attorney, to make a purchase on his behalf, drawing on the remittances that he had already entrusted to his care. As for the location, he would trust Ossian's judgment. Above all, the money should on no account be left in the hands of bankers, except the Bank of England. Bankers were not to be trusted. As he explained to Ossian in 1786,

> My fortune is not so large as to enable me to play with a considerable share of it, nor so small as to oblige me to run many risks—with respect to Bankers, I positively enjoin my attornies not to leave a shilling of mine in their hands.

'[A]s an individual,' he told Ossian, 'I would trust you with anything in the world'—but as a banker? Why, Allan would not trust even himself!

Early in 1785, Warren Hastings left India forever. Through an unexpected accident (the death of his deputy), the office of Governor-General fell to the next most senior member of the Supreme Council, John Macpherson. This lifted the spirits of Allan and Eliza Macpherson. John Macpherson had often expressed a wish to help his kinsman, and had shown (so Allan assumed) particular friendship in securing him the appointment of Quartermaster General as well as lucrative contracts.

Except in name, John Macpherson was not really a kinsman of Allan and Ossian. Born on the Isle of Skye, he was a scion of the Skye Macphersons, a branch remote from the Cluny Macphersons of Badenoch, of which Allan and Ossian were proud clansmen. The son of a clergyman, he had worked his way to India in 1767, where he had ingratiated himself into the good offices of the Nawab of Arcot and feathered his own nest before returning to England a decade later. Back home he had purchased a seat in Parliament, with the express purpose of looking after the interests of

Sir John Macpherson, Bart. Miniature by Ozias Humphry, 1785–87. CLAN MACPHERSON MUSEUM, NEWTONMORE

Warren Hastings and the Nawab. His bearing was aristocratic, an effect more readily achieved by his handsome features and considerable height, reckoned by some to be 6 feet 6 inches (nearly 2 metres). Fluent in several languages, he was generally understood to possess exceptional intelligence. He was also a favourite with the ladies (though apparently not susceptible to their allurements), and exuded great charm. Allan Macpherson was certainly charmed by him (though it might be said that Allan was easily charmed by anyone who offered friendship). So too was Warren Hastings (though Hastings was not always the best judge of character). For many years John Macpherson had maintained an intimate correspondence with Hastings, though not so intimate as his frequent exchanges with his best friend Ossian.

On becoming Governor-General, John Macpherson appointed Allan Macpherson confidential secretary and interpreter, an office which offered no additional salary but which placed its occupant in an ideal situation to pick up any money that happened to be lying around. Allan hoped that further advantages would come his way. Yet the sad truth was that John Macpherson, since his return to India in 1781, had proven less friendly than his friends thought proper. In particular, he seemed reluctant to favour his namesakes or anyone who might appear to be related to him. Allan conceded that this was a laudable policy, but apt to be enforced too rigidly: so long as a job was effectively done, what did it matter to the state who did it? Ossian was more forthright, lambasting John from afar for conduct perverse and unfriendly. What is the use of being in India, he asked, if not to make money for yourself and look after your friends? 'For God's sake have done with foolishness!' he wrote (in Gaelic), 'And be as you used to be—pleasant, brave, friendly and wise.' Ossian would attend to their 'big friends', meaning Hastings, while he was still in India, and men of influence at home; but John Macpherson must do something for the 'little friends', meaning Allan Macpherson and Macintyre, and others who had been loyal to his cause. '[M]y whole expectation is centered on what you will do for my little friends … Do good for yourself & for your friends.'

But John Macpherson seemed incapable of rising to the occasion. 'There are not worthier men than Allan and Macintyre', he told Ossian. But what more could he do? Money in Calcutta was short, and his own influence, even as Governor-General, was limited. Indeed, he was expressly prohibited from favouring kinsmen. His main interest appeared to be in cutting costs, even to the extent of depriving himself of a salary. Once again, Allan was disappointed: he would have to be satisfied with the money he had accrued from his various contracts, which certainly offered more than his salary but would never amount to a great fortune.

Then more bad luck struck. Lord Cornwallis, famous for his valiant endeavours against the rebellious Americans (and the unhappy defeat at Yorktown), arrived from England with authority to take charge of the government in place of John Macpherson, who had served as Governor-General for just two years. Allan thought his friend had been given rough treatment, and wrote to Ossian and Macintyre with uncharacteristic warmth: 'the most virtuous endeavours for our employers is not sufficient to secure us from supercession and removal'. The lesson was clear: 'we ought therefore to take care of ourselves whilst in office as the only chance of being comfortable the remainder of our lives'. The treatment that John Macpherson had received suggested that loyal servants of the Company should do as their predecessors did—'that is to get Money, Honestly if we can—'.

The only question was: how?

5

SCOUNDRELS

 $\mathcal{T}$ HE EAST INDIAMAN *BERRINGTON* OFFERED THE FINEST accommodation to officers and gentlemen and their families travelling between India and England. In 1785 it carried Warren Hastings home to face his detractors. Two years later, in January 1787, passengers embarking at Calcutta included Hastings' short-lived successor as Governor-General, Mr John Macpherson; and Lieutenant-Colonel Allan Macpherson, his lady and two infant children. John Macpherson occupied the best appointed cabin, on the starboard side of the roundhouse (the port side being reserved for the captain). Allan Macpherson and his family, together with their three servants, occupied the starboard side of the great cabin, immediately below.

As the *Berrington* sailed down the Hooghly and into the Bay of Bengal, Allan Macpherson rejoiced in the prospect of returning home to enjoy the modest rewards of his twenty-three years in the East. He left India and the friends he had acquired there with some regret, but happy in the knowledge that good friends awaited him at home, and that others who remained would eventually join him. John Macpherson was equally keen to escape what had become for him an invidious situation. Since Lord Cornwallis had unceremoniously displaced him as Governor-General a few months earlier, he had waited to see how he might, through his intimate knowledge of India, be of service to the new regime. But Cornwallis (having promptly arrived at the conclusion that Macpherson was 'certainly the most contemptible and contemned Governor that ever pretended to govern') studiously ignored him. Macpherson took to his budgerow in 'a nervous fever' and remained very sore.

At least Allan Macpherson's company on the voyage offered John something of a balm. Allan harboured a sense of outrage even stronger than that of his friend, the injured party. Despite what John Macpherson's critics said, Allan was convinced that the measures his friend had introduced had been the saving of India, and that he had sacrificed a great deal in the interests of the Company. No person who had occupied his position had profited so little from his appointment. What irked Allan most was that so much loyalty by John to his employers could be met with such ingratitude, an offence for which there could be no forgiving.

There are, however, remedies for ingratitude. As he stepped aboard the *Berrington*, Allan Macpherson knew that his friend would be justly rewarded. This was a deep secret: no one must be told, least of all John Macpherson. So in the many hours the two Macphersons spent together during the six months' voyage home, Allan gave away nothing, concealing information that was much to his friend's advantage. His secret kept him awake at night—but whether through elation or anxiety, who is to say?

SECRETS

Allan and Eliza Macpherson took back with them to England all their worldly possessions, apart from their houses, carriages, palanquins and horses and other items that could not be carried except at great expense. Altogether there were five large chests, ten trunks, a picture case, a chest of drawers, a writing bureau, a small dressing box, and three cots, or sofas, each with drawers, and constructed to Allan's specifications by Messrs Steuart & Co., coachmakers, so that they would swing as required in heavy weather. One of the trunks was packed with books that attest to Allan's interest in the cultures of India; another contained the bundles of letters and documents that have allowed this story so far to be written. The picture case conveyed several paintings, including Seton's portraits of Allan and Eliza. The chests were packed with clothing, all clearly marked: 187 shirts (ruffled and plain), forty-nine long drawers (likewise ruffled and plain), thirty-six children's night caps, sixteen dozen clouts (or nappies), and so on, sufficient to get from one port to the next—Madras, the Cape, St Helena and Southampton—without having to do much washing aboard ship. The washing bill when they reached England was enormous—£9/18/6.

This much was relatively easy. The far greater challenge was how to get money home. Several opportunities offered, but none without worry and risk. The most straightforward way was through bills drawn on the

East India Company; but the availability of bills was limited, and in any case there were widespread fears that the Company was overextended, and might not be able to meet its obligations. Diamonds might seem a safer option; but they were hard to come by (though Warren Hastings found it easier than most), and once again, a satisfactory return was never guaranteed. Allan Macpherson managed to remit much of his wealth by this means, but when he sent home a bulse of diamonds in 1786, his agent Ossian was so disgusted with the price offered that he sent them back to be disposed of in Madras.

Then there was the opportunity to remit money, in the form of bills of exchange or goods, under the flag of another country, probably Dutch, Danish or Portuguese. But this meant putting trust in foreign ship owners and—far more dangerous in Allan Macpherson's view—bankers. He lost £1000 in 1786 when his bankers became insolvent, and might have lost much more had Ossian not been vigilant.

Another possibility involved taking advantage of the Company's growing trade with China. While there was a strict prohibition on individuals trading with Europe for their private advantage, no such constraints applied to trade with the East. Indeed, Company officers were positively encouraged to send their wealth to China, where it was needed to buy tea for export to England. Remittances by this means promised good returns—and if it seemed desirable, for one reason or another, that a transaction be kept secret, this was as good a way as any of ensuring that it remained so.

So Allan Macpherson and his friend John Macintyre decided to send most of their money home via China. Macintyre, who was scheduled to leave Calcutta first, would take the rest with him directly as a bulse of diamonds. The 'China plan', as they called it, needed expert help. So they engaged, on Macintyre's recommendation, the partnership of Turnbull & Macintyre, comprising two Macintyre brothers (probably unrelated to John), and Adam Turnbull, who possessed, by his own testimony, a peculiar genius for managing complex transactions of this nature. Confident that the firm of Turnbull & Macintyre could be absolutely relied upon, Macpherson and Macintyre took their advice and invested their money in cargoes of wheat, pine goods, saltpetre and especially opium, as well as a consignment of pearls. In several vessels, around the end of 1785 and early 1786, the cargoes were sent to Canton, where they would be transformed into bills of exchange, payable in London at a handsome premium.

When Allan Macpherson reached London in August 1787, the bills had not yet arrived. As yet, this was no cause for alarm: anyone engaged in mercantile transactions with the East knew that remittances could take a long time. Nevertheless, Allan admitted to Ossian that 'To see all safe home will be the happiest moment of my life'. As the weeks passed, Macintyre, who had arrived some months before Macpherson, became increasingly jittery, and started to wonder whether their agents in the East were 'not the men I supposed them'.

The weeks gave way to months, and then a year. By early 1789 Allan Macpherson had still heard nothing. His patience left him: he started to panic.

Then came the blow. News arrived from China that Turnbull & Macintyre were bankrupt. The partnership had broken up, with Turnbull escaping to Serampore, a Danish settlement across the river from Barrackpore, where he was out of reach of English law. John Macintyre, now back in India, catalogued the disasters: two vessels carrying cargoes for Macpherson and Macintyre had been lost, and Turnbull & Macintyre had failed to insure them; other ships had been mortgaged; cargoes that arrived in China had been sold at half their value. John Macintyre concluded that Turnbull was no better than a highwayman. Except perhaps for the return on the pearls, the China project had yielded nothing. Turnbull had even mortgaged Macpherson's garden house at Calcutta, which he had undertaken to sell. The little money Macpherson had left in India was gone, and the chances of recovering any of it were at best uncertain.

This was clearly a disaster—but how much of a disaster was not clear. All the money Allan had managed to save before 1782 had already been safely remitted, so his losses through Turnbull & Macintyre were mercifully confined to the assets he had acquired since that date, including his £550 from 'the Rohilla donation'. All in all, he calculated that the failed partnership owed him about £7000. This sum could readily be explained, if anyone had bothered to ask, by reference to the services he had performed for the Company during his several years as Quartermaster General, as well as the sale of his various properties in Bengal. The amount was also consistent with his modest expectations. Four months before embarking on the *Berrington*, he calculated that his income at home was unlikely to exceed the £2000 a year which would allow him to live 'Genteely without Extravagance'.

Yet just as he heard the dreadful news of Turnbull's insolvency, rumours began to circulate around London that Allan Macpherson had lost a fortune—

not a mere £7000, but closer to £30,000, with an equal amount to come; and that his friend John Macintyre had suffered similar losses. This news was potentially far more damaging than the effects of the bankruptcy in the East. Who could doubt where the money had come from? The amounts that people were gossiping about were far greater than the two friends could have acquired through honest means. Surely they had accepted presents in India. The timing of the rumour was appalling: it was only a matter of weeks since Edmund Burke, during Hastings' trial, had railed against the receipt of presents, denouncing them as 'the most abominable and prostituted bribery'.

'The poor Colonel is frightened out of his wits', said Ossian. 'Some accounts have come home that he has been receiving presents in India, which he declares he never did.' But Ossian said nothing to calm him, urging him instead to leave the country until he received word that the danger had passed. Surrounded, as he thought, by knowing glances and wagging tongues, Allan Macpherson and his wife Eliza left the children with relatives in London and fled to France where, amid the tumult of revolution, they waited for people in England to lose interest in their private misfortunes and Allan's alleged misdeeds.

This brief escape achieved nothing. Back in London, in mid-1790, they were confronted with the same dismal prospects. Macintyre, writing from Bengal, suggested that Allan come back to India. But Macintyre did not understand. How could Macpherson contemplate returning to a country he had been so eager to leave, without any of the advantages he had once enjoyed or friends in high places to promote his interests? Certainly, the current Governor-General, Lord Cornwallis, had shown no wish to serve him. Allan began to despair, confessing to Ossian that he was 'almost unfit for any thing'.

There was an even stronger reason, secret and mysterious, for not returning to India. How could he explain what had happened to *duinne dù*, Gaelic for 'the native man', or as Ossian called him, the *chori-chin duh*, 'the black man', who appeared obscurely in letters between them? How could he tell the native man that 'what *he meant for a certain friend, never reached him*, nor was he even made acquainted with his *kindness towards him*'? The prospect filled Allan with terror.

PRESENTS

Allan Macpherson's financial arrangements around this time are almost impenetrable. A figure totalling £62,500—half evidently in his own name, the other half in the name of John Macintyre—appears in fragments of accounts, seemingly out of nowhere. There was even the hint that this was the first of two equal instalments. Where could it have come from? And where, before it sank with the rest of the money and property entrusted to Turnbull & Macintyre, had it been headed? The second question is the harder to answer. The first is easier, but it requires a trip back to the *durbar* of the Nawab Wazir of Oudh.

Shuja ad-Daula, the 'hero' of the Rohilla campaign, had about 700 wives and concubines, and numerous progeny. But when he died ingloriously in 1775 he left just one legitimate son, who succeeded with the title Asaf ad-Daula. By all accounts, Asaf, then aged twenty-six, was the sort of son that only his mother could love—and even she had to concede that he had shortcomings. He was, said the Begum, 'entirely inexperienced in the affairs of the world and ignorant of what is good or bad'. Where his father had been cast in the traditional warrior mould, Asaf was a sybarite: obese and degenerate, too partial, it was said, to claret and cherry brandy, addicted to vulgar amusements, and given (as his father had been) to violent outbursts of ill temper. He kept a vast harem of women (though they were universally assumed to be of no use or interest to him), thousands of servants, and an immense menagerie of 1200 elephants, 200 or 300 horses and 1000 dogs, many of which, according to one of his underlings, were unfit to take part in his twice yearly hunting expeditions and therefore served no better purpose than to satisfy his acquisitive nature.

Hastings told John Macpherson that Asaf was a 'cheerful, good tempered and pliant creature', with an 'excellent but unapplied understanding'. But an English visitor to the court in 1794 described him in more familiar terms as 'a curious inexplicable compound of absurdity, generosity, candour, leniency, childish curiosity; devoid of taste, affable, polite, good-humoured, weak, ignorant, and often detestably brutish in his private pleasures'. On becoming Nawab, he had moved the durbar to the then small town of Lucknow, where he indulged a passion for building, creating through his minions a city of palaces and mosques that rivalled in splendour imperial Delhi. As befitted his exalted status, he was munificent to those in need (as well as to those who were not): it was popularly said that 'To those whom even God denieth, Asaf-ud-daula giveth'.

Asaf ad-Daula had no time for the routines of administration, which he left in the hands of his ministers. The most influential was Hyder Beg Khan, a man of humble origins whom some in court regarded as an upstart, but whose aptitude for business far exceeded those around him. Well-informed, shrewd, and skilled in the arts of diplomacy (including pragmatism, deceit and subterfuge), he effectively controlled all the financial and military affairs of the province. Like his nominal master, the Wazir, he was both extravagant and munificent, his generosity much influenced by the advice of astrologers, who sometimes (for a consideration) instructed him to distribute coppers to the poor—the effect of which, according to one disgruntled source, was to multiply the number of beggars in Lucknow.

Early in 1786 Asaf ad-Daula, Nawab Wazir of Oudh, fell off his elephant. Mercifully for those around him at the time, and still more so for the hapless elephant, His Excellency sustained no serious injury. Nevertheless, it was appropriate that the Governor-General in Calcutta, John Macpherson, should write to the Nawab expressing his concern for his welfare and relief that he should survive the ordeal unscathed:

> When God shows his kindness in a distinguished manner to a particular friend, our acknowledgement thereof should be discovered by a charitable deed. Permit me, therefore, to entreat your acceptance of the accompanying 1001 Rupees to be distributed to the poor and needy that they may join in the general joy.

Asaf ad-Daula, Nawab Wazir of Oudh. Watercolour by an unknown Lucknow artist, about 1780. BRITISH LIBRARY

Hyder Beg Khan, Asaf ad-Daula's influential minister. Watercolour miniature on ivory by Ozias Humphry, 1786.
VICTORIA & ALBERT MUSEUM

Such earnest expressions of solicitation were in keeping with the elaborate rituals of communication between the British and the nawabs. Likewise, the exchange of gifts and ornate compliments was as much a part of East Indian life as eating *chapattis* and smoking the *hookah*. As one of the Rohilla chieftains had once explained to Colonel Champion after he had churlishly declined to accept the chieftain's gift: 'The custom of the People of Indostan is this, That when Hearts are United in Friendship, presents are always the consequence'. Company representatives knew that if they were to have an influence beyond the blunt display of military force they had to assimilate themselves to the conventions and expectations of the Mughal courts.

Allan Macpherson, with many years experience as an interpreter, had an expert knowledge of what was appropriate on this occasion or that. As secretary and interpreter to the Governor-General, he was assigned particular responsibility for 'country business', meaning corresponding with the ministers and *vakeels* of potentates beyond Bengal. This included arranging interviews with dignitaries and supplicants, and ensuring that they were welcomed and complimented appropriately to their status. This meant that a *vakeel* of the Nawab Wazir of Oudh was embraced and seated on a chair alongside the Governor-General, and presented with gifts of 'otter' (or *attar*, a perfumed oil) and 'beetle' (or *paan*); while Peera Mull, the agent of the Lucknow banker, Cashmeery Mull, received merely the otter and beetle, with neither embrace nor chair. As and when appropriate, Allan Macpherson organised the presentation of gifts: the gift of rupees to the Nawab Wazir so that the poor might share in the general rejoicing; and to the Maratha *Peshwa*, now aged about twelve, two young elephants, five ponies, a pair of rhinoceroses and four pictures, which the *Peshwa's vakeel* had intimated would be well received.

The Europeans were presented with gifts in return. When the envoy of the Emperor Shah Alam waited on the Governor-General, he presented Allan Macpherson, who was acting as interpreter, with a silver seal and an emerald engraved in Persian with an inscription which suggested past associations:

> Dignitary of State, helper of the country, the honourable Colonel Allan Macpherson, Isfandiyar [hero] in war, servant of the conquering king, Shah Alam, in the 28th year [of his reign], 1200.

Warren Hastings, during his later years as Governor-General, encouraged the local potentates to accept portraits as expressions of friendship and respect, and to offer portraits of themselves in return. As well as providing employment for the growing coterie of European artists who had come to India in search of a fortune, this suggested an effort to influence the rituals of present giving. Although the nawabs were sometimes slow to take up the invitation (and slower to pay the artists' bills), the result was a flourishing of European-style painting in the various durbars.

There were large gifts too. In the time of Robert Clive these had been enormous: a Select Committee of the House of Commons identified gifts totalling over £2 million between 1757 and 1765, and perhaps much more exchanged hands in secret. Gifts were generally measured in lakhs of rupees. (Clive's toast to life in Bengal of 'alas and alack-a-day', though seemingly apt, has been dismissed as apocryphal.) In 1764 the Company forbade the acceptance of money, but to little effect, as officers continued to assume that it was appropriate to receive gifts so long as they had not asked for them. By the 1780s the mood had changed, with successive acts of parliament identifying all corruption as misdemeanours punishable by law, and specifying rules by which alleged offenders could be prosecuted.

Nevertheless, temptations remained. In 1781 the Nawab Wazir expressed his satisfaction with a new treaty with the Company by presenting Warren Hastings with ten lakhs of rupees, including a lakh intended for Mrs Hastings. Hastings used the money to replenish the Company's coffers, then sought to recover it, arguing that it represented an appropriate reward for his long service. The Directors were unmoved. A year later, the Wazir again offered him another ten lakhs. The money was never paid, but the smell of this and other presents, offered and received, stayed with Hastings during his long trial for impeachment.

Hastings, who had spent more than thirty years in India, the last sixteen of them without interruption, might well be excused for unfamiliarity with changing attitudes in London to ways of making money, especially since those attitudes were still clouded in ambiguity. John Macpherson, on the other hand, had been in the thick of British politics as recently as 1780, when he had been re-elected to the House of Commons. After the election campaign, he and others had been charged with accepting bribes, charges that were eventually sustained. But by that time he was safely in India, where he resolved to follow a hitherto unfamiliar path of public virtue, denying himself presents and avoiding favours to his kinsmen—the policy that caused Ossian so much disgust. Observing too that the Company's finances in India were headed for ruin, with expenditure far exceeding revenue and insufficient funds to keep the service running, he determined to make his mark as a reformer. Costs had to be cut: so when he became Governor-General he slashed salaries to civil and military officers. This measure had the predictable effect of encouraging officers to look after themselves as best they could. Corruption flourished; and John Macpherson, far from winning honour as a reformer, secured a reputation for corruption and incompetence that historians have rarely bothered to dispute.

Allan Macpherson and John Macintyre, steeped in the ways of India, had little understanding of how far the acceptance of presents might get them into trouble at home. Certainly, they had heard from Ossian about the growing prejudice against 'East Indians' and calls for reform; but Ossian had also assured them that reform was a ruse, and that the so-called reformers' real purpose was to secure to themselves the patronage of India. Without realising it, they were caught between old and new ways of seeing the world. While they might agree with John Macpherson's assertion that 'Nothing but reform can save India', they also accepted Ossian's conviction that patronage was 'the eternal nature of things'.

Ossian also taught that time must be grasped by the forelock; and there was plenty of evidence around to prove this true, including the sad fate of Allan's brother John, who had served twenty-two years in India with little except ill health to show for it. 'Honest John', as his friend Alexander Murray called him, had died in 1784, leaving his widow with next to nothing to live on. Where was the justice? And now their friend, the other John Macpherson, was bent on pursuing a policy which, while admirable in theory, would probably win him no credit and certainly no money. But his messages were mixed, for simultaneously he was expressing to Allan an 'earnest wish' that something might be done for their mutual friend Ossian. Allan and Macintyre decided that they must act. 'We shall do well,' Macintyre told Ossian, 'we must do well altogether in spite of fate.'

So Allan Macpherson 'fell upon a plan which gave me a prospect of serving both my friends': firstly the Governor-General, John Macpherson, whose own misguided sense of honour prevented him from taking advantage of what was properly due to him; and secondly Ossian, in fulfilment of promises made several years earlier and reiterated each time Ossian professed his determination to help them. This, after all, was what friendship was about. And when the two grateful recipients were settled on lands in Scotland, they would undoubtedly make provision for their loyal friends who had made the arrangement possible. Allan Macpherson and Macintyre would retain some money for themselves, sufficient to cover the public losses they had sustained while in India—but this was secondary to the main object of serving their friends.

Macintyre, with the help of his connections Turnbull & Macintyre, had attended to the complicated arrangements for getting the money to China, while Allan approached the Wazir and his minister, Hyder Beg Khan, whom they referred to as *duinne dù*, the native man. The Wazir, pleased with recent concessions offered by the Company, or perhaps in anticipation of future ones, readily agreed, and a transfer of funds was arranged through the Lucknow bankers Cashmeery Mull. Probably the Wazir or his minister had offered the money without Allan even having to ask for it. What could be more straightforward, or more proper?

We can only guess at the objectives of the Wazir and Hyder Beg, though we can be certain that they intended most of the money should go to John Macpherson, the Governor-General. Hence the need for absolute secrecy, and Allan's silence during the long passage home. Had John Macpherson known about the plan, he would surely have tried to forestall it. The only way to persuade him to take the money was by presenting it to him as a done deed.

But the villain Turnbull blabbed, no doubt intending to publicly compromise Allan so that he could not pursue him through the courts of law. Word spread not merely that Allan had accepted money from 'a native man', but that he had accepted it on behalf of the former Governor-General. This was the cruellest cut: 'I would almost sooner die than do any thing to destroy his happiness', Allan told Ossian. He need not have worried, for John Macpherson was well capable of looking after himself. After complaining in the right circles that his displacement by Cornwallis amounted to foul play, he was compensated with a baronetcy; and to prevent him from acting on a threat to return to India, the government rewarded him with a gratuity of £15,000. He soon learned about his friends' misjudged efforts to enrich him and decided to undertake a tour of the Continent (though whether there was any connection between the discovery and the tour must remain a matter of conjecture). There he remained for several years, his ingratiating manner and fluency in European languages making him a favourite among people who mattered.

More than two decades after Allan Macpherson's return from India, his elder son William, struggling to find his way through the morass of his parents' finances, came upon a reference to £62,000 and tried to persuade his father to explain how he could have acquired so large a sum of money in so short a time. Allan responded by detailing the various contracts he had undertaken as Quartermaster General which, as he put it, increased his circumstances considerably. He said nothing about presents. Perhaps, at the age of seventy-three, he had succeeded in forgetting the source of so much misery.

His wife Eliza, writing to William the next day, said nothing in response to his inquiries, merely observing, as if in reference to nothing in particular, that 'ill-gotten wealth never thrives'.

'MAKE YOUR MIND EASY'

When all their plans seemed to be falling apart, at least Allan Macpherson and John Macintyre had Ossian to turn to. Ever reliable, and wise in the ways of the world he would, they were sure, be able to find some way around their problems, or at least relieve their anxieties. Long before the two friends knew of their misfortunes, Macintyre had written from London to tell Allan what to expect in the cousin he had not seen in over twenty years: he was 'exactly the man you would take him for from the style of his correspondence, friendly and sincere, and with a brotherly affection for us both'. He lived most of the time in a small house near the House of Commons, economically and without show, yet as well as any man in London. Outside the capital he owned a handsome country retreat, where Macintyre was invited to stay.

So when Allan Macpherson heard in mid-1789 the terrible news about Turnbull & Macintyre's bankruptcy and the still worse news that he was being accused of accepting presents while in Bengal, he came to Ossian for advice. Ossian immediately grasped the seriousness of the problem, reminding Allan that Warren Hastings was currently being castigated in the dock for alleged misdeeds and telling him that, however honourable his conduct might have been, he had much to dread from minute inquiry into his financial affairs. Mercifully, Ossian was able to offer a solution. The only way of avoiding prosecution, he said, was by providing accounts that demonstrated that Allan possessed no significant fortune—and here too Ossian could help. Allan should make over to him 'certain receipts and discharges' which, although fictitious, would give the impression

KNAVE of DIAMONDS.

A critical view of Warren Hastings after Edmund Burke had charged him with 'high crimes and misdemeanours'. Etching by an unknown artist, 1786. BRITISH MUSEUM

that any questionable money Allan possessed in fact belonged to Ossian. In due course, when there was no longer anything to fear from Edmund Burke and his fellow tormenters, the accounts would be appropriately reconciled between them. And in further proof of his friendship, Ossian told Allan that he intended to leave a considerable portion of his estate to him in his will.

Ossian then dictated a letter, which Allan wrote and signed, setting out the fictitious accounts which testified that Ossian and not Allan owned much of the money that Allan had sent back from India. 'Colonel,' said Ossian, 'this is only a temporary settlement ... when this blows over, we will finally settle our accounts.' If Allan had any doubts about this solution, they were expunged by his fear of prosecution and absolute trust in Ossian: 'my friendship & my feelings for him,' he later explained, 'were so warm & sincere, that I could not refuse him any thing he asked'. The arrangements completed, Ossian assured Allan that all would be well. 'Make your mind easy', he said (but in the meantime, he should get out of the country as soon as possible and reside for a while on the Continent).

Although Ossian was invariably encouraging, he often appeared to be weighed down by financial problems of his own. In fact, he had managed over the years to accumulate a substantial fortune through various enterprises, chief of which were his services as vakeel to the Nawab of Arcot. His accounts hint at the nature of his duties as the Nawab's representative: the publication and distribution of a pamphlet defending the Nawab in the face of charges against him; payments to writers and newspapers for rebutting attacks made on the Nawab by the East India Company's Directors; 'Secret Service money' for obtaining information; and 'H—of C—Expenses', an imprecise category suggesting that some other members of parliament were indirectly in the Nawab's pay. His salary from the Nawab was about £4800 per annum, with generous provision for expenses.

He also offered his services to officers of the Company stationed in India who wished to remit money to Britain. Having acted in this capacity for his two kinsmen, and recognising that many 'Gentlemen in India' lacked 'Confidential Friends' to whom they might remit their property with safety, he formed in 1784 a partnership with Sir Samuel Hannay, Baronet, and Samuel's brother John to assist in transactions of this nature. John Hannay was an 'East Indian', then on his way back to London. Sir Samuel was a member of parliament, representing the same borough as Ossian in the House of Commons; he was also a successful drug merchant, whose products included 'an infallible preventive for a certain disease'. Another brother, Alexander (Burke's 'bloated leech'), was no more, but it was well known that he had accumulated a vast fortune in Oudh which had presumably found its way back to the family in London. Allan complimented Ossian on the initiative: people would trust Ossian's integrity and have confidence in Sir Samuel Hannay's resources.

But Ossian was a busy man; so in 1788 he persuaded Allan Macpherson, lately returned from India, to take his place in the partnership, along with John Macintyre and William Duncan, who had helped Ossian for many years manage his Indian affairs. Allan was not entirely comfortable with this arrangement, and was not exactly sure what it entailed, but he deferred as ever to Ossian's judgment.

Late in 1790 Sir Samuel Hannay suddenly died, leaving confusion and heavy debt, including £24,000 owing to the house of Hannay Macpherson. Hannay had long been assumed to be extremely rich—in fact he appears to have made several fortunes, all of which he managed to gamble away or squander through keeping open house for his relatives and friends. Allan, recognising at once the potential for disaster, wrote despondently to Ossian: 'for Godsake write me as soon as possible the state of affairs—I never received one halfpenny advantage from this house that threatens to involve me in distress'.

Ossian urged Allan not to despair—the fortunes of the house would surely turn around in time. But Allan *was* despairing: 'what shall become of me and my helpless family!' Where would he find the £5000 that Ossian told him he would have to contribute towards keeping the house afloat? Allan's letter arrived at the wrong moment, for Ossian was preoccupied with his own problems: he too stood to lose money from his earlier involvement in Hannay Macpherson & Co.; and to make matters worse, he was 'tormented' with a troublesome despatch from India. This was not the moment to settle their accounts. Instead, Ossian would lend him £5000 in return for Allan granting him a heritable bond (a common form of loan which bound the borrower and his successors in perpetuity), assuring him that there was not the least chance of his asking for the interest or principal, which would no doubt be met when all the money was collected from Hannay's debtors. In making this concession, Ossian begged him 'to show less anxiety in your letters' and to be 'as brief as possible in anything you will [find] it absolutely necessary to write'. The Hannay business continued to annoy him, so much so that, by the end of the year, he told Allan to address any letters on that subject elsewhere, 'for my mind is harassed and occupied so much with other matters, that it has not room for more'.

Allan's consolations through all these troubles were his family and his estate. Eliza was the model of a devoted wife, sharing his every hope and anxiety. In 1788 she gave birth to a second son, Allan, who, like his brother and sister, showed every sign of remaining strong and healthy.

Then there was the estate. While the family were still in India, Ossian had fulfilled his promise to Allan by acquiring for him a Highland property near their old home at Ruthven. Ever solicitous for his friend's welfare, he had purchased the estate in his own name, urging Allan to keep the matter a secret. As Macintyre explained, this was a better method than buying lands for a nabob (meaning Allan), who was assumed to be able to pay double the price, as he had gained his wealth through plunder and rapine. If Allan approved the purchase, the papers would be made over to him; if not, Ossian would probably retain the property as his own estate.

Once back in Britain, Allan and Eliza remained firm in the view that land closer to Edinburgh would suit them better, especially for the children's education. So when an estate in Perthshire became available that appeared to fit his budget and meet all the family's needs, Allan seized the opportunity. Ossian advised against the purchase, lecturing Allan on the folly of spending all his available money on lands that promised only future advantage, and adding that the proposed property did not include a suitable house. Nevertheless, Allan proceeded with the sale, becoming towards the end of 1788 the proud owner of a fine estate at Blairgowrie, in the foothills of the Highlands, and a little over 40 miles as the crow flies north of Edinburgh. Henceforth Blairgowrie became the family's anchor in turbulent times; and when disaster followed disaster in the following years, the prospect of selling Blairgowrie was always looked to only as a final resort.

'THE DECEPTION OF THE CROCODILE'

The causes of the disaster confronting Allan in the early 1790s were plain to see: the incompetence and perfidy of Turnbull and his partners, and the villainy of Hannay the embezzler. Yet those misfortunes were passed, with no prospect of reversing them. The immediate problems were his continuing debts, most of which were to Ossian. Ossian had helped him out in times of need. But now the relationship between them was so complicated that it was not at all clear who owed what to whom. Other friends were tied into a tangle of financial relationships that was almost impossible to unravel. These included Macintyre and William Duncan, both of whom had granted Allan heritable bonds to meet obligations acquired in India.

Each time Allan begged Ossian to consider the matter, he replied that he was overwhelmed with business, and there was no need to worry as everything would soon be put right. In mid-1794 Allan made the long journey to London and determined to remain there until everything was settled. But Ossian seemed reluctant to see him. Eventually, in desperation, Allan wrote begging that he accept the heritable bonds that Macintyre and Duncan had made out to him, in substitution for his own bond; and declaring that he was prepared to sell his land to pay off his debts. This drew an immediate response: he should come to Ossian's town house 'on Wednesday the 4th of June at a quarter before 3 oClock'.

Ossian began the interview abruptly: 'Who advised you Colonel to write me the letter you sent me on Saturday—it made me very angry very uneasy'.

'I had no persons advice', said Allan.

> The feelings of my own heart dictated every word of it—the feelings of a fond parent & an affectionate Husband to a valuable woman were the guides of my thoughts & the cause of my letter—alas I am overwhelmed in distress & trouble—

Ossian then declared: 'Macintyre and Duncan's bonds are not worth a Sixpence' (which, given that the same might be said of Allan's own bond, was scarcely calculated to reassure him).

> I will not give up your bond but make your mind at ease— Have I troubled you for the Interest or principal; I will not trouble you for it unless distress & difficulties drive me to it, but do not shew a want of confidence in me.

And so the conversation went on for several minutes longer, with Ossian repeatedly saying 'tig lu mi', 'you understand me', delivered more in the form of a command than a question. By the end of the interview, he had managed to convey the impression that he was deeply injured by Allan's evident distrust; and Allan came away promising to tell Mrs Macpherson that she 'should be at ease also'.

There was no one moment when Allan Macpherson realised that Ossian was not the true friend he had ever since their childhood taken him to be. His disillusionment came incrementally, as a series of numbing shocks; and with each, a sharp assault on his understanding of the meaning of friendship. The interview in 1794 was a blow, confirmed by the care with which he recorded the exchange word for word afterwards, concluding his testimony: 'I solemnly declare the above to be the truth'. But even then he clung to the hope that he might have been mistaken and that the old Ossian, in whom he had placed so much trust and confidence, might return, and at least release him from interest on the bond, which he could never see any prospect of paying.

But Ossian, apart from being perpetually busy, had his own financial worries, which had lately been augmented by a building project he was undertaking in Badenoch, on the estate he had purchased for Allan and probably paid for with Allan's money. Here he built a neo-classical mansion which he called Belleville where, according to a neighbour, 'now that he had got all his schemes of interest and ambition fulfilled, he seemed to reflect and grow domestic', though remaining 'a stranger to the comforts of domestic life, from which his unhappy connexions excluded him'.

He died at Belleville early in 1796, in his sixtieth year. His coffin was carried to London to be interred, by his own request and at his own expense, near Poets' Corner in Westminster Abbey. Before the stone had been laid, some of his enemies suggested that any epitaph should begin: 'Here continueth to lie'.

The reading of his will removed any lingering doubts that Allan Macpherson might have harboured: far from inheriting a fortune, he had been left a mere £2000—certainly a sum worth having, but so much less than he thought he had been promised. The estate, valued in excess of £150,000, went to the eldest son, the child of one of his 'unhappy connexions', young James Macpherson. Allan had the galling task of acting as an executor and writing to young James, then in India, that his father had died leaving him sole heir, and suggesting that he return home.

Allan's disillusionment was complete. At last all was clear: Ossian had exploited Allan's innocence and ignorance, misrepresenting his own needs, retaining monies that had been sent to him in trust, extracting even more through fraud and intimidation, and enlisting him in a partnership that he knew to be verging on bankruptcy. What hurt most was the betrayal of friendship. Six years after Ossian's death a sense of injustice still burned within him, when he wrote from Blairgowrie to his wife, who was then in London:

> We have my dearest Eliza met with heavy misfortunes, & I confess, my love, that my confidence in a man who at least

owed me everlasting *gratitude* for my *generosity* and *kindness to him*, was the principal cause—if in place of gratitude, I found in him the deception of the cro[co]dile for the destruction of the wearied traveller on the banks of *the Nile* …

Yes, he had been gullible. All he could plead, in extenuation, was his long period in His Majesty's service in India, and consequent ignorance of matters of business, or the laws and customs of Britain. And he could take some consolation from knowing that he was not the only friend to have been duped. William Duncan had likewise come to recognise that: 'My confidence in one man has been my ruin, but he acted like a father to me in my younger days'. John Macintyre was more forgiving: 'whatever his failings may have been, I shall ever speak gratefully of him for his friendly attention to me through life, and I regret exceedingly, that you have cause to think otherwise of him latterly'.

At least Allan remained confident of his own rectitude, telling his son William:

I have thank my god in my deepest troubles & greatest difficulties felt a conviction in my *own breast* that I never intentionally neglected a trust or knowingly deprived an other of the Right he ought to possess— They are my dear comforts which the world cannot deprive a man of; nor can all the Riches of the universe remove the *pangs* of a conscience loaded with guilt.

Perhaps he had forgotten the secret transactions in India; or perhaps he made no connection between money made on one continent and lost on another. Remembering India, though, we might wonder, as Eliza later appeared to do, if the justice Allan received was in any degree poetic.

6

LOTTERY

MONG THE CROWD GATHERED ONE DAY IN 1802 AT London's Guildhall to observe the drawing of the state lottery are two ladies, one scarcely more than a girl, the other a good deal older, both respectably attired, and both watching the proceedings with eager interest. The event, which extends over many days, is conducted with much theatre. At the centre of an elevated stage, important looking men are seated at a long table; they are flanked by two large iron wheels, each about 6 feet in diameter and 12 to 18 inches thick, and emblazoned with the royal cipher; one wheel contains duplicates of the tickets that have been sold to the public, the other prizes or blanks. These 'wheels of fortune', as they are called, are rotated three times a day, with elaborate ceremony. At regular intervals, the presiding officer drops his gavel onto the table, which is the signal for two small boys, one standing alongside each wheel, to reach through a hole into the wheel's cavity and remove a ticket. An official standing besides one boy reads out the number, while a corresponding official at the other wheel reads from the other ticket whether it is a prize or a blank.

At this announcement, one or more of the audience might respond with cries of despair or delight.

The two ladies who attract our attention are Miss Harriot Macpherson, aged fifteen, the only daughter of Colonel Allan Macpherson of Blairgowrie, and Harriot's grandmother, Mrs Fraser. This might seem an odd place for Mrs Fraser to bring her grandchild, as their fellow spectators are far from universally genteel, a circumstance that might be gathered both from their appearance and from the rowdiness of their behaviour, especially when one of their number decides that, through accident or mischief, they have been done an injustice. At least the respectable

Drawing of the Lottery in Guildhall, 1751. The happy 'adventurer' in the left foreground is about to have his pocket picked.

classes are separated from the noisy and boisterous riffraff. Harriot and her grandmother are seated in a ladies' gallery, while the common people stand in the pit below. Yet while these physical arrangements maintain the necessary social distinctions, the lottery is in fact a great leveller, for by one lucky draw from the wheel, a footman might become a master, or a seamstress a fine lady; and even before the draw, the classes are publicly united in the common hope of bettering their condition. They are all officially described as 'adventurers', a term that once simply meant that they ventured their money, but which now is associated with risk. Some say that people who spend their hard-won earnings on lottery tickets are knaves and fools; but that does not stop them from hoping, especially when there is little or nothing else left to hope for.

Allan and Eliza Macpherson are in the habit of buying lottery tickets. In 1800 they purchased one-sixteenth of a ticket, which probably cost about a guinea and promised them, if they were lucky, a share in a prize of up to £30,000. A sixteenth of this sum might not restore entirely their faded fortunes, but it could forestall what seemed at times to be an inevitable slide into ruin. And it would certainly lift their spirits by demonstrating, at least this once, that fate was on their side.

In Eliza's view, fate governed their every move. Win or lose in the short term, their future was in the hands of an 'All Wise Father, who rules every good design agreeable to his Will: and although mysterious to us at times, invariably turns out perfect'. Their purpose in life was to obey God's will; and should his will lead them away from their expectations, they must nevertheless yield unquestioningly to it, confident that the treatment they received in God's hands would inevitably prove to be right and just.

Allan, though he shared his wife's faith, was more inclined to attribute their misfortunes to earthly deeds and misdeeds. Their fate now was shaped by the villainy of others, especially his pretended friends, and his own gullibility. Such was the extent of his misfortunes and the magnitude of his folly that he was sometimes thrown into a deep melancholy, from which only his wife's solicitations and a devotion to his family could rescue him. They continued to hope for a win at the lottery until even a guinea for a sixteenth of a ticket seemed beyond their means.

BLAIRGOWRIE

How far the family's fortunes had fallen! Over a decade earlier, when they had returned from India, Allan had rejoiced in the prospect of becoming a landed proprietor and enjoying the comfort and respect to which his life of service had entitled him. The purchase of the estate at Blairgowrie was a first bold step towards realising this dream.

According to Reverend James Johnston, a local clergyman who prepared a detailed account of the parish of Blairgowrie in the early 1790s, Allan's purchase was likely to turn out a good bargain. The estate comprised about 2000 acres, or a quarter of the whole parish, and extended from the foothills of the Grampians to the fertile valley of Strathmore. A fast-flowing river, the Ericht, ran through the property, offering some of the finest salmon and trout fishing in the country. Allan's lands included farms and forests, and uncultivated areas of heath and moor, as well as most of the village of Blairgowrie, which nestled alongside the river. This was the only substantial village in the parish, and was home to over 400 people.

Halfway up the hill, with a commanding view of the village and the valley and hills beyond, was a four-storey mansion known as Newton. Built during the second half of the sixteenth century, its outside walls had survived a fire during the turmoil in Scotland at the time of the English Civil War. The interior had been restored around 1700. Newton was in fact a small castle, wanting the customary battlements, but with walls sufficiently thick and solid to keep at bay the most determined brigands (meaning unfriendly neighbours). 'To be sure', Allan told Eliza, 'the house is entirely in the old fashion, with low ceiling, small windows and the whole upon a very ancient plan, but I must own, that the accommodations are upon the whole not so very bad as I expected.' Once a few initial problems had been resolved, such as a leaking roof and the gardener's pigs running loose through the kitchen, Newton promised to serve well enough, at least for the time being.

What was really needed, though, was a modern house, more suitable for entertaining and accommodating visitors, and more appropriate to Allan's status as laird. So he set about building a new mansion on a flat site beside the river, about half a mile from the village. Blairgowrie House, as he named it, was completed in 1797, and was altogether on a grander scale than Newton, with three public rooms, nine bedrooms, a kitchen and servants' quarters, as well as coach houses and stabling for ten horses. Reverend James Johnston, who watched the house being built, anticipated that it would be 'a most delightful habitation'.

The houses—first Newton, then Blairgowrie—were elegantly furnished with various items brought back from India, and other goods purchased from some of Britain's most fashionable merchants. Soon after their return from the East, Allan and Eliza went shopping in London for various essentials, such as a silver cutlery set engraved with the crest and motto of Clan Macpherson, and with sufficient places to entertain twenty guests; a bronze balloon tea urn with inserted tube heater; an eight-day clock in a mahogany case; and so on. All this cost a great deal of money, which they parted with before realising the extent of their financial woes.

The other requisite for any landed proprietor was a coach, essential both as a means of conveyance and as a statement of gentility. Allan ordered a new one soon after his arrival in London, finely varnished and polished, with superior fittings and ornamentation, including crest and motto. The carriage cost £140, increased to £157/15 by the addition of several improvements, including a pair of reflecting lamps and a raised footman's cushion.

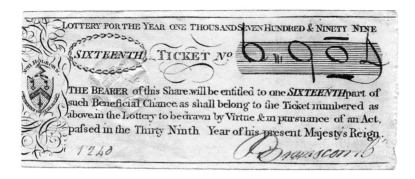

Lottery ticket purchased by William and Eliza Macpherson in 1800. Like every other ticket they purchased, it drew a blank. MACPHERSON COLLECTION

But there was much more to being a laird than merely looking the part. As proprietor and landlord, Allan's relationship with the farmers and villagers on his estate had not changed much from feudal times. His experience as a sahib in the East had scarcely prepared him for exercising the traditional rights and duties of a Scottish laird, which might include collecting rents, maintaining order, or encouraging improvements for the benefit of the community at large. A fellow proprietor, who resided some distance to the north, offered helpful advice:

> it is absolutely necessary to make the villagers sensible that they ought and must be under your controul and patronage, where they will meet with justice, candour and firmness on your part, and every proper desire and inclination for the encouragement of the village [— then] they will find it their interest to coincide in your plan and directions.

There was much to be done. To get the most out of his own lands, he advertised farms for lease and ground to be feued, an arrangement which enabled farmers or labourers to take small areas of land and repay the proprietor with their labour or produce. According to the minister, James Johnston, the parish was lagging in introducing improvements that were common in other parts of Britain. Only a quarter of the lands had been enclosed, and many areas needed to be properly drained and cleared of stones; and there was insufficient attention to the proper rotation of crops from one season to the next. Allan, as the only resident proprietor in the parish, was expected to lead by example.

He was also expected, and declared his intention, to do 'every thing in his power to encourage the improvement of the Village'. In the early 1790s, Blairgowrie village comprised about twenty shops, including grocers, butchers and a baker, as well as several blacksmiths, carpenters, wheelwrights and tailors. Several mills had been established along the river for weaving flax, both locally grown and imported, and these were the village's largest employers, especially of women. Manufacturing was set to grow, with Allan soon approving construction of the village's first linen spinning mill.

Johnston was pleased to report that the people of Blairgowrie were 'sober, industrious, attentive to their respective callings, and exemplarily regular in their attendance on divine ordinances'. Nine out of ten of them worshipped at the Church of Scotland: most of the rest were a group of dissenters known as Antiburgher Seceders. There were no beggars in the parish, and just a dozen or so on the poor list, who therefore received monthly charity payments—though parishioners were burdened by beggars and vagrants from other districts, many of whom were 'very worthless'. There was one parish school, attended by between thirty and fifty scholars, together with a charity school and several small private schools in remote parts of the parish. All in all, wrote the minister, the people enjoyed, 'in a reasonable degree, the benefits and comforts of society', and seemed 'contented with their condition'.

Blairgowrie, in other words, was a highly desirable place in which to live. There was, however, a significant defect: an excessive number of dram-shops—nineteen in all—which Johnston remarked 'must be attended with bad consequences to the morals of the people'. In mitigation, this could be explained by the village's location at the intersection of roads built and used by the military (for travelling soldiers needed refreshment), and the ease of obtaining a licence to sell spirits and ale on a military road.

The military were often out in force, ever since the beginnings of the long-drawn-out wars with France in 1793. Fearing invasion, the government established throughout Scotland a system of lords lieutenant, modelled on the arrangements long existing in England, and gave them the task of raising local defence forces. Allan was appointed Deputy Lieutenant for Blairgowrie, with responsibility for recruiting volunteers and otherwise contributing to the war effort. In 1797, when French manoeuvres off the Scottish coast stimulated both patriotism and panic, Blairgowrie and nearby parishes contributed generously with horses and carts. But the government went too far: a *Militia Act* introduced that year was intended to press men into service by means of a ballot. In many parishes the people protested, regarding the measure as a tax on the poor and a devious means of forcing men into the regular army. When Allan and two fellow officers tried to implement the measures in Blairgowrie, they were mobbed and jostled by an angry crowd. This was an unfamiliar and unnerving experience. In circumstances repeated many times across the Lowlands, the officers yielded to force and swore an oath declaring that they would have nothing further to do with carrying out the odious act. Some of the rioters were later thrown into gaol; only three put their names to a written apology.

There was no difficulty, though, in recruiting volunteers. Allan became commanding officer of a battalion that drew men from several parishes. Armed with firelock (flintlock) guns and bayonets, the volunteers stood at the ready until Britain and France signed the Treaty of Amiens in 1802. But the peace was short-lived. Hostilities resumed a little over a year later; and with invasion threatening, Allan responded again to the call of duty, and offered to raise a new battalion. Within weeks he had succeeded in assembling four companies, each about sixty men strong.

The commanding officer's job was hard work, mostly paperwork perhaps, but nevertheless hard on a man in his mid-sixties and not so strong as he used to be. Late in 1805, when news arrived of Lord Nelson's great victory at Trafalgar, Allan wrote to the town council, encouraging the people of Blairgowrie 'to testify their Joy on this happy occasion' and contributing five guineas towards drinking His Majesty's health. But his own health prevented him from attending the celebrations. A few months earlier he had resigned his commission. Others would have to defend the country against Napoleon; all his energies were needed to save his own family from ruin.

'GOD GRANT ME A RELIEF FROM THE LAW'

To protect his family, Allan looked to the law. A decade earlier, when James 'Ossian' Macpherson had revealed himself as a false friend, Allan decided to institute legal action. What motivated him was not just the need to recover the monies owing to him (though there was no doubt of his need); he was equally impelled by a deep sense of injustice, a conviction that right was on his side, and a blind confidence that the law would set things straight. Just as he had once put his trust in friendship, now he put his faith in the law.

John Murray, who had once given such wise advice on matrimonial matters, urged him to be careful: 'I hope you have had the soundest opinions of the most eminent men of the law in favour of the Law suit you mention, otherwise that is an unpleasant & expensive lottery'.

But Allan was not listening. And when Ossian died in 1796, leaving him (relatively speaking) a pittance in his will, he was more than ever determined to seek justice. Ossian's beneficiary, his eldest natural son, also James, appears to have inherited, along with the estate, his father's proficiency in looking after himself. Although Allan had acted as a parent to him in India, young James, suddenly elevated to the role of landed proprietor, showed no inclination to share his good fortune. When Allan came to Belleville in 1798 to beg for a modest sum which he said was owing to him, James replied that he needed his money to plant 100,000 trees and perhaps to purchase an estate for which the owner would accept nothing less than £40,000, which left no money to spare.

So Allan set forth on a quixotic search for justice and £4600, a small proportion, he said, of what the estate actually owed him. Young James responded with a counter claim for £8000. Allan's lawyers portrayed their client as an innocent who had lived all his life in an army camp, as ignorant of business as any schoolboy in Scotland, and actuated by an 'ardour of family-attachment'. This 'mine of ingenuity' was easy prey for Ossian, who worked his subtle arts on his 'credulity and simplicity'. For Allan to lose would be 'palpably inconsistent with justice', 'an indelible blot on our jurisprudence'.

None of this was flattering to Allan, and still less to Ossian's reputation. That reputation had long been fragile. The controversy about Ossian's literary endeavours, in which Dr Johnson had played so prominent a part, continued after his death. In 1800 the historian Malcolm Laing inquired minutely into the sources of the alleged 'translation' and concluded that they were in fact 'a composition of scraps; an accumulation of crude, undigested similes, transcribed with a few exceptions' from other authors—'the stock of books with which the supposed translator retired to the Highlands in quest of epic poems'. A report published five years later by the Highland Society of Scotland offered a more even-handed account of his writings; but questions remained about whether he was a genius or a fraud. Against this background, young James Macpherson took it upon himself to defend his late father's reputation against all comers; and seeing his memory 'so grossly attacked' by Allan's charges, declared himself *absolutely determined* in vindication both of that memory and his own conduct, that the Business shall be *probed to the very bottom*'.

Which meant much work for the lawyers. The proceedings ground on, so that within a few years Allan was wishing he had never started the process and begging that 'God grant me a relief from the law'.

But there was no relief in sight. Allan's optimism waxed and waned, more in response to any hint of movement among the lawyers than genuine evidence that the case might go one way or the other. The family's fortunes were reflected in their coaches. In 1802 they ordered 'a strong plain genteel Second Hand carriage' costing not more than £100, hinting to the coachmaker that he should pay more attention to economy than to fashion. The following year they were obliged to give up one carriage 'until matters become clear'. Then it seemed they might have to part with carriages entirely. By 1808 they were able to afford a new post chaise, but with special provision for it to be driven by just one servant rather than the usual two, so that the one servant might alternate as postilion and coachman, thereby giving relief to 'our old horses'. In due course this carriage needed repairs, and the coachmaker was instructed to do whatever was necessary to ensure its strength and security; but the 'unlucky scratches' it had received when almost new would have to wait until the family's finances improved.

As the extent of their misfortunes became obvious, Allan convinced himself that he was subjected to constant humiliation. Some people ignored them entirely; others merely made a show of politeness. Even the servants looked at them askance. The coachman, he told Eliza,

> is grown to be so fine a Gentleman, that his notions are by far too high for my humble situation in life—He is the third Brother I have raised from Common Ploughmen to be Coachmen & all grew too proud for my service the moment they were taught.

Allan became reclusive. 'I find more pleasure in looking at the progress of nature in the smallest bush in my garden than the finest prospects, objects or things all the world can produce.' No longer did he have any interest in travel, whether to make new friends or suffer indifference from old ones. In any case, the threat of invasion and his responsibilities to the volunteer militia kept him close to home. Here he and Eliza parted company, for Eliza loved to travel, to see new sights, to attend musical performances and the opera, and to go sea-bathing. Allan tried to indulge her, keeping careful track of every penny spent.

Misfortune made him philosophical, especially about the nature of friendship: 'If our good luck had continued we should not have known the difference between the friends of our *splendor* and our *real* friends'. He urged Eliza not to be surprised by the depravity of mankind and to be grateful for the true friends they still had. And they should try not to think of the fortune they had lost.

EDUCATING WILLIAM

Even as the prospect of ruin hung over them, Allan and Eliza were determined that their children should receive the best possible education. Like most Scots of their class and generation, they believed that a sound education promised wealth and happiness. In their present desperate situation, it offered an opportunity to lay a hand on fortune's wheel and turn it in their favour.

They had returned from India with two children, both born in Calcutta: William in 1784, and Harriot in 1786. The second son, Allan, had been born in 1788, after their arrival in London.

Eliza took charge of their early upbringing, introducing them to the elements of reading, writing and arithmetic, and inculcating the principles of religion. When William left his mother for the first time at the age of six, in the care of his father, she sent him a series of instructions. 'Your duty to God', she wrote, 'is your first study; and by praying to him, he will strengthen you against the Temptation of the World.' The little boy should obey his mother and father, and never tell a lie. He should practise his spelling, reading and spelling some words to his father every day, and taking care not to read too quickly or in a monotone. He should also practise writing—but 'mind how you hold your dear little hand'. And he must be careful about what he ate, 'because you are like at present a little tender Plant that will die if great care is not taken when it is very young & first put into the ground'. He should avoid drinking too much milk, which disagreed with him, and cheese, which made him thirsty after dinner (and opened the way to bad habits); and he must shun sugar entirely, 'as it will destroy your teeth my dear, and probably inflict a tooth-ache on you as long as you have one in your head'.

As well as prayer books, hymns and sermons, William at the age of eight studied works of history. His favourite characters were the Duke of Marlborough, scourge of the French nearly a century earlier, 'whose military achievements gave so much glory to the British nation', and the thirteenth century Scottish hero William Wallace, 'who came forth such a champion for his country and was so ill treated by Edward the III who made a Glorious English reign to the sorrow of the Scotch and French'. This mix of heroes required some agility—but it was hard enough to remember the right king (he meant Edward I rather than Edward III) without having to probe too deeply into the complex of allegiances that allowed Scots to be loyal to Scotland, England and Britain simultaneously, or one by one, as occasion demanded.

About this time, Eliza decided that there was nothing more she could teach William. The preferred course for the son of a laird would now be to entrust his education to a private tutor, who would supervise his intellectual, physical and moral development and give the lad his undivided attention. But good tutors, apart from being hard to find, did not come cheap. Happily, Allan and Eliza had chosen at least one of William's godfathers wisely (the others, John Macintyre and Ossian, had turned out to be signal failures when it came to financial support, and Ossian a downright liability): Peter Murray, who was still in Bengal and on his way to accumulating a vast fortune, and who had no children of his own, insisted on paying the first five years of his godson's education. Allan, elated by this expression of genuine friendship, approached the principal of Edinburgh University for advice; and on his recommendation, appointed a young clergyman, James Grierson, as tutor to the two boys. Eliza continued to look after Harriot's educational needs, which were, of course, held to be quite different from those of her brothers. As a dutiful daughter, she naturally expected to serve as her mother's companion until she should enter the happy state of matrimony.

The chief object in the education of young men, as it was promulgated by men of learning at that time and discussed in the coffee shops of Edinburgh, was the inculcation of virtue. Allan Macpherson, residing far from the metropolis, did not frequent coffee shops; but as a solicitous father, he well understood what a sound education should entail. 'Yes! My dear Boy', he told William,

> Virtue & a good Education are the true & lasting Sources of real
> happiness ... Persevere my dear Boy in true Virtue to pursue
> your Education with diligence & attention as the certain road,
> not only to honour & wealth, but likewise lasting happiness to
> yourself & those who fondly love you.

This was a far cry from the philosophy he had been familiar with in India,
where moral values rarely interfered with the pursuit of fortune. When
Allan, in Calcutta, had told his friends Ossian and John Macintyre that
their task now was 'to get Money', adding the qualification, 'Honestly if
we can', these last few words probably seemed an unnecessary scruple.
Back in Scotland, he quickly embraced the enlightened view that virtue
brought its own rewards, both spiritual and material.

But virtue was not easily attained. The great English philosopher John
Locke had argued a century earlier that: 'The Principle of all Vertue and
Excellency lies in a power of denying our selves the satisfaction of our
own Desires, where Reason does not authorize them'. The pursuit of
virtue entailed sacrifice; and without sacrifice, the consequences could be
dire, as William's tutor neatly explained:

> Convinced of the infinite importance of religion and virtue,
> it has ever been my anxious endeavour to exhibit them in
> this light to the minds of youth, and to represent the way of
> goodness as the only possible one to the attainment of solid
> happiness;—as on the contrary ... the way of vice will infallibly
> sooner or later lead to misery, wretchedness and contempt.

Under Mr Grierson's watchful eye, the boys first spent a term at the
university town of St Andrews, which was closer than Edinburgh to
Blairgowrie, and less expensive. As William was not yet ready to attend
university classes, Grierson suggested that he should enrol at the St
Andrews grammar school. He had received assurances that it was well
regulated and that the boys there were 'not by any means addicted to
any remarkable viciousness'. Nevertheless, the tutor remained vigilant,
always endeavouring to spend as much time with his charge as possible,
without giving the impression that he was especially anxious to do so, and
inquiring discreetly about his companions at other times, including the
hours he spent on the golf links. He was both tutor and spy. Temptation

was everywhere; but happily Mr Grierson could soon report that William was strictly attentive to his classes and study periods, sure evidence of his incorruptibility: 'for I have always observed that irregularity in these respects is the first symptom of the contagion of vice and dissipation'.

Education also helped confirm a young man's social standing. Writing from Bengal, Colonel Peter Murray urged his godson to attend very closely to his books: 'for unless you do that you will never become a respectable character in society—you may be a very honest Cobler or a Taylor, but will never be a good & respectable Gentleman unless you mind your book'. There was, of course, no real prospect of William becoming a tradesman, so long as he remained heir to the estate at Blairgowrie (and so long as his father was able to retain it). What Murray meant was that, if a man were rightly to call himself a gentleman, he needed a good liberal education. So William studied Latin and Greek, and mathematics and French (in which he proved to be especially proficient); and he read works of history, following perhaps Colonel Murray's advice that he note down 'the good and the bad qualities of the Princes you are reading about'.

After William had successfully completed a term at St Andrews, Mr Grierson suggested that he should attend classes at Edinburgh University. According to Dugald Stewart, one of the University's most distinguished professors, Scotland after the rebellion of 1745 had experienced a 'sudden burst of genius, which to a foreigner must have seemed sprung up in this country by a sort of enchantment'. The most obvious evidence was a remarkable assemblage of philosophers, historians, natural scientists, architects—Thomas Reid, Lord Kames, David Hume, Robert Adam, James Watt, Adam Smith, William Robertson, and many more—who contributed in one way or another to what became known as the Scottish Enlightenment. Edinburgh was at the centre of this cultural and intellectual awakening; and its university, when sixteen-year-old William Macpherson arrived there towards the end of 1800, was widely regarded as pre-eminent in Britain and among the finest in Europe.

Scottish universities at that time differed from their English counterparts in significant ways. First, many students attended for a term of lectures without any intention of taking a degree—so William was by no means unusual in enrolling for a term without a precise idea of what might happen next. Second, universities were organised around the professoriate rather than colleges, as at Oxford and Cambridge. Students at Edinburgh paid two and three guineas to attend a term of lectures on a particular subject given by a particular professor. The more students a professor attracted to his classes, the more money he received—which no doubt contributed to the strong emphasis on providing superior teaching. When, as occasionally happened, the teaching did not measure up, some students expressed their dissatisfaction by hissing or stamping their feet—though it is hard to imagine young William Macpherson, always obedient to his parents' strictures about proper conduct, participating in any sort of unruly behaviour. Classes were well attended, with some professors attracting nearly 500 students (and more on medical subjects), including the sons of Scottish gentlemen, merchants and tradesmen, as well as a fair proportion of young men attracted from England by the university's high reputation, lack of religious tests and low fees. Many who attended Edinburgh University around this time distinguished themselves in later years, including the founders of the great liberal journal, the *Edinburgh Review*, and others who made a mark in English politics.

William purchased class tickets for five series of lectures, which entitled him to attend a one-hour lecture each weekday in each subject: Physics, or Natural Philosophy; Mathematics; Logic and Metaphysics; Classical Greek; and Moral Philosophy. All five professors were highly regarded; but none more so than Dugald Stewart, who had occupied the chair of Moral Philosophy since 1785. Stewart's lectures, one of his students recalled, 'were like the opening of the heavens. I felt that I had a soul. His noble views, unfolded in glorious sentences, elevated me into a higher world'.

Stewart's subject matter was vast. He explored the teachings of the great philosophers, from Socrates to David Hume; he introduced his

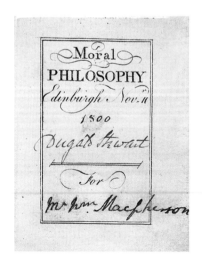

William Macpherson's ticket to attend Professor Dugald Stewart's classes in Moral Philosophy, 1800. MACPHERSON COLLECTION

students to philosophical issues, such as the relationship between mind and matter, the nature of truth, and the exercise of free will; and he invited them to consider their duty to God and to their fellow creatures, as well as the duty that they owed to themselves to promote their own happiness. He advocated the philosophy of commonsense, which emphasised the role of personal experience in providing guidance through life. He spoke with infectious optimism about the individual's capacity for self-improvement, urging his students to acquire 'all the intellectual and moral improvement of which their nature is possible'. He offered specific advice about proper modes of behaviour, arguing, for example, that: 'We ought to suppress as far [as] possible the external signs of peevishness or resentment'. And he confirmed what William Macpherson's father had told his son about virtue as a means of attaining wealth and happiness.

Stewart and the Professor of Logic, John Playfair, were members of the Whig party in politics, with a reputation for encouraging students to engage in political debate. Another of William's instructors, the art teacher Alexander Nasmyth (later known as the founder of the Scottish school of landscape art) was a well known Radical. But there is no evidence that any of the strong political opinions he encountered at Edinburgh rubbed off on William. While he left University brimming with virtue and confident of his capacity for self-improvement, he did not come away with a burning desire to save the world.

At the end of the term, William returned to Blairgowrie, his university studies seemingly at an end. His tutor, James Grierson, had gone on to higher things, having received a generous invitation to serve a noble family; and the five years during which his godfather had promised to support his education had passed. In any case, he was ready to go out into the world, both to make his own fortune and, as a dutiful son, to repay his parents' care and solicitude by helping relieve their financial worries. As to the exact course he might pursue, that was for him to decide. His parents, while always ready to offer advice, avoided pushing him in a particular direction, beyond reiterating that the way ahead involved behaving virtuously and seeking the assistance of influential connections and friends.

For William, as for many young Scots of his age, the colonies beckoned. He had grown up hearing about India, especially when one of the 'East Indian' camaraderie visited Blairgowrie and conversation turned to the old times; and when letters arrived from Major Macintyre (as he had now become) or Dr Dick, or some other friend still in the East, describing progress in the campaigns against Hyder Ali's son, Tipu Sultan, the legendary Tiger of Mysore, who threatened British interests in India during much of the 1790s, or mentioning some friend who was headed home with a large fortune. But India also appeared to be the source of the family's perpetual financial troubles, so that when William or his brother Allan wondered aloud about following their father into the East India Company's service, the response was at best lukewarm.

Perhaps the *West* Indies held out greater promise. William knew almost nothing about that part of the world, except that there were fortunes to be made there. His father likewise had little information to offer, but discovered someone who did—a kinsman on William's mother's side, James Fraser, proprietor of the estate of Belladrum, a couple of hours' ride from the town of Inverness. Fraser had been conducting business in the West Indies for several years, and was rumoured to have made from his last trip £40,000.

So in the late summer of 1801, when the days were still long and the sun warm, William set out on horseback for Inverness, a journey of several days across unformed roads and rough tracks; and as he travelled—across the Grampians, through the Badenoch valleys that his father had frequented as a child, then down through the Strathdearn Forest to the Moray Firth— he dreamed of life as a gentleman planter, and of returning after several years to Scotland as a rich man. At Belladrum he was welcomed warmly by James Fraser and his eldest son, also called James, who had himself spent several years in the West Indies. Young James was full of enthusiasm about their venture in Demerara, a colony on the South American mainland. His father decided that William was 'a most promising young man', who would certainly succeed in Demerara—'if he is spared'.

Now, said young James Fraser, was the time to go, so as to arrive in Demerara during 'the cool season'; and he too was about to head in that direction. At once William began the return journey to Blairgowrie, pausing there just long enough to receive his father's blessings and say goodbye to his brother Allan. By happy coincidence, Dr and Mrs Dick, lately returned from Bengal, were about to travel to London, and they welcomed William into their carriage, the doctor providing during the journey much earnest advice about how he should preserve his health in the tropics. In London William rejoined his mother and his sister Harriot, who were staying with Eliza's mother, Mrs Fraser; and eleven days later he boarded the coach for Portsmouth, his mother pressing him tearfully with last minute advice: to purchase some aromatic vinegar (always valuable as a general restorative); to remember not to leave his sheets behind at Portsmouth; and (as if he could forget) to 'Persevere in goodness against every temptation that may come in your way'.

William, as the smell of the sea grew stronger along the Portsmouth road, tried to put his regrets and anxieties aside. This was no time for tears: he was embarking on a great adventure, armed through his upbringing and education with all the confidence he needed to take a hand to fortune's wheel. Back in Blairgowrie, his father agonised over a letter he had received from Eliza's uncle, Simon Fraser of Fairfield, written soon after William had left Inverness. Simon had just heard news about Demerara, the country where William was headed:

> of 14 Young Men who went out there together the End of last
> or the beginning of this Year, 13 had dropt into their Graves.
> This melancholy acct is further Corroborated from Doctor
> Chisholm ... who terms it a *Sink*.

But this news came too late: William had made up his mind to chance it.

A LETTER FROM COLONEL ALLAN MACPHERSON TO HIS SON WILLIAM

Blairgowrie, 15th October 1801

My dear William

You are now upon the eve of entering into the world, at a distance from the Eye & advice of your Parents, who from the earliest period of your life, studied with anxiety & care to watch over all your actions, & to inculcate you in the principles of Religion & Virtue; & to give you an education which qualifies you for any Line of life not a specific profession—And they have true happiness in acknowledging to you that their fond Wishes have hitherto been accomplished, by your dutiful, studious, Virtuous, & Religious demeanour; & that the Almighty who never leaves or forsakes those who put their trust in him, & earnestly supplicate his support & protection, be your guide & your guard in every moment of your life is my most fervent prayer in which your truly dear & most valuable Mother now in London will most earnestly & affectionately unite when you see her.

In your deportment through life, be civil & polite to all, even to the lower class of people; be assured altho' Necessity may oblige you to enforce the law or a severe order, yet doing this with softness & even feeling for the misfortunes of those who suffer, will have a wonderful effect for the humanity discovered for their troubles; although you could not, or had not the power of mitigating their sufferings.

You are soon my dear boy to be in a situation where obedience & diligence will be expected from you—that is, attention & obedience to the orders of your superior; & diligence in carrying these orders into execution, with firmness, steadiness, & at the same time mildness: for as I have already observed, be assured that this conduct will gain you the approbation of your Employers & the love & willing obedience of those under your Command—At least it was by such conduct that I who lost my Father & Mother very early & went out into the world, without Parents or friends to guide or help me, made myself many valuable friends, who promoted my interest to the first situations to which my rank in life could entitle me.

Be strictly honourable & steady to the Interest of your Employer; & if you should at any time find yourself from bad advice or any other cause or motive, inclined to neglect your duty or to do any act of Injustice to your Employer however small; I implore & enjoin you as a father loves you as he does himself, that you will that instant check the rising evil in your breast that by Satan's guidance wants to ensnare you; & ask your own Conscience this simple question—Would I do, or omit, this or that if my Employer or superior were present upon the spot—If your conscience tells you, that you would not do or omit this or that in the presence of your Employer or Superior—that instant avoid such conduct, as you would do the serpent that would sting you to death—This one Rule observed you will never have cause to blush for your actions—Your Employer cannot be blind to your merit & will in due time promote your interest & regard your integrity; but at all events you have a reward in your own breast, of which the world cannot deprive you, that happy reflection of having acted with honour in the trust reposed in you.

If at any time you discover an opportunity of being serviceable to yourself without injury to your Employer, explain the object you have in view to him; & if he approves, he will encourage & assist you; but if he disapproves, feel yourself above acting in any clandestine manner that may subject you to future reproof; & be assured if your master is a reasonable man he will soon see your merits & reward your diligence, Integrity & moderation—But if he should in due time appear insensible to your merit & the just claims you may have upon him, endeavour by a mild & modest representation to induce him to render you that justice which your services to him entitle you to—He must be a bad character indeed upon whom such conduct has not its wished effect. Be circumspect & studiously upon your guard against the company of bad men or women; be assured once they get hold of you, that they will endeavour by every wicked means to secure you to themselves; or do all in their power to ruin you when you attempt to part with them—also avoid low company—it is only weak & insignificant men that can adopt such conduct—look for the Company of respectable men more particularly amongst your equals & occasionally your superiors.

Keep from Drinking or Eating, as much as you can, except at your regular meals; & particularly in the forenoon avoid drinking spirits or spirits & water; for I never saw a man give up to this practice that did not soon die wretchedly.

Avoid as much as possible the night dews & the violent heat of the sun—Encourage perspiration & have an undershirt of thin soft cotton to absorb it & to prevent your upper shirt from sticking cold to the skin, which will be apt to check perspiration & bring on a fever—Change your linen as often as necessary in such circumstance; & upon all occasions as I have already observed, endeavour to encourage a moderate degree of moistness upon your skin; & be particularly careful at all times never to drink cold water when you are very hot & perspiring—there is nothing so dangerous—avoid drinking of all kinds at such a time, but if you cannot do without something moist, take a little drop of Spirits & water pretty strong; But for godsake do not make a regular custom of this, as it will be certainly your ruin if you do.

You are my dear William likely to be in London for a month before you sail; & let me earnestly intreat that you will be most circumspect & careful in all your actions,

& particularly be not out in the streets late at night—& I most earnestly implore you as a father that truly loves you, to avoid any connection with women in London, with cards, with Dice, or with Billiards, except a game of Cards for amusement with your own Relations—Be assured if once you should be entangled with either of the others you will be completely ruined, let me therefore Guard you over & over again in the name of our almighty Father against the irreparable ruin that must be the companion of such transactions; therefore keep out of their way.

Never my dear boy omit morning & Evening praying to our almighty God through the merits of our dear Saviour to guide & protect you in all your actions & to keep you out of all harm—he never forsakes those who earnestly implore his blessing & protection—and that he may always Guide, Guard & protect you in health happiness & prosperity through life is the truly earnest prayer of your ever fond & affectionate father,

An Macpherson.

7

....

MUD

$\mathcal{T}$HE WIND BLEW HARD; AND IT CONTINUED BLOWING LONG after the *Sophia* had weighed anchor, forcing the vessel to take shelter in the lee of the Isle of Wight and repair damage to the mainmast. Already this West Indian venture is seeming like a bad idea. Apart from James Fraser, the eldest son of James Fraser of Belladrum, William knows no one. Fortunately Mr Fraser recommends William to the captain, Mr Ashington, who promises to look after him, offering him a couch in the roundhouse, and a place to stow the clothing that Fraser had suggested he bring with him: two cloth coats, four cotton jackets, twelve pairs of loose pantaloons, three dozen shirts, three dozen pairs of cotton stockings, six pairs of stout shoes, and so on.

As spray lashes the roundhouse windows, he lies on the couch, reading and rereading his father's letter. 'I hope you will often read this letter', the Colonel has written, '& think of me as I shall ever do of you with fondness & true love & affection.' Then, as his father has requested, he transcribes it carefully and sends the copy back to its anxious author, along with a lock of his hair.

His other reading matter includes letters from his mother reminding him of his duty to his Maker, a volume of Blair's sermons, and some practical advice that Dr Dick has kindly put to paper. The doctor tells him that he should live in a dry and airy situation, at least half a mile from woods or swampy ground; that in the rainy season he should dry his sheets every night before the fire; that he should avoid the pulpy part of the pineapple, which is apt to cause fluxes; and that he may take with safety and advantage a moderate quantity of wine, say five or six glasses, every night at dinnertime. As William possesses 'an uncommon share of good sense & prudence' and the benefits of a strictly virtuous education, the doctor considers it unnecessary to point out (as he would to most young men) 'the great danger of a promiscuous intercourse with the female sex', or to mention that 'one half of the Young Men who go abroad are destroyed by the disease contracted from bad women or by the mercury injudiciously taken to cure it'. He describes the symptoms of fever, advising that if the pain is acute, blood should be drawn immediately and freely. Dr Dick, having spent most of his life in Bengal, is unfamiliar with the West Indies, let alone the particular part of the Caribbean where William is headed. If he had lived there, he would know, for example, that for many months of the year, during the two wet seasons, there is no avoiding swampy ground. Nevertheless, he is well acquainted with tropical ailments; and Captain Ashington, who *is* very familiar with Demerara, believes that the doctor's warnings and remedies will serve William well.

Beyond the optimistic stories he heard at Inverness, William has little idea of what to expect when he reaches his destination. While his father has offered sound advice about how to avoid losing a fortune, he is less clear about how he might go about making one, apart from taking advantage of those opportunities that life and his employers might offer. So when the captain asks solicitously whether he is going out a bound apprentice, William is uncertain how to reply. On hearing of this, his father, alarmed that his son should suspect him of duplicity, writes immediately to reassure him: 'No! My dear Boy—you are going out ... bound by nothing my dear Son, but the ties of friendship, honour & Gratitude'. Hard work and loyalty, says the Colonel, will bind employer and employee tenfold more than all the indentures in the world can do. William takes heart from his father's advice, reminding himself that many young men have voyaged far in similar circumstances and returned with great fortunes and tales of adventure to entertain young ladies around the drawing room.

The gale eventually eases, allowing the *Sophia* to escape England's shores. On New Year's Day 1802 they pass the French fleet. England is still at war with France and its allies, but hostilities have abated, and the captain has secured French passports, so there is no cause for alarm. But they do not carry passports from the Spaniards, so 'if we fall in with them,' writes William, 'we must either fight or run away'. Then there is talk of pirates, an ever-present threat, especially as the ship approaches Caribbean waters. This time they are lucky: the voyage passes uneventfully, and after six weeks at sea the vessel anchors in the muddy mouth of the Demerara River.

Shortly after landing, Mr Fraser suggests that William accompany him on an excursion up the river; but Captain Ashington intervenes, and arranges for him to travel to the neighbouring colony of Berbice. 'My dear Mac', he says:

> I will do for you as I would for my own son, I hope you will not think that I wish to hurry you away from your fellow passengers, but I have your interest at heart my dear Boy and I do not think that you ought to stay any where near town at present.

William is not quite sure why the captain is so concerned; but in any event, the Berbice schooner arrives that night and is due to sail on the return voyage the following morning. Embarking with his few belongings, he arranges to be set down near the Frasers' 'Golden Fleece' plantation. Here he is destined to learn 'the planting business'.

BERBICE SOCIETY

Berbice was part of Guiana, or Guyana, a land which had long excited the European imagination. This was the home of the legendary El Dorado, the man who like a golden statue was covered in gold-dust from head to foot (an apparel so uncomfortable that he had to undergo frequent washing). Queen Elizabeth's sometime favourite, the explorer and adventurer Sir Walter Raleigh, had made the story famous to English readers in *The Discoverie of the large, rich, and bewtiful Empire of Guiana* (1596); and although two centuries later the tale had lost much of its glitter, Guiana still held out allure as a place where there were fortunes to be made; if not from gold, then through luxuriant plantations of cotton, sugar and coffee.

Raleigh had prophesied that one day the whole expanse of South America would belong to the English people. When William set out, however, the only parts of the continent that were formally British were the three small colonies of Essequibo, Demerara and Berbice that straddled part of the northern coastline, each with its own great river that reached south into impenetrable jungles, rugged mountains and mighty waterfalls and, beyond these, Brazil and the Amazon. Whether they ought to be regarded as part of the West Indies, which were generally perceived as islands, was never quite clear. The three colonies had an erratic history of possession, chiefly by the Dutch, briefly by the French, and intermittently by the British. Since 1796 they had been British; but William had scarcely time to get his bearings before they were restored to the Dutch following the Treaty of Amiens in 1802, only to be seized again by the British when hostilities with Bonaparte resumed in the following year.

Over the previous half century, the Dutch had welcomed settlers from other nations—and they had come from all over Europe and from the United States. English and Scottish planters were prominent among recent arrivals, some coming straight from home, others abandoning the Caribbean islands whose soil had withered through excessive cultivation. Around the turn of the century, in all three colonies, the British outnumbered the rest of the white population, perhaps by two to one. But this white population was vastly outnumbered by the blacks: the slaves who had been herded across the Atlantic from west and central Africa during the last century, and their children, black and coloured, born in the colony. In Berbice, less populous than the other two, there were estimated around 1810 to be just 550 whites, 240 'coloureds' and over 25,000 blacks—or about forty-five blacks to every white. With access to British markets, slave labour (rapidly increasing since the British took control) and a steady influx of British capital, the colonies around the turn of the century were thriving, such that for a short period they were the greatest producers of cotton in the world.

The Berbice schooner heads east along the muddy coastline towards Golden Fleece plantation. Here it drops anchor and William and his few possessions are carried by rowboat closer to shore, where he steps into squelchy mud. In drenching rain, he makes his way through the mangroves and into the cotton fields, and then to the manager's house, where he is met by James Fraser's younger brother, Evan. Golden Fleece is one of the recently settled plantations that extend along the Berbice coastline, all of them almost entirely given over to growing cotton. A few have Dutch names; others are named after places in Scotland—Foulis, New Belladrum, Ross—reflecting the strong Highland presence; a few more project their owners' optimism—Paradise, El Dorado, Hope and, more prosaically, Profit.

Each plantation, except where it has been subdivided or combined with another allotment, is a long narrow strip of about 500 acres. The 600 yard frontage, known as the façade, invariably faces the river or the sea.

The property then extends back across an alluvial plain, almost perfectly flat, with coconut palms, plantains and cabbage trees scattered here and there, until the cultivated land melts into marshy country, known as savannah, and then into impenetrable jungle, or 'bush'. The official depth of each plantation is 4000 yards, but in fact the rear boundary is notional: if a planter wishes, he can cultivate as far back as his means allow. Few planters venture far from the waterfront, though, partly because this is the only means of transporting their crops, but also because of the supposed dangers from Indians and gangs of runaway blacks, the dreaded 'maroons', who have colonised the interior.

First sight of the countryside confirms William's worst fears. It rains incessantly, forcing him to wallow in mud up to his knees. Shoes are useless so, despite the presence of rattlesnakes, he goes barefooted until half a dozen pairs of boots arrive from home. What had possessed him to come here? Perhaps, he confesses to Colonel Murray in Bengal, a rather foolish desire to see 'wild and savage countries'. Whatever the case,

> nothing now could induce me to remain here but the fear of being thought fickle and unsteady were I to return home, and the prospect of being able to make a fortune here in a shorter time than I could either at home, or even in the East Indies.

A fortune seems a long way off. Certainly a number of planters have made a vast amount of money—but these are generally those who already have money to spend: people like Lord Seaforth who, struggling to maintain the upkeep of his Scottish estates, is prepared to venture £12,000 on several allotments in Berbice and dozens of slaves to work them. Seaforth's investments quickly pay off, yielding in 1802 a satisfactory profit of £3000. William, however, has arrived with a little over £40 in his pocket. Like other young men in his position, all he can look forward to in the short term is employment as an overseer at just £50 a year, which—given the exorbitant cost of living (it costs three to five shillings to send a letter home) and the rate at which clothes rot in the wet—is scarcely sufficient to keep him properly clad. Furthermore, he quickly learns that there is a well understood hierarchy of planter, attorney and manager, with a sharp descent to the position of overseer. His status as the son of landed gentry counts for nothing—here, it is only money that matters.

William's father, always punctilious on matters of etiquette, understands his lowly status, and gently instructs Eliza about how she should address her letters to her son:

> in directing your letters I beg of you my dear, not to direct
> to him William Macpherson Esqr.—only plain Mr. William
> Macpherson at E.D. Fraser's Esqr. Golden Fleece Berbice ...
> it is full time enough to give the title of Esquire, when he has
> something of his own, & out of the employ of others; or in a
> situation that may entitle him to such distinction—at present
> my dear he would be laughed at for receiving such a title.

William is soon transferred from Golden Fleece to Union, another Fraser plantation about 7 miles to the east, where Evan Fraser has been appointed manager. This is one of the grandest estates along the coast,

A Map of Part of Dutch Guyana, London, W. Faden, 1804. This detail shows the coastline of Demerara and Berbice, stretching some 50 miles east from Stabroek on the River Demerara to New Amsterdam on the River Berbice. 'Golden Fleece' plantation, where young William Macpherson arrived in 1802, is one of the long, narrow allotments stretching back from the coast. BRITISH LIBRARY

comprising three allotments, with a three-storey house built on 7 feet high brick pillars, a manager's house, an overseers' house, and twenty-three 'Negroe Houses', which together accommodate over 300 slaves. In addition there are several other outhouses, a kitchen, a 'sick house', fifteen cotton gins, and various items of equipment. James Fraser and his wife reside here, and do their best to maintain an elegant lifestyle, importing the finest clothing, crockery and cutlery from Europe, and entertaining their neighbours in an extravagant manner. But their house, though larger than most, is still made of timber. It does not compare with the palatial mansions on plantations in the United States; and however great their pretensions, whenever they step outside during the wet seasons there is no escaping the mud and rain.

At Union William is one of three overseers, subject to the routines of managing slaves. Every day, rain or shine, he is required to be up at dawn to start the slaves on their day's work. He comes in from the field once or twice during the day, finally returning with the slaves when they stop work at dusk. At times James Fraser requires him to help with the plantation correspondence and bookkeeping, so that every moment he is not in the field he is engaged in clerical work. The slaves are made to work even on Sunday mornings, after which the overseers distribute their rations for the week. This leaves only Sunday afternoon free, for slaves and overseers alike. In the evenings, all the whites on the estate dine together; but just in case William momentarily forgets his proper place, he and his fellow overseers withdraw, in accordance with established custom, as soon as the cheese is brought to the table. Since candles are expensive, he then retires to his hammock, where a thin muslin curtain affords feeble protection against swarms of mosquitoes.

All the conventions he is used to are turned on their head. 'As to Religion, Virtue, Regard of the Sabbath,' he tells his parents, 'I believe there is no such thing in this country;'

> even in the hour of sickness and death, religion seems to
> be forgot: and in the last moments, the ... raillery of man is
> more feared than the punishment of God: and his name never
> mentioned but to violate it.

Most of the Europeans spend Sunday afternoon visiting, drinking or shooting, or gambling at cards, backgammon, billiards, cockfighting, and any other way they can find to amuse themselves. William stays in the overseers' hut, consoling himself by reading one of Blair's sermons, and remembering the precepts his mother taught him.

A public road, bordered on each side by a ditch or canal, runs almost in a straight line through the estates, several hundred yards back from the seashore. As well as linking the plantations, this creates interdependence between them, as each planter is responsible for maintaining his section—a demanding task, since the canals need constant clearing and the road is often potholed by rain and high tides, and undermined by crabs. The road carries frequent travellers from one estate to another, mostly blacks sent on some errand or another, but also the occasional European. There are no roadside inns, and travellers are accustomed to slinging their hammock at any plantation along the way, where they expect to be well fed and watered. According to William, such visits are accompanied by much carousing, with the host generally endeavouring to get the traveller as drunk as possible.

William rarely escapes the confines of the plantation. His first venture abroad is a long day's walk and a ferry crossing to New Amsterdam, the only town in Berbice, located several miles from the broad mouth of the Berbice River. There is little to see here: a scattering of timber houses surrounded by open drains, a couple of taverns, and Government House, which has the rare distinction in the colony of being made of brick.

More than eighteen months pass before he visits the much larger town of Stabroek, the capital of Demerara and the principal port for the three colonies. Stabroek has a population of several thousand, perhaps a fifth of whom are white. It bears no resemblance to any Scottish or English town William has ever seen, but reminds him of what he has read of Holland. The main street, which is roughly paved, runs back from the Demerara River for about a mile, with widely scattered houses on either side, backed by canals and drains. The white timber houses are of one or two storeys, and jut out in different directions, as in a cross, to take maximum advantage of sea breezes. Some have warehouses between them, and casks and bales lie about as if every road is a wharf. Groups of Europeans loiter outside the town's few taverns, some of them hopelessly drunk. William now understands why Captain Ashington was so keen to bundle him off to the relative civility of the plantation. The occasional white man sits beneath an umbrella, smoking his cigar and issuing commands to his own slaves or perhaps to some of the fifty or so blacks who, having committed

View of New Amsterdam on the Berbice River. Hand-coloured engraving. Published by C. Sepp Jansz, Amsterdam, 1807. JOHN CARTER BROWN ARCHIVE OF EARLY AMERICAN IMAGES, BROWN UNIVERSITY, PROVIDENCE

....

some criminal offence, are retained in heavy chains to labour around the town for the common good. The town has a dilapidated government house; a church, the only one in the colony, and little frequented; and a courthouse, whose decaying floor, according to one observer, 'is a perfect emblem of the state of laws in this colony'.

Disease is rife in the towns and on the plantations alike. But William obeys Dr Dick's instructions, and although he is often forced to stand all day in the pouring rain, remains perfectly healthy. Others are dying around him, which he attributes chiefly to intemperance. Others again succumb to a depression in the spirits that seems to infest the whole coastline, even during the good times.

In such circumstances it is difficult to remain optimistic. William's father begs him not to give way to melancholy, for 'that will serve no good purpose—You have far more favourable prospects than I had &

yet I did very well, if I had prudence to take care of what providence put in my way—But alas!' Overcoming his initial miseries, William does his job well, and in 1803 James Fraser appoints him manager of Union at a salary of £166, much lower than it should be given the size of the estate, but nevertheless a step up. The following year he is offered a more desirable appointment to the smaller plantation of Paradise, another Fraser estate adjacent to Golden Fleece. He makes friends, including another young Scot, Edward Satchwell Fraser of Reelig, near Inverness, whose family is connected to the Frasers of Belladrum by blood and commerce. Edward Fraser, who arrives in 1803, serves first as an overseer in Berbice. A sensitive and reflective young man with a love of music, he loathes the country and the 'vulgar' people— meaning the whites—who inhabit it; but his father has invested heavily in plantations, leaving him little choice but to stay here. He consoles himself by playing a flute and later, when he moves to one of the Union allotments, a piano. On many matters, including religious observance,

Edward Satchwell Fraser of Reelig, William Macpherson's contemporary in Berbice. Oil by Henry Raeburn, completed in 1803, shortly before the young Fraser set out to make his fortune in the West Indies. TAFT MUSEUM OF ART, CINCINNATI

temperance and filial duty, he and William are of similar minds; but as they and other potential friends can rarely leave their plantations, their conversations are few and far between.

William knows he cannot escape this dreary existence without making money; and that the only way he can make money is by himself becoming a proprietor of land and slaves. His father promises to help him:

> Be assured my dear boy that your fond and affectionate father will do all in his power to promote your welfare & Success in life and that I will Study every possible means to furnish you with three or four thousand pounds, as soon as it will be Safe by your Experience & Situation to invest it ...

The best starting point is to acquire a few slaves. A 'good field negro' costs £100 and could return £25 per year. This handsome profit could be used to purchase additional slaves until he has sufficient to form a task gang of fifteen or twenty. The gang could then be assigned to larger undertakings, such as clearing and draining an area of land, for which the slave owner is paid by the acre. In no time at all there should be sufficient funds to purchase land. It seems a sure investment.

So the Colonel, even though he is weighed down with concerns about his claim against Ossian's son, responds promptly to William's appeals and authorises him to purchase slaves to the value of £500. William rejoices at his father's generosity and, even before he has been promoted to the position of manager, purchases from Evan Fraser four 'prime negroes' and two 'inferior' ones.

The Colonel congratulates him: 'I sincerely hope my dear son that your Negroes will be a happy beginning to your future prosperity'.

SLAVES

When the Europeans on the larger plantations gathered at the end of their day's work, conversation around the dinner table was often lively. Sometimes it turned on events back home—especially the ups and downs of the wars with Bonaparte—which they heard about many weeks after the events occurred. More often the subject matter was close at hand: the potential for a good cotton crop, the planting of new seeds in the vegetable garden, the arrival of a new overseer at a nearby plantation, and when, if ever, the rains would start or stop.

Then there was the tittle-tattle that a small community invariably generates. In 1804 Governor van Batenburg's wife caused a great scandal by 'eloping' with the local commander of British troops, Major Hardiman. Simon Fraser, who was married to one of the van Batenburgs' daughters, challenged the Major to a duel, from which both emerged unscathed. As everyone already knew, but had previously not dared to say, the offending lady had once been an opera dancer in France or Holland—so what could you expect? Before the gossips ran out of things to say, the Governor provided more fuel for the cauldron by remarrying, a milliner thirty years his junior. They are 'all love and affectionate', Edward Satchwell Fraser told his mother; he is 'an old fool'.

They talked often about slaves—the behaviour of particular slaves on the estates, some violent crime committed down the road, the pursuit of runaways—and larger questions relating to the necessity or morality of slavery and the slave trade. For many planters, a future without slaves was unimaginable, given that the plantation economy was built around unpaid labour. In London, though, the power of William Wilberforce and the abolitionists was growing, and in 1807 the House of Commons, ignoring desperate pleadings from sections of the West Indies interest, outlawed the slave trade on British ships.

On the Fraser estates, conversation at dinner time often became heated. At the head of the table was James Fraser (the younger) of Belladrum, with his wife at the opposite end. At the sides were the two Fraser of Reelig brothers—James Baillie Fraser and Edward Satchwell Fraser; the Frasers' attorney Lewis Cameron; and perhaps (until the customary time for their withdrawal) two or three overseers and tradesmen. Edward made no secret of his opposition to slavery—but he had difficulty getting a word in. Whenever he said anything against the system, his brother, who was a few years his senior, subjected him to such a browbeating that he decided to hold his tongue. The others, wrote Edward, then continued to argue, 'all trying who can drown the other's voice and on the same side of the question—with a gentle contradiction now and then from Mrs Fraser—she and I generally laughing at the other three, in our sleeve'.

Behind the joviality was a deep fear—not just of the economic consequences should slavery be abolished or the supply of slaves dry up, but also of the risks of maintaining the slaves in subjection. 'I think we may be in continual dread as long as we live in a slave country',

Edward Fraser told his mother. Owners, managers and overseers knew only too well that things could get out of hand. There were many stories of rebellion, including a bloody insurrection in 1762 and 1763, when slaves overwhelmed the white population and held the colony for nearly a year. While English and Scottish planters might congratulate themselves that they were more humane than the Dutch, slaves still rebelled against their conditions, perhaps by refusing to work or by escaping into the savannah, as they did at Golden Fleece plantation in 1807. Violence was endemic. Just before that conversation around the Fraser dinner table, a mulatto man had been found dead on the public road with three stab wounds in his head and neck. Suicide among the slaves was commonplace. 'There surely must be something radically wrong', wrote Edward Fraser, 'in a thing that is the source of so many miseries and crimes.'

Nearly everyone in the plantation households agreed that managing slaves demanded much skill. Some owners and overseers maintained control through brute force, punishing the smallest misdemeanour or slackening

The mode of flogging slaves. From an album published in 1828 for the Birmingham Female Society for … the relief of British negro slaves. Engraving printed by Benjamin Hudson.
CORBIS IMAGES

of pace. Their chief instrument was the whip, and they used it mercilessly. More astute planters recognised that the effective management of slaves required more than mere coercion. While a thorough flogging might sometimes be called for, greater profits would accrue through the subtle use of carrot and stick. This was achieved through the 'task system'. As William Macpherson explained to his sister Harriot, a slave had no hope of bettering his situation, however strenuously he might exert himself; therefore, the best way of getting the work done was to give him each day a specific task to perform, and once he had carried it out satisfactorily, to allow him the rest of the day off.

People who did not demonstrate the necessary management skills were considered a threat to the system. As well as upsetting the relative harmony on the estates, they gave slavery a bad name. In 1812, on one of the Fraser estates that had once formed part of Union, the attorney Lewis Cameron sacked the manager, James McDougall, for treating a 'Negro' family 'in a most Wanton & Cruel manner'. According to McDougall, the Negro carpenter Willitick and his wife Dobie were troublesome and insolent, so he was obliged 'to lick them'. When Cameron returned from a visit to Stabroek, he discovered from the other slaves what this meant. The manager, who was given to 'Violent passions', had beaten Willitick to the ground with a stick, thrown him into the stocks and then had him flogged; and he had forced Dobie to lie stretched out on the ground, tied to pickets, leaving her there for two hours (the other Negroes said four) before having her flogged. Two days later he had repeated the punishment; and when the three children, terrified by what was happening to their parents, left work to plead on their behalf, they too were subjected to brutal treatment.

McDougall protested that Cameron had no right to interfere in such a trifling matter. But Cameron was adamant: 'in my opinion *nothing* can justify such inhumanity'—and rather than connive at such treatment he would instantly resign the charge of any estate. McDougall, he said, might have known how to plant cotton, but he had no idea of how to manage Negroes. 'I am very sensible how necessary it is to support proper order & discipline amongst Negroes', he told Edward Satchwell Fraser; 'but the facts that I have related are very wide of my ideas on that subject'. Two of the neighbours reported the case to the colony's legal officer, but Cameron in any case had no doubt that McDougall was 'finished' in the colony: no other planter would give him a job.

There was nothing especially remarkable about McDougall's brutality, any more than there was anything untoward about the reporting of it. Some masters were sadistic, others compassionate, most influenced by the realisation—made sharper after the abolition of the slave trade—that slaves were essential to their prosperity, a valuable commodity who yielded the highest returns when they were healthy and compliant. Edward Satchwell Fraser was unusually compassionate. When he had shown distress at the sight of a grieving mother whose baby died in her arms of lockjaw, he guessed that his manager ('a capricious conceited little body' called Mr Arthur) would laugh at him. But most owners, and employees who had their owners' interests at heart, would have been distressed when a slave died, if only because they were losing a productive, or potentially productive, member of their workforce.

William Macpherson no doubt heard about McDougall's dismissal— news travelled fast along the Berbice coastline. But he left no record of his reactions to this or any similar incident that might provide clues to his views on slavery. Like other young men who came to Berbice to make their fortune, he had brought with him prejudices and preconceptions that were the product of how he had been raised and what he had been taught. He had seen blacks in Britain, possibly as liveried footmen on one of the great estates near home, certainly as musicians or domestics on the streets of London. He had read about them in books, including Mungo Park's just published story of his travels in Africa, which told how the intrepid explorer had been held prisoner by 'Moors', how he had been tormented and humiliated, and how he had eventually escaped, taking care to avoid the 'Mahometan Negroes' who were, by William's recounting, every bit as bad. Park wrote about slavery without condemning it, and suggested that there was little to be gained from abolishing the slave trade.

At the University of Edinburgh, William had listened attentively to Professor Dugald Stewart expound the various theories relating to the origins of the different races—European, Samoyed, Tartar, Hindu, Negro and the Aborigines of the New World. Physically, opined the professor, the Negroes, while 'on the whole not ill-shaped', were 'greatly inferior to the Europeans in correctness and elegance of form'.

On the matter of their mental attributes, he said, philosophers were divided; but he was sure Thomas Jefferson was mistaken in arguing that Negroes were equal to Europeans in memory but not in powers of understanding. 'Mr Stewart', William had noted in his lecture book, 'thinks that their inferiority to us is owing to the miserable situation in which we commonly see them rather than to any natural defect.' But Stewart appears to have said nothing, except by implication, about slavery and the slave trade.

Similarly, the Colonel, in his parting advice to William, had not mentioned slaves, but he obviously had them in mind when he wrote:

> altho' Necessity may oblige you to enforce the law or a severe order, yet doing this with softness and even feeling for the misfortunes of those who suffer, will have a wonderful effect for the humanity discovered for their troubles; although you could not, or had not the power of mitigating their sufferings.

If William had doubts about the morality of depriving fellow humans of their freedom, he could console himself in the knowledge that there was nothing he could do about it.

His mother was more deeply troubled about the evident contradiction between slavery and her religious beliefs, and more responsive to the movement for abolition. Her usual practice was to offer spiritual and moral advice in the form of passages from the scriptures or any other worthy source that she came across; so when she chanced on these lines written, she said, by 'a little African Slave girl' (in fact the young Boston slave, Phillis Wheatley, who was later celebrated as the first African American to publish a book, in 1773), she copied them out carefully for William's edification:

> 'Twas *mercy* brought me from my *Pagan* land,
> Taught my benighted soul to understand
> That there's a God, that there's a *Saviour* too:
> Once I redemption neither sought nor knew.
> Some view our sable race with scornful eye,
> "Their Colour is a diabolic die."
> Remember, *Christians*, *Negroes*, black as *Cain*,
> May be refin'd, and join th'angelic train.

When the House of Commons took its momentous decision to outlaw the slave trade, Eliza remarked approvingly that abolition would 'soften the ferocious treatment of these poor unhappy creatures'—for it was certain, she said, that more were treated cruelly than kindly.

But William had already absorbed the prevailing view among the white population that the abolitionists were armchair theorists, with little understanding of what life on the plantations was actually like. What really mattered was the potentially disastrous impact of abolition on the colony's economy. If he remembered Professor Stewart's teachings or was moved by his parents' guidance, his letters did not let on. Soon after his arrival in the colony (and before he received his mother's exhortations), he concluded that the negroes were 'an obstinate ungrateful race; and I have never yet seen an instance of a negroe's being grateful to you any longer than you have the power of conferring more favors on them'. The relationship between planter and slave was quite different from his memories of home, where landlord and peasant were traditionally bound to one another (at least in theory) by bonds of duty and obedience.

Edward Satchwell Fraser had no time for such comparisons.

> I do not believe that there ever exists any sincere or disinterested attachment between negroes and their masters, nor do I think that the negroes *owe* that attachment, even to the kindest of masters at least to any that I have seen.

People who compared the condition of slaves with that of the peasantry in Britain 'ought to have known, and must have known better'.

But might it not also be said that he, like William Macpherson and all the other planters, attorneys, managers and overseers in Berbice, ought to have known better than to have been there? Among the Europeans, Edward Fraser's views were nevertheless exceptional. As the mud washed over the plantations, threatening to ruin the cotton crop, William Macpherson went with the flow.

COUNTESS

Early in 1805, three years after his arrival in Berbice, William's spirits were lifted when he was joined by his brother Allan. Unlike William, whose optimism had carried him at least as far as London, Allan was desperately unhappy about the prospect of becoming a planter. Now in his sixteenth

Phillis Wheatley, c1753–1785, author of the first book published by an African-American woman. Eliza Macpherson might not have known her name, but she was certainly moved by her verse. Frontispiece to Wheatley's *Poems on various subjects, religious and moral,* London, A. Bell, 1773. BRITISH LIBRARY

year, he had set his heart on following their father into a military career in the East Indies or, failing that, a writership with the East India Company. But the Colonel could not afford a commission, and writerships were hard to come by. So, with penury hanging over the family's head, Allan had little choice but to follow his brother, tearfully, to the Fraser estates in Berbice. 'If I should be so lucky as to make a little fortune', he told his father, 'I shall give every farthing of it to you.'

But there was never much prospect of Allan making a fortune, even if Berbice had been equipped to offer more. He was flighty, with (by his own testimony) a 'passionate and open temper', and prone to fits. William managed to get him a job as overseer on a nearby estate, but before long he had decided to join a West Indian Regiment. For his father, this was an appalling prospect, as serving in the Caribbean was generally understood to be much more dangerous than serving in the East, and it was no way to make a fortune. Just in time, Allan changed his mind—but his parents and brother continued to worry that he was incapable of remaining 'steady'.

Allan had brought with him to Berbice a letter from his father similar to the one the Colonel had previously prepared for William's guidance. The Colonel earnestly advised his younger son to be faithful to God, obedient to his employers, careful in his choice of companions and, this time explicitly, compassionate to the Negroes under his care. As in his letter to William, he implored him to avoid loose women (who would be 'certain destruction to your health, character, money & happiness in this world & ruin to your Soul in the world to come'); and whether in recognition that Allan was less steady than his brother, or simply in acknowledgment that it would be helpful to suggest other means of satisfying his desires, he offered some additional advice: 'I by all means recommend to you to keep a decent Native woman of the Country where you may be as your constant concubine in preference to running after the loose & debauched Females'. He did not elaborate on what he meant by 'a decent Native woman', but probably had in mind some Caribbean equivalent of 'a Hindostanee lady' without giving thought to whether she was of African or American descent.

Allan appears to have been slow in following this recommendation—but for William, who no doubt read the letter, as his father had intended him to do, it provided either welcome encouragement of an appealing prospect or happy endorsement of an arrangement already entered into. For when—or soon after—Allan arrived in the colony, William had chosen a slave who would serve the purpose his father intended.

Her name was Countess, a name that suggests much but tells us little. Did she acquire it as a haughty infant as she issued instructions to her mother or playmates during her few years of relative freedom, before she was set to work in the fields around the age of nine? Was it bestowed on her as a young and beautiful woman, self-possessed and stately in bearing? More likely it had nothing at all to do with her personal attributes, being instead just one of those names—sometimes classical, sometimes Christian, sometimes absurd—that 'da massas' gave their slaves, which served to confirm their own power over them. The 300 or so slaves at Union, for example, had names that said much about their Scottish masters and hardly anything about their own personal attributes, other than whether they were male or female. There were Tom, Ned and Frederick; Dundee, Berbice and Belladrum; Caesar, Horace and Othello; and among the more valuable men—drivers, carpenters, boatmen and the like—a few with names such as Bano, Abbae and (the brutal McDougall's nemesis) Willitick that were intended, perhaps, to acknowledge their African origins. The women were mostly given Christian names—Emma, Charlotte, Prudence, Deborah, Dolly; but there were also Cleopatra and Bathsheba, Agongo and Doquissa. Although most names on the estate were probably assigned arbitrarily, there were exceptions, including a child that Edward Satchwell Fraser took a particular liking to and named after himself.

So Countess' name does nothing, in itself, to rescue her from anonymity. We know that she was 'attached' to James Fraser's Paradise plantation in 1807. She may well have been there when William was appointed manager three years earlier—which might account for his telling his father in mid-1805 that life in Berbice was not really so bad at all. We know too that she was black, as she would otherwise have been described in documents as 'mulatto', 'mestee', 'quadroon' or some other indicator of colour and descent. Probably she had arrived some time over the past decade as part of the influx of slave ships from west Africa. Possibly she was a Creole, whose parents, grandparents and even great-grandparents had been born in Berbice or some other part of Guiana. Perhaps she had parents or brothers or sisters at Paradise or on a nearby plantation; perhaps she was alone. Nor can we guess at her age, beyond noting that slave girls tended to become 'concubines' around the age of fifteen. What we do know for sure is that William chose her from the many slaves on Paradise and neighbouring estates and that he had a deep affection for her—though not for her name.

In taking a concubine, he was merely following a practice generally accepted throughout the Caribbean. Relationships between European men and black or partly black women, whether slave or free, were so commonplace that one observer remarked in the early 1790s that it was considered a disgrace for a European *not* to take a concubine. There were exceptions: in Barbados, for example, some owners of grand plantations with several hundred slaves introduced strict rules to dissuade their white employees from engaging in 'improper intercourse'. But in the three colonies of Guiana the English and Scottish planters inherited more relaxed mores from the Dutch, so that it was reported that when a gentleman in Stabroek attended a ball or a concert, which took place every few weeks, his ticket also introduced 'two ladies of colour'. John Wray, who arrived in Demerara in 1808 to represent the London Missionary Society, was appalled that as many as nineteen white men out of twenty were living in fornication.

On the plantations it was expected that a European should have a housekeeper or mistress who would take charge of his household and fulfil all the duties of a wife. According to Henry Bolingbroke, an observant traveller not much older than William, who was employed by a merchant house in Stabroek about this time, once such attachments were formed the ladies regarded them as inviolable. 'The strictest scrutiny of their conduct in general cannot glean one particle of impropriety, by which their fidelity or constancy can be brought into question.' The only domestic activity normally barred to them was presiding at table (assuming there was a table to preside at); and by this distinction, decorum was maintained. Bolingbroke reported that ladies were in such short supply that some enterprising 'women of colour' in Stabroek were doing a brisk trade bringing additional ladies, both free and enslaved, from Barbados and other well-populated islands, to serve the needs of gentlemen in the town and on the plantations. A good 'housekeeper' was much valued, and could bring between £100 and £150.

So Countess became mistress of the manager's cottage at Paradise, greeting William each evening when he came in from the fields, preparing his meals, sewing his clothes, pouring his lime juice to ward off the mosquitoes, and playing the role of a dutiful wife. Early in 1807 she gave birth to a daughter, whom William thought first to call Harriot, after his sister, but then decided should be called Eliza, after his mother. And as Countess was no proper name for the mother of his child, he decided that *she* should be called Harriot—although in his letters to his brother he continued to call her Countess. In an environment where so much else was alien and hostile, he fashioned, consciously or otherwise, within his own domestic regime, comforts and relationships that reminded him of Home.

By this time William had been in the West Indies without a break for five years. A visit home was long overdue, both to see his ageing parents and to look for ways of making the fortune that had thus far eluded him. Leaving Countess and his newborn infant would be a wrench; but at least his brother, who was now employed as an overseer at Paradise, would keep a close eye on them and make sure they were being well treated. William arranged for them to live with a trusted male slave in a house on a nearby estate; and he instructed Allan to see that Countess received regular rations: three pounds of beef or pork and three pounds of salt fish each week, and a little sugar or rum whenever she asked for it—'In fact whatever Coffee, Vinegar, Soap, Candles, butter or any thing else in the eatables way'. If the house required repairing, Allan was to hire slaves to attend to it on Sundays; and if timber was needed, Allan was to purchase it. In short, William begged his brother 'to act towards her and my child as you would wish me to do towards yours were you in my situation'; and he pleaded with him 'to let me hear how she is by every letter which I expect once a month'.

Before he could leave he had to await the return of James Fraser, who was expected back shortly from a trip to Scotland. Fraser's arrival enabled him to resign as manager of Paradise without causing inconvenience and offence, but also to complete the arrangements for Countess' care. Although Fraser was initially reluctant, William persuaded him to part with her for the sum of £120. The bill of sale was signed in Stabroek in March 1807, just as he was about to sail. Before embarking he sent her 8 yards of Irish linen to make clothes, as well as six strings of blue and black beads, three red chequered handkerchiefs, and a frock and pair of shoes for Eliza.

William made an anxious crossing—this time, as England was again at war with France, in a convoy of four vessels. Although stories abounded of ships being taken and their passengers imprisoned, this voyage was uneventful. Several times sails were seen on the horizon—but mostly they turned out to be British men-of-war or American merchantmen, one of which misleadingly reported that the French armies had succumbed to the Russians. As the ship sailed north William, accustomed now to tropical weather, began to feel the cold—but the captain would allow no fire on board, owing to the large number of children travelling, many of them no doubt the progeny of planters and their concubines.

Six weeks after leaving Stabroek he stepped ashore at Liverpool, where he rested for several days before starting out on the first of several coaches that would take him home. During that time he purchased clothing to send to Countess (as he still sometimes called her) and 'poor little Eliza', reminding Allan to take good care of them and let him know how they were keeping. 'Any letter in which you mention Countess,' he added, 'direct to me; my father and mother know nothing of the business, but I should like to see what you write about her before they see it.' This was a matter that would have to be handled with care.

8
·················
LOVE

$\mathcal{M}$ISS HARRIOT MACPHERSON, THE ONLY DAUGHTER OF Colonel and Mrs Allan Macpherson of Blairgowrie, had all the usual accomplishments. On the grand piano in the drawing room of Blairgowrie House she could play the works of Haydn and Mozart (her mother's favourites), as well as popular songs, with an ease and depth of feeling that delighted her ageing parents and could not fail to impress the occasional visitor. She painted watercolours that capably represented the surrounding landscape, such as a fine view of the River Ericht and the nearby hills that she composed for her brother William to remind him of home. She had read widely, including—on her mother's advice—books that were morally improving and spiritually uplifting. And far from living a cloistered life on an isolated Scottish estate, she knew something of the world, having travelled often with her mother to London, where she attended the theatre, exhibitions in Vauxhall Gardens and other entertainments for which the capital was famous. Her manners were modest and becoming, her appearance comely, with dark curly hair and slightly pursed lips. All in all, she was a young lady whom any young man of suitable family and fortune might regard as a fine catch.

Yet as the aspiring English novelist Jane Austen remarked a few years later, 'there certainly are not so many men of large fortune in the world, as there are pretty women to deserve them'. Many potential husbands were away at the wars, and the eligible men who remained could reasonably expect to marry into money. This essential qualification Harriot Macpherson lacked; and as the years rolled by, with her father still fretting about the law suit and agonising about whether they should part with their carriage, the prospect of the family ever recovering its fortunes seemed increasingly remote.

Harriot Macintyre 1786–1874, oil by Thomas Phillips, 1812, four or five years
after her marriage to John MacIntyre. MACPHERSON COLLECTION

So when, at the age of twenty, she received a proposal of marriage
from Colonel John Macintyre, her father's oldest and dearest friend, she
recognised an opportunity to relieve her parents of their anxieties about
her future, avoid a life of spinsterhood, and attain a home of her own.
Never mind that the Colonel was thirty-six years her senior and had
difficulty bending his knee owing to the pain of extreme gout—Harriot
Macpherson fancied herself in love.

PRUDENCE

Born in Badenoch about 1750, John Macintyre was the son of surgeon
Donald Macintyre and his wife Isobel, who was James 'Ossian'
Macpherson's sister. He came to India as a cadet in the Company's army

in 1771, bringing with him a letter from Ossian to Allan Macpherson that urged Allan to look after him. Although there was a decade between them, the two became the closest of friends, sharing adventures and frustrations and, for a short time when they were together in Calcutta in the early 1780s, a house. Where Allan Macpherson was earnest and reticent, and always careful to say the right thing, Macintyre was forthright and gregarious. Among his fellow officers he was witty and sometimes ribald, and with the ladies always charming. In Calcutta he took a *bibi* and had by her at least four children, including two sons whom he sent back to be educated in various parts of Scotland. That relationship appears to have lasted more than twenty years, until he finally returned to England in 1804. There he acquired at least three more children by a white mistress. Eliza Macpherson esteemed him as a brother, though she did not approve of his 'lamentable female connexion' (meaning, at that time, the white one). Allan was more understanding, acting as guardian to one of the 'Indian' sons.

Macintyre was perpetually plagued by a 'tremor in the nerves' and violent headaches, which he attributed to a severe fever he had contracted many years earlier in Bombay. The treatment for his problems included mercury, which suggests that he might have been suffering from syphilis (though mercury was used for other serious ailments as well). Patients who took this medication were apt to complain that the cure was worse than the disease: Macintyre blamed the mercury for his sore gums, which he was prepared to put up with so long as it worked. It might also have caused loosening of the teeth, dribbling, heavy sweating, loss of appetite, insomnia, irritability and the 'dejection of spirits' that often overwhelmed him. His melancholy might also have been attributable to the gout, which caused such swelling of the feet and ankles that he was often unable to get out of bed.

'What am I to do?' he pleaded to Allan. 'How am I to act? My mind is distracted—my very brain is boiling—my heart is broken—my existence not worth the keeping.' This was after he had proposed to Harriot, and she had accepted, and Allan had begun to address him as 'My dear son'.

Harriot too, according to her doting parents, had her health problems, which perhaps encouraged them to think that marriage to an older and (so to speak) less robust man might be in their daughter's best interest. After the lovers had committed themselves to one another, Allan suggested to his friend, then in London, that the marriage should not be rushed.

'Your health is delicate', he wrote, searching carefully for the right form of words:

> & my beloved Harriot, although upon the whole better than
> [she] has been for years past, yet still is delicate, that were you
> & she united immediately & it should be Gods will to put her
> in a way of increasing your family, that from the very delicacy
> of her constitution there would be a great chance of her not
> surviving her first Child Birth ...

Therefore the union might best be delayed; and when Macintyre was in a fit condition to come to Scotland, he and Harriot might 'enjoy the Society of each other with your truly fond & affectionate parents, who will nurse and cherish you with the truest love & best endeavours'.

As it turned out, Harriot's parents need not have worried about her health—she lived to the age of eighty-eight. In the short term, though, her prospects for a happy marriage seemed unpropitious. Long before the wedding day she had told her future husband that her happiest days were over.

Macintyre appears to have accepted readily enough his prospective father-in-law's advice about Harriot's delicacy, without trying too hard to discover exactly what it meant. He was more concerned about money, an issue rarely absent when marriage was under discussion. He, like Allan, was beset by financial worries. He too had given away thousands of pounds to Ossian and become embroiled in the disastrous affairs of Sir Samuel Hannay. He had retained hefty investments in India, so that long after his return to England he was still looking anxiously to each arriving ship for news of his affairs in the East. Unlike Allan, he had no property at home to fall back on. To make matters worse, he was a big spender: when not laid low with gout or melancholy, he was fond of lavish entertainments, and seemed incapable of drawing in the reins.

So while he was attracted to Harriot chiefly by loneliness and the prospect of domestic felicity in his advancing years, he also hoped a favourable marriage settlement might relieve him of some of his financial woes. Within weeks of Harriot having accepted his proposal, he indicated that he would settle £5000 from his estate on his new wife and suggested that his prospective father-in-law should do the same. Allan carelessly acceded, before realising that he could do nothing before his law suit

Major-General (later Lieutenant-General) John Macintyre 1750–1828,
oil by Thomas Phillips, 1817. MACPHERSON COLLECTION

was resolved. When he explained these circumstances and apologised
for his 'great error', Macintyre flew into 'a violent passion'. Eventually he
recovered his composure and proposed that the wedding should proceed
without a settlement, which Allan took as the end of the matter. In truth,
though, the financial issue was left to brew.

The marriage took place at Blairgowrie House in August 1807, a quiet
affair attended only by the bride's parents and a few close friends. Her
brother William was there too, having arrived back from the West Indies
early in June. The whole family then set out on a tour of the nearby towns
and countryside, after which the newlyweds travelled unchaperoned
through the Highlands as far as Inverness. So far everything appeared
to be proceeding smoothly, with Macintyre at his jovial best and Harriot
responding well to the exertions of travel.

But it was too good to last. When they returned to Blairgowrie in
October, Macintyre succumbed to gout, and from his sick-bed revived

the matter of the marriage settlement and again lost his temper. As the days grew shorter, the atmosphere at Blairgowrie House became increasingly tense.

Then William, having waited perhaps for the appropriate moment that never came and now about to set out on his return journey, revealed his secret: shortly before he had sailed from the West Indies a black slave girl had given birth to his child. This should have come as no surprise to his father, who had encouraged such a liaison, or to Macintyre, who had fathered children in the East; and presumably they were neither affronted nor perturbed. Eliza, however, was shocked and thrown into confusion, torn between her love for her son and wretchedness at his parting, and anguish that he had acted contrary to God's law: 'Oh my dear fellow what I feel, I cannot express; but God of his infinite mercy preserve you for me; I do not know what to write, or what to think'.

William left Blairgowrie shortly after Christmas Day. On New Year's Eve, Allan and Eliza, Macintyre and Harriot, sat around the fire after dinner, playing cards, reading, writing letters, and conversing in their usual way. Eliza, distressed about William's leaving, was more than usually tense, Macintyre irritable, and Harriot and her father eager to keep the peace.

What exactly was said that evening was never divulged—except that, according to Eliza, 'Col Macintyre spoke disrespectfully on Religion'. This was unforgivable. Always deeply religious, her piety had increased over the years. None of those present ever let on exactly what Macintyre had said, but as William had just told his astonishing (for Eliza, at least) news and promptly left for the West Indies, we might reasonably conclude that it related to his indiscretion and the temptations to which young people were exposed when abroad. Whatever the words and whatever their origin, Eliza 'was roused to say he or I must leave the room'; and as the Colonel showed no sign of doing so, she stormed out in a huff.

The following day there was some sort of reconciliation; and here the matter might have ended had Eliza wished it. But clearly she did not, for reasons that went beyond Macintyre's impious words. In Eliza's eyes, her old friend had stolen her beloved daughter—and now he had signalled his intention of 'cruelly taking her away' to England. She continued to seethe until late January, when mother and daughter parted amid a sea of tears and the couple headed south, Macintyre in the meantime having caused still greater offence, this time to both mother and daughter, by refusing to allow Harriot's maid to accompany her. More sharp words were exchanged, with Eliza accusing Macintyre of mistreating her daughter, and Macintyre declaring that Eliza was trying to control his affairs. Harriot, caught in the middle, begged for a reconciliation; and Allan wrote a short affectionate letter to Macintyre, addressed 'My dear John' and hoping that his health would quickly improve. Eliza wrote an equally short note, beginning 'Dear Sir' and alluding to 'the return of my beloved Harriot', but otherwise incomprehensible, beyond conveying the impression that Macintyre had much to answer for. Macintyre thanked Allan for his kindness—but as to Eliza, 'I cannot make out what she means—the Idiom may be French, Dutch, or German, but it is not English'. If she was expecting an apology, there was no chance whatever of her getting one—and if he did, as he put it, act so absurdly, he deserved to be put in a straightjacket and locked up in a madhouse. Thus both parties assumed positions from which they would have great difficulty extricating themselves, even if they had wished to do so.

The newlyweds arrived in London, where Macintyre was met by bad news from India. Some of his investments had failed; and here in London, one of his natural children had got himself into difficulties that would cost him money. If he could not borrow from somewhere, he told Harriot, he would surely be dragged away to the King's Bench prison. Harriot was in despair. She suffered from headaches, her courses came early, she succumbed to melancholy. 'I sometimes wish I never was married', she told

THE

L A D I E S

ANNUAL JOURNAL;

OR,

COMPLETE POCKET-BOOK,

For the YEAR 1780.

An Useful Register of Business and Amusement.

CONTAINING,

I. Days for buying, &c. the several Stocks, and receiving the Interest due.	VIII. 108 ruled Pages for Memorandums.
II. Holidays at the public Offices.	IX. Rules for promoting matrimonial Happiness.
III. Capitals of the public Funds.	X. Dissertation on Pride.
IV. Royal Family of Great-Britain.	XI. Approved Receipts.
	XII. Laws at Quadrille.
	XIII. New Songs.
V. Regal Tables of the Kings and Queens of England.	XIV Country Dances.
	XV. Perpetual Diary.
VI. Birth-days of the Sovereigns of Europe.	XVI. Marketing Tables.
	XVII. Interest Tables.
VII. Table of the Roads from London to Edinburgh.	XV.II. Rates of Hackney Coachmen, Chairmen, and Watermen.

London: Printed for J. Russel, Successor to E. Stevens, No. 2, Stationers-Court, Ludgate-street; and J. Taylor, nearly opposite Great-Turnstile, Holborn. [Price 1s.]

[To be continued Annually.]

Eliza Macpherson's copy of the *Ladies Annual Journal* for 1780, 'An Useful Register of Business and Amusement', is still useful three decades later to her daughter Harriot.

MACPHERSON COLLECTION

her mother, 'and then I could live with you constantly—I certainly never was made to be separated from you.'

Harriot was perfectly aware of her expected role as a wife. Her mother had given her, before she had married, her copy of the *Ladies Annual Journal* for 1780—the same little volume that Eliza had taken with her to India and which had (more or less) guided her conduct over the past twenty-five years. 'Remember always', instructed the author of the journal,

> that whatever misfortunes may happen to either [husband or wife], they are not to be charged to the account of matrimony, but to the accidents and infirmities of human life ... Therefore instead of murmurs, reflections, and disagreement, whereby the weight is rendered abundantly more grievous, readily put your shoulder to the yoke, and make it easier to both.

And the young bride should re-read frequently the matrimonial service, taking care 'not to overlook the word *obey*'.

There were other views of marriage. In 1792, when Harriot turned six, Mary Wollstonecraft had published *A Vindication of the Rights of Women*, a scarifying text which challenged the notions that 'all women are to be levelled, by meekness and docility, into one character of yielding softness and gentle compliance', and that a married woman should yield with blind obedience to her husband's will. This book quickly became one of the most talked about in Britain, and was surely mentioned in the drawing room at Blairgowrie House—though probably only in passing, as Eliza Macpherson had no time for revolutionary ideas of any sort.

Nevertheless, Harriot could not fail to notice that relations between the sexes were changing. Take, for example, her good friend Eliza Dick, Dr Dick's daughter, who had become engaged in London to a young man whom Harriot (by this time Mrs Colonel Macintyre) thought would make her a good husband—'but I cannot help thinking she is too free with him before Marriage'. Eliza had shown her some of the letters she had written to her betrothed, which began 'My Dearest George', and then addressed him often as 'My Darling, My Love ... and such like endearing expressions; which I think is very well from a Gentleman to a Lady, but not altogether so proper, from a young Lady to a Gentleman'. Harriot sought her mother's reassurance:

I think my own reserved mode of correspondence with Col. M—the best—and I am certain he loves me a great deal more now, than he did before marriage—as he has felt my Love for him much more sincere than he ever thought before, from my reserved manner to him as a Lover—whereas Eliza is so free, and uses so many endearing expressions now, that her Love will appear to diminish after she is married, and all the nonsensical & ridiculous part of it done away—.

Thus Harriot eschewed subversive trends and sought to play the role of an obedient wife.

But it was hard to obey when her husband was so stubborn. She confessed to her mother that she was sometimes very warm with him, which provoked him to say things that he later regretted. Part of the problem, she admitted, was the age difference: 'he looks upon me in many respects more as his Child, than his Wife, and thinks I am not competent to advise him in any thing'. He did not share his secrets or show her his letters, which Harriot took to be 'inconsistent with true love'. The couple argued often about where they were going to live. Harriot wanted to be near her parents in Scotland, but Macintyre could not abide the cold (not to mention proximity to his mother-in-law). She would not have minded the English countryside, but he thought 'there is no sociability amongst the neighbours—we might almost as well be buried alive'. He preferred London, but they could not afford to buy there.

So for several years after the couple were married they moved from one lodging house in London to the next, Harriot disconsolate, and Macintyre all the time looking over his shoulder in case his creditors were on his tail. We find them towards the end of winter in 1810 in what Eliza calls 'a common boarding house', Macintyre confined to his room with gout and Harriot sitting in her own small room, without a fire and wrapped in a shawl, determined on principle not to go down to the drawing room which they shared with other guests. She escapes whenever she can to visit her grandmother, aunt and uncle, who live in London, and a few close friends: 'if my husband does not give me a home I can be happy in', she tells her mother, 'it is natural for me to go where I can find happiness, which at present is in other peoples homes'. Macintyre, when he is up to it, also likes to go visiting; but Harriot believes that visiting beyond their closest relatives and friends leads to debts that they are not in a position to repay. Just the other day he embarrassed her by accepting an invitation from new acquaintances who are 'people inferior in rank to ourselves, which in my opinion, throws us under greater obligations, than if they were our superiors'.

Across the Atlantic, as Countess—the other Harriot—tenderly massages his shoulders to ease his aching muscles, William reads his mother's accounts of the unhappy couple and wonders if they should separate. Divorce is never mentioned, though both separation and divorce are by no means unknown at the time. But Harriot is determined to make the best of her situation, not just because the alternative might be worse, but also because she is convinced that her husband sincerely loves her and that likewise she loves him. 'I firmly believe he loves me as well as it is possible for a Man to Love his Wife—& mine for him is equally strong, altho' I may say little things against him sometimes ...' In other words, everything is as society expects in a relationship between man and wife; and if occasionally things are not exactly as they should be, she will put her shoulder to the yoke and act the part in life that Providence has assigned her.

FOLLY

Allan and Eliza are determined that any strains in their daughter's marriage must be concealed from the rest of the world. A family's status in the community and among their friends rested not only on the extent of their estate, the splendour of their house and the number of their carriages, but also in their proper adherence to religion and morals, so that a gentleman and his lady had not merely to *look* the part, they had to *behave* the part as well. As the Macphersons struggled to make ends meet and keep up appearances, their adherence to proper codes of conduct was more necessary than ever.

In particular, any signs of discord must be kept from the servants. The family's reduced circumstances made it hard enough to maintain the proper class distinctions without any misbehaviour or impropriety getting in the way; and once the servants knew of any problem within the family, nothing would stop them gossiping among themselves and spreading stories far and wide. So in order to keep their private thoughts and affairs away from prying eyes, Eliza and William, before he returned to the West Indies, invented a 'secret language', which involved substituting for each letter the following one in the alphabet. Although a literate servant with

William Macpherson, on his way back to Guiana, writes to his mother using their secret code. MACPHERSON COLLECTION

....

sufficient curiosity would have had little difficulty deciphering this code, the task of translating long passages required application and time, so that there was little likelihood of a servant chancing upon a private letter on Eliza's dressing table and instantly discovering its meaning—even if they might quickly gather that 'Dpm Nbdjouzsf' was the main subject of their coded exchanges.

At the time of the initial rupture, Allan and Eliza had just four household servants: Mrs Margaret Cameron, who acted as cook and housekeeper, and who had two young children; Mary Forsythe, the maidservant whom Macintyre refused to allow to accompany his wife when they moved to London; Betty Macpherson (no obvious relation to the family), who served as undercook, and also milked the cows; and James Kennedy, a young coachman who had joined the family's service the previous spring. Kennedy was like most coachmen—he did not know his place, and in April 1808 Allan was forced to discharge him 'as fractious & ill-tempered'. Such decisions were never taken lightly, because good male servants were hard to find, and then they had to be trained to the appropriate standard— which cost money. Fortunately, Allan was able to replace Kennedy with his cowherd, Alexander Stewart; but Stewart had to be sent south for a month for training, which cost Allan three guineas, about a quarter of a coachman's annual salary.

Margaret the housekeeper, otherwise known as Peggy, was going too, to join her husband Ensign Cameron, who was in the militia and now based

Colonel Allan Macpherson dismisses his fractious coachman and retains another, at considerable expense. A page from his Servants' Wage Book. MACPHERSON COLLECTION

in Edinburgh. Eliza was sad to see her go, as she had served the family faithfully for eight years and understood their particular requirements. Fortunately, Peggy had a younger unmarried sister, Anny, who could be trained to fill the vacancy. Eliza was pleased with this prospect, as Anny, like her sister, was from her own birthplace of Inverness, and she knew that Inverness girls were brought up in accordance with strict moral and religious principles.

So Anny visited Blairgowrie, where Eliza was pleased to find that her expectations of her good character and seemly manners were confirmed. She then arranged for her to be sent to a lady in Yorkshire, who would instruct her in the duties of a housekeeper, and then to Edinburgh, where she would attend pastry school while staying with her sister and brother-in-law. 'I hope through time', Eliza told Peggy,

> Anny will be my right hand for everything thrifty in my
> family.—I would have her learn to make a good Curry
> [a taste that many 'East Indians' had brought home with them
> from the East], a hash [of] Calves-head—a Harrico [ragout]
> of mutton—a nice veal cutlet—and I would recommend
> her going to the Butcher's to see a good Beef Stake cut, and
> a nice mutton chop—and to make nice pancakes—and also
> apple-fritters.

If Anny performed and behaved as she should, Eliza trusted that she would one day turn out, as Peggy had done, a useful wife. But in the meantime, she should take particular care in her conduct, especially in her relations with the other household servants, over whom she would have charge. Although she would be obliged to eat and spend much time with them in the kitchen and back parlour, she must work hard to win their respect, a task made more difficult because she was young. 'I hope', said Eliza, 'Anny will observe all the advice given her about not being too familiar.'

But the warnings came too late. During her visit to Blairgowrie around the end of 1807 Anny had become excessively familiar with James Kennedy, the insolent coachman. Even, perhaps, on New Year's Eve, as Eliza and Macintyre were exchanging sharp words in the drawing room about religion and morality, Kennedy was having his way with Anny in the barn—which, evidently, no one was aware of until six or seven months later, when the Camerons' landlady in Edinburgh raised her suspicions with Peggy. Anny, confronted by her distressed sister, immediately confessed that she was with child, and that Kennedy was the father.

Ensign Cameron wrote promptly to Allan to ask what should be done about the 'poor unfortunate Girl', who had 'ruined herself at the time when she had in her power to be of credit to herself and Satisfaction to her friends'. She could not stay any longer in Edinburgh, said Cameron, without his regiment finding out; and 'we have enough to do to Keep ourselves and our Children in a respectable way these hard times'. At least Kennedy had, according to Anny, promised faithfully to marry her—and indeed, 'as she is so unfortunate as to be with child with him, I do not know what better they can do'. Eliza was not so sure that Anny should marry the man who had 'seduced her virtue', and Allan thought she would do better to seek asylum with her mother. But Anny, who had a mind of her own, had no intention of returning home.

By the time Allan learned of Anny's situation, he had already sent Kennedy packing. But the unfortunate encounter had taken place under his roof, which implied a certain responsibility, additional to any desire he might have felt to assist Peggy's family in their time of need. So he tracked Kennedy down to an estate just 20 miles away, where he had quickly secured another appointment as a coachman. When Ensign Cameron wrote to ask him his intentions, Kennedy readily agreed to marry Anny, and the ceremony was performed without delay, a month or two before the baby was due.

There was, of course, no prospect now of Anny taking up a position at Blairgowrie House. Fortunately for Eliza, Ensign Cameron was shortly called to the line, so his wife Peggy offered to return with her children to help Eliza out, and so make amends for her sister's 'shameful behaviour'. Eliza was prepared to be forgiving: 'I trust ... they will both implore God's mercy for pardon', she told Peggy; that Kennedy would mend his manners so that he could improve his situation, and that Anny, through her future conduct, would seek redemption for her past folly.

For Allan, it had been an expensive business—there was the cost of Anny's classes, and coach tickets and upkeep—all in all more than £20. At least it provided a distraction from his own family's embarrassments, proving (if proof were needed) that the servants were as likely as their masters to be afflicted by matters of the heart, and as much concerned to protect their reputations.

LOOKING AFTER COUNTESS

William spent the whole of his visit to Scotland in the second half of 1807 at Blairgowrie House, except for the short tour of the local region with his parents and the newlyweds, and a futile trip to Edinburgh to see his father's lawyers. The time passed slowly, with his thoughts often turning to Countess and his newborn child on the other side of the Atlantic, and how they were managing without him. At least his brother Allan was there to see that they were being well looked after, that they were well supplied with food and clothing, and that their house was in good order. From Edinburgh he sent Allan another consignment of goods for Countess, chiefly textiles for making clothing for herself and the baby: 8 yards of blue printed cotton, 4 yards of white spotted muslin, several handkerchiefs, made of muslin, cotton and silk, several rolls of tape and thread, and so on.

He worried that Allan could not be relied upon—and with good cause. Two months after William had sailed from Stabroek, his brother, supposedly on doctor's orders, followed him in a convoy bound for London. Then came a series of remarkable adventures and misfortunes: a fortnight out of Stabroek, Allan's brig was seized by a French privateer; during the ensuing melee he lost all his money; while on its way to the French colony of Guadeloupe, the brig was recaptured by a British man-of-war and escorted to British territory at Grenada; there a kindly Colonel offered him a commission in a West Indian regiment; but soon he found that life as a subaltern was far from what he had imagined; mercifully, his commission was not confirmed, which freed him to return to Stabroek. All these events happened in quick succession, so that the ship that delivered him to Demerara coincidentally dropped anchor on the same day that William arrived back from Scotland.

If Allan had hoped for his brother's sympathy, he was disappointed. William, annoyed that his brother had abandoned Countess and the baby, had long since concluded that Allan was his own worst enemy: 'how often', he asked, 'have you promised and declared that you would be *careful, thoughtful,* and *steady?*' Allan was abject and promised once again to mend his ways.

William, having left his management position at Paradise, had no specific job to return to; but at least he had a little money in his pocket and a reputation throughout the colonies for honesty and application. What was more, convinced that this time he could make a success of planting if only he had the capital to start with, he had persuaded his father to allow him to draw against his name a total of up to £2000, money that the Colonel did not have and was forced to borrow, but that William was confident he would be able to repay with the profits of wise investment and hard work.

As there was no prospect of the colony acquiring more slaves from Africa, he hurried to purchase ten while they were still to be had, each at a cost of £100, which he proceeded to hire out at £27/10/0 per year. Then, when a property known as Rising Sun, several estates east of Paradise, was offered for purchase, he went into partnership with his old friend from Union estate, the attorney Lewis Cameron, to purchase jointly a half share, totalling 250 acres. By this bargain William incurred a debt of £5000, repayable at the standard rate in the colony of 6 per cent—but as the vendor, a wealthy and long-established planter by the name of

John Tapin, did not require the first repayment of one-half the sum (plus interest) until mid-1812, and the second half until mid-1816, there was surely little to worry about. After all, mid-1812 was four years away.

With regard to Cameron, though, William should have taken heed of his father's earlier advice, based on bitter experience, that entering into any partnership was 'a most dangerous business'. Within a year the two were engaged in 'a long and tedious dispute' which ultimately resulted in their separation, with William taking on the full debt of £10,000, together with an additional burden to cover the cost of additional slaves. This change involved him, as he put it, a great deal more deeply than he wished to be; but he hoped soon to take in another partner, whose contribution would reduce the debt to more manageable proportions.

If only he had read the signs—the chief of which was the unreliability of the weather. In a normal year, there were expected to be two wet and two dry seasons, yielding two crops of cotton. In 1803, however, the year after he had first set foot in Berbice, the 'long dry' from September to November extended well into the new year, with a devastating effect on the first crop. Then came the rains, sometimes accompanied by destructive winds, with each season seeming worse than the last. No planter, large or small, was spared. Early in 1806 the deluge was worse than ever, with dire effects on profits. Some planters went bankrupt; some investors in Britain decided to cut and run. Lord Seaforth delivered a sardonic warning to his long-suffering manager, suggesting that his river estate Seawell should more properly be called 'We'll see'.

William was perfectly aware that yields were low before he sailed for Scotland in 1807. Back in Berbice he admitted to his father, 'I most anxiously wish I had not come out at all this last time, for misfortune has attended me ever since'. But that was several years later. At the time of his return, like every other European along the Guianan coast, he was certain that the weather could never again be as bad and that their fortunes must inevitably get better. In any case, he could not think of deserting Countess, his newly acquired possession, and 'poor little Eliza'.

Before setting out from London on the return journey, William had purchased a supply of household goods including crockery and a dozen green-handled knives and forks, a salt cellar, and pots and pans; and one of his uncles had given him 'a very excellent Dining Table'. With these and other goods acquired in the colonies, he and Countess managed to make the planter's house at Rising Sun estate look like a home. Soon he had thirty or so slaves, one of whom helped Countess about the house, with the remainder working in the fields. As he could afford no overseer, he too spent six days a week from daybreak to dusk in the fields, which he claimed to enjoy because of his inclination for 'the country life'.

Like other 'concubines', 'housekeepers', 'secondary wives', or whatever they might be called in various parts of the West Indies, Harriot (as he reminded himself to call her) enjoyed a special status. On the one hand, their relationship was one of exploitation—William chose Countess as his concubine, and there is little likelihood that she had any choice in the matter. Once he had paid his £120 to James Fraser, he owned her, enjoying much the same rights of property that extended to his material possessions; and within the bounds of a loosely administered law and lax colonial morality, he could do with her as he wished, from changing her name to controlling her every move. But ownership did not deny affection—and William provided ample evidence that he loved her with emotions similar to those any young lover might feel for his more conventional mistress or bride, the most obvious evidence of which was his determination to act as her protector.

Nor did the fact that Harriot was owned mean that she was powerless. Rather to the contrary, it was a common complaint among whites throughout the West Indies that some female slaves had too much control over their masters. The brutal James McDougall alleged that the real reason Lewis Cameron had discharged him as manager was not that he had treated the slaves harshly, but that Nancy, Cameron's housekeeper, had conspired against him, and exercised 'undue influence' over the other slaves. And William's hapless brother Allan, having returned from his Caribbean adventures and obtained a manager's job (promising yet again to remain steady), was promptly forced to give it up owing, he said, to 'the ill temper of a coloured woman' and his new employer taking her side.

Although Harriot spoke English, or the local patois, which was part-English and part-Dutch, she was unable to read and write. None of her words survive to tell us what she thought about her master or the situation in which she was kept. She had escaped the labour and oppression of life in the field; she was protected and looked after; she enjoyed an influence with 'da massa' that would enable her to win favours for her family or friends; she was regarded with deep affection, especially after she became mother of the master's child. But we can only guess how much, if at all, that affection was returned.

Contemporaries in the West Indies found such relationships hard to define: 'husband and wife' inferred too much, 'master and slave' too little. So they spoke of 'keeper and concubine', which fell somewhere in between. Within that category, the exact nature of specific relationships might extend from brutality and exploitation to protection and affection. One ingredient, though, they shared in common: the relationship was almost invariably temporary. Often it terminated in the death of the master, so that it was said that 'tropical ladies and tropical mosquitoes have an instinctive preference for newly arrived Europeans'. And if death did not intervene, it ended when the master eventually sold or abandoned his Guianan interests and headed for home.

William thought often about death—it was hard not to when so many were dying around him. In 1809 the birth of a second daughter, whom he named Matilda after his favourite cousin, prompted him to tell his parents, in code, that he intended to send them an abstract of his affairs in Berbice, so that 'should any accident happen to me this knowledge will perhaps enable you to prevent at least some of the losses which too frequently attend a mans property in this country, when he unfortunately happens to die'.

The following year Harriot gave birth to another child, this time a boy, whom William named Allan after his father. This prompted a momentous decision: he would set them all free.

FREEDOM

Manumission throughout the West Indies was far from common. While there were significant variations from one colony to the next, it tended to occur more in the towns than on the plantations, and more often than not took the form of a slave purchasing his own freedom than receiving it as a gift from a white man. In the three colonies of Guiana, where slaves had long been in short supply, it was especially rare: in Berbice from 1808 to 1810 just seventeen slaves—about one in 5000—were recorded as having received their freedom. William's deed of gift to Harriot and their three children accounted for four of them.

A month after Allan's birth, he visited New Amsterdam and there, before the notary public and seven planters, including his brother Allan,

Evan Fraser and his creditor John Tapin, signed a 'Deed of Gift of Harriot & her three children to themselves', which announced to the world that he had 'manumitted, enfranchised, renounced and redeemed from Slavery and for ever set [them] free':

> To have, and to hold, to them the said black female slave named Harriot, and the said mulatto children named Eliza, Matilda and Allan and their future increase or issue for ever, their full free Manumission, Enfranchisement, Emancipation and Freedom from the day of the date hereof—fully, freely and absolutely for their own proper use, behoof and benefit, for ever—subject to no labour, service, or servitude, in or for the benefit, or profit of him the said William Macpherson, his Heirs, Executors, Administrators, or Assigns or any, or either of them, or any other person or persons whomsoever ...

And to ensure that they all were looked after, especially in the event of his death, he appointed ('with the approbation of the said Black woman named Harriot') no fewer than nine guardians and trustees: his father, sister, brother and his aunt's husband, all in Scotland; and four planters, first of whom was his friend Alexander Simpson of Seafield estate, between Union and Rising Sun. Apart from sacrificing what was in the eyes of the law valuable property, the transaction cost him money: a fee of 200 guilders for Harriot and 100 for each of the children (a total of about £40), and an unspecified sum to be paid into the colony's poor chest to prevent them, should the need arise, from becoming a burden on colonial funds.

Perhaps to satisfy the curiosity of his fellow planters, some of whom might well think he was setting a bad example, William included in the Deed of Gift an explanation of his magnanimity. He was moved, he said, by 'divers good causes and considerations', as well as 'the regard he entertains for his black female slave named Harriot'. The last part was clear: Harriot had been his friend and companion for at least six years, had borne his children, and made a lonely life tolerable. The manumission offered proof of his affection. But his 'regard' was accompanied by perpetual anxiety— the 'divers good causes and considerations'—about what might happen if he were to die. And what if he were unable to repay his mounting debts? The prospect of Harriot and the children being sequestered and perhaps ill-used by one of his creditors was too awful to contemplate.

His financial woes were increasing, with one bad season following another. Even when he did manage to send cotton home, the price was low because of competition from American planters and Napoleon's blockade of the continental ports. Misfortune, he told his parents, 'has pursued this wretched colony with a heavy hand'. Planters in all three colonies told the same story, begging relief from their creditors and petitioning the government for help. Property decreased in value to almost nothing. As July 1812, the date for the first repayment on Rising Sun, drew nearer, all hopes of making a fortune had long disappeared. All he had to show for more than a decade's hard work was sinking into the mangroves.

In the meantime, life in Blairgowrie was descending into unrelieved misery. After nearly a decade of intermittent but expensive haggling, the court case against Ossian's son was still unresolved (though the lawyers remained, as ever, optimistic); and Macintyre was threatening legal action regarding the marriage settlement. The family's circumstances were reduced to one domestic servant, one two-wheeled carriage, and two horses to pull it. Increasingly desperate, the Colonel begged both his sons to return: 'I feel I cannot be happy without you—I feel I cannot be happy to divide you—I feel I cannot be happy at the little I have to give you'.

William anguished over his parents' plaintive letters. One possible solution, open to all young men in distressed circumstances, was marriage. His principal creditor, John Tapin, had a daughter named Betsy; and William had heard a rumour that Tapin might be willing to make over Plantation Rising Sun to him if he married Betsy and promised to settle half of it on her. Betsy had lately returned from England, where she had been living for four or five years. William remembered her from many years earlier, but had not yet seen her since her return. Now aged twenty-one, she was reputed to be well educated, and of irreproachable character.

But there was a hitch. Betsy was a 'mulatto', half white and half black; and notwithstanding her qualities, William felt 'considerable repugnance towards a match with a coloured girl'. Evidently he felt no repugnance to his own mulatto children, nor to the black slave whose freedom he had purchased. But the idea of *marriage* to a coloured lady, however manifest her virtues and advantageous the match, involved bridging two moral universes. Each universe had its own rules, the chief of which was that the one should have as little as possible to do with the other. Happily, for most of the time an ocean kept the two apart. William had conformed to the mores of colonial society in taking Countess as his mistress and housekeeper—

there had never been any question of marriage. And now, when he chose to marry, he would do so in accordance with the genteel expectations of Scottish society (the society of his sister Harriot and Colonel Macintyre) and choose someone who was unambiguously white.

Before he had talked himself out of marriage to Betsy, he had asked his parents for their views. His father said nothing about colour, but questioned his motives:

> no doubt money is necessary to afford the comforts of life— But my own ideas of Matrimony were and still are, first, true love to the object of my affection & her character & manners & lastly the respectability of her parents & connections of which a man should be fully satisfied with before he fixes his love— and I am truly grateful to the almighty that to the outmost wishes of my heart I have been successful in all ...

Tellingly, his mother said nothing.

With that option closed, William searched desperately for other ways of repaying his debts. These included a doctor's bill totalling over 250 guilders (about £20), made up of 140 guilders for the slaves, 40 for William and 70 for Harriot and the children. Fortunately the doctor, who visited the estate at regular intervals, was prepared to accept in payment the green-handled knives, damask tablecloths, sideboard, and other items that William had brought back with him from Britain. Other creditors reluctantly agreed to extend their terms. But Tapin, his largest creditor by far, believing that he was heir to a great fortune (and remembering perhaps that he had spurned his daughter Betsy), demanded that he surrender the estate and pay an additional £5000. He is 'a hard hearted old miser', said William, 'and has neither honour nor generosity'.

But Tapin held the upper hand: Berbice law gave creditors the right to prevent their debtors from leaving the colony, so there was a real risk that William might be forced to stay there forever. The obstacle was removed after he obtained legal opinions (at a cost of £18/3/4) which obliged Tapin to accept as payment in full the estate and the remaining thirty slaves. This left him with so little that he had to borrow money from his father to buy a passage home. But at least he was free.

Early in 1813 he sailed from Stabroek (recently renamed George Town in honour of George III, and so confirming the fact that the colonies of

Guiana had become more British than Dutch). He escaped in time to miss an exceptionally bad season for illness, which carried away many planters, including his old friend Evan Fraser. Many had left before him, including James Baillie Fraser and Edward Satchwell Fraser of Reelig, their father having concluded that 'Berbice is a poison'. After a short stay in Scotland, they now set out for India, hoping to redeem the family's fortunes: James travelled extensively through much of Asia, winning fame as a fine painter of people and places; the sensitive Edward reached Delhi but soon showed symptoms of consumption. Sent to sea for his health, he died at St Helena. A few more planters, including Lewis Cameron, stayed longer in Berbice, suing one another to recover debts and yielding to an increased sense of hopelessness with each passing season. Allan, whose erratic conduct had prevented him from acquiring property and massive debts, also remained behind, installed as manager at Plantation Hope, a name that now sounded less optimistic than pathetic.

William took with him on the journey his two daughters, Eliza approaching six and Matilda about three and a half. Although he knew that many other planters abandoned their children, he could not bear the thought of leaving them in a country to which he might never return. Little Allan, who had only recently turned two and was therefore too young to travel, stayed with his mother. Two other young children were also in his care, a son and daughter of Alexander Simpson of Plantation Seafield, who had given him sufficient money to look after them. Such arrangements were common practice, so that William could safely assume that Simpson or another planter would bring his own son home as soon as he was old enough.

The ship was packed with passengers escaping the colonies, and with cotton, no indicator of a successful season, but rather that fewer vessels were making the journey as there were fewer goods to carry. Once at sea they joined a convoy of fourteen other merchantmen accompanied by a sloop of war—an essential precaution, thought William, as Britain was now at war with the United States.

Nearly forty years later, William remembered his excitement as the ship made its way slowly up the Clyde. Unable to wait for the change of tide, he took a rowboat ashore a dozen or so miles short of Glasgow. There, on a beach, he 'lay down and kissed the earth, and ejaculated a short prayer to Almighty God thanking him for my safe return to the loved land of my early years'.

And what of Countess? As a free woman, she had some choice in her future. She might, as often happened, have become 'housekeeper' to another 'buckra'; or perhaps a huckster, purchasing food and goods from merchants in New Amsterdam or Stabroek and selling them at plantations around the Guianan colonies. A single clue suggests that she remained where William had left her: on Alexander Simpson's Seafield estate. According to the register of slaves for Berbice, a female domestic called 'Mary', aged twenty-two and born in Africa, lived at Seafield in 1817. Her owner, who left her mark on the register, was 'Harriet McFarson', close enough to how William would have pronounced his own name.

By that time little Allan had followed his father home. We can only guess at Harriot's misery at parting with her children and losing the life she had led for at least six years. Did she have more children? Did she remain on the plantations or move to the town? Did she see and hear the Christian missionary John Wray, who arrived in Berbice in 1816? Where was she when nearly all the 12,000 slaves in neighbouring Demerara rose up and were violently suppressed in 1823? Did she ever think of her former keeper and the children, taken to some place that William had often spoken of but was for her barely imaginable?

William, in his surviving letters, seems never to have mentioned Countess, and rarely anything of his West Indian years. Perhaps, though, he occasionally reflected on life in Berbice; and like James Baillie Fraser during his long, lonely voyage to India, admitted to himself how much he missed 'the good creature who lived with me & made my life comfortable so long'.

9

....

SHAME

As their ship sailed north, William and his two little girls, as well as Mr Simpson's two children, rugged up against the cold. He had already told his parents that he was bringing his children with him; and now, finding a quiet moment and a cramped space between the cotton bales, he wrote to ask them to find a clergyman's widow or some other suitable person who might bring the girls up carefully and religiously, and teach them, with as little expense as possible, reading, writing, sewing and arithmetic, so that they might one day become good housewives. 'I should not wish them', he added, 'to be more than thirty miles from Blairgowrie.'

The letter was sent from Glasgow the moment he landed.

His father, though, had already written to suggest that it would be best 'to leave them a little at Glasgow' until he, William, had resolved upon a plan for their future care; for

> although I believe in my heart that there cannot be a more
> affectionate parent than your beloved mother, yet from the
> pure delicacy natural to her heart it would grieve her [—Allan
> corrected himself and substituted 'Us'—] to see you introduce
> them with yourself at our home—at the same time should any
> accident happen to you, which God forbid, I am confident no
> parent on earth, would be more anxious than she would be, for
> the care of any person or thing connected with you our dearly
> beloved son.

The two letters passed in the post, so that when William arrived at the portico of Blairgowrie House with not just two but four half-black children in tow, he was quite unprepared for the effect their appearance might have on his mother. For Eliza, the shock was almost too much to bear.

THE HOMECOMING

William found there a scene of misery and inertia. The law suit dragged on, with nothing appearing to happen beyond the accrual of more debts to the lawyers. His father, having fallen behind in paying his taxes, soon received a threatening demand for nearly £100. He owed money to some of the tenants (several of whom were far better off than their landlord). Worst of all, he had lately received a summons to appear in court for failing to pay servants' wages. The sum was trifling, said Eliza—but the embarrassment was enormous.

The only good news was that the breach with Macintyre appeared to be healed, albeit at a substantial cost. As his own circumstances had worsened, Macintyre had pursued his supposed rights under the marriage settlement relentlessly, as well as a large sum of money that he claimed Allan owed him from Indian days. None of this, he insisted, was for himself, but solely to ensure that Harriot would be adequately provided for; and after all, his father-in-law had not given 'a single shilling towards her maintenance' since they had been married. When Allan failed to respond to his letters, Macintyre had threatened to take him to court. This was the cruellest blow: 'nothing', Allan lamented, 'can compensate for the sorrow he has occasioned me'. Worn down by attrition and concern for his daughter, he agreed to sign a bond to his son-in-law for £10,000 to be paid twelve months after his death. This improved Macintyre's mood considerably, as did his elevation to the rank of Major-General (which demonstrated that, while he had left active service far behind, he still had some good friends in government). Eventually father and son-in-law embraced, though without the warmth they had felt for one another in years gone by. That reconciliation achieved, Macintyre held out an olive branch to Eliza, who responded that *she* certainly felt no ill-will towards Macintyre and that the hostility was therefore all on his side. In any case, she added, 'Ladies cannot, or at least should not war' but should rather, through faith in God, summon fortitude in defence of virtue—and more along these lines, which Macintyre evidently deemed sufficient to allow a return to speaking terms and accept an invitation to visit Blairgowrie again for the coming season.

None of this was a recipe for happiness. We find the four of them in mid-1812 (nine months before William's return), all under the one roof, but mostly living separate lives. Allan rises in good time, takes breakfast, and then has dinner at one o'clock. Macintyre has a late breakfast, which means that he prefers to delay dinner until five. Allan in the meantime sleeps from two to four, then walks in the garden, and retires to his bedroom at five, just as Macintyre is sitting down to dinner. Eliza doesn't rise from her bed until eleven or twelve, and then doesn't leave her bedroom until six or seven in the evening. Macintyre is then ready to settle down for an evening of cards, mostly with Harriot as the only other player. All the old routines of morning and evening prayers have been abandoned. There are no visitors—even the neighbours stay away. They still have a carriage, but it is never taken out of the barn, not even for drives.

William promptly set out to do what he could to rectify the financial situation. First, he tried to understand the law suit, gently prodding his father's failing memory for anything about his transactions with Ossian, and visiting Edinburgh to attend the hearings at the Court of Session. Whether through his persistence or because the lawyers realised that they had nothing more to gain by prolonging the case any further, the matter was quickly brought to judgment. For a moment, William thought the decision might go in their favour—but as even he had difficulty making sense of his father's explanation of where his money had come from, and why he and Ossian had compiled fictitious accounts, the result was hardly surprising. In mid-1813, the Court ruled against the Colonel, ending a case that had now lasted over a decade and leaving him with a hefty debt to Ossian's son. Once costs had been taken into account, Allan owed nearly £32,000, on top of continuing liabilities of £450 per annum.

There could be only one solution: he had to sell part of Blairgowrie estate, the only question being whether he should sell all of it. Allan could not bring himself to sign the necessary documents; but firmly told by William that he had no choice, he eventually agreed to sell sufficient of the land to cover immediate debts. This left them, by Allan's calculation, with £5/7/6½ a year to live on—less than half the wages of his coachman.

Next, William confronted Macintyre, arguing that the General was as much responsible as his father for their joint financial miseries, and that in fact it was he who owed his father money rather than the opposite. Macintyre proposed independent arbitration, until William pointed out that, given what he had learned—or at least suspected—of their dealings in India, they might both lose their East India Company pensions. No one, least of all Harriot, had any appetite for reviving the dispute, so

William Macpherson 1784–1866, oil by an unknown artist. MACPHERSON COLLECTION

a compromise was reached by which Allan's bond to Macintyre was cut from £10,000 to £6000—though they continued to haggle about payment of the interest.

These most pressing problems solved, another large one remained. No sooner had William returned to Blairgowrie than his parents were secretly making plans to leave. Everyone—servants, neighbours, villagers—knew of their desperate circumstances; and now, thought Eliza, everyone knew of the shame William had brought upon their household with his two half-black girls. Allan arranged lodgings at Callander, a small village far enough away for no one to recognise them, where they might, he said, look forward to 'a little comfortable quiet retirement free of Bustle and care'. One morning after breakfast they told Harriot they were leaving, and the next moment they had gone.

William was furious. How could they think of living at Callander when their property was unattended, their horses, carriage and servants 'perfectly idle and useless'? It was all his mother's doing, with her 'whimsical passion for travelling and living in inns and lodging [houses]'. His father, broken in spirit, appeared to do exactly as he was told. They had begged William to return to Scotland, and now they claimed to be anxious to keep him at home: but how could he believe they had any concern or affection for him 'when your actions seem to shew that you do not care what becomes of me'? If they returned promptly to Blairgowrie, he said, and made an effort to live prudently, he would remain there until Christmas, but no longer.

After several weeks' standoff and more harsh words, Allan and Eliza yielded to pressure and returned to the family home. William relented and stayed on beyond Christmas 1813 to get the farm in order, clearing stones, pruning hedges, planting trees and pursuing the 'daring impudent fellows' who were stealing wood from the estate. The farm might furnish a modest living, but certainly not enough to repay debts; so he looked for some form of government employment in the district, writing to the Duke of Atholl (John Murray, whose daughter was married to the son of one of the Murray brothers) and other potential patrons, but each time meeting with disappointment. He was still there in mid-1814, 'dull and solitary' during the long summer evenings. His only consolation was meeting more people in the local community—including a number of young ladies, some of whom were obviously on the lookout for an appropriate match.

'MOONLIGHT SHADES'

William's sudden arrival with the children had thrown his mother into confusion. Now he retained the initiative, arranging for the housekeeper, Mrs Cameron, to look after them at home, together with her own young children, and enrolling them at the local school, where the infant Matilda was considered just old enough to attend morning sessions. His sister Harriot, who had often longed for children of her own, took overall charge while she and General Macintyre were in Blairgowrie, ensuring that they were always clean and well fed and never exposed to the sun without their bonnets, tippets and sleeves.

His mother kept her distance, which was easily done by following her usual practice of spending most of each day in her bedroom, and then by retreating with the Colonel to Callander. But William's indiscretions, as she regarded them, preyed on her mind. She avoided calling the children by their names, referring to them instead as 'the little moonlight shades', as if to shroud their origins in the mystery of the night. The Colonel followed her lead, so that when he carelessly wrote in a list of household expenses 'My dear William's children', he corrected himself by substituting 'The children'.

As summer in 1814 approached, Eliza persuaded herself and the Colonel that it was essential for his peace of mind to travel, this time to London. A few days before they were due to leave, she suggested to William that *she* should now take charge of the moonlight shades and ensure that they receive a proper education in England.

This was an astonishing turnabout. 'After thirteen months of almost total neglect', William confided to Harriot, 'such a proposal could not but appear suspicious.' What his mother was obviously trying to do was to get the children away from Blairgowrie, and probably bring them up as servants. This was not at all what he had in mind for them:

> It has never been my intention my dear Harriot to bring them forward or to introduce them in life in the same manner that I would have done my lawful children—but I can never consent to educate them as servants in any capacity … My present scanty means obliges me to be as economical as possible in regard both to them and myself but if Providence shall afford me the means, I wish them to learn all the useful branches of female education but none or at least not much of the ornamental.

While he was unsure what line of life he would eventually choose for them, his present object was to help them acquire the skills to maintain themselves virtuously and respectably. Little Eliza had already shown herself fond of needlework, and perhaps this would determine her future direction. He said nothing more about them becoming 'good housewives', having realised perhaps, after a year back home, that marriage might be hard to achieve.

Yet despite his suspicions about his mother's motives, William yielded to her wishes and let her take them south. The arrangements in Blairgowrie, he told Harriot, left much to be desired. Although Mrs Cameron was extremely kind to them, she lacked 'that method and regularity' that a person taking charge of children should have; and they were not making good progress at the schoolhouse, having acquired there 'a shocking dialect' which a short residence in England would remove (providing further proof of Dr Johnson's dictum that 'the noblest prospect that a Scotchman ever sees, is the high road that leads him to London'). The children were bundled into the Colonel's carriage, with Eliza promising faithfully to keep them close to wherever they chose to live. Mr Simpson's two children appear to have remained in Blairgowrie.

Travelling south, the party paused at Stevenage, several hours short of London, where Eliza learned from the mistress of the inn that there was a plain but good moral school nearby where her own children had been educated. Eliza booked the girls in there for six months, before proceeding with the Colonel to London, where they took unfurnished lodgings in Oxford Street for 60 guineas a year and purchased a few articles of furniture. The horses and carriage had to go, and they dismissed their male servant, Francis, for being insolent (which servants tended to become when their masters fell behind in paying them), leaving them with just one servant, Mary. But Eliza remained restless; and within three months they had moved again to an upstairs room in Charing Cross for 2 guineas a week, with use of the kitchen fire for cooking.

William was fast losing patience with his parents' frequent moves and constant complaints. He longed to hear of his little girls: 'who they are with, what they are learning, the terms on which they are boarded—if they are well—if they are comfortable & happy'. He worried that his mother had put them into the care of an entire stranger, and remained suspicious of her intentions, especially in relation to their name. 'I hope you have not made any change in their name', he told her, 'as I will not consent to it.' While he had said many times that he would not 'introduce them into life' as he would his lawful children, he was nevertheless deeply attached to them:

> perhaps the attachment may have been increased by want of success in my own efforts to gain a competency—but the true and best reason of my attachment to them is—first they are my children if not lawfully so it is not *their* fault, but their misfortune—secondly their helpless unprotected condition.

Eliza responded that she wouldn't presume to go against his wishes; and that while she did indeed have misgivings about him 'giving them your name', she did not mean that it should lessen his duty towards them—'only to keep it in a right line'.

But this was not the time to press the matter. She had noticed that, since his return from the colonies, William's manner of expression had changed. He had become more assertive, less respectful of his parents, and less obedient to the principles of religion. Voltaire, she concluded, was partly to blame, with his notions of freedom and equality, without reference to the Holy Writ. After all, the Bible had nothing to say about removing distinctions between the ranks. The colonies too were a bad influence, introducing young men to despotic power 'without observance of pure delicacy which can only be the result of a pure Religion'. If she were to win the battle she would have wait for the right moment, and then proceed with great care.

She was determined to defend the family name—but where, in her view, lay the greater danger: the stigma of illegitimacy or the stain of colour? Not colour, she protested—if anything their colour would induce her to be kinder to them than otherwise, should their conduct warrant it. Although they were 'in the line of Egyptian Bondage', they could nevertheless through God's grace become heirs to an immortal crown. Colour was only a problem in that it stamped them as being 'brought into the world with Shame', in defiance of Holy Wedlock—for while God had made no distinction between Gentile and Jew, he had certainly 'drawn a line for Virtue & for Shame'. In other words, because of their colour, the children were to be pitied; because of their illegitimacy, the family was shamed. Giving them the family name would merely confirm their illegitimacy. Better therefore that they should be known simply as Eliza and Matilda, until William could be made to see reason.

The neighbourhood around Blairgowrie, encompassing the area it was possible to reach in a day, included many genteel and sociable families who competed in the generosity and joviality of their entertainments. William received numerous invitations to dinner parties, which were often accompanied by dancing into the early morning. Rumours began to circulate that he was courting half a dozen young ladies. There was no truth in them, he told his mother—though he did have an interest in one, Miss Cecilia Kinloch, who was undoubtedly 'the handsomest in this neighbourhood'.

But Miss Kinloch was well beyond his reach, as indeed were many of the ladies whom he might have fancied. There was not much chance that any of them would 'run way with me after a few interviews' or that their fathers would accept a man who had so little to offer. His failure in the West Indies and continuing frustrations in finding employment had shaken his confidence, leaving him unprepared to risk rejection and the sense of humiliation that would certainly follow.

Yet there was one young lady who might well serve as a substitute for the gorgeous but unattainable Miss Kinloch. This was Miss Jessy Chalmers, aged twenty-four, the elder daughter of William Chalmers, the Town Clerk at Dundee, who had acquired a fortune sufficient to purchase one half of the property that the Colonel had recently put up for sale. The gossips were saying that William fancied Chalmers' much younger daughter, Margaret, who was her father's favourite and generally considered the prettier of the two. But while the younger sister, said William, 'possesses some amiable qualities, yet she is not altogether to my taste and besides suffers by comparison with one whom I fear I have scarcely any chance of ever obtaining'. Jessy was more to his liking, and probably more within his reach:

> she appears to have a good temper and to be of a very mild and obliging disposition, fond of retirement, of reading and of needlework; she has not much taste or inclination for music but plays very tolerably also seems rather to dislike dancing but can acquit herself well enough. I have sometimes thought her rather inclined to melancholy but in conversation she does not shew anything of it—she has no pretensions to beauty but has rather a pleasing countenance and figure.

As he wrote these words, thoughts of Miss Kinloch evidently came to mind, for the next moment he declared that he was 'very lukewarm in the affair [and] indeed am not inclined to marriage at all—at present'. But then he changed his mind again, and sent the letter to his parents with a request for their approval to seek her hand.

Here was the opportunity Eliza had been waiting for. She responded at length—managing, though, to avoid entirely any direct reference to Miss Chalmers or William's request. Instead, after reflecting broadly on love and happiness, and quoting from suitable verses, she returned to the issue of what name would be given to the moonlight shades. She approached the subject coyly, alluding first to the Colonel's business anxieties and their implications for William's future. 'I am sensible', she wrote, 'you must give up yourself for a humble life—but humble life can be dignified with grace my dear and let this be your dignity my son—and God will bless you when you call on him.' Then she eased herself into her main theme:

> now that I am on the topic of Grace I must treat another subject that may give you pain until you are able to calm your mind for reflection ... relative to your little moonlight shades—I mean as to their assuming your name My Dear—which I have not or cannot approve—I have not spoken of this to the person with whom they are placed but it is my own resolve not to have anything further to do in their direction unless your name is laid aside.

This decision, she insisted, was founded on 'pure delicacy'. While he should not contemplate forsaking his offspring, he should nevertheless do his best to conceal 'the shame in which they have no blame'. This 'trait of modesty', she suggested, 'will rather encourage attention from any amiable character who may become your wife than otherwise'. On the other hand, if he were to give the children his name, he would dishonour his wife and offend the blessed sacrament of marriage. 'Therefore My Dear William let me have the name of Macpherson laid aside with them.'

This was a bold ultimatum from a position of strength. Eliza's language was, as usual, convoluted, and her arguments were opaque, but William had no difficulty understanding her meaning. There were two threats: one—to abandon the children—perfectly explicit; the other thinly disguised—if he insisted that the illegitimate children should carry his name, his parents would withhold their blessing from his proposed marriage.

What she did not say, at least in as many words, was that the status and respect the family had once enjoyed were so fragile that any deviation from the strict rules of propriety—or what she called 'pure delicacy'— might undermine them entirely. They were clinging to gentility by a thread. Apart from the land, which they might yet have to part with, they owned next to nothing; the Colonel was dispirited and unable to come to a decision about anything; the servants with whom they had been forced to part were no doubt telling stories about them. Yet if they could not enjoy the trappings of wealth, they could at least keep their heads high by adhering strictly to the rules of proper conduct, as defined by Holy Writ—which, in Eliza's view, prescribed the exact course she should take in relation to the moonlight shades.

His mother's response—or pointed lack of response to the question William had asked—seemed to increase his ardour for Jessy and stiffen his resolve. Another visit to the Chalmers family 'completely restored Miss Chalmers power over me to its original force'. 'The more I become acquainted with her', he told his parents, 'the more I esteem her'. 'I shall be very much distressed indeed if you refuse your consent and aid towards my accomplishing my wishes.'

But what could he do about the children, given that his mother was adamant? Reluctantly, he yielded before her insistence, so that henceforth they were known as William's children Eliza and Matilda—in other words, Eliza and Matilda Williams.

So far he had said nothing to Jessy—indeed he had concealed every sign of affection. Now he decided to approach her parents, taking first her mother aside during an afternoon walk in the garden. She was easily won over; but Jessy's father needed more persuading. Had William fully considered the cost of supporting a family? How did he intend to maintain his daughter? How much did he expect the farm to yield each year? William confessed that it was unlikely to be worth more than £250 if the seasons remained fair, with a chance of £300 in a good year. This, said Mr Chalmers, was scarcely enough to keep a family in any comfort; then, after a long pause, 'he said that he was inclined to think very favourably of me—and that Mrs Chalmers was very much my friend'. So far as he could tell, William was not extravagant, and nor was Jessy, so with a little help they might just be able to get by. He promised to do whatever he could to support the arrangement—provided that Jessy was happy to marry him and that his father made over part of the estate, as he had long promised to do. Jessy was to know nothing of his intentions until his parents had approved the match.

This should have been straightforward. Eliza, though, now that the children were safely out of sight, had evidently concluded that the son of a laird, however straitened his circumstances, deserved better than the daughter of a town clerk. The Colonel begged him to come to London, to discuss the matter face to face; Eliza urged him not to rush into anything, but to look around more carefully before becoming entangled in a relationship he might later regret.

William was exasperated beyond endurance. How could his parents question Miss Chalmers' birth and connections? One of her uncles was a Major-General; another belonged to the illustrious Mackenzie family (whose branches included many members of the nobility). What more could he hope for?

> It is now very near two years since I arrived in Britain and during that period I know not what I have been doing ... I have now [the] prospect of uniting myself to a young lady of birth fortune and expectations fully equal to what I have any right to expect, provided only you will perform the promises you have always been making.

Jessy Macpherson 1789–1847, oil by an unknown artist. MACPHERSON COLLECTION

He begged for their support—and if they refused to give it, he would return to the West Indies. This was the ultimate threat, and it worked—though Eliza's blessing came grudgingly.

All that now remained was for William to reveal himself to Jessy as her lover and offer his hand. Evidently she took no offence at being the last to learn about her possible future, for she accepted his proposal without hesitation and they were married within weeks, early in 1815. There was little time for romance—but, unlike the earlier arrangements between Harriot and Colonel Macintyre, at least the prudential side of the relationship appeared to be all in order. Romance could wait.

The newlyweds settled into Blairgowrie House, with William assuring Jessy that she might regard the home as her own. No sooner had they done so than Eliza discovered a new enthusiasm for their old home and decided that she and the Colonel should return from London and assert their rights of occupancy. While the house was large enough to accommodate both couples easily, neither was prepared to live there as guests. A tense situation followed, with William accusing his father of fickleness and Eliza complaining of her son's 'unkind disrespect'. The young couple moved out for a time to live with Jessy's parents. Eventually the Colonel relented, and in mid-1815 made over the estate to William, and along with it the diminished status of Laird of Blairgowrie.

The Colonel and Eliza passed the following winter in London, where they joined the crowds who came to see Bonaparte's carriage that had been taken at the battle of Waterloo, which ended the Napoleonic Wars. Returning to Blairgowrie in the spring of 1816, they stayed disconsolately at Blairgowrie House, hoping in the meantime to restore their dignity by regaining possession of the old house at Newton, which was currently occupied by a tenant on a long lease. Each consoled the other in their miseries. Eliza, troubled by headaches and rheumatic pains, reflected as ever on the role of fate, remarking that while some things 'appear dark & mysterious', an all-seeing God would one day restore their happiness and make everything clear. Allan, now in his seventy-sixth year, while healthy in body, constantly berated himself for the folly that had led them to sink to this condition, lamenting that his dear wife was reduced 'even to cooking the victuals I eat'.

In March a letter from a retired soldier and student of the Highland regiments asking for information about the role of the Black Watch during the Seven Years War reminded Allan of happier days—but he feared his memory was failing, so he was unable to tell his inquirer anything that he did not already know. In May the Hannay affair came back to haunt him, with General Macintyre insisting that *he* was not responsible for the partnership's debts; and while Allan was convinced otherwise, he was 'determined to bear the loss of this money, rather than sign any Deed that will tend to hurt or injure my old friend & now my son in Law'. He worried about his younger son Allan, still in the West Indies and falling deeper into debt; and he continued to write to his friends and connections in the hope that one of them would find William a job. He fretted about the worsening economic conditions prevailing in the country and feared they would lead them all to absolute ruin.

One evening at the end of May 1816 Allan suffered a double blow: the rents from the estate had come in and were far short of what was due; and the tenant at Newton was refusing to budge unless he received large compensation. He went to bed at the usual time, according to William 'very greatly depressed'. The next morning William found him lying in a pool of blood in the front room of the house, having evidently suffered a stroke—perhaps, thought William, owing to 'the great agitation of his mind'. The doctor was summoned and made some perfunctory attempts to revive him—but in a short time Colonel Allan Macpherson was dead.

For many months Blairgowrie House was immersed in misery even deeper than usual.

A USEFUL EDUCATION
The school at Stevenage where Eliza had enrolled the moonlight shades fitted Jane Austen's description of:

> a real, honest, old-fashioned Boarding-school, where a reasonable quantity of accomplishments were sold at a reasonable price, and where girls might be sent to be out of the way and scramble themselves into a little education, without any danger of coming back prodigies.

It was run by a Miss Fisher, a well-meaning woman who appeared to have a genuine affection for the children in her care. She took an immediate liking to Eliza and Matilda Williams, telling their grandmother that she found 'these sweet children' very manageable. Although English dame schools around this time have often been derided as little more than child-minding institutions, Miss Fisher ran regular classes and expected her twenty or so pupils to show signs of steady improvement. The cost for the two children together, including board and classes, was £60 a year—a sum that William could scarcely afford.

Soon after the children arrived, Miss Fisher committed a faux pas by asking Eliza whether they should be taught to acknowledge her as their grandmama or their mama? Eliza, in her customary fashion, avoided answering the question directly, while making it clear that the children were her wards and she was their guardian, with the implication that any blood connection was an unfortunate accident that need not be mentioned. So the children were taught to address her as 'dear Madam' or 'Honoured Madam', and to see themselves as her 'affectionate and dutiful wards'. At least their father made no effort to disguise his relationship to them, and insisted that they should continue to call him 'Papa'.

'I think you have misunderstood my mother', Harriot told William. 'She does not seem to have an idea of making servants of them at present. She rather talks of giving them a finished education to make them fit for keeping a school or being a private governess.' Certainly Eliza, once she had won the battle over the children's name, applied herself diligently to their education. She now lived most of the time in London and visited them regularly, carefully assessing their progress and offering advice on what they should learn. 'I recommend they should be interrogated as to the parts of speech, when they read their daily lesson', she told Miss Fisher; 'and I also beg that the catechism of Sacred Questions may be regularly & particularly attended to, as a proper groundwork and sense of Religion surpasses all other reading for Children of their age.' As well as reading, writing, arithmetic and religion, she arranged for them to attend lessons in dancing and music; and whenever opportunity offered, she took it upon herself to introduce them to French.

Some people, she told William, thought that 'my ideas for your little girls are too elevated for you and them—and that I do wrong not to place them in business' (meaning setting them up as seamstresses, or some similar occupation). 'Some people' probably meant one person in particular, her son-in-law General Macintyre, who ever since their rapprochement seemed to have taken a particular delight in rubbing her up the wrong way. Eliza stood her ground: 'the little moonlight shades' were more worthy of particular care than 'Handsome fair ones from an unprincipled woman'. There was, in other words, a scale of culpability, in which an illicit liaison with an ignorant heathen in some distant colony was less reprehensible than an affair with a white woman who ought to have known better. This was probably a thinly veiled attack on Macintyre, who had fathered illegitimate white offspring as well as the children of his Indian *bibis*.

So the moonlight shades should be given 'every necessary advantage for a genteel livelihood'. Like William, Eliza said nothing about their chances of getting married. Girls (or at least coloured ones) should be able to look after themselves; and this meant that they should, like boys, be given the best education their father's money could buy. As well-educated young women, they might look forward to being placed as governesses in respectable households, or as teachers in schools of their own. 'Business', Eliza warned William, was too risky: better to set them up at Blairgowrie with a cottage and a cow's grass (a small parcel of land), sufficient to guarantee that they would not starve in their old age.

The girls continued at Miss Fisher's for several years, learning how to become 'industrious & fit for the world—& not fine Ladies', and being steadily inculcated with the principles of virtue and religion. Through their handwriting exercises they learned to 'Avoid whatever is unbecoming' (Matilda) and 'Commend virtuous actions' (Eliza), that 'Shame accompanies mean actions' (Matilda) and that 'Innumerable annoyances accompany mankind' (Eliza). When it seemed that they would have to be taken away, as their father could not afford the fees, Miss Fisher kindly allowed them to contribute to their upkeep by sewing fine shirts for sale, and assisting with the younger boarders. They were constantly reminded of their place in the world; and if they should chance to forget it, Eliza was quick to refer them to appropriate references in the scriptures and suitable sermons about duty, humility and obedience.

Under her firm guidance, the girls made good progress. Yet there was one persistent problem (apart from the cost of their fees): however much their grandmother cajoled and scolded them, they refused to open their mouths wide when they were speaking, reading or singing. How, she asked them, could they expect to become governesses or teachers if they could not be heard? Annoyingly, General Macintyre remarked on the problem when the girls were staying with her on one occasion, and asked why they spoke so softly. Eliza retorted that it was common for children to be bashful at their age (little Eliza was then eleven, and Matilda nine), 'particularly when they were under a proper sense of deference, & obedience & discipline'. Then, on reflection, she decided that their timidity was in fact a virtue, as it signified their growing awareness that they were 'not Honorable Children', and in

Eliza Macpherson in 'widow's weeds', oil by an unknown artist.
MACPHERSON COLLECTION

such circumstances modesty was more likely than excessive confidence to win them friends.

Nevertheless, their persistent refusal to open their mouths continued to vex her, especially when Macintyre gave the impression that she was in some way to blame. So she accosted little Eliza, who by the age of twelve had outgrown Miss Fisher's school and come to live with her grandmother in London:

> I ask her if she hates me for the trouble I take with her, & then she falls a crying & says no; & I tell her it looks like it, & that if I send her away again in displeasure as I did last time, I will take no more trouble about her,—that it is all for her own good & to make her get bread genteely & like a gentlewoman. She promises to mind me & do better.

In such ways Eliza Macpherson confirmed the misfortunes of her granddaughter's birth.

While the two girls were acquiring a useful education at Stevenage, their younger brother Allan was growing up in Berbice, presumably with his mother on Plantation Seafield. As he approached the age of six, he was considered old enough to leave her and make the Atlantic crossing. Like other children who made the same journey, he was probably accompanied by a returning planter or merchant at least as far as Glasgow, where his escort put him on a coach for Perth, addressed to the care of William's agent, Thomas Whitson. He arrived at the Whitsons' towards the end of autumn 1816, a few months after the death of the Colonel. As young Allan had a bad cold, the Whitsons kept him for a couple of days until he was well enough to be taken by gig the 20 miles to Blairgowrie. He is 'a fine smart sensible Child,' said Whitson, '& is already quite at home in our house'.

Eliza had got her way with the girls—but this time William was not prepared to part with his youngest, not so much because he was a boy but rather because Eliza, with enough to keep her busy in London, was in no position to persuade him otherwise. In any case, now that her son was married, there was less reason for her to try to do so: if his wife could tolerate his indiscretions, why should his mother worry? So William kept Allan at home, and when he was a little older enrolled him as a boarder at Mr Peddie's school near Perth, on the Blairgowrie side of the River Tay. While his sisters in England were learning much about obedience and little about love, Allan grew up close to an affectionate father and stepmother who seemed untroubled by what the neighbours thought about his shady origins or the colour of his skin. He was also spared any ambiguity about his name: following the precedent set for his sisters, he was known from his arrival in Scotland as Allan Williams.

None of the little 'West Indians', though, could claim first place in their father's affections. That place was reserved in anticipation of William and Jessy being blessed with legitimate offspring. For a time it seemed that this was not to be. But in autumn 1818, two years after Allan Williams had arrived from Berbice, Jessy gave birth to a son, in circumstances that nicely presaged his turbulent career.

Thirty-seven years later, on the other side of the world, William told his son about the night of his birth. The events were 'as fresh in my mind as if they had happened only yesterday'. Jessy had a hard time of it: she went into labour around six o'clock in the evening, and was attended by two doctors (one of whom spent the most of the evening dozing in front of the fire) and a midwife from Dundee. The baby did not arrive until around four or five in the morning, and for a terrifying moment it seemed to be stillborn. William recalled that one of the doctors:

> desired me to bring a large Wash-hand bason full of whiskey, which I immediately procured, and you were plunged into it up to your neck; signs of life soon appeared, and in a few minutes you acquired strength, and began to cry; the sound of your voice seemed to give fresh life and spirits to your anxious mother; in a short time you became a stout hearty brawling little fellow, but so cross and impatient if not indulged in your own way, that I could hardly prevent the Monthly Nurse from giving you some cross shakes and slaps sometimes ...

Jessy survived the birth, but only just—she had no more children. Naturally, the son and heir was called Allan, ensuring that the other Allan would continue to be called Allan Williams, as if it were a single Christian name.

PATRONAGE

Mr Chalmers, William's father-in-law, had been right: the farm at Blairgowrie was scarcely sufficient to keep a family in comfort. It might just have been—but then the long wars against Napoleon finally came to an end and the victors, instead of reaping vast rewards, were left with economic turmoil and huge debts. The poor suffered most: in Perth a Committee of Manufacturers and Operative Weavers reported that the situation of the manufacturing and labouring classes was so dire that 'unless *immediate relief* is afforded, beggary and starvation must be the inevitable consequences'. Farmers were also under duress, unable to get a reasonable return for their produce. So when the workers in Perth asked local landholders to help, William struggled to find a guinea.

What he wanted—what he *had* to have if he were to maintain 'the situation in society to which I have been accustomed'—was a job with a regular salary. He asked for an appointment as factor on the Duke of Atholl's vast estates, but the Duke wanted someone from England, free from any local connections. When the Barrack Master at Perth suddenly dropped dead, William quickly put his name forward, but was beaten to it by another Barrack Master on half pay.

The family's old patrons, especially the Duke and Duchess of Atholl, seemed to offer the best chance of success. Over many years they had offered William's father, and now William himself, 'much politeness and attention and even promises of support'. In return, the Macphersons had been their loyal supporters, voting for their candidates at parliamentary elections. William knew that his vote was a valuable commodity, not something to be squandered on account of a candidate's professed political principles (not that he had ever shown much interest in politics), but rather as an exchange for favours promised or given. But the system rarely operated smoothly, and sometimes caused anxiety and embarrassment.

So when in 1818 a candidate at the forthcoming election asked for his support, William had to declare his obligations to the Duke while making it clear that he would switch his allegiance if the candidate gave him reason to do so:

> I much fear I should seriously offend these valuable friends if I were to promise you my vote—in opposition to the wishes of the Duke of Atholl—Yet had you succeeded in procuring for me any situation that would have relieved me from the

very straitened and embarrassed situation in which the nature
of my father's settlements has placed me they could not and
would not I am sure have been offended at my making you
the only return in my power for a benefit of which they know
I stand so very much in need—

Again the colonies beckoned. He tried for a government position in
Berbice, but without success. Then he heard enthusiastic talk about
sheep farming in the Australian colonies. Perhaps wool in Australia would
be what cotton had once been in the West Indies. In 1824 a group of
wealthy London bankers, spurred by the prospect of free land grants and
cheap convict labour, formed the Australian Agricultural Company to
grow fine wool in New South Wales. William rushed to the capital to
put his name forward for the position of superintendent. He was too late;
but another company was about to be formed with similar objectives in
Van Diemen's Land (later known as Tasmania). Given his experience of
planting cotton and managing slaves, he thought he had a good chance
of success, especially since one of his local members of parliament, Sir
George Murray (from another branch of the Murray Clan), had said
a word in his favour. But the company's promoters wanted someone with
an extensive practical knowledge of sheep farming, especially of the
Merino and Saxon varieties that apparently showed exceptional promise;
and as William could not pretend to know much about such matters, his
chances were slim. He remained in London, waiting for the outcome to
be confirmed, and walking each day 4 miles into the city to 'enquire the
news and seek for new hopes and prospects'.

   While he was thus gloomily occupied—or unoccupied—in the capital,
an unexpected death came to the rescue. Through Donald Macintyre,
one of General Macintyre's sons by his white mistress, he learned that
a partner in the mercantile firm of McLachlan Macintyre & Co, which
traded on behalf of the East India Company, had died. Donald, who was
himself a partner in the house, was ready to promote William for the
vacancy, which was said to be worth £1000 a year. This was a far more
attractive prospect than going to a distant colony, especially since his
sister Harriot had calculated that his family could get by in London on
half that income. So William seized the chance he had been waiting for,
withdrew his application for the situation in Van Diemen's Land and put
the Blairgowrie estate up for lease for fifteen years. Soon the family—

William, Jessy and the two Allans—were on their way to begin a new life in London, where the future seemed so much brighter.

The move to London enabled the extended family to see more of one another than they had done for many years. William and Jessy lived modestly—however much he might earn, the encumbrances on Blairgowrie left no room for extravagance. By contrast, the Macintyres lived lavishly—much too well, according to the ageing Eliza. Macintyre, who had received an additional promotion to the rank of Lieutenant-General, spent most of his time in bed or playing cards. Harriot, when she was not waiting on her husband's needs, devoted herself to an adopted daughter, Isabella (about whose parentage nothing is known). Occasionally she held a party for the children, to which little Allan Macpherson, who attended a nearby boarding school, and the three moonlight shades were all invited.

Whenever Eliza and Macintyre were present in the same room there was potential for disaster, with Eliza tending increasingly towards 'Methodistical notions' and her son-in-law always ready to bait her. Eliza had devoted most of her time in the preceding few years to supervising her 'wards' and looking after them during their frequent illnesses. Early in the 1820s Matilda Williams, who was the brighter of the two, disappeared from the record—perhaps she was carried off by a childhood illness; perhaps she married; perhaps she remained at Stevenage to assist Miss Fisher with the younger children and then, as her father and grandmother had hoped, found a place as governess in a respectable family or teacher in a small school of her own. Eliza Williams, after a period with her grandmother, moved to a school for older children near Dulwich, south-east of the city, where her guardian took increasing satisfaction in moulding her in her own image as 'a well bred woman'. There was to be no more needlework—now she was to devote her time to 'superior accomplishments', including music, drawing, geography and Latin, and her schoolmistress was to pay 'every attention to polite exterior', especially her manner of speaking, deportment and 'easy elegant address'. Eventually she came to live with her grandmother, accompanying her to church and indulging her fondness for sacred music by playing and singing for her every day. The grandmother was pleased with her handiwork: 'most people', she

The Reverend Allan Macpherson, William's younger brother, in the 1820s. This unassuming portrait on cardboard was probably painted before he set out with his wife on their ill-fated voyage to the East Indies. MACPHERSON COLLECTION

said, 'seem very dissatisfied with the progress of their children—but I have my own ideas on this subject—and think much is their own fault'. Whatever the consequences for Eliza Williams, her grandmother had now evidently acknowledged her as her own.

Allan Williams, the youngest of the moonlight shades, was nearly fifteen when the family moved to London. He probably finished his schooling and then found employment with his father at McLachlan Macintyre's or some other counting house. He must have met his sister—or sisters, if Matilda was still living; but we can only guess whether their contact was ever more than fleeting.

One other family member who attended an occasional gathering in London was Allan—William and Harriot's long-lost brother who had returned from Berbice in 1820 after seventeen years abroad. He would have left the colony long before, had there been anything for a younger son to come home to. But as there certainly was not, he tried to make the best of it in Berbice, investing in horses and then breeding cattle to supply the local garrison with meat. When all his enterprises had failed, he paid for the manumission of his slave concubine and their child, as his brother had done before him, and sailed for home. There he married Jessy's amiable younger sister Margaret. Heading south to England, he flirted with political radicalism (offending the Duke of Atholl), took holy orders (often the last refuge of a younger son) and through some happy act of patronage won a curacy in Wiltshire, a little over a hundred miles from the capital. But Allan had evidently inherited his mother's restless spirit, and before long he and his wife were on their way to India, where he served as a chaplain with the East India Company.

Within a few years of William and Jessy's move to London, it was clear that things were not going according to plan. The McLachlan Macintyre venture, far from yielding William £1000 a year, was forcing him even deeper into a pit of misery and debt. In 1828, nearly three years after joining the firm, he decided that enough was enough: he would resign as a partner, whatever the consequences might be. He was now in his mid-forties.

But there was cause for hope. At the end of May, around the time William made this decision, Sir George Murray—the same Murray who had supported his application to join the Van Diemen's Land Company a few years earlier—was appointed Secretary of State for the Colonies, an office which carried with it huge opportunities for patronage. Within a few weeks William waited on Murray in Downing Street and told him frankly of his predicament—that he had lost heavily as a cotton planter in Berbice; that he had inherited an estate that was burdened with debt; that he had tried farming for twelve years, but with insufficient capital to move ahead; that his recent commercial venture had failed to meet expectations—and that now he had 'really nothing whatever to support myself or my family'. He told Sir George of his varied experience, as planter, farmer, merchant and justice of the peace. While he would prefer a position in London, his needs were so pressing that he would willingly accept whatever offered.

Murray, an affable character best known for his achievements on the battlefield and in the boudoir (having been involved some years earlier in a scandalous liaison), listened patiently and promised to do his best. During the next two and a half years, while he was in charge of the Colonial Office, he would distinguish himself by saturating the colonies with Scots much as Ossian had done for India nearly half a century earlier. Now, as he settled into office, he was overwhelmed with applications and requests for help. There could be no question though that William, as a Perthshire landholder who had fallen on hard times, the son of a distinguished officer, and friend of his own political friends, including the Duke of Atholl, deserved his support. Moreover, William appeared to know something about business, and to be capable and honest (and if his failure to get rich cast doubts on his capacity, at least it proved his honesty); and his manner was pleasant and reserved, suggesting that he was unlikely to engage in the squabbling to which colonists seemed remarkably prone. Above all, it seemed unlikely that his nomination to a position in the colonies would, as so often happened, come back to haunt those who had appointed him.

William left the meeting as optimistically as he dared allow himself to be. Then he waited anxiously, first for weeks, then for months, until one day in November or early December he was summoned to the Colonial Office where he appears to have been offered not just one job, but a choice of two: superintendent (the name had yet to be decided) of a new settlement at Swan River, on the west coast of the Australian continent, or Collector of Internal Revenue in New South Wales. For various reasons, the west Australian prospect seemed uncertain. William had had enough of uncertainty; so he eagerly accepted the position in the well known and well established colony of New South Wales. His appointment was formally announced to the New South Wales governor in mid-December 1828.

The family—William, Jessy, young Allan Macpherson and Allan Williams—scrambled to prepare for their departure. They visited Blairgowrie, where William arranged for the estate to be put into the hands of trustees. There was a momentary panic when it seemed that he would be unable to raise the necessary sureties to allow him to accept an office of trust, but the Colonial Office softened its demands and his sister Harriot and some friends came to the rescue.

William asked his mother if she would come with them, but Eliza, now approaching seventy, regretfully said no, with accompanying reflections on 'fickle fortune' and the emptiness of pursuing 'the dross of this world'. She looked forward to seeing them in the next, she said, for there was little chance of their meeting again in this one. And she was right: faithfully attended by Eliza Williams, she died within two years of their departure.

Harriot had already lost General Macintyre, mid-way through 1827. With the help of Colonel Allan's legacy, he left her comfortably off. Within a few years she had married another former officer of the East India Company, Lieutenant-Colonel Edmund Craigie, who was much closer than Macintyre had been to her own age. Her adopted child, Isabella, remained her constant companion.

After Eliza's death, Eliza Williams probably returned to Blairgowrie, or at least to somewhere in Perthshire, and found employment as a governess or teacher. She never married. William continued to support her with £50 annually, until Harriot and their brother Allan, now back from the East, offered to ease his burden by each paying her £10 a year. He gratefully accepted their help: 'I do not wish her to be encouraged in idleness or luxury, altho' I should be very sorry to see her deprived of necessary comforts; especially in the event of her health continuing delicate'. After a painful illness extending over many weeks, Eliza Williams died in Perth early in 1837, in her thirtieth year. Someone, presumably William's agent in Perth, ensured that she was well attended by a doctor and nurses, and given a good funeral, at a cost of £15/0/6.

William did his duty—or paid for his pleasures—until the end. Whether he shed a tear at her passing, or whether her brother Allan Williams or half-brother Allan Macpherson were ever aware of it, we shall never know.

10

COLONISTS

BOARD THE BRIG *ELIZABETH*, 1829. DURING THE LONG AND tedious passage from England to New South Wales, William Macpherson insists that his younger son Allan, now aged ten, should spend a few hours each day in the open air, for the benefit of his health. Twice a day for nearly six months father and son pace the deck, a distance from fore to aft about the length of a cricket pitch. Sometimes Allan's mother Jessy joins them, but only when the sea is calm and then never for long. Allan's half-brother, Allan Williams, who turns nineteen during the voyage, is old enough to look after himself. He is more interested in playing cards with other young gentlemen and passing judgment among his shipboard chums on the few young ladies among their fellow passengers.

William is determined that Allan should not fall behind in his education. For nearly four hours every day between breakfast and dinner, he supervises his younger son's lessons. In the evenings the lad has time to himself: the ship's carpenter has made him the hull of a model vessel, leaving him to add the masts and rigging. Sometimes he reads the books he has brought with him, including a book of stories, intended by their author 'to encourage in children the love of reading'; and *Scenes of British Wealth*, which introduces its young readers to the wonders of modern Britain, in proof of 'the superiority of industry over idleness'. 'Who can tell,' writes its author, an English clergyman, 'but some child, only old enough now to read this book, may, by reading it, begin to think: "Now, what shall I do?" and "What shall I be?" and so, in time, become something famous, or, better still, useful ...'

On their walks around the deck, William tells Allan as much as he knows of the colony where they are headed: that it was first settled in 1788, just about the time his late grandfather, Colonel Macpherson, took up the land at Blairgowrie; that its prospects are especially promising, owing to the fine wool that is grown there; and that while many of its inhabitants are convicts and soldiers, there are now numerous free settlers (including members of the respectable classes) and a growing number of native born. There is also, he says, a race of Aboriginal people, backward and uncivilised, yet equal to themselves in God's eyes.

Allan listens intently to all his father tells him, as an obedient son should. Who could doubt that he will grow up to be a fine young man and a credit to his doting parents?

SYDNEY

It is raining when the ship arrives, so torrentially that William might have thought for a moment that he was back in Demerara or Berbice. But Sydney is quite different from the desolate townships of Stabroek and New Amsterdam that he had encountered nearly thirty years earlier. For a start, it has hills. When the rain eases, the men of the family leave the temporary lodgings near their landing place and take a stroll up George Street, the muddy main thoroughfare which rises gently from the waterfront. There are one-, two- and even three-storey buildings on either side, a disorderly mix of public houses, government offices, military barracks, shops, warehouses and private homes, many of them solidly built from local sandstone. Free men and women go about their business, the old hands easily distinguishable from the 'new chums' by their casual manner and appearance; a few convicts shuffle past in chains, though most of them work as servants assigned to a settler or government officer, and look much the same as free men of their class; soldiers lean against veranda poles or saunter down the street with no particular object in view; and a few Aborigines stand or sit in the thoroughfare, sometimes arguing among themselves, sometimes drinking and sometimes begging for tobacco from passers-by, who, if they notice them at all, generally regard them with disdain.

William goes house hunting, and soon the family take up residence in a comfortable two-storey dwelling in Castlereagh Street, less than a mile from Sydney Cove and close to the government offices. Rents, like most other things in Sydney, are expensive, and this house will cost him £100 a year, a fifth of his salary. But what choice does he have? After presenting himself to the Governor, General Ralph Darling, he is ready to start work—and the sooner the better, for until then he cannot draw a full salary.

George Street from the Wharf, engraving by John Carmichael, 1829. NATIONAL LIBRARY
OF AUSTRALIA

When William took office towards the end of 1829, the position of
Collector of Internal Revenue was a new one, with responsibility for
collecting all the moneys due to the government, excepting customs duties
(which made up the largest proportion). In all the colonies there were
sinecures, but this was not one of them. William discovered there were
'enormous arrears', with some of the colony's most successful merchants
and landholders not having paid taxes for a decade or more. As every
potential taxpayer in the colony knew, there was no real need to pay taxes;
for while the Collector might send out cajoling letters, the only way he
could force debtors to pay was through the Crown Solicitor, who was,
declared Governor Darling, 'one of the most idle Men living', and who
did, according to William, 'nothing, literally and absolutely nothing'.

This did not stop William from throwing himself into his duties
with a degree of zeal that left his less energetic colleagues gaping with
astonishment. The one clerk assigned to him could not even keep up with
current business, so William set Allan Williams to work as an 'Extra Clerk',
paying him from his own salary £80 per annum. Then, when the work was

still overwhelming, he retained another clerk at his own expense. This was a big risk; yet, having been so often told in his youth about the duty an employee owed to his employer, and having been assured by his late father that diligence would be rewarded, he concluded that the risk was worth taking: that his hard work would surely be noticed and his expenses one day reimbursed.

So he and his three loyal clerks immersed themselves in correspondence and calculations, working in the summer from nine o'clock in the morning to six or seven in the evening, and as the days grew shorter, for as long as there was sufficient daylight (candles being expensive and in short supply). In his first full year of work he personally drafted nearly 2000 letters, addressed to 'every Public Office—every Bench of Magistrates—and almost every individual of any consequence in the Colony'. With the help of his clerks, he compiled detailed information about all the sources and potential sources of local revenue, including land rents in town and country, tolls on roads and ferries, publicans' licences, duties on spirits produced in the colony, auction duties, magistrates' fees, fines, and postal revenue. All this activity gave him an intimate view of the colony, the rules and regulations that governed it, the people who administered it, the officials who were diligent and those who were lazy, the magistrates who were fair and those who were corrupt, the merchants and landholders who were thriving and those who were struggling, the honest men and women who paid their taxes and those who tried every means to avoid doing so. He also learned about the colony's geography—the rich farming and grazing lands along the Hawkesbury River within a day's ride of Sydney, the expanding pastoral regions across the Blue Mountains, and the small settlements along the Hunter River, 100 miles by sea to the north. But none of this he saw for himself: for well over a year after his arrival in the colony, he saw nothing of New South Wales beyond the streets of Sydney, except for one day's dreary ride to Parramatta, the colony's second largest town.

He asked the Governor for more clerical assistance, or at least for money to cover the cost of the clerks he was meeting from his own salary. But Darling, apart from being naturally parsimonious, had been strictly instructed by the Colonial Office to avoid additional expenditure. So William wrote to his patron, Sir George Murray (as Murray had invited him to do), detailing the work he had done to date, suggesting ways of making the system of land rents work, and gently pointing out that it made no sense to limit colonial revenues by starving the office

that was supposed to collect them. This won him a partial victory: the
new Secretary of State, Viscount Goderich, agreed that he should be
reimbursed for his expenses to date; but as the additional clerks had
presumably brought the situation under control, there was no further
need for them. Better to hand the duties of Collector of Internal Revenue
to the office of the Colonial Treasurer who, by William's own testimony,
appeared to be underemployed. Evidently William had talked himself out
of a job. There were lessons here: that a letter sent from Sydney might
not reach the patron for whom it was intended; that cries for economy in
Downing Street tended to drown out arguments based on logic and local
knowledge; and that no position in the colonies was ever secure.

Nevertheless, his efforts were not in vain. Lord Goderich, having
observed that 'Mr. Macpherson's Letters display so much ability and so
correct a judgment on the present situation of the Colony', instructed the
Governor to find him a job that would make best use of his talents; and
Sir Richard Bourke, who succeeded Darling as Governor in 1831, decided
that, whatever the Secretary of State might say, the job of Collector was
indispensable and that William Macpherson was unquestionably the best
man to fill it. Here, for William, was further proof that loyalty and hard
work were the surest means of securing his and his family's future.

That future appeared to lie in the colony, at least for the next ten
to fifteen years. His unhappy association in London with the house of
McLachlan Macintyre came back to haunt him when it collapsed entirely,
owing him almost £3000. Most of his salary disappeared in repaying debts,
including those inherited from his father. In 1832, in words reminiscent of
the Colonel's lamentations, he wrote of the 'almost hopeless and desperate
situation of my affairs'. He came close to selling Blairgowrie, but was saved
just in time by a small legacy following his mother's death, which gave
him enough to cover immediate debts.

Apart from these worries about money, life in Sydney was pleasant.
The days for much of the year were mild (a happy balance between the
cold of Scotland and the oppressive heat of Berbice), the skies were blue,
and he was making friends among his fellow colonists, many of whom
(needless to say) were Scots: the Colonial Secretary, Alexander Macleay;
the Clerk of the Legislative and Executive Councils, Edward Deas
Thomson; the Surveyor-General (and another of Sir George Murray's
protégés), Major Thomas Mitchell; and many more. In 1836 William and
a group of friends organised the first St Andrew's Day Ball, where he and

a Mrs Barker were observed dancing a Highland reel 'with great glee' (and presumably perfect propriety).

He was becoming a pillar of the colonial establishment. Deas Thomson described him as 'an excellent man of business ... universally esteemed and respected', compliments that had particular force as they were delivered behind his back. He accepted honorary appointments appropriate to his status in the community, including Trustee of the Savings Bank of New South Wales (the only one of nine trustees, he said, who knew anything about savings bank business); and Secretary of the Emigrants' Friend Society, which helped newcomers find jobs, as well as, occasionally, husbands and wives. Balancing the responsibilities of Collector of Internal Revenue and Emigrants' Friend was no easy task. As Collector, he was expected to ensure that government-sponsored emigrants repaid part of the cost of their passages. As Secretary to the Emigrants' Friend Society, he knew that many of the newcomers, including 'poor young friendless destitute females', were surviving on a pittance. 'If I had the means,' he declared, 'I would rather pay these debts myself, than stand forward as the prosecutor of these unprotected young women.' True enough, many emigrants, male and female, were 'drunken, idle, profligate spendthrifts' who should not have been given help to emigrate in the first place. But now that they were here, what possible benefit could there be in throwing them into prison? Surely it would serve only to discourage emigration— and emigrants were exactly what the colony needed. Already, a few years after arriving, he was speaking as if his own prospects were linked to the colony's future prosperity.

Governors of different political hues came and went, but William retained the respect of each of them. When the Tory Darling was replaced by Richard Bourke, an Irish Whig, some supporters of the former Governor fell out of favour. Although William, if pressed to offer an opinion, favoured the Tories over the Whigs (the proposed Reform Bill back home filled him with 'anxious forebodings'), he and the new Governor were soon on the best of terms. Bourke thought he would make a good Colonial Secretary, the most senior civil officer in the colony after the Governor, and put his name forward to Downing Street, before deciding that his son-in-law, Deas Thomson, would make a better one. He compensated William by appointing him to the position Thomson had vacated of Clerk of the Executive and Legislative Councils, at a salary of £600 a year, as well as Agent for the Estates of the Church and Schools Corporation, which brought in another £300. Although the latter position soon disappeared, by 1839, after ten years in the colony, William had enough money in the bank to provide a sense of security that he had never before experienced. All he had to do was remain careful and avoid any extravagance.

While William was poring over his ledgers and pursuing reluctant debtors to the Crown, Jessy played the role of a dutiful wife and mother. She made sure that dinner was on the table when her husband and Allan Williams returned from work, and her son from school. She paid the customary visits to the wives of various government officers, acquired a large circle of friends and took up various charitable causes. Quiet and unassuming—perhaps even a little timid—she was just as happy at home with her needlework as joining in Sydney's social whirl.

One spring afternoon in 1835, when William and Allan Williams were as usual at the office, her simple pleasures were violently interrupted by a bolt of lightning. She and young Allan were seated near a large window at opposite ends of their dining room table as a storm raged outside. Just as she removed her spectacles and laid down her knitting lest, she said, the needles should attract the lightning, a bolt shot down the chimney, followed immediately by a tremendous thunderclap. Plaster fell from the ceiling and the window shutters were wrenched from their hinges, so that it seemed for an instant that the house was falling apart around them. The lightning struck the chair on which Allan was sitting, singeing the haircloth and melting the metal frame, and leaving his legs numb below the knees, but causing him no permanent injury. His mother was thrown to the floor and struck on the forehead by a brass handle that had broken from one of the shutters. Her clothes caught fire, leaving her with severe burns to both legs and unable to walk for many months without the aid of a chair to push in front of her. She was never the same again, and always terrified whenever a storm threatened.

Allan Williams, having received a sound basic education in Scotland and practical experience of commerce in London, was well equipped for an accounting career. He worked hard under his father's tutelage, trusting that steady application would bring promotion and financial rewards. No doubt it helped that his father was his employer; but William was a hard taskmaster, and not one to give credit where it was not due, especially when he could be called to task for the work of those under him. By 1834 Allan Williams had risen to the rank of Chief Clerk on £200 a year. Three years later, his salary was £300, a handsome income for a young man of twenty-seven, and sufficient to allow him to contemplate marriage. The young lady who caught his eye was Miss Sophia Crowther, who was several years younger than he, and the daughter of a Captain in the 39th Regiment—though as the Captain's name does not appear where it should in the regimental history or army musters, some doubt must remain about her parentage. New South Wales was, after all, still a convict colony, where too close an inquiry into such matters might reveal things you did not want to hear. The couple were married quietly in 1837.

Never one to create a stir, Allan Williams kept his head down. In New South Wales, though, as so often in the colonies, there was so much sniping between the Governor and local officials that it was difficult to avoid being hit by a stray shot. When his father had been promoted from Collector of Internal Revenue to Clerk of the Councils, the Revenue department was finally absorbed within the office of the Colonial Treasurer. Allan Williams moved across to the Treasury, where he now had another Chief Clerk (a clerk of the First Class) above him. The Treasury was now effectively divided into two, with the Chief Clerk responsible, as in the past, for the expenditure branch, and Allan Williams in charge of the revenue department.

About the time Allan Williams married, the Chief Clerk in the Treasury died. According to recently promulgated regulations, designed to ensure that senior officials should not promote family members or favourites, Allan Williams, as the next most senior clerk, should have slipped easily into his shoes. However, the Colonial Treasurer, Campbell Drummond Riddell, a cherubic-looking Scot with aristocratic pretensions and a direct line to Downing Street, decided to bring in 'a stranger'. Governor Bourke, who regarded Riddell as an insubordinate dullard, insisted that the new rules be followed. Riddell stood firm, reasoning that while Allan Williams was up to heading the branch that collected revenue—the department 'in which he had been bred' (a sly dig, perhaps, at the cosy arrangement when his father was Collector)—he was incompetent to head the branch that spent it, where, given the confidential nature of its duties, the Treasurer needed someone he could absolutely trust.

This was nonsense, said Bourke. Mr Williams was 'a gentleman of considerable ability and official knowledge', as the Treasurer had himself conceded; and, as to the matter of trust, there were various mechanisms in place to ensure that none of the clerks would run away with the Treasury funds. What Riddell really wanted to do was keep the patronage of his office in his own hands, contrary to his government's regulations and the public good. An additional reason, which Riddell had let slip in an earlier conversation with the Governor, was that Mr Williams was 'a man of Colour'. It seemed that while the Treasurer could tolerate such a person in charge of the Revenue Branch, with which he had little to do, and was even prepared, if the Governor insisted, to see him promoted to a clerk of the first class, this was as far as he could go. The prospect of a man of colour being elevated to the status of Chief Clerk, and therefore his most intimate subordinate, was out of the question.

Bourke had no time for such arguments, declaring that he looked to 'integrity and ability rather than to complexion as the qualifications for office'. Riddell, though, had already scored a partial victory against the Governor through his influence at the Colonial Office. Rather than risk having Allan Williams' appointment overruled, Bourke decided to leave the matter to the Secretary of State. In any case, he was about to quit the colony, fed up with its political shenanigans and peeved that the Secretary of State had let his enemy get away with insubordination.

Allan Williams was probably left guessing why he was not allowed to succeed as Chief Clerk, though surely he would have suspected that the colour of his skin and questionable parentage had got in the way. Through intelligence and hard work (and with the help of a fatherly employer) he had won the respect of his superiors and had stepped up the clerical ladder. Yet just as he was within reach of the final rung, he found that somebody—the Colonial Treasurer—had taken it away.

The same thing happened two years later, though this time he would have been less likely to be aware of it. The semi-detached and newly settled district of Port Phillip, otherwise known as Australia Felix and later as the colony of Victoria, needed a Treasurer; and someone—perhaps his father—suggested to the new Governor, Sir George Gipps, that Allan Williams might be the man for the job. Gipps knew a lot about human foibles and follies, including those that related to the colour of a man's skin. The son of a country curate, he prided himself on having achieved high rank through ability alone. After training as a Royal Engineer, he had served with distinction during the later years of the Napoleonic Wars. In 1824 he had been posted to the West Indies as Commander of

Sir George Gipps, Governor of New South Wales from 1838 to 1846. Sketch by
William Nicholas, 1847. NATIONAL LIBRARY OF AUSTRALIA

Engineers in Demerara and Berbice, arriving at Georgetown, once known
as Stabroek, over a decade after William Macpherson had left there for
the last time, taking his two half-black girls with him but leaving the
infant Allan Williams to follow when he was old enough to be parted from
his mother. Gipps, during his four-year posting, often travelled by horse
and ferry from Georgetown in Demerara to New Amsterdam in Berbice,
which must have taken him through William's old haunts of Golden
Fleece, Union, Paradise and Rising Sun. His reports to superiors included
a plan which might allow slaves employed by the government to win their
freedom, thereby helping to recover 'the lost Rights of their Race'. Like
William Macpherson, Gipps had taken a slave mistress, had a child by her
and, when he left the colony, had paid for her manumission, along with
that of the young male slave who had acted as his domestic servant.

Gipps, intelligent and humane, saw nothing in Allan Williams'
complexion and background that might prevent him from serving as

Treasurer in the Port Phillip District. So he promptly put the suggestion to his friend in Melbourne, Lieutenant-Governor La Trobe—but then immediately thought better of it. 'Mr. Williams', he wrote:

> is a very fit man in every respect but one—which is that he is a *Demarara Half-Caste*, his Father being Mr. Macpherson the Clerk of our Councils. I do not myself attach much importance to this, except under one point of view—

namely, that Port Phillip might soon become a separate colony with a separate council, in which case Allan Williams, as Treasurer, would become a member of it—'and how you, or your Austral Felicians wd. like to see a Man of Color at your Council Board I am hardly prepared to say'.

In any case, he concluded, Allan Williams was engaged in farming, and would be unlikely to accept the position for less than £400 a year. Two years earlier, when Riddell had refused to have him as Chief Clerk, Allan Williams had taken the hint and responded to the call of the bush, where everyone said there were vast amounts of money to be made, and where he could reasonably expect that 'a Man of Colour' had as good a chance of getting ahead as the next man.

A COLONIAL EDUCATION

Allan Macpherson had the good fortune to arrive in Sydney with his parents and half-brother just as young Mr Cape was opening an academy in King Street, across the road from St James' Church and the old racecourse, which was now grandiosely known as Hyde Park. William Timothy Cape had already acquired a reputation as a fine teacher, and his school, which soon evolved into the Sydney College, attracted the best and brightest in the colony. Many of them were the sons of ex-convicts who had made good in trade or pastoral pursuits; and while Allan's father may have worried that his son was mixing with the wrong sorts of boys, there was not much he could do about it. Mr Cape had no time for snobbery; and where, against his best efforts, distinctions did exist among his pupils, it was the native-born, regardless of any convict connections, who were likely to have the upper hand, while the likes of Allan Macpherson, as 'new chums', had to prove themselves among their peers.

Mr Cape, while much admired by his students, was a strict disciplinarian. The boys were expected to attend classes each day from nine to three, with

King Street looking east, ca. 1843. The view looks up the hill towards the convict barracks and St James's Church. Mr Cape's school is nearby. A convict road gang is behind the carriage, which is driving along George Street, towards Sydney Cove. Watercolour by Frederick Garling. MITCHELL LIBRARY, STATE LIBRARY OF NEW SOUTH WALES

half an hour for lunch, and to apply themselves diligently to their lessons. There were rules governing bad behaviour, and a boy could be expelled for lying, swearing, indecency, or persistently playing in the streets with low company. Yet however conscientiously a young lad might avoid the riff-raff outside the gates of the college and avert his eyes from improper conduct, there could be no avoiding the truth that Sydney was a rough and often violent town. After all, the racecourse, open to all and sundry, was their playground, and Hyde Park Barracks, which accommodated prisoners working for the government, was just across the road. Down George Street near the quay, the gaol was the venue for public hangings, which took place so often that 'the mob' was supposedly becoming bored with the spectacle. Brawls and beatings were commonplace, with Aboriginal people often the targets. One evening, shortly before the Macphersons had arrived in the colony, a gang of ruffians had been seen 'thumping the heads of a party of Aborigines' who were soliciting tobacco and rum in Market Street, just a stone's throw from where Mr Cape was about to start his new school.

William monitored his son's progress closely and kept him hard at work. The college offered a classical and commercial education: Latin and Greek; English grammar, elocution and composition; writing, arithmetic, bookkeeping, geography and drawing; and mathematics and natural philosophy. This was all good; but there was not enough emphasis, said William, on law, chemistry, botany and mineralogy, so he gave Allan lessons in these subjects at home.

Outside school, the most popular pastimes among Allan's friends were cricket, shooting and fishing. Cricket bored him. Shooting might have been fun were there something more interesting than native magpies to shoot at, the kangaroos having retreated beyond the town—and in any case his father refused to let him own a gun because he was too careless. Fishing, though, was great fun. He passed many hours with his friends perched on rocks above the water, listening to the gentle lapping against the shoreline and hauling in good catches of mullet and bream. He asked his father if he might take swimming lessons, but William said no—walking

Hyde Park, Museum, Darlinghurst Gaol, Sydney Grammar School, Burdekin's and Lyons' Terraces, 1842. When Allan Macpherson was attending Mr Cape's academy in the early 1830s, Hyde Park served as a playground. The boys here are playing cricket, which Allan considered boring. Watercolour by John Rae. MITCHELL LIBRARY, STATE LIBRARY OF NEW SOUTH WALES

was better exercise and safer than swimming. So he learned to swim by jumping from the rocks and scrambling ashore, becoming as comfortable in the water as he was on dry land.

His indulgent father, when the family's finances improved, bought him a skiff, which he and his friends sailed across the harbour and up the Parramatta River, exploring isolated beaches and hidden coves, and experiencing an unfamiliar sense of freedom from parental expectations and academic pursuits. Sometimes he and his closest friend and schoolmate, William Forster, sailed halfway up the river to Meadowbank, where they climbed the hill to Brush Farm, a grand mansion built by one of the colony's first rich free settlers, Gregory Blaxland, and now owned by Forster's father, a former army surgeon. As well as having birth dates just eight days apart, the two boys had much in common: an Indian connection, Forster having been born in Madras; a similar status as new chums, both having arrived in the colony with their parents in 1829; a quick intelligence; and a sometimes cutting wit, which they sharpened during classroom debates. Both acquired from Mr Cape a love of the classics and poetry and, with his encouragement, imagined for themselves an illustrious future.

Allan, inspired perhaps by accounts of his grandfather's successes in India (which, in his father's retelling, glossed over his failures), as well as romantic images conjured up by Forster and other students, set his heart on joining the East India Company as a writer. By 1835, though, he had given up on the idea, as 'Mama would have taken it hard', and he had learned in any case that writerships were not as lucrative as they once had been. His father suggested that he become an advocate in Scotland, but not until the family was ready to return home. In the meantime he would learn English law in the office of a Sydney solicitor, a prospect that did not appeal to him. Addressing his Aunt Harriot in Scotland (but writing chiefly for his father's benefit, as William edited his letters home), he calculated that it might be fifteen years before he qualified as an advocate, and that even then he would be unlikely to earn much money. This was very hard, he told his aunt: but 'my best way is to submit in silence'.

Nearly three years later his obedience was starting to waver. He had been sixteen months in the solicitor's office, dabbling in the law or walking from one part of town to another delivering legal papers—and 'such another sixteen months I would not spend for the wealth of the Indies or the pleasures of the happy valley'. His father, though, was determined that he should take articles; and (still for his father's benefit), 'as his experience and knowledge of the world are necessarily far greater than mine, I am resolved to turn my whole heart & attention to his choice whatever it may be'. At least 'I shall in the end have the satisfaction of knowing that I have sacrificed my own wishes for the sake of my duty'.

What Allan really wanted was to become a sheep farmer. Declarations of martyrdom were merely a tactic in what was becoming a battle of wills between father and son (with Allan's mother, disabled by the lightning strike, watching on helplessly). After all, who in the late 1830s did *not* want to become a sheep farmer or, to use the term that had lately acquired respectability, a 'squatter'? Wool was the colonial obsession, with exports quadrupling between 1830 and 1835. The naturalist Charles Darwin, who visited the colony in 1836, commented that the whole population, rich and poor, were bent on acquiring wealth, and that 'amongst the higher orders wool and sheep-grazing form the constant subject of conversation'. Just as his father had been lured by the prospect of making a fortune from cotton, Allan imagined himself as a grand proprietor and exporter of fleece. Many of his old school friends were talking about heading for the bush. Yet his father wanted to condemn him to a life of legal drudgery. It simply wasn't fair.

To make a start as a squatter Allan would need capital—not for the purchase of land which (ignoring the Aboriginal owners) appeared to be there for the taking, or at worst, for the payment of a £10 licence fee. But sheep were expensive, perhaps 25 shillings a head. He begged his father to advance him £1000, which would set him on his way. William was not convinced. Sheep and cattle required constant superintendence; and if thieves did not get down on his flocks, there was a fair chance they would succumb to catarrh or some other devastating disease. If he kept cattle he would have to associate with butchers, who were a low class of men. True, he might make a fortune if he stuck with squatting for fifteen or twenty years. But his own speculations had never been successful, and Allan would do well to learn from his father's unhappy experiences.

In 1838 father and son took the mail coach to Goulburn, an inland village of a dozen or so houses in rich pastoral country south-west of Sydney. Heavy rains had extended the expected two-day journey to nearly three. While William was conducting government business, Allan went walking and shooting with the two sons of the local squire, Captain Rossi, which made him even more enthusiastic for the pastoral life and the freedom that appeared to come with it. William, inspired perhaps by the lushness of the countryside, or worn down by his son's nagging, was starting to yield. Back in Sydney, he decided to give Allan a chance: he would allow him to spend a year learning about wool growing at Mr White's pastoral station, Edinglassie, on the Hunter River, 100 miles north of the capital, and easily accessible by a regular steamer service from Sydney; and if he remained steady for at least twelve months, he might then consider advancing him money for stock. If he didn't measure up, he wouldn't get a farthing.

The sad truth was that Allan, as he approached the age of twenty-one, was becoming quite a handful. Before setting out for the Hunter he behaved so badly that William had to deliver a stern lecture:

> your excessive devotion to pleasure, to the total neglect of duty to your God, to your Parents, to your Friends,—of attention to business, or matters requiring to be attended to … Your dilatoriness and off-putting even to the last day, or hour I may say of your stay … [Yet] I will still address you as my dear Allan anxiously hoping that at some time or other you will become really and deservedly dear to me—altho' at present the prospects of such being the case are not very promising.

On reaching Edinglassie, Allan endeavoured to make amends by proving himself a good correspondent. But here too he caused offence by writing in the wrong place the addresses of letters that had to be forwarded, or enclosing one sealed letter inside another, requiring William to pay additional postage. Worse still, in one letter he made sarcastic comments about the new Governor, Sir George Gipps. William said he would do well to curb his tongue, as such comments, if made in public, tended to find their way back to the Governor or those around him. As the son of a government officer, Allan should be defending the government rather than lampooning it.

> I have often told you that your disposition to find fault with others was a fault, and a very great fault, in your character, which you should use every means in your power to repress: be content with acting rightly yourself if you can, and let the faults of others when you perceive them be a warning to you,

but do not take upon yourself to express harsh opinions upon them, which will never gain you friends even among those who may gratify your vanity, by laughing at, or joining in, your *Jokes* and criticisms.

William feared that his advice would fall on deaf ears. But he would go on doing his duty as a father and trying to set his son straight.

Allan bridled at the reprimands, before returning to pleasanter thoughts of country life. After all, he had won the battle. With the misery of enslavement in a lawyer's office behind him, the argument between father and son (for now it seemed that there always had to be an argument of some sort) had become whether Allan should try his hand on the land in the north or south of the colony. William won this debate by negotiating to take over a squatting lease about 400 miles to the north, on the western slopes of the long range of mountains that separated the coastal districts from the interior. The station was situated on the Big River, also known as the Gwydir or Bundarra River, and was stocked with several hundred cattle, along with seven bullocks and a dray, but as yet with no sheep. Evidently William too had been swept up by 'wool mania', so confident of success that he was prepared to invest £3000 in the venture, 'the whole fruits of my ten years labour in this Colony'. He would immediately settle a half share of the station on Allan Williams, and the other half on young Allan once he had proven himself worthy of taking on the responsibility. William decided that the two brothers should manage the station on a rotating basis, so that neither was removed for too long from the benefits of religion and civilisation.

Allan Williams, though, was unimpressed by his father's largesse. Having escaped from the Colonial Treasury, he was now working a small farm near the village of Invermein in the Hunter Valley, scarcely half a day's ride from Edinglassie. As his wife had lately given birth to their first child and had another on the way, he had no intention of venturing so far from the relative safety and comfort of the Hunter. His brother would have to go alone.

So, early in 1840 Allan prepared for the long journey north, leaving William worrying whether he had made a mistake. He urged his son to take particular care: study the scriptures and remember the Sabbath; avoid smoking and drinking to excess; keep moving if he chanced to get wet; and avoid every unnecessary expense. Above all, he must try to remain on fair terms with the Aboriginal inhabitants, without too much familiarity: 'Let me again earnestly beg that you will not be rash in any rencontres with the Blacks, should any such unfortunately occur'.

Allan wondered if his father's lectures would ever cease.

HEROES

Young gentlemen about the age of Allan Macpherson and William Forster, recently out of school and with the world at their feet, tended to see themselves as heroes—or, if they were not heroic already, they would surely become so. In Sydney they imagined themselves as heroes to the young ladies they encountered at social occasions, such as the annual St Andrew's Day Ball (which Forster referred to disrespectfully as 'the Mac Ball'). It was here in 1836 that Allan made his debut among 'the fashionable of Sydney', several months before he had turned eighteen. This premature coming out would not have been allowed had the ball been held in Government House, where the proprieties had to be observed. He was unable to attend the 1839 ball, as he was up the country at Edinglassie. 'Oh! Unhappy wanderer', wrote Forster,

> what are you losing? The hearts you touched will be given away to others and the girls you left behind you will leave you in the lurch ... Shall I offer your love to any best and brightest in Sydney?

Not that Forster was much impressed with the occasion. It was, he told Allan,

> a perpendicular jam. We were squeezed out of all shape. I pitied several unhappy moist people who appeared in an incessant state of wash and wipe ... I particularly noticed a lady in yellow who flung herself about as if [she] intended to make presents of her legs and arms for the benefit of anatomy.

But there was more to life than being a hero of the dance floor. The real opportunities for heroic endeavour were in the bush, far beyond the boundaries of colonial civilisation. So Forster, like Allan, persuaded his father to give him the money to take a party north to another 'Big River', soon to be renamed the Clarence, in a region even harder to reach by land than

Allan's proposed destination, but easily accessible by sea; and he wanted Allan to accompany him. His language of persuasion was mock-heroic:

> I am bravely resolved to undergo what are sometimes designated 'almost incredible hardships'. Do meet me somewhere if possible 'by moonlight alone' if you like. If you should have no stock come with me as compagnon de guerre. Whatever I take with me though rude is at your service but I should recommend you to provide yourself with a horse and gun.

He rhapsodised on this new country—its proximity to water transport, its climate, its beauty, its fertility, so that he could look forward to being stationed one day with all his family on the banks of one of the finest rivers in the colony. 'But in the mean time old chap let us enjoy ourselves—who can tell what geological or mythological and all other -logical discoveries we may make together, besides shooting blacks which is reckoned a pleasant amusement in cool weather.'

If, like William Forster and Allan Macpherson, you were well schooled in the classics, the bush seemed fashioned for the mock-heroic. Even Brush Farm, the Forsters' Palladian mansion nestled incongruously in the bush above the Parramatta River, could be seen as a joke, the unkempt landscape laughing at its classical pretensions. But it was also a statement of sober respectability. That was the problem with the mock-heroic: it was sometimes hard to tell where the joke ended and serious conversation began.

Allan was keen to join his friend on the excursion and possibly exchange the inland property for land on the coast. His father, though, was not ready to trust him with managing a property himself, and the Clarence seemed so remote that neither he nor Allan Williams would have any chance of pulling him into line, should the need arise. Already, before setting out for the Big River, Allan had offended by ordering expensive household supplies. 'We had begun to have better hopes of you', said William, signing himself 'Your Unhappy Father.' There could now be no prospect of him moving to the coast unless he was under the control of a manager whom William could trust. For Allan, such a suggestion was intolerable: 'no consideration on earth not even actual destitution would ever induce me to accept of your offer'. If his father did not trust him, he would try to buy stock with the help of someone who did.

Brush Farm, home of the Forster family from 1831 to 1880. A later watercolour by G. T. F. Mann, painted in 1932. STATE LIBRARY OF NEW SOUTH WALES

These quarrels were heated, but they never lasted long. The compromise agreed to was that Allan should proceed as before to the Big River as if the altercation over the Clarence had never happened; and that he would establish a station and take charge of the stock, on his father's behalf, for a salary of £100 a year. So William Forster and Allan Macpherson prepared to go their separate ways to 'Big Rivers' on either side of the Dividing Range, each determined to make a fortune from the land and each expecting remarkable adventures.

Allan's first adventure was neither welcome nor pleasant. In May 1840, he set out alone from Maitland, the largest town on the Hunter River, to join the small party of men who were to accompany him to the Big River. No sooner was he on the road than he was bailed up by four armed bushrangers, the name applied in the colony to outlaws and highwaymen. It was nearly nightfall and the rain was pelting down. One of them 'put a musket close to my heart requesting me to hold up my hands'. Being completely unarmed, Allan immediately complied, allowing the thieves to help themselves to all his money and most of his goods and chattels, and leaving him with only the clothes he was

Liverpool Plains at Warrah in the 1850s. Having climbed the Dividing Range, Allan Macpherson drove his sheep north across the Liverpool Plains towards Tamworth. Watercolour by John Andrew Bonar in his *Views in New South Wales and Queensland.*
MITCHELL LIBRARY, STATE LIBRARY OF NEW SOUTH WALES

standing in. Oddly, they did not take his horses, so he could return to Maitland and report the incident and, drawing on his father, buy more clothing. 'I shall take care in future', he wrote, 'never to be so foolish as to travel without my pistols.'

Joining his men at Allan Williams' farm at Invermein, he made his way across the Dividing Range and on to the Liverpool Plains, a vast expanse of undulating country already given over to squatting runs. The party included at least two bullock teams, sufficient supplies for the journey and a year or more in the bush, and several hundred bedraggled sheep, which Allan Williams, according to his father, had purchased at an inflated price. Allan Williams had been rebuked for his troubles, and had responded with what his father called 'an ebullition of intemperate feeling'. Eventually they made up, but only after Allan Williams, who was about to reach his thirtieth year, had made it clear that he would no longer jump to orders.

So many aspiring squatters were heading inland around 1840 that there was a fair chance of encountering another party on the road. Not far across the Liverpool Plains they were spotted by two new chums, Pemberton Hodgson and Henry Russell, whom Allan had met in Sydney and who were now travelling to join Hodgson's brother on the Darling Downs, west of the coastal town later known as Brisbane. 'How are you, Macpherson[?]' asked Hodgson, remarking that he was carrying heavy loads. 'Yes, I'm not going to live like a savage', Allan replied. 'I have a good cellar, a piano, cigars, *eau de cologne*, scented soap.'

Henry Russell, recounting this story many years later, was exaggerating: there was no piano—yet. But he was right in suggesting that Allan intended to live well. Squatters were lairds of the bush, so they had to look and act the part. But there were many obstacles, the first of which was revealed in further conversation with Hodgson and Russell. 'I'm miserable', said Allan. 'I can't leave my tent for an hour but these ruffians of mine spring my plant and drink my brandy.' Now they were all ill, leaving him to do all the work about the camp himself. Then, roaring with laughter, he described the reason for their illness. In order to catch the thief, he had dosed a bottle of brandy with an emetic and then put it where the offender was sure to find it. The stratagem worked, but unhappily it revealed that *all* his men were thieves. What was he to do? 'I must have men.' In coming years, this was to be a frequent refrain.

The party paused at Tamworth, a village taking shape at the head of the Liverpool Plains. Within the last few months it had acquired a postmaster, a blacksmith and a police lock-up. Here there was a fork in the road. One path climbed through a pass on to the New England plateau, leading eventually to the Clarence River valley or the Darling Downs—this was the route that Forster, and Hodgson and Russell, would shortly follow. Another reached into a broad valley that skirted the tableland from south to north. This was Allan's route. There were still over 90 miles to go before they reached the Big River. Although a few explorers and squatters had traversed the country before him, it was still thinly settled, and inhabited, so it was said, by hostile tribes of blacks. Checking his pistols, Allan stepped into the unknown.

11

SQUATTING

*A*FTER SEVERAL MORE WEEKS ON THE TRACK, THE PARTY CLIMBED a low but rugged range of mountains. Allan rode on ahead to the edge of the plateau, where suddenly his squatting run (or strictly speaking his father's run—but who was here to quibble?) opened up before him. He looked out over a valley which stretched several miles north, apparently surrounded by heavily wooded mountains. The river flats were lush and green after recent rains, covered with kangaroo and spear grasses, and thinly treed, except for the graceful swamp oaks that lined the banks of several creeks. The most prominent of these creeks snaked north until it joined a broad river, which flowed into view from behind a distant hill. This was the Big River, and it marked the northern boundary of his run.

Descending steeply from the plateau, he followed the valley until he reached a few roughly built huts beside the creek half a mile or so short of the junction with the river, but close enough to hear its rushing waters. Here were the cattle and bullocks that his father had purchased. Downstream, just beyond the river junction, another hill, smaller but almost perfectly rounded, gave this part of the valley a distinctive character and presented an unambiguous marker for anyone arriving for the first time. This seemed an ideal place for Allan to set up his 'head station'.

Over the following months the new squatter explored his estate. The total area was between 70,000 and 80,000 acres, stretching some 22 miles from south to north, and up to 12 miles from east to west. Only about a third of it was suitable for grazing, the rest being what Allan described as 'masses of mountains' and 'rugged granite country', densely covered with eucalypts, native pines and heavy undergrowth, and interspersed with rocky outcrops and gullies. In heavy weather, the creeks swelled

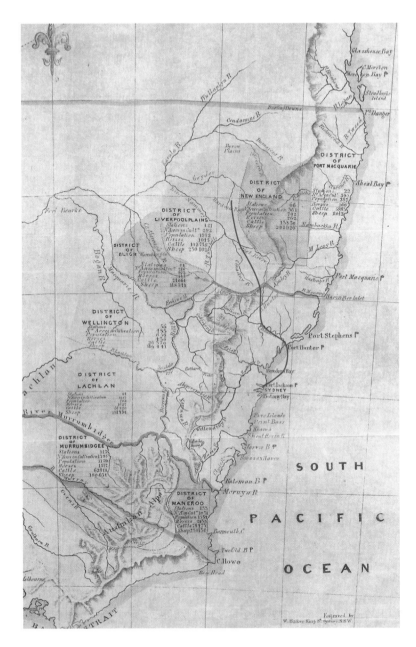

Map of a portion of Australia showing the area of the twenty located counties of New South Wales with the eight adjoining pastoral districts. The added red line shows Allan Macpherson's route to Keera in 1840. Engraving by William Baker, 1841.
NATIONAL LIBRARY OF AUSTRALIA

with water from the New England tableland, making the country almost impassable. When the sun shone and the days were warm, Allan, with sextant and compass to guide him, mapped the area comprehensively, measuring distances by the steady pace of his horse.

An early task of any new squatter, once he had identified the boundaries of his run and secured his sheep and cattle, was to give it a name. So far Allan had known it simply as the Big River station. But other estates that straddled the river up or downstream could lay equal claim to that title; and in any case, the name was full of ambiguities. Apart from the possibility of confusion with the coastal Big River (the Clarence), Allan's Big River was by now officially designated the Gwydir. For his own run, he wanted another name. The choices were English or Scottish, or Aboriginal. On the road north there had been roughly as many of one as the other—Invermein (lately renamed Scone), Murrurundi, Currabubula, Tamworth, and so on. He discovered that the local blacks often used the word 'Keera', which supposedly meant 'shrimps' (though whether they used it to describe the watercourse or the locality is anyone's guess). Allan evidently decided that it sounded distinctive and melodious, and started to write his address as 'Keera Creek'. By that act of naming, he confirmed, in his own mind at least, that this fine estate was his.

KEERA

Keera, at first sight, was everything an aspiring squatter might hope for. Its one obvious failing was that it was so hard to get to. Although the Gwydir was an impressive stream, its waters were not navigable, and in any case they flowed in the wrong direction, if not to an inland sea, then perhaps a thousand miles to the continent's southern coastline. Everything—flour, soap, sugar, tea, boots, tools, nails, paper, candles, gunpowder—had to come from Sydney by land; or rather, by colonial steamer to the Hunter River, and the remaining few hundred miles by the overland route that Allan had followed to get here; and everything the station produced—chiefly wool, and fattened sheep and cattle—had to be sent all the way by land to Sydney.

This was an expensive business—which did not matter if markets were strong and the produce brought good prices. In the early 1840s, though, the same bad luck that had so often visited the Macpherson family returned to plague Allan, just as he was starting out on his squatting career. The booming British market for wool plummeted and the colony's overreaching economy fell into a deep depression. Sheep that William had paid more than 17 shillings for in 1840 were worth as little as sixpence in 1843. To make matters worse, across much of the colony it stopped raining. At Keera, as one dry season followed another, the waters of the Gwydir slowed to a trickle, the creeks became stagnant and once green paddocks became brown and parched. Allan sent cattle to Sydney, but by the time they reached there they were in such poor condition that they fetched a feeble price. He sent bales of wool for export, only to have them rejected as 'short grown & heavy', badly washed, and contaminated by burrs and grass seeds.

Not that these misfortunes stopped him from pursuing plans to become a grand squatter. He built a long, low timber house near the creek, laid out a garden, planted fruit trees and vines, and acquired from Sydney the appurtenances essential to living in the style of a gentleman. He ordered a piano, which fell overboard as it was being transported across the Hunter River. Eventually it arrived at Keera, but with strings missing and completely out of tune. He put himself forward for appointment as a magistrate, or justice of the peace, and was soon entitled to put the initials 'JP' after his name. In the colonial context, where higher honours were beyond reach, this afforded proof of gentility. As one cynic later put it, being appointed a magistrate was rather like being vaccinated against smallpox, in that once the honour was conferred the recipient remained a gentleman forever—unless he should be declared bankrupt.

That, said William, was exactly where the family was headed. Poring over account books in Sydney, he was horrified to see the evidence of his son's extravagance, especially when set alongside the station's miserable returns. While he and Jessy were living frugally and depriving themselves of every luxury, their son was spending money on brandy and sherry, fine crockery and expensive cigars. 'It is very painful to me my dearest Allan', he wrote, 'to have to fill letter after letter with complaints of your expenses but I cannot help it.' Within a year the expedition had incurred debts approaching £7000. William was forced to borrow from his local Scottish friends, offering the Blairgowrie estate as security. But now, in the depths of the depression, his creditors, including the Surveyor-General, Sir Thomas Mitchell, were pressing, and there was no more money to be obtained from anywhere in the colony. His estate manager in Scotland came to the rescue with a loan of £400, though at a high rate of interest. It was small consolation to know that almost everyone

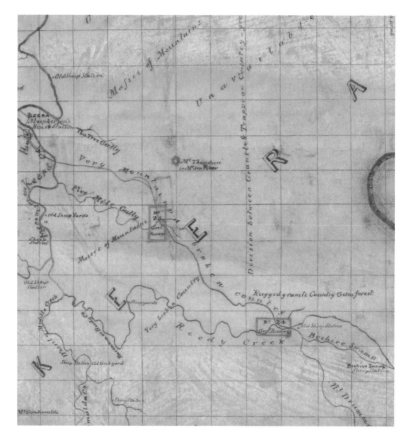

Keera in the late 1840s, as surveyed and drawn by Allan Macpherson. 'I can't draw,', he told his Aunt Harriot, 'but I understand some of the principles of surveying and I can plot.' The head station is situated near the junction of the Gwydir River and Keera Creek, at the top left of the map. The two rectangular areas in red are Government Reserves, presumably set aside for use by the Aboriginal people in accordance with directions from the Secretary of State, Earl Grey, in 1848. MACPHERSON COLLECTION

in the colony was suffering, especially those who had invested in sheep and cattle. Late in 1841 Sheriff Macquoid was declared bankrupt and shot himself the morning before his estate was due to be put up for sale. William assured Allan that he would never do such a thing; but he feared he would be the next government officer to be declared insolvent unless Allan mended his ways.

Rumours reached Sydney that Allan was a bad manager. James Bowman, a surgeon who had married into colonial money and acquired a grand estate in the Hunter Valley, hinted to William that his son left too much business to his employees, and that 'if things were well managed the Station ought to yield a handsome Return even in bad times'. This was too much for Allan to bear. It was one thing to have to put up with his father's constant carping—but if Dr Bowman, a jumped up squatter with aristocratic pretensions, dared to repeat to his face what he had said to his father, 'I shall find that a Horsewhip will at once level all differences real and supposed between our respective ranks in society'.

Allan kept his horsewhip handy. Yet such criticisms, whatever their source, made him more determined than ever to succeed. The depression eased, though slowly, and the rains came, giving Allan, and others like him who had survived on borrowed money, a glimmer of hope. An inventive squatter provided a new reason for optimism by discovering that he could get a much higher return from his sheep by boiling them down for tallow, which could be exported to Britain and used for making candles. Allan ordered boilers and buckets (his father refused his request for a pump) and cashed in on this new market. He was less successful when he tried to sell gelatine to India and China, and the venture ended up costing more than it yielded in returns.

William, at the end of his tether, urged Allan in 1845 to give up the station. Here we are, he declared, living in the most inexpensive manner 'while you are unprofitably throwing away money for the sake of appearance'. It is 'really extremely imprudent, as respects yourself, and unjust and unkind, as respects your Father and Mother, to be spending money *at their expense*, to gratify your own feelings, on an object that makes so poor a return'.

All Allan wanted, and begged to be allowed to do, was to get on with managing the station without interference. After all, what could his father know about the challenges facing a squatter and the hardships of life in the bush?

SOLITUDE

Allan's trips from Keera to Sydney were few, perhaps once every twelve to eighteen months. On such journeys he generally brought down sheep and cattle for sale, conducted business in town and visited old friends, before returning by steamer to the Hunter and then onwards to Tamworth and home. The rest of the time he communicated by mail, writing conscientiously to his parents every ten days to a fortnight and telling them about conditions on the run and anything of interest that happened in the district. He also kept a daily diary, which he sent down every six to eight weeks. His parents responded with equal regularity, William—the main correspondent—sending details about stock sales and events around the town, and invariably reminding his son about the need to maintain the strictest economies. Sometimes when Allan or one of his employees visited the post office at Tamworth several letters were waiting for him. Although the cost of postage was high, this was one expense that William did not mind paying for.

Allan wrote his letters late at night by candlelight. (This was bad for the eyes, advised William: he should get up every morning between four and five and go to bed no later than ten.) William wrote many of *his* letters at the table of the Legislative Council, dressed in his black robes of office, while a member was delivering a long (and presumably tedious) speech. Father and son therefore acquired quite different views of colonial life, one shaped within the council chamber and the government offices, the other determined by the harsh realities of life in the bush.

One of the harshest realities was the solitude. Not that Allan was entirely alone—he employed several shepherds and labourers, and each year before Christmas the station was transformed by the arrival of a team of itinerant shearers. Like most squatters, though, he kept his distance from the men, who could easily take advantage of excessive familiarity. After two years at Keera, another squatter and fellow magistrate took up a run just 25 miles away; but Allan got into an argument with him about a horse and caused such offence ('no wonder', said Allan Williams) that relations remained frosty for some time.

Allan had long been used to getting his own way, and when he did not the experience tended to sharpen his temper. So did life in the bush. As the poet Henry Lawson put it a few decades later, the 'grand Australian bush' was 'the nurse and tutor of eccentric minds'. Some squatters succumbed to depression, others went mad. Allan did neither; but confronted by the loneliness, the unremitting demands of looking after his stock, a miserable return for his labours, too much or too little rain, and a barrage of complaints from his father, he often let his temper get the better of him. A few years later he was allegedly known as 'Cranky Macpherson', which he might reasonably have taken exception to had not his father and his closest friend, William Forster, said much the same thing.

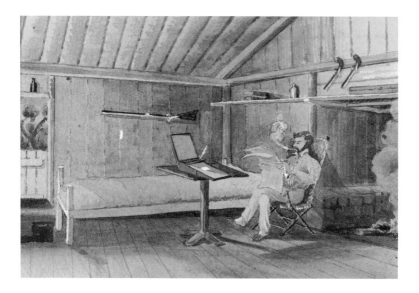

Solitude. This is the homestead of another squatter, located on the Dividing Range within a hundred miles of Brisbane. Like Keera it has timber floors, ceiling and walls. A rifle and pistols are within easy reach. Charles Archer, *The squatter taking his ease: a room in Waroogundie Homestead*, about 1845–47. JOHN OXLEY LIBRARY, STATE LIBRARY OF QUEENSLAND

At least Forster understood him. Although they were separated by the Great Dividing Range, the two young men remained intimates. They corresponded often, Allan's letters travelling overland to Maitland or Sydney, then north to the Clarence by sea, and Forster's by the same route in the opposite direction. 'I know of no one', wrote Forster, 'who understands me as you do or to whom I can talk so entirely without reserve.' Unlike Allan, Forster never claimed to enjoy the squatting life, though ultimately he made more of a success of it. He carved a station out of the dense forests beside a tributary of the Clarence, built a fine house and garden, and called it, with sardonic wit, Purgatory, 'in the middle of all the romance of uncomfortable solitude'.

They shared an interest in politics and literature. They both read widely—the newspapers, with the news from Sydney several weeks old, and from London several months old, and extracts from the latest Dickens novel; the works of Carlyle, 'a truly original genius', said Forster, 'though quaint and fantastical sometimes absurd'; and de Tocqueville's *Democracy in America*, Forster forewarning Allan that it would cause some of his dreams to grow dim. They reflected on the decline of civilisations, the constraints on individual action and the evils of democracy, and commiserated with one another about life in the bush.

'I own the greatest danger I fear from a bush life', wrote Forster, 'is the direction it is apt to give to our passions.'

> Passions all young men must have. In the bush avarice is the only one susceptible of gratification. And this one passion, the most debasing to the human soul and most detestable in youth, may in time be strengthened by the borrowed forces of all those other desires which we are compelled to smother.

Frustration, in other words, fed greed. And the frustrations were many: the government, the weather, the blacks, the absence of women ... 'I'm like Miss Squeers—I hate everything and everybody'. He hated 'the horrid b[east]s that have the form of women on this river'. But he hated himself even more for wanting them. Not that there were many European women for him to take a dislike to—in the mid-1840s probably fewer than a hundred, married and unmarried, along and near the Clarence, including the tiny settlement of Grafton. One of the few was Polly Oakes, the daughter of the Commissioner for Crown Lands, whom he described as brusque and awkward in manner, 'large, languid, and lubberly—a flabby looking damsel and puffy everywhere but in the right place'. And yet 'she was female flesh and consequently became a kind of heroine'. He was often getting himself into what he called 'love-scrapes', with unhappy outcomes. Allan warned him against marriage, opining that it had an injurious effect on the energies of young men. But what was his friend to do? 'I have just recovered from a second edition of the clap which most fortunately in my constitution is very slight and goes away without medicine—but I find it excessively inconvenient.'

Allan was more circumspect about his love life—or more probably, the lack of it. (I don't know, said Forster cryptically, 'where your recumbent pieces come from ... unless they walk in beauty like the night'.) If European women were few around the Clarence, where homesteads were within relatively easy reach of one another, at Keera they were almost non-existent, except perhaps for the wife of a shepherd or labourer. Rumour had it that Allan was corresponding with a young lady in Sydney, Miss Fanny Wentworth, the daughter of William Charles Wentworth, a lawyer, absentee grazier and political firebrand who for many years had promoted the cause of the colony's native-born. Such a relationship was sure to raise eyebrows, as Wentworth had been born on the wrong side of the sheets to a convict mother and a father who might also have become a convict had he not had friends in high places. Allan's father, when he heard the rumours, wrote stiffly to his son that any connection with 'that family' would be very distressing, not only to his parents but to his nearest and dearest relatives in Britain, meaning Aunt Harriot and Uncle Allan, and anyone who still treasured the family name. Echoing his own father's advice to him three decades earlier, he urged Allan to:

> select a wife from a family every branch of which you have no cause to be ashamed of—If she has money so much the better, but above all, let not only her own individual character, but also that of her family be untainted.

Be patient, said William, and within a few years we should be able to afford to send you to find a wife in Britain, where there could be little chance of being disappointed.

Allan deferred to his father's advice, and Fanny Wentworth disappeared into the arms of another. But he stubbornly resisted William's other advice that he give up the station and pursue some other career that brought in a steady income. It had been his decision to become a squatter and he would see it through to the end. Just as William had hung on in Berbice when all the signs pointed to disaster, Allan clung to the hope that things would get better. There were many young men like him. Across the Great Dividing Range his friend Forster felt the bush a prison: 'I see no end of this damned squatting ... I may live to be as old as Methuselah without being blessed with a chance of what you term strengthening my position in life'. In the meantime, after they returned alone to their homesteads after a hard day's work, they had plenty of time to reflect on their misfortunes and all the obstacles that seemed to frustrate their legitimate ambitions.

REBELLION

Someone, or something, must be to blame. The weather was an obvious target: the cruel extremes of drought and flood that led many a squatter into black despair. In autumn 1848 it rained at Keera for weeks on end, so heavily that the Gwydir broke its banks and the paddocks disappeared beneath fast-flowing waters. Allan watched helplessly as his cattle became bogged and hundreds of the last season's lambs were drowned and washed away. Rumours reached Forster on his Purgatory estate that his friend had become so frantic that he fired his pistols into the sky, crying out that he would 'shoot the God who sent such rain'.

Then there were the blacks. Events at Keera followed a familiar pattern of European occupation of Aboriginal lands: the squatters arrived with their flocks, forcing the kangaroos further inland or into the bush; the Aborigines, deprived of their staple meat supply, speared sheep and cattle; the squatters responded with force. How much force, and how it was applied, varied from one occasion to the next, and depended on the character, mood and motivation of the individual squatter, as well as how he rated the risks of getting caught. A squatter might intend to use just enough force to protect his flocks, and plan his attack accordingly. He was equally likely, though, to be driven by frustration and a desire for retribution. Once in pursuit, the original reasons hardly seemed to matter as Aborigines were 'dispersed', which often meant shot. Such attacks were called 'punitive expeditions', and they were commonplace across the moving frontier of pastoral expansion.

Allan Macpherson gathered his men and led such an expedition in autumn 1843, three years after he had arrived at Keera. The surviving records do not tell us whether his actions were a first resort or a last, whether he employed force or merely threatened it, whether there was any loss of life, or whether firing his pistols did anything to ease his frustrations. We do know, though, that his father, when Allan told him of his plans, was consumed with anxiety. We know, too, that this first expedition was not his last.

Then there were the workers. They required more subtle management. In the early years, employers prospered with the help of cheap convict labour. But now transportation and the system of convict assignment were at an end, and immigration could not keep up with the demand. So servants had the upper hand, and employers, if they wanted to succeed, had to look to the workers' needs and welfare. Allan paid his workers well: £16 to £20 a year for shepherds and £18 to £26 for labourers and bullock drivers, with generous rations of beef, flour, tea and sugar. He congratulated himself that his servants were generally of a better character than those of some of his neighbours, which he attributed to laying down clear rules and enforcing them fairly. He preferred to employ ex-convicts rather than new arrivals, who tended, he said, to be lazy and less trustworthy. Whatever their backgrounds, though, station workers could be insolent and demanding, and could threaten to walk out if they did not get their way. Such, Allan lamented to his Aunt Harriot back in Scotland, was the lot of 'the unhappy employers of labour in New South Wales', where workers were fond of saying to one another that masters *dare not call their souls their own*.

This was all too true, in more ways than one. Apart from fearing that their workers might force them off their land simply by withdrawing their labour, they were vulnerable to covetous neighbours. While their squatting licence (if they bothered to pay for it) gave them a right to graze sheep and cattle, it did not guarantee the boundaries of their runs. On this score, Allan Macpherson was in no position to complain. No sooner had he arrived at Keera than he occupied an adjacent run while the squatter who had previously claimed it was absent. Allan Williams, still at Invermein, thought this unneighbourly, but was not surprised, for 'I know *you* have impudence for any thing'.

But the squatters' greatest worry was that while they might think the land they occupied was theirs, they were in fact merely tenants, with little more security of tenure than lodgers in a boarding house. Technically the land belonged to the Crown; and if the Crown chose to change the rules of occupancy, they could be evicted at a moment's notice, without compensation for the buildings and fences and all the work they had put into the property to make it pay. Hence William's dismay that all the improvements his son was making at Keera were 'more suited to land belonging to yourself than to Government land'.

The government! There, according to almost every squatter who had anything to say on the subject, was the root of the problem. While they saw themselves, with some justification, as essential to the colony's prosperity, the government was constantly getting in their way. Sir George Gipps, who governed the colony through the toughest years of drought and depression, was seen as the chief villain. Cartoons showed him boiling down squatters for tallow and squashing them in a wool press, unconcerned about his victims' suffering: 'This is as bad as the drought', cried one squatter jammed in a wool press; 'the Blacks are a joke to it'.

Gipps—astute, honest and irascible—believed that the Crown lands should be held in trust 'for the benefit of the people of the whole British Empire'. Under the present system, as set out by Governor Bourke several

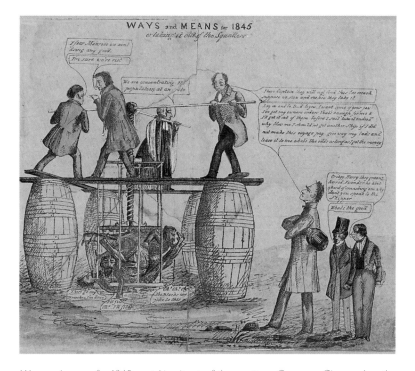

Ways and means for 1845, or taking it out of the squatters. Governor Gipps orders the members of his executive council who are working the wool press to show no mercy to the squatters. Lithograph by Edward Winstanley and others, 1845. MITCHELL LIBRARY, STATE LIBRARY OF NEW SOUTH WALES

years earlier, 'monster squatters' (as Gipps called them) could occupy vast tracts for a £10 licence fee, plus a penny a head for their sheep and cattle. William Charles Wentworth, for example, could control perhaps half a million acres in four squatting districts with four licence fees, costing just £40. Gipps feared that the 800 or so squatters who currently happened to hold land beyond the settled districts might end up dominating the colony's pastoral interior forever. Of course nothing could be done to prevent them spreading wherever there was a blade of grass for their sheep and cattle to graze on, but they should at least be made to pay for the privilege. The additional revenue could then be used to fund immigration, and so provide the labour that the squatters were crying out for. What could be more reasonable, and more in keeping with the needs of the whole colony? So in 1844 he introduced regulations which required squatters to pay a £10 licence fee for every run of 20 square miles or, where the land was of inferior quality, an area sufficient to graze 4000 sheep or 500 cattle.

The squatters were outraged. Most of them would now have to pay far more for their land than they considered it was worth. Wentworth calculated that he would be forced to take out twenty licences to cover all his holdings, costing him £200 rather than £40. A week after the regulations appeared, a large and rowdy crowd met at a hotel in Sydney's George Street to protest against the changes. Speaker after speaker denounced Gipps and his imperial masters, insisting that the regulations would ruin them and declaring that they were being treated no better than Russian serfs. Forming themselves into a Pastoral Association, they signed petitions to the Queen and the House of Commons. Wentworth told them they were the 'rightful inheritors' of the lands they occupied. The audience cheered. He referred ominously to a 'unanimous feeling of revolt against injustice and tyranny'. In the Legislative Council, a turbulent majority rushed to set up a committee to inquire into grievances relating to Crown lands. Gipps prepared further regulations to soften the blow, but it was too late. The issue had become a test between the authority of government and the power of the squatters.

Far away on their stations, solitary squatters devoured the latest newspapers from Sydney and waited anxiously to see what would happen next. Although the main battle was being waged in town, led by non-resident grandees such as Wentworth, many smaller proprietors who lived on their own squatting runs were just as concerned about the outcome and just as eager to play a part in the campaign. Allan Macpherson and William Forster wrote to one another about the tyranny of the local government and its agents, the Commissioners for Crown Lands. But what was to be done? The squatters on the Clarence, said Forster, were 'a degenerate race', and nothing could be expected of them. 'We want some New England or Liverpool Plains hero ... to lead us to victory or death!' Would Allan Macpherson, the man of action, come to the rescue?

Short of heroic deeds, the pen offered isolated squatters their only means of resistance. When the committee set up by the legislature went trawling for grievances, Allan responded with a long and thoughtful submission denouncing the new regulations and proposing that they be replaced entirely by a system more favourable to the squatters. They were the ones, he wrote, who had made the land available. They had spent their capital on improvements. They had braved the risks to life and property from hostile tribes of Aborigines. Now they deserved security of tenure; and security would encourage them to make permanent improvements, which would undoubtedly benefit the colony at large:

> it would change large portions of the country districts, from rich but uncultivated wastes, into fertile fields and blooming gardens; it would convert rude bark huts into substantial houses; it would raise up churches and schools in the desert; and it would make a wandering, unsettled, and discontented race, an industrious, and happy people.

The key to this Arcadian dream was a pre-emptive right of purchase. Granting this boon 'would serve to make the government which is now loathed for its exactions, loved for its liberality'; and it would nip in the bud 'feelings of disaffection' that had disrupted peace and harmony in other parts of the empire.

Back in Sydney, William Macpherson read his son's submission and was impressed by the obvious care he had taken in preparing it. (It was he, in his capacity of clerk of the Legislative Council, who had written on behalf of the committee inviting Allan and other squatters living far from Sydney to express their opinions.) But he did not like this talk about 'loathing' and 'disaffection'. While he did not agree with all the Governor was trying to do, he respected his office and regarded him as a patron and friend. (Surely there were idle moments, when the ladies were out of earshot, when they shared memories of old times and places in Demerara and Berbice?)

William chanced to meet young Forster's father, Dr Thomas Forster, in a Sydney street, and the two chatted for several minutes, commiserating with one another about their recalcitrant sons. Dr Forster told William that his own son had lately spoken 'very intemperately' against the Governor, and suggested that his behaviour had not much been improved by association with young Allan. It was quite wrong, said the doctor, for young men to talk in so unbecoming a manner of a person so much their senior in age and superior in rank and station, especially on an issue such as squatting, on which they were so unfitted, through their personal interests, to offer an unbiased opinion. William entirely agreed. If the government complied with the squatters' exorbitant demands, there would be no prospect of encouraging further immigration. But what could you do? It seemed to be 'a distinguishing characteristic of the present generation to talk as much treason ... as they could venture on without being hanged'.

Dr Forster was no doubt right in suspecting that his son's connection with Allan Macpherson had done nothing to improve his manners. Young Forster, though, was quite capable of generating his own invective. His metier was satire. At school he had been an outstanding poet, and his solitary life at Purgatory gave him plenty of time to sharpen his political acumen and cultivate his writing skills. He found an ideal outlet in the *Atlas*, a 'weekly journal of politics, commerce and literature', which launched in Sydney late in 1844 under the editorship of Robert Lowe, a passing luminary in colonial politics. Lowe was a lawyer, an Oxford man and an albino, who had come to Sydney in the hope of improving his failing eyesight. His brilliant and often savage wit led readers of the *Atlas*, then and since, to suppose that he was the author of most of the journal's political commentary and satirical verse. Forster, though, probably wrote more than he was given credit for, including some of the most caustic and perceptive lines. Gipps was said to have anticipated his contributions with trepidation.

In 'The Devil and the Governor. A dramatic sketch', Forster imagined the Devil visiting Gipps late at night and warning him that the squatters, if pressed too hard, might rebel. 'Rebel! ha, ha!', the Governor responds, 'you're surely in joke ...'

> A handful of troops would put them down,
> and the higher classes would join the Crown.

But the Devil persists:

> It might be so; but just mark my friend—
> Who come to be losers in the end?
> No doubt there'd be fun well worth enjoying—
> Burning and plundering, and destroying ...

It was an adolescent rebellion, and the squatters knew it. However much they might rail against 'imperial despotism' and the oppressive policies of Governor Gipps, there was never any chance of 'burning and plundering'. Rather than being in open rebellion, they were, as the *Atlas* put it, in 'a civil, constitutional, gentlemanly state of disgust'. After all, Britain—

the mother country—provided nearly all their markets, their capital and their future population. Like Allan Macpherson and William Forster, and other young squatters determined to get their way, the pastoralists and their supporters pushed parental tolerance to the limits; but they also knew that without parental support they would have no hope of realising their ambitions.

There was, in any case, a safety valve. Rebellion erupts when conditions become intolerable and where there is no hope of escape. In New South Wales though, in the late 1840s, squatters could still imagine new lands to conquer, distant fields that were, if not necessarily greener, invariably vaster; places where, whatever misadventures might have taken place in the past, fortunes were still to be made. They had learned to think big—convinced that they could only succeed with a substantial minimum number of sheep and cattle, and that the more sheep and cattle they owned beyond that minimum, the greater their potential for success. Allan Macpherson's Keera might seem a large estate, but by comparison with the vast acreages of Wentworth, Dr Bowman and the like, it was small; and in any case, much of it was rugged, and either useless for grazing or requiring too many shepherds to look after the flocks. More land would allow his sheep and cattle to run free, multiply, and magnify his profits.

New hope came from an unexpected direction. Late in 1846, just as Allan was reflecting despondently that his father might be right and Keera might never pay its way, the Surveyor-General, Sir Thomas Mitchell, family friend and sometime creditor, returned from a year-long journey of exploration of the inland region far north of the Gwydir, including an area that he named the Fitzroy Downs. Mitchell thought he had found a river that flowed eventually to the continent's northern shore. He was mistaken; but he did find what he referred to as 'the finest and most extensive pastoral regions' he had ever seen, the 'El Dorado of Australia', with vast grasslands and majestic rivers. Everything was in abundance—so much so that in his journal of the expedition, published in 1848, he repeated the word more than fifty times, not including the hill to which he gave the name Mount Abundance. From this elevation, he wrote, he beheld the finest country he had ever seen in a primeval state: 'A champaign region, spotted with wood, stretching as far as human vision, or even the telescope, could reach'.

Allan Macpherson heard these exuberant reports, even perhaps before the news reached Sydney. Faced with the prospect of abandoning squatting entirely, he needed little encouragement. Forgetting that most explorers had a vested interest in exaggerating the significance of their discoveries, and that Sir Thomas in particular had a tendency to hyperbole; forgetting too that the wet and verdant countryside that he described might not always be so, Allan started making plans to head for Mount Abundance.

Forster warned him to be careful, reminding him of his 'propensity to annihilate practical difficulties by too great an ingenuity in laying plans'. But Allan was utterly confident that the potential for success far outweighed unspecified obstacles. In any case, there was no time to worry about matters of detail. Word of Mitchell's discoveries would soon be out; and based on past experience, the plains would soon be crowded with squatters droving their flocks into the new country in a rush to claim the best lands for themselves. He had the advantages of knowledge and relative proximity, and he was not about to sacrifice them.

A sad event delayed his progress. In June 1847, just as his preparations for the journey were almost completed, his mother Jessy died in Sydney at the age of fifty-eight. Ever since the lightning strike a dozen years earlier, she had endured chronic rheumatism and other ailments. Her final weeks were especially painful. William, devastated, had her entombed in a lead coffin in anticipation of eventually laying her to rest in the family graveyard at Blairgowrie; and in an obituary for the *Sydney Morning Herald*, he praised her as 'the untiring friend of the poor and distressed', a 'perfect image of meekness, simplicity, gentleness, and contentment'. Allan, who seems to have inherited none of these attributes, hurried to the capital to attend the funeral and grieve with his father. But he did not stay long. By early July he was back at Keera and ready to leave for the north. There was no time now for talk of rebellion. The call of Mitchell's boundless acres was urgent and irresistible.

233

12

WAR WITH THE BLACKS

*J*T WAS A VAST EXPEDITION, COMPRISING OVER 10,000 SHEEP, several hundred cattle, four drays each drawn by ten bullocks, and another dray drawn by a team of horses. There were twenty-seven men in all, including Allan and his superintendent. As skilled sheep dogs were yet to become essential members of any droving team, the sheep spilled out into the valleys and across the plains, sometimes disappearing into the scrub, where they had to be pursued on foot or horseback by one or more of the men. The bullocks and horses strayed, and had to be rounded up each morning before the party could move on.

Little wonder that they made slow progress, averaging for week after week just two and a half miles a day. They followed as closely as they could Sir Thomas Mitchell's recent maps, watching eagerly for traces of his dray wheels in the sandy soil. After a few weeks, Allan left the party and veered east towards the relatively well-settled Darling Downs, where he hoped to buy additional supplies. In his absence half the bullocks went missing, meaning that two of the drays had to be abandoned. By the time he returned, the lambing season was fast approaching, so he decided to split the party in two. Leaving 5000 ewes with the superintendent, he moved on with the rest of the party, and then, accompanied by just one of the men, struck out to survey the route ahead. In mid-October 1847 he reached Mount Abundance and the Fitzroy Downs.

'A glorious prospect!' he recorded in his diary. 'Certainly the most magnificent country burst upon view that it has ever been my lot to see in the colony of New South Wales.' Thirty years later, in a pamphlet telling the story of the expedition, he found new superlatives for English and Scottish readers: 'the most beautiful land that ever sheep's eyes travelled over', resembling 'a few scores or hundreds of gentlemen's parks rolled

'A glorious prospect!' Allan Macpherson gazed towards Mount Abundance and saw 'a few scores or hundreds of gentlemen's parks rolled into one'. There had recently been plenty of rain. H.G. Lloyd, *Mt. Abundance*, watercolour, from his *Views in Queensland*, c 1864–1894. MITCHELL LIBRARY, STATE LIBRARY OF NEW SOUTH WALES

into one'. By now Sir Thomas Mitchell's 'champaign region' (meaning an expanse of open country) had become a 'champagne region'. Perhaps the error was in the printing; but it was also in Allan's imagination. As he gazed across the grassy plains towards the distant hummock that now gloried in the name of Mount Abundance, he dreamed of himself as the squatter-laird relaxing on the veranda of his stately homestead, surveying his magnificent acres and drinking a toast to his own success. Even better, he saw in Mount Abundance the means to achieving his ultimate ambition: to return to Scotland, reclaim Blairgowrie on his father's behalf, and eventually succeed to his estates, and the titles and dignity that accompanied them.

SAVAGES

Sir Thomas Mitchell, as well as inspiring many squatters like Allan Macpherson to drive their flocks further and further into the colony's interior, helped fashion their opinions of the Aboriginal people who lived there. In the 1830s (as Major Mitchell, Surveyor-General of New South

Wales), he had led three exploring expeditions into remote parts of the colony, and then described his journeys in a two-volume work published in London in 1838. Here he lamented that the Aboriginal tribes would inevitably succumb to 'invasion' by the 'civilised intruder'. They must surely realise, he wrote, that the advance of so powerful a race as the European must lead to the extirpation of their own.

Mitchell drew a distinction between 'half civilised' Aborigines and those who were still in 'a savage state'—naturally ferocious and not to be trusted. Anyone who ventured into the remote regions, he warned, must be constantly vigilant, and travel 'with arms forever at hand'. He also offered implicit advice on how to deal with the savages should the need arise, as it had for him on the Murray River in May 1836. Threatened by 'a vast body' of hostile blacks, all armed with bunches of spears, he had prepared an ambush. When a barking dog thwarted his plans, one of his men fired at the blacks, who 'fled as usual, to their citadel, the river, pursued and fired upon by the party from the scrub'. Mitchell reported that seven Aborigines died and four were wounded. The killing was regrettable, but it 'afforded unspeakable relief' to his men, and assured 'the permanent deliverance of the party from imminent danger'. 'I gave to the little hill which witnessed this overthrow of our enemies and was to us the harbinger of peace and tranquillity the name of Mount Dispersion.' An accompanying illustration provided graphic evidence of the blacks in retreat.

Returning from his fourth expedition at the end of 1846, Mitchell gave the Aborigines around Fitzroy Downs an especially fearsome reputation, which he later reported in another book. By the time Allan Macpherson's party was on the track to Mount Abundance, his warnings had already been widely circulated. The men, huddled around their campfires, recounted stories of explorers and squatters brutally murdered by savages. With each retelling, they became more fearful of the unknown, and more alert to unfamiliar sounds and shadows in the night.

Allan was not about to let exaggerated fears about a few blacks get in the way of fulfilling his dreams. During the journey north they came across two or three small groups, who seemed to him 'harmless enough'. As the advance party approached Mount Abundance, they encountered another group 'who fairly frightened my men into convulsions'. Allan laughed off their fears, calling them 'cowards and faint-hearted creatures'; and to show them they had nothing to worry about, he said he would go on ahead and camp out two or three nights alone. During this solo expedition he met a party

'The Murray 27th. Of May 1836'. Mitchell wrote: 'I gave to the little hill which witnessed this overthrow of our enemies and was to us the harbinger of peace and tranquillity the name of Mount Dispersion.' Lithograph by J. Brandard & G. Bernard from drawing by T.L. Mitchell, in Mitchell's *Three expeditions into the interior of eastern Australia*, vol.II, London, T.&W. Boone, 1839.

of thirty-two Aboriginal men, all armed, with whom he exchanged green bushes as a sign of peace. They knew two words of English, 'white fellow' and 'wheelbarrow' (meaning dray), which he gathered they had learned from 'semi-civilised tribes' to the south. Somehow they had also learned that white men were to be feared, as they appeared terrified of Allan, his horse and his double-barrelled carbine. He told this story to his men, but it did nothing to reassure them. They remained, he said, in a state of almost constant mutiny, and ready to abandon him if the going got too rough.

Around the beginning of November 1847 the advance party reached Mount Abundance and quickly set about building huts, fences and sheep and cattle yards. No sooner had they arrived than Allan was retracing their path back to Keera to replace the provisions they had lost on the trip north. By now the countryside was in flood, so that much of the journey involved wading and swimming, including a dangerous crossing of the fast-flowing Gwydir, where he was helped by 'kindly blacks'. Returning to Mount Abundance, he congratulated himself that, despite all the problems they had encountered in getting there, all his expectations had so far been

Sir Thomas Mitchell, Surveyor-General of New South Wales, whose extravagant accounts of his discoveries encouraged many aspiring squatters to head further into the bush. Hand-coloured calotype by William Hetzer, 1850s? STATE LIBRARY OF NEW SOUTH WALES

realised. Stock numbers were increasing, and soon he would be able to send the station's first bales of wool to the Sydney markets. There had been no conflict with the blacks, and nor was there likely to be, the two parties, he said, being so terrified of one another that they would keep well apart. Thus reassured, and with his mind on fat profits, he retraced his route to Keera and then onwards to Sydney, remaining away from the new station for over six months.

He had been too sanguine by far. On the way back to Mount Abundance he met two of his old hands heading as fast as they could in the opposite direction. They had a terrible story to tell. Three weeks earlier the blacks had attacked a flock of about 2000 ewes in lamb and had murdered their shepherd. Then they had gone to an outstation about 3 miles from the head station, taken away with them 800 to 1000 sheep and killed the hutkeeper. His men had abandoned the property entirely and headed south without making any effort 'to deal with any of the blacks' or to recover the stolen sheep, taking the remaining sheep and stores with them, but leaving behind all the cattle and thirty or forty bales of wool.

Allan was furious, his rage directed as much at his own men, these 'faint-hearted pioneers', as at the blacks. His workers quaked in trepidation: smaller misfortunes had caused him to lash out wildly, sometimes to his own cost. Stories were told of how one morning he and his men, having left their camp to round up their horses, could not find their way back to their saddles and provisions through the long grass. After an extended search, Allan lost his patience. 'I will soon find them', he said, and set fire to the long dry grass. They found the camp soon enough—but all their possessions were burned to a cinder. On another occasion the cattle broke out of the yard, so he grabbed his rifle and took his revenge on the sliprails. Then there was the time when, after a sleepless night tormented by fleas, he threw his blanket over a fence and fired at it with a shotgun.

There is no record of how he reacted the moment he heard of the blacks' attack on his sheep and his men. Recovering from the immediate shock, he realised that his first task was to reach the station and assess the damage; but when he asked who among his men would accompany him there was a sullen silence—except for Black Charley, an Aboriginal man from the south who was supposed to speak 'a good many native dialects' as well as English, and whom Allan had recruited in the hope that he would help maintain good relations with the 'wild blacks'. Charley, much to Allan's satisfaction, succeeded in shaming the other men, pronouncing that 'neither master nor he wanted such cowardly wretches with us'. But his contempt could not persuade any of them to change their minds. So the two set out on their perilous journey, accompanied only by a 'semi-wild' local black known as Friday (who presumably had no choice).

In the early afternoon of the second day of their journey they encountered a group of blacks whom Allan took to be the advance division of a larger party bent on further destruction. He 'dealt with them', and blood was spilt. More conflicts followed, evidently with similar outcomes, before the party arrived two days later at Mount Abundance. Allan was relieved to find that the bales of wool had not been torched and that a few cattle were still grazing in the vicinity. It could have been worse.

Nearly a decade earlier, when he was embarking on his career as a squatter, his father had begged that 'you will not be rash in any rencontres with the Blacks'. And in 1843, when he wrote from Keera to say that he was about to take action against them, without saying why, William was as much anxious about what he might do to the blacks as what the blacks might do to him. The killing of Aborigines, wrote William, could be justified only if it were shown to be in self-defence. But how could this possibly be proved when you led an expedition against them? And you could hardly plead that your own lives were in danger if the Aborigines were forced by your pursuit to take up arms in their own defence—but 'my advice will now my dearest Allan come too late'.

Now, on hearing about the events at Mount Abundance, he again entreated him to be cautious:

> Circumstanced as you at present are, amidst numerous hostile tribes of these wretched beings, I do not at all doubt that it may be necessary occasionally to kill some of them to deter the others from taking advantage of the small number of your party, and coming treacherously upon you and killing you.

The blacks should first be warned that if they came too close to the station they would be given a severe flogging. If they failed to heed the warning, then he might be forced to take human life, but only when 'they actually make an attack upon you, or it is evident from the circumstances under which they are met with, that they design an attack'.

> It would be most dreadful if you should in any way subject yourself to criminal proceedings my dearest Allan; and moreover if you in any case take human life when not absolutely necessary for the safety of yourself, or those dependent on you, the feelings you will be subjected to in after life will not be of a pleasant kind.

William's concerns about criminal proceedings were well grounded; and no one knew better how such matters were regarded in government circles. In the late 1830s, soon after he had been appointed Clerk of the Councils, there had been agonised discussions about the best way of combating the upsurge of violence beyond the boundaries of settlement. In London, the Secretary of State was insisting that Aborigines be treated with humanity and justice. In Sydney, Sir George Gipps and some senior officials were determined to halt the atrocities on both sides. The issue came to a head in mid-1838, when news arrived of the murder of twenty-eight Aboriginal men, women and children by eleven white station hands on Myall Creek Station, a short day's ride from Keera (which Allan was yet to occupy). Gipps described the event as 'a most atrocious massacre'; and his Attorney-General, John Hubert Plunkett, pursued the offenders with such resolve that seven were eventually found guilty and hanged. This was the first time white men in the colony had been executed for murdering

Aborigines, and Gipps trusted that the lesson was clear: aggressors of either race or colour would be brought to 'equal and indiscriminate justice'.

But how could such warnings be enforced? According to the squatters, *they* were the ones who needed protection against the Aborigines. They, after all, were 'the pioneers of civilisation', 'engaged in the laudable and enterprising pursuit of a pastoral life in the interior', and if the government was unable to protect them against murder and outrages committed by 'savages', who could blame them for taking matters into their own hands? Gipps conceded that the squatters were entitled to protection and was ready to provide it; but it was obvious, he told them, that 'every wanderer in search of pasturage cannot be attended by a military force'. The best the government could do was issue stern warnings and assign the task of maintaining order to the Commissioners of Crown Lands and small bands of mounted police in each of the pastoral districts. Given the vast areas they had to cover, the Commissioners could do little more than pursue aggressors, black or white, after the violence had already occurred. And this could only happen if the outrages were reported or in some way became public knowledge. While the Myall Creek case showed that whites could swing for killing blacks, squatters could just as easily draw the lesson that they might continue to take matters into their own hands so long as they kept quiet about it. This is precisely what happened. Myall Creek was not only the first time whites in the colony were hanged for killing blacks following acts of frontier violence, but also the last.

In 1848, when Allan came to blows with the Aborigines at Mount Abundance, the events of Myall Creek seemed long in the past. But the squatters still had to watch their steps. When William Forster was confronted with hostile Aborigines—these 'wretched protégés of Plunkett', he called them—he was accused of 'shooting a black-fellow'. Some zealous neighbours told the local Commissioner, who conscientiously reported the incident to his superiors in Sydney—but, wrote Forster dismissively, 'without any important result'. The squatters might have been apprehensive about what could happen if they broke the law, but they were much more concerned about defending their property. They had asked for help, but the government had been unable or unwilling to provide it. Now they had no choice but to protect themselves in circumstances where, as Allan put it, the 'majesty of the law is entirely powerless'.

If the law were a feeble deterrent, what of religion? Allan, like most other young squatters, had been brought up in a good Christian family. His mother, Jessy, had been a model of piety; and while William might have deviated (on his father's advice) from the strict path of morality during his years in Berbice, he never questioned his parents' religious teachings or neglected the rituals of the Church. In Sydney they were among the most regular worshippers at divine service until Jessy's declining health prevented her from leaving home.

But there were other influences beyond the family; and however hard William and Jessy might try to infuse their son with 'the everlasting and supereminent importance' of religion, Allan could scarcely fail to witness the prevalence of vice and immorality on the streets of Sydney. Nor could he fail to notice that many esteemed gentlemen and ladies in colonial society were lax in matters of religious observance, nor to be influenced by the indifference to religion among many of his old school friends. William knew that his son was at risk, and warned him about venturing too far from civilised society. Once in the bush he might ignore the Almighty Being, forget the Sabbath, and yield entirely to worldly pursuits and pleasures, 'without once reflecting on what you have been so often taught, that Worldly gains are dearly bought, if obtained by the sacrifice or neglect of our duty to God'.

These fears proved to be well founded. Arriving at Keera, 90 miles from the nearest clergyman, Allan called his men together every Sunday morning and read to them from the scriptures—but this ritual was probably more intended to allay his parents' concerns and encourage a proper sense of duty and obedience among the men than to satisfy any spiritual longing. He promised William and Jessy that he would join them in taking the blessed sacrament when next he visited Sydney, but made excuses when the time came. His father was disappointed—though given Allan's behaviour on that occasion, he thought it just as well to wait until he should have his 'temper and passions more under control'. If parental expectations and religious obligations had so little effect on Allan in the town, what chance did they have of influencing him in the bush?

'SUNDRY CONFLICTS'

Having reclaimed Mount Abundance and having persuaded, with the help of the loyal Charley, most of his men to return there, Allan set out for the Darling Downs, hoping to map a path that could be used to transport goods to and from the port of Brisbane. He took with him Charley, the local black known as Friday, and a stockkeeper called Dublin

Jack. Before they had progressed far they came across a white man's grave, and soon they learned that other squatters had lately arrived in the district, only to be scared away by Aboriginal attacks on their men and their stock.

Nevertheless, the expedition so far had gone smoothly. On the return journey, though, they came across 'a considerable number of hostile blacks'. A conflict followed—Allan called it a 'skirmish'—'in which we had so far the best of it that they eventually retreated'. Then, encouraged by this victory and reassured that there were now just thirty of forty warriors remaining, Allan committed what he confessed to his diary was an act of 'reckless foolhardiness': rather than returning directly to the relative safety of Mount Abundance, he decided to rest a short while in the blacks' camp beside a creek. Setting loose the horses, the party prepared for an 'unusually sumptuous' feast of fish, bandicoots, possums and snakes, which the blacks had been cooking when the intruders came upon them.

Suddenly, Charley noticed a warrior in the distance and called out, 'You had best get up the horses, as I think there are a *mob* coming'. Allan and the others ran for their horses, just as a line of warriors—Allan guessed there were over 150—appeared before them. The blacks 'set up a tremendous war shout' and began to advance in their customary manner, two steps forward and one step back. As Allan mounted his horse, one warrior rushed towards him and hurled his nulla-nulla (or club), grazing his hat, while Allan at the same instant fired his pistol. With no other means of escape, he charged through the ring past a shower of spears, one of which just cleared his horse's mane. Dublin Jack also escaped unscathed—but Charley and Friday were missing. Hoping that their black companions had managed to escape, the two Europeans rode on towards Mount Abundance, reaching there early the following morning.

There was no sign of Charley or Friday. Allan hoped (without much reason) that Friday, as a local black, might have been spared. But he was determined to find Charley, whom he regarded as a loyal friend. Over the next five days, he, Dublin Jack and two other men searched for him, engaging in what he called 'sundry conflicts with hostile blacks'. Eventually they found Friday's body, mutilated almost beyond recognition. They also found Charley's horse, without its rider. Later Allan learned that he had been killed some miles from the scene of conflict.

Long before these misfortunes, Allan had resolved to return to Scotland just as soon as the station was secure. But his shepherds, who were becoming more terrified by the day about what the blacks might do to them, had ideas of their own, and made it clear that they would not stay an hour longer than their contracts obliged them to. Allan's only option was to sacrifice the sheep in favour of cattle, which required fewer men to look after them. So in March 1849 his superintendent started with all the sheep on the long journey back to Keera. Allan calculated that at least 10,000 sheep had been lost to spearings, dingoes and other causes, so that there were fewer sheep returning than had set out from Keera twenty months earlier. In the meantime he arranged for more cattle to be sent in the opposite direction, ensuring that he would leave behind a well-stocked cattle station while he pursued his interests on the other side of the world.

His troubles, though, were far from over. Twenty miles short of Mount Abundance the party of five men bringing cattle was attacked and three of them, including Dublin Jack, were killed. The remaining men at Mount Abundance were now more terrified than ever, and desperate to leave the station. At least help was now at hand. Far away in Sydney it had become obvious that the violence on the Fitzroy Downs could not be allowed to continue; so urgent and persistent were the squatters' cries for help that the government decided to appoint a Commissioner of Crown Lands and a small band of police to try to bring peace to the region. Impatient as ever and 'armed to the teeth' with his smooth bore carbine and pair of pistols, Allan rode out alone on a hazardous journey of 70 miles or more to meet the new Commissioner, a fellow Scot by the name of John Durbin. Allan was determined to enlist Durbin's help not just to protect his men and his sheep and cattle, but to pull his men into line. Soon he returned with the Commissioner, who promised to escort his wool drays south to relative safety—too late though to save two bullockies, whose mutilated and decomposing bodies were discovered beneath the wool that had been torn from their bales and scattered in piles on the ground.

There could be no doubt about it: any further investment in Mount Abundance would have to wait until the region was more secure. In the meantime Allan would follow his resolve to return to Scotland, taking what profits he could muster from the wool, leaving a few men to retain possession of the station and look after the cattle, and hoping that he would have something to come back to in future years.

More than three decades later, when he published the story of his experiences at Mount Abundance, Allan left much for his readers to imagine. His description of the first conflict, in October 1848, quotes from his journal, but cuts short mid-sentence just as the first gun is about to be fired or the first spear about to be thrown, offering no clue as to which happened first and only a hint of what happened next. He elides the 'skirmish' that 'left us masters in the field', passes over 'sundry conflicts', and hurries to the end of the story just as he and Commissioner Durbin and his small band of police gain the ascendancy. His narrative, in relation to these encounters, is sober and reflective. There is no hint of the man who, after the Aborigines on one occasion were found killing and eating sheep, was alleged to have instructed his men 'to shoot every thing that was black if only a black bullock'. This story was hearsay, but the words, and the frustration and rage that evidently lay behind them, sound familiar.

The puzzle is not why Allan omitted certain things from his published story, but why he troubled to describe the events at all, so long after they had happened. The fact is, he had submitted his diary for publication some time during the 1850s, but the prospective publisher had told him that his accounts of narrow escapes and unequal encounters with the Aborigines were so far-fetched that readers would not believe them. He would therefore do well to leave the more remarkable parts out. Allan put the manuscript aside; and there it remained for at least two decades until 1879 when he received a letter from an old friend, the Crown Lands Commissioner John Durbin, who was now living in England. Durbin alerted him to an article in the latest issue of the *Gentleman's Magazine*, entitled 'On a Sheep Station'—and the station was none other than Mount Abundance! Now it was owned, so the article said, by the Scottish Australian Investment Company. There was a town, grandly called Roma (after the then Governor's wife), close by, and it was possible to travel much of the way there by train. The station itself, although in drought, was thriving, and yielding handsome returns to investors on the other side of the world.

Reading the account, Allan reflected wistfully on what might have been. There was no disguising the fact that his efforts to tame the wilderness and make a fortune had failed dismally. He owed it to himself and his descendants to explain what had gone wrong. And of course there was a story to tell—an adventure story along the lines that he and Forster had half-jokingly imagined for themselves when, as young men, they had first set out on their squatting careers, ready to endure 'almost incredible hardships'. Now Allan could see the adventure in Biblical terms, as he led his small party into the 'Land of Promise' (where the children of Israel had been forced to wander in the wilderness for forty years), only to be eventually cast forth from 'the stronghold of the Philistines'. It was a story of remarkable bravery, with a dash of bravado: the hero, assuming the role of pioneer of civilisation, ventures into the wilderness, defends himself against hostile tribes of wild natives, finds loyal support in 'Black Charley' ('as brave as he was intelligent, and faithful to the death'), and is eventually thwarted by the ferocity of the blacks and the rascality and cowardice of his own men. In the end he and other pioneers gained little from their adventures, while those who followed profited 'by the labours and toils of those who had borne the first heat and burden on the day'.

The story must be preserved. Yet from previous tellings, perhaps at the occasional public lecture in Scotland or to family and friends around the supper table, Allan had evidently realised that some of his listeners found some of the detail unpalatable. Perhaps this is what the publisher had been hinting at many years earlier when he suggested that readers would not believe him. The whole story was there in his journal, but not all of it need be told. So in the published pamphlet he included long extracts, but cut them short before they reached a violent climax.

The journal disappeared. No one knows whether it was accidentally mislaid or, in defiance of the family tradition, deliberately destroyed; and if the latter, whether the perpetrator was Allan himself, or one of his children, or some other party who hoped to rewrite the past. No one can say how much detail was missing from the printed account. All that is certain is that there was much more than Allan was prepared to tell. As soon as the pamphlet was published, he sent copies to relatives and friends, and received some appreciative replies. One came from his friend and brother-in-law (he had now been married many years), the Reverend Thomas Pearce, who expressed much interest in his adventures but regretted that 'an evil spirit' at his side had suppressed 'the way in which I am quite sure you walked into the blessed blacks with your smooth bore [carbine]'. 'I dare say', he added, 'that the same evil spirits at your elbow said "pray don't put that in" when you came to this appalling part':

'CALLING THINGS BY RIGHT NAMES'

'To any person of proper feelings,' wrote Allan in his pamphlet, 'the remembrance of taking human life must always be a painful one.' Yet surely justice was on his side. Recalling, perhaps, his father's advice many years earlier, he cited the need to act in self-defence or to protect the lives of others. It was also appropriate, he wrote (and here he parted from his father's advice), to punish murderers where the formal instruments of the law held no sway. Therefore, after he and Charley and Friday had first clashed with the blacks near Mount Abundance, it was 'a great consolation' when Charley found on the body of one of the men they had shot a pocket knife belonging to the hutkeeper whom the blacks had murdered a month earlier. Here was proof that they had exacted just retribution.

In the eyes of the squatters, the scale of violence provided its own justification. The Aboriginal people around Fitzroy Downs—the Mandandanjari—were indeed a formidable enemy. They knew their country—the course of every creek and gully, the thickness of the scrub, the lie of the land beyond each rise and clump of trees. They could track the movements of the white men by day and lie in wait to ambush them by night. They were well led: a squatter who followed close on Allan Macpherson observed that a warrior whom he called 'Old Billy' was held in such respect that he was able to induce five tribes to act together in an effort to throw the whites out of their country. They certainly were far more numerous than the intruders; and while their weapons might seem no match for guns, a volley of spears and nulla-nullas could inflict a lot of damage while the white fellows were desperately reloading their unreliable muskets.

The other justification was that they were engaged in war. When Dublin Jack accused the blacks who had ambushed them of treachery, Allan tried to set him straight. They were 'at war with the blacks', and in war, treachery had no meaning. But what was the point of endeavouring to explain 'the law and practice of civilised and uncivilised races to an Australian stockman'?

Allan had more success explaining such matters to his English wife Emma, whom he married in 1853 during his trip home, and brought to Australia in 1856. While he had so far little to show from his long pursuit of material gain, in finding a partner in life he succeeded brilliantly. Emma, as we shall see, was everything he could have hoped for—young, beautiful, perceptive, perfectly capable of forming her own opinions and expressing them, and in every way well suited to her ambitious, intelligent and sometimes irascible husband. She also proved to be her husband's staunchest defender. In the book of her Australian travels that she published in 1860, she insisted on 'Calling things by right names'; and the right name for the violent encounters on the edge of European settlement was 'border warfare' or 'guerilla warfare'. Admittedly, 'horrible atrocities' had been committed in certain districts (perhaps she was thinking here of stories she had heard about killing the blacks with poisoned flour). But the conflict her husband was engaged in was 'as fair legitimate fighting as may be', differing from more familiar warfare in that it concerned 'the lives and properties of a few unknown individuals instead of those of powerful nations' and that the loss of life was measured in units rather than thousands. To call the conflicts murder was 'simply absurd, unless all acts of defence, not to speak of warfare, are to be invariably so termed when attended with loss of life'.

There was nothing new about this argument. Squatters had long seen themselves as engaged in warfare, comparable with the warlike conflicts that had been or were then taking place in India, Africa and the Americas. Allan, when he reflected in his pamphlet on the ambush beside the creek, hinted at the similarity of the occasion with recent events in Zululand. There was some looseness in the squatters' language, as they usually described their adversaries as murderers. But *they* (as they saw it) were engaged in warfare, and war made their actions both morally and legally legitimate.

That was not how the government saw the situation. In 1839 Governor Gipps had warned colonists that the natives were not aliens but subjects of the Queen, against whom it was therefore impossible to wage war or 'exercise belligerent rights'; and ten years later, shortly after Allan left Mount Abundance, the Colonial Secretary was warning one of its officers in the field (the newly appointed and over-zealous Commandant of Native

Police) that his job was to maintain peace and order, not to carry war into an enemy's country. The squatters protested: 'Why does the government not acknowledge that there is a war, when it is so notorious?' Far away in Sydney, though, the humanitarians—Plunkett and a few other men of influence—knew that if they called the conflicts war the squatters could get away with murder.

The squatters had another problem. Having persuaded themselves they were engaged in warfare, they had to justify it, to themselves as well as to others. A punitive expedition against Aborigines who had attacked their sheep and cattle, and perhaps committed murders, could be easily explained away in terms of just retribution. But war demanded something more. The obvious justification was that they were defending their property. But here many squatters recognised they were on slippery ground. Had the blacks simply accepted the white fellows' dominance and yielded peacefully before them, the issue might not have arisen. But they had not. Their resistance (while it varied in intensity from one region to the next) was fierce and determined; and there could be no mistaking their intentions: they wanted the invaders off their lands.

Allan was not so sure. The blacks, he told his journal, had killed his men and driven away vast numbers of sheep and cattle 'without any provocation on our part, but simply from the desire to plunder'. But then he seemed to waver.

> We certainly only wanted that our sheep and cattle should eat some of the grass which was of no use to them; but then, on the other hand, they no doubt thought they had a better right to the land than we had.

Emma, having heard her husband recount his perilous adventures, and having resided for a while near the Aboriginal people at Keera, was more forthright. She was not one to put up with 'the nonsense talked by those who know nothing about the matter'.

> If it be argued that we have no right to any portion of their land, this principle, if admitted anywhere, must for consistency's sake be carried out everywhere. ... The land on which Sydney itself is built, how did it become ours?

If the first explorers and settlers had been right in taking possession of one acre of soil, was it not equally right for the squatters to occupy and cultivate the lands now? Did it not seem that Providence had opened up a fair new land for the hardworking emigrant, to relieve overcrowding in the old world? Surely, then, the Europeans' claim to the land accorded with 'the interests of humanity and the cause of civilization and progress'. The resulting war was the inevitable result of the march of civilisation, reflected in the portentous words of the American poet William Cullen Bryant, which Emma quoted at the outset of her chapter:

> Look now abroad! Another race has filled
> Those populous borders—wide the wood recedes,
> And towns shoot up and fertile realms are tilled.

The fate of the Aborigines consumed many hours of conversation around colonial dinner tables, much as the rights and wrongs of slavery had been argued over when Allan's father was in the West Indies. One of the best informed people on such matters was her husband's old friend William Forster, with whom Emma likewise formed a warm friendship. Having long ago forsaken the misogyny of his youth, Forster was now a married man with a growing family, living at his parents' old mansion, Brush Farm, on the fringes of Sydney. During his thirteen or fourteen years in the bush, he had been involved, in one way or another, in many encounters with Aborigines, sometimes pursuing them in reprisal for a raid on his sheep, and once as a magistrate calling to account one of his neighbours who had given them poisoned flour. Soon after Allan had embarked on his expedition to Mount Abundance, Forster had set out in search of his own greener and vaster pastures far north of Brisbane, though remaining near to the coast. As one of the first squatters in the Wide Bay district, at a station called Gin Gin, he was engaged, as he put it, in guarding the northern frontier—evidently with some success, as he managed to persuade the blacks to keep their distance. 'To speak in bush style', he told Allan, 'the climate of Gingin does not agree with their constitutions.' He gave up on squatting, ruefully, in 1855; and by the time he and his wife Eliza, and Allan and Emma, were discussing the war against the blacks a year or two later, he had thrown himself into colonial politics, while still aspiring to literary greatness.

Like Emma, he believed that conflict was inevitable. He agreed with her too that the violence, in its early stages, should be classified as war; but unlike her he had no compunction in using the term 'murder'. Murders, he said, 'must always be expected on the frontier of a Colony like this', wherever enterprising men, induced by large profit (or the appearance of profit), went beyond the reach of the law. They were 'a necessity almost of that sort of colonization'. The object of government, he implied, should be to limit unwarranted violence, such as poisoning the blacks or shooting them without just cause. He agreed with Emma too that claims of ownership of the land must rest on something more than the strong arm of the colonisers. 'By what right or authority', he asked, 'had the people of this country to occupy the land? Not by the right of conquest from the aboriginal population, but by the right to civilize and put the land to some use.'

Yet was that sufficient justification? A decade or so on, mellowed perhaps by age, experience and philosophy, and possibly seeking to expunge his own evil spirits, Forster wondered if the benefits of civilisation outweighed the melancholy impact of conquest:

Tis thus—a fatal race—where'er we go,
Some phase of fitful tragedy appears.
We strew the earth with murder, crime, and woe,
Marching as in monumental show
Begirt with mourning years.
We pave our path with terror, blood, and tears—
We wade through tears and blood.
Our track is as the ruthless track of fires.
Our passage as the havoc of a flood,
When from the wasted levels it retires.
Thus with whatever good
Our conquest brings, or seems to bring,
Perpetual evil mingles or conspires.
Pale death and ruin round our footsteps spring,
And desolation dogs our civilized desires.

He called these musings 'Lines on a young kangaroo'.

13

HOME AND AWAY

ALLAN MACPHERSON BELIEVED THAT NEW SOUTH WALES HAD treated him badly. While his career as a squatter had not lacked adventure, this scarcely made up for nearly a decade of hardship, loneliness and frustrated ambitions. He arrived back in Sydney late in 1849 no better off than when he had first set out for the bush—much as his father had returned from the West Indies a generation earlier with nothing but the lessons of bitter experience (and three young children).

So when he sailed for England aboard the *Royal Emperor* in March 1850, Allan farewelled the colony with few regrets, certain that he would never set foot there again. In Scotland more than two years later he was still sure there was no chance whatever of his returning. And yet, he confessed to Allan Williams that 'my heart would warm to a sick monkey if it had ever been in New South Wales'. Now, sitting alone beside the fire in the living room at Blairgowrie House, he had to admit that despite all her faults and annoyances, he loved 'dear old New South Wales' still. Was this homesickness? If so, Allan would not have admitted it; for while he might refer to New South Wales as 'my country', Scotland was unequivocally 'home'. Sometimes the expression would subconsciously be extended to include the rest of Britain, or at least England—though really England was merely a staging post on the road north to Scotland.

His father, too, had no doubts about the meaning of home. William's heart had always been in Scotland, even though by 1850, when he turned sixty-six, he had spent over two decades in New South Wales. From the moment of his arrival in Sydney, he had always assumed that he would return to Blairgowrie. And now, when Allan set out for the ancestral home, William confidently expected to follow him within a few years.

William had to admit, though, that life in the colony had its attractions: a wide circle of friends and acquaintances, and the respect in which he was held by the community. These might be replicated in Scotland. But there was no prospect of transferring to Blairgowrie Sydney's climate; and when a wintry wind blew across the harbour and chilled his ageing bones, he was reminded that back home the weather would be much more severe. Moreover, while he had no intention of remarrying, his domestic situation was comfortable—a circumstance reinforced before Christmas in 1850 when he was brought down by a severe fever. For over a fortnight his housekeeper, Mrs Egan, nursed him day and night, rubbing his forehead with vinegar and water every fifteen minutes during the height of the fever, and moving into Master Allan's now vacant room to be adjacent to him. Back on the mend, William purchased an insurance bond to guarantee that Mrs Egan would receive £30 a year after his death, for as long as she should live. A more warm-hearted woman he never knew.

Allan Williams probably picked up the habit of calling Scotland home; but unlike his father and half-brother he had no choice about where he might live. Although he might have had some faint memory of parting from his mother and crossing a vast ocean at the age of five, it is unlikely that Berbice—now part of British Guiana—had any claim on his affections. In 1850, at the age of forty, he had spent half his life in New South Wales, and there was no prospect of him moving elsewhere. By the end of that year his wife Sophia had given birth to eight children—five boys and three girls. The two eldest, confusingly named William Williams and Allan Williams, lived in Sydney with his father, who in 1847 had assumed responsibility for their education and upbringing—a welcome distraction from his miseries after the loss of his wife Jessy. But that still left Allan Williams to provide for Jessie Eliza (a name that, aside from the errant spelling of Jessy, must have pleased his father), Laura, Henry, Frank, Frederick and Emily. As William Forster put it, 'a man may carry a tolerable weight on dry land which in the water must sink him irretrievably'. Allan Williams was often on the verge of sinking.

Allan Macpherson's adventures occasionally offered Allan Williams a lifeline. Allan, before setting out on the first expedition to Mount Abundance, had persuaded Allan Williams to take over the running of Keera in his absence; and Allan Williams, who was not enjoying much success as a farmer in the Hunter Valley and who generally tended to go along with his half-brother's proposals, readily complied. When Allan

Allan Macpherson 1818–1891, oil by an unknown artist. This is the earliest surviving portrait of Allan and might well be the one he had painted when he returned to Britain in 1851. If so, he is prematurely bald, as he was in that year just thirty-two years old. MACPHERSON COLLECTION

....

Macpherson abandoned Mount Abundance and headed for Scotland, Allan Williams remained at Keera with his wife and family. Accepting what life offered him, his notion of home rarely extended beyond the backyard clothesline where the baby napkins were hung out to dry.

TRANSITION STATES

As soon as Allan Macpherson reached London he arranged to sit for his portrait in oils. The artist worked quickly; and Allan, anxious as ever to please his father, despatched the finished work by the *Royal Emperor* on its return voyage to Sydney. William received the package with 'inexpressible pleasure; but not unaccompanied with a sigh', for it must have cost a great deal of money. 'You know I must pay for it My dearest Allan; for I asked you in Sydney to get it done, some time when convenient, but I did not expect you would get it so soon done.' Allan gritted his teeth. But at least his father conceded it was an excellent likeness, and everyone who saw it admired it. The housekeeper, Ellen (or Mrs Egan, as she preferred to be called), was in raptures.

Allan's other pressing assignment was to marry, as much to please his father as himself. William was generous with his advice, urging his son, as his own father had urged him, not to set his heart on money—for tens of thousands could not compensate for the want of solid virtues. If the lady had money, so much the better; but 'to use a law phrase, let it be an agreeable appurtenance, but not an essential requisite'. Allan applied himself to the task with such diligence that before he reached London he had (according to rumour) fallen 'desperately in love' with one of his fellow passengers. His friend Forster had warned him against shipboard romances. He proposed, and the young lady spurned him, leaving him resentful and forlorn. He consoled himself by making sardonic comments about 'domestic felicity', which earned him a sharp rebuke from his happily married friend.

Thwarted in love, he still had Blairgowrie to look forward to. It was twenty-five years since the family had last been there. Several times over that period William, struggling to make ends meet, had contemplated selling the property, managing on each occasion to stave off the dreaded day. The estate had not done well—William attributed this to bad management by useless trustees. Now Allan's job was to pull things into line, farming the lands as he had done just before he had left there. He was to leave as many acres as possible for grazing, keeping a single plough and pair of horses; and while he would need a horse for riding, or for driving himself and his prospective wife in a gig, there was to be no extravagance. If Allan followed these principles, William trusted that the property would yield on average £300 a year, after payment of essential expenses, just allowing him to live as 'a plain country gentleman, and farmer, as I was before him'.

This was not exactly what Allan had in mind. When in the Australian bush he had imagined himself as laird of Blairgowrie, his thoughts had turned more to entertaining local notables in grand style and distributing largesse among his tenants than to keeping the farm free of gorse and broom. He had seen himself in the House of Commons, or perhaps as a figure in the world of literature. Whatever he might have aspired to, there was as much chance of him becoming a '*plain* country gentleman' as there was of his father leading an exploring party into the Australian wilds. Nevertheless, for the moment at least, Allan submitted to his father's will, yoked himself to the (solitary) plough and looked forward to a brighter future.

'I am in a transition state,' he told Allan Williams, 'which can be interpreted in many ways.' The same, he said, applied to Blairgowrie. Over the past quarter century or so the town, like many others in central Scotland, had been transformed. In the mid-1840s the population was estimated at 2600, many of whom had moved there from the surrounding countryside as small farms were consolidated into large estates. Manufacturing had taken over from farming as the main activity. The traditional domestic spinning wheel had given way to large water-powered textile mills along the river. Together these employed some 200 people. Another 350 workers were engaged in weaving into cloth the yarn produced by the mills, some of which was exported to France and North and South America. Scattered thatched houses had been replaced by orderly rows of cottages along well-formed gas-lit streets. Now, wrote Allan, the community was in 'agonies of suspense' about whether Blairgowrie or the neighbouring town of Rattray, on the other side of the River Ericht, would be chosen as the terminus of a branch line that would link them to the network of railways that was reaching out across the whole country, and making it so much easier for the towns' products to reach their markets.

Back in New South Wales, William wondered at the transformation: 'I have no idea what sort of carriages Railway carriages are', he mused; 'are they in any respect very much different from the Stage-coaches, and Omnibuses that used to travel with horses[?]'. But changes were not only happening at home: the colony too was changing as never before. In May 1851 significant gold deposits were discovered just beyond the mountains west of Sydney, and within weeks half the population seemed to be heading for the diggings. Many thought their moment had come. Others reacted with alarm. At Government House Sir Charles FitzRoy, who had succeeded Governor Gipps in 1846, complained that both his footmen had given notice. 'The hall porter went last week. Where will it all end?'

More rushes followed in quick succession, first to the Port Phillip District, now the separate colony of Victoria, where the goldfields proved to be exceptionally rich; and then to the north along the New England tableland. In mid-1852, about a year after the initial rushes, a promising field was found at Bingara, just 15 miles from Keera. There, according to the local Crown Lands Commissioner, one fossicker, using just a tin dish and a spear blade, extracted over several days 22 ounces of gold, including a 4 ounce nugget, while another scraped a pound weight in two days with the help of a knife and spoon.

Allan Williams heard the clatter of the gold cradles and listened intently to the many stories of fossickers who had struck it rich. Whatever the prospects of success on the diggings, anything would seem better than remaining at Keera. The station continued to yield miserable returns, with the predictable result of his father accusing him of extravagance and bad management. Instead of increasing the numbers of sheep as William had instructed him to do, he had allowed them to fall; he had sent wool to Sydney which was covered in grass seeds and could not be sold; he had failed to round up the stray cattle; he had employed more workers than the station needed; and so on and so on. William concluded that Allan Williams was 'too apathetic; too indolent; too devoid of activity and energy' to manage a sheep or cattle station. If he could find a buyer for Keera he would accept whatever he could get for it; and as for Allan Williams, he could become 'an overseer to some more fortunate Stock-holder, or a Shepherd, or a Stockman, or what he pleases, for I will no longer submit to have my life made a perfect burden to me by such an unprofitable, thankless Concern'.

So Allan Williams took the hint, grabbed a pan, pick and shovel, and headed for the Bingara diggings, leaving Keera in charge of a manager more to his father's liking, and his wife and children at a friend's station nearby. There Sophia gave birth to another child. And despite his threats to abandon his son, William came to the rescue with a promise of £100 a year, grumbling that this would cost him less than leaving him in charge of Keera. Allan Macpherson wrote from Scotland to wish his half-brother well; and as the diggings were reputed to be lawless places, he sent a brace of pistols. 'Sincerely I do hope that you may have less occasion for using the pistols at the "diggings" than I had to use guns at the "[Fitzroy] Downs".'

For every digger who struck it rich there were many who failed. After a year of scraping a few meagre specks from the ground, Allan Williams had had enough of fossicking and begged his father to send him £20 so that he could bring his family to Sydney. William would have none of it. Where would the family live? *He* could not be expected to support them. Allan Williams was really 'a most unfortunate fellow; and his two boys with me, will, I am afraid not turn out well; they are far too fond of the company of low Street boys—and neither Ellen nor I can keep them from them'.

But there were other ways of benefiting from the gold rushes than by finding gold. The booming colonial economy led to new government appointments, including an additional clerk in William's office of Clerk of the Legislative Council. William put his son's name forward, and his old friend the Colonial Secretary readily agreed to his appointment. The salary was just £200 a year, two-thirds of what Allan Williams had been earning when he had abandoned the public service in the late 1830s to take up farming on the Hunter. But the income was regular and the position secure. Of course there could be no question of him living in town, where prices were outrageous. But he managed to rent a four-room cottage for 8 shillings a week in the village of Ashfield, about 7 miles to the west of town along the Parramatta Road; and from there he took a coach to and from the office for a total cost of 5 shillings a week.

Allan Williams' life began to improve. Towards the end of 1853 he secured a more satisfactory position as clerk in the Surveyor-General's office, initially at the same salary level but soon rising to £300 a year. With a lot of help from his father, he purchased a block of land at Cooks River, not far from his current rented cottage; and, using skills he had acquired in the bush, built and furnished a comfortable timber dwelling—nothing grand, but roomy enough to accommodate his large family. There Sophia gave birth to a tenth child, a boy, in 1855. He has 'too many by far', complained William, 'by one half at least'. There was one more to come: another daughter was born in 1858 in what had now become the family's permanent home.

After Allan Macpherson left New South Wales in 1850, William had to wait more than three years to hear the news he had so much yearned for: that his son had found a suitable bride. When it came he was ecstatic. As well as knowing that Allan was at last settled in life, he could look forward to a continuance of the family line. What was more, he had been told that his son could not anywhere have found 'a more excellent, more accomplished, and more beautiful young lady'.

Emma Blake was indeed a brilliant catch. At the time of their marriage early in 1853 she was aged nineteen, and therefore Allan's junior by fifteen

Emma Macpherson 1833–1916, oil by an unknown artist. This probably captures her around the time of her marriage to Allan Macpherson, when she was nineteen years of age. BLAKE-ESPITALIÉ COLLECTION/QUERCY-PHOTOGRAPHIE

years. She had an older sister, married to the Reverend Mr Thomas Pearce, and two younger brothers. The family had close Indian connections. Emma had been born in a village about 60 miles north of Calcutta and had spent her infancy in Bengal. Her father, Charles Blake, had also been born in India, where he had acquired sugar mills and a distillery. Now, at the time of Emma's marriage, he was a successful London merchant. Her father's father, Benjamin Blake, had served as a naval captain with the East India Company. Benjamin's wife was the daughter of a Captain Powney and a woman of whom nothing is known other than that her name was Mary and that she was Indian, a fact that Emma did not advertise but did not attempt to disguise. Another distant branch of the family appears to have had French lineage.

At the age of three, Emma accompanied her parents to England, where she lived for eight years with two unmarried aunts. She then spent four years at school in London, where she devoured the great works of English literature and won a prize for proficiency in history. At some stage she taught herself Latin and Greek. A youthful portrait, probably painted about the time she was married, shows her to be round faced and dark haired, with large, intelligent brown eyes looking directly at the viewer. While the pursed lips and tilted head hinted at something coquettish in her manner, further acquaintance would prove that Emma was a young lady not to be trifled with.

If Emma had any deficiency, it was that she was not a Scot—a misfortune that neither Allan nor his father alluded to. But she certainly came from a good family. Her father promised to settle on her £200 a year during his own and his wife's lifetime (not a vast amount, but certainly an 'agreeable appurtenance'), and he proposed that after his death his property should be divided fairly (which Allan took to mean equally) among his four children.

The couple married in London at the end of April 1853 and the same afternoon caught the train to Dover for a holiday in France. Allan recorded in his diary: 'The happiest day of my life'.

IMPERIAL TRAVELLERS

The gold rushes coincided with a revolution in communications between Britain and the Australian colonies. Immigrants arrived in their tens of thousands—86,000 in 1852, many more than in any previous year—and with them came new incentives for transporting people and goods to the colonies in the shortest time possible, and carrying the wealth of the colonies by the quickest means home. In that year the first mail steamer arrived in Sydney, bringing the expectation of improved postal services. But William Macpherson was unimpressed. 'I had hoped the introduction of Steam would have facilitated our correspondence,' he told Allan testily, 'but hitherto it has had quite a contrary effect.'

Although steam was here to stay, sail remained the fastest means of traversing the oceans. A new generation of American-style clipper ships followed the 'great circle' route through southern latitudes, breaking speed records between British and Australian ports. A record was set in August

1853 when the *Walter Hood*, newly launched in Aberdeen, and the largest ship built in that city to date, arrived in Sydney Harbour from London after a passage of just eighty days.

Among the *Walter Hood*'s score of first class passengers disembarking at Circular Quay was Snodgrass Chalmers, the only surviving son of William Macpherson's brother-in-law, Sir William Chalmers, who had fought with great distinction at Waterloo. Snod, as he was affectionately known, had a problem: he was irresistibly attracted to the demon drink. He was, nevertheless, a cheerful and affectionate young man, disarmingly honest, and invariably popular among those who came to know him. Allan Macpherson, renewing acquaintance with his mother's side of the family, had met him soon after returning to Britain; and as his uncle, Sir William, was at his wits' end over what to do about his dissolute son, Allan proposed that Snod should make the journey to New South Wales, where his own father would do his best to set him straight.

Striding up from Circular Quay, Snodgrass found his way to the legislative chambers in Macquarie Street and presented himself to his uncle who, having been forewarned by Allan that Snod was on the way, was looking forward to meeting him. He was, wrote William, 'a fine looking man of very pleasing appearance, and manners, and bears so strong a resemblance to his worthy Father, that he had no need of an introduction'. Eager to be of service to any member of his late and much lamented wife's family, William assigned the younger Allan Williams to look after him, and arranged to meet him later in the day. Snodgrass, after taking some food and a tumbler of port, proceeded with twelve-year-old Allan to see the sights of Sydney. Before long, though, he chanced upon some of his erstwhile fellow passengers, and with them sidled into a nearby public house, telling young Allan that he would be home in time for tea.

That was the last any member of the family saw of him for two days, until suddenly he appeared at his uncle's office asking for a few shillings to pay for a boat to bring his luggage ashore, and telling him that he would sleep aboard ship that night but see him the following morning. After another two days he resurfaced and came again in quest of money. Already he was slipping into a routine of appearances and disappearances that left no one in doubt about the nature of his problem, but everyone short of ideas about how to solve it. He became devious, waiting until his uncle had left for work before approaching the housekeeper for a crown for a bottle of brandy, telling her that 'if she did not give him Spirits, or money to buy some, he would absolutely die'. William tried to reason with him, telling him that he was wasting his life and reminding him of his duty to his family. Snodgrass listened attentively, pressed his uncle's hand, and promised to try his hardest 'to break himself from his vicious course'. They agreed that he should limit himself to some spirits in the morning and three of four glasses of wine a day. But this achieved nothing; and however hard William might try to remove him from temptation, including by sending him up-country, he still managed to find means of satisfying his unquenchable thirst.

Back in Blairgowrie, Allan Macpherson apologised for giving his father such a troublesome charge and suggested that he send Snodgrass home, preferably on a ship travelling directly to Dundee, to avoid the temptations of London. In retrospect it was obvious that New South Wales, where public houses far outnumbered places of worship, and where, according to one observer, not to drink was considered a crime, was no place to sober up; and the long sea voyage did not help. Only recently Allan's old school friend Roderick—'Roddy'—Mitchell, the son of the Surveyor-General, had drowned after jumping overboard on a trip from Moreton Bay to Sydney during a fit of delirium tremens. Allan should have known better.

The colonies, though, were often regarded as a solution to problems that could not be solved at home, or at least as a means of putting them out of sight and mind. Snodgrass Chalmers was one of many travellers later referred to as 'remittance men'—sent to the colonies for their country's (or their family's) good, and sustained by modest remittances from home; except that in Snodgrass' case, Sir William (whom Allan Macpherson regarded as 'a shabby dog') gave him so little that Allan, through his father, had to come to the rescue. Many years later one of Allan's children remarked that Snodgrass eventually 'made a good recovery with the help of a good wife'. So the story had a happy ending. In the meantime, though, Snod's travels left Allan out of pocket and William upbraiding his son for inflicting the young reprobate on him.

Snodgrass, though, was among the least of Allan's misdemeanours. The marriage to Emma had been splendid news; but it was difficult for William to sustain his happiness when he learned of Allan's 'enormous' expenditure. 'I am much afraid you will soon run through Blairgowrie,' he despaired, 'and every other means [of income] that may chance to be drawn into your bottomless pit.' Surely by now he should have redeemed 'the follies of your youth'. The station at Keera, William declared, would have yielded a large annual return had Allan not always been 'playing the fine gentleman, keeping the best table in the district, and winning popularity'; and Mount Abundance should also have been profitable. But for his son's bad management and extravagance, William might by now have been able to return to Scotland with £10,000 in his pocket. Now it seemed likely that 'all my endeavours, and my prolonged toils and labours in a foreign and far distant land, will prove to have been in vain'. He would not be available forever for his son to call upon; and when he was gone, Allan would be forced to return penniless to Australia, or travel to some other part of the world. No doubt Allan had plans to reform, but William had heard them all before: 'Will', he remarked scathingly, 'is a very favorite word in all your reforming resolutions; am, and have have been quite discarded from your vocabulary'.

As it happened, Allan in his newly married state was behaving with uncustomary restraint and propriety. While his father was fulminating in Sydney about his supposed excesses, he was setting out for his own benefit a 'Proposed division of day in general during winter and spring':

9 to 10—Prayers and Breakfast
10 to 11—Reading letters and newspapers
11 to 1—Looking about Farm and Improvements etc.
1 to 3—Writing business etc.
3 to 4—Walking and driving with Dear Emma
4 to 5—Dinner—
5 to 6—Reading letters and newspapers
6 to 7:30—Light business
7:30 to 8—Tea
8 to 9—Reading (to self)
9 to 10—Reading aloud
10 to 11—Prayers and retiring to rest

Now that he had disposed of the useless trustees, the prospects for Blairgowrie were promising. If the farm was slow to yield profits, at least the land was proving increasingly valuable. He negotiated a lease with the Scottish Midland Railway, which had chosen Blairgowrie over Rattray as the terminus for its new branch line; and imagining the growth that the

Detail from Plan of Newton Villa and Town Feus, on the Estate of William Macpherson, Esquire, of Blairgowrie. 1854. Allan advertises sixty-nine villa and sixty-three town allotments. 'Views from the ground are very extensive', while mills and factories along the River Ericht suggest that the town is making impressive progress. MACPHERSON COLLECTION

railway would bring, he drew up plans for subdividing part of the estate and making 130 or so building lots available for long-term rental. But it was not to be. Chastened by his father's admonitions, he wrote back instantly: 'All my improvements are *absolutely at an end*'.

William's comments had cut to the quick. Allan expressed contrition, urged understanding, begged for forgiveness. Yes, he had spent more than he should have done—but was this not excusable, when he was starting out on a new line of life as a married man? Yes, his father's whole existence had been and still was 'a continuing act of self sacrifice for my sake'. But surely only 'the blackest ingratitude on my part' could justify William's threat never to return to Scotland. How could so 'kind and good and just Father' make him forever miserable by loading his sail with the guilt of being a recipient of 'blood money'? Emma hurried to his side, assuring her father-in-law how carefully they were managing their household expenses and how they avoided all extravagance: 'You do not know how we long to see you—it is Allan's only wish'. If only William could see him as she had often done, 'looking at your miniature or letters with tears in his eyes', he would know that no son could regard his father with deeper gratitude and affection.

Which was no doubt true. Having been from the day of his birth the first object of his father's affections, and having been indulged in effect as an only child, now he was bound to him by tangled ties of love, duty and obedience. His father had always intended to come home to Blairgowrie. Now Allan was obliged to make sure that happened. The thought that he, the dutiful son, might be the cause of his father being unable to fulfil his deepest desires was a burden too heavy to bear.

It was equally true that if his father maintained this level of irritability something might go seriously wrong. William had already announced that he intended to dispose of Keera and Mount Abundance, and there was a risk he might let them go for a song. And what of Allan's inheritance? There had never been any question that he should inherit the Blairgowrie estate; but with a careless promise here, and a legacy there, anything could happen. Allan knew what he had to do: he must return to New South Wales, take charge of selling the properties and try his hardest to bring his father home. Only thus could he expect to assuage his guilt and allay his anxieties.

Emma was determined to come too; but this was not the moment. In 1854 she gave birth to their first child, whom they named Jessie Harriet, after Allan's mother and his much-loved aunt. They would need to wait for Jessie to be old enough to undertake the long voyage. The following year Emma gave birth to a son, whom they named William Charles, after the two grandfathers. In March 1856, as little Willie approached his first birthday, they could wait no longer. Leaving him in the care of Aunt Harriot, Allan, Emma and the infant Jessie sailed for New South Wales, intending to remain there just long enough for Allan to sell the properties and persuade his father to accompany them home.

SCANDAL

After twenty-five years in New South Wales, William Macpherson's ties to the old country were becoming frayed, as past friends died and others receded into distant memory. Two strong links remained: his sister Harriot and brother Allan. Allan had lost his beloved wife Margaret, Jessy's sister, from fever while they were on the way to the East Indies in 1828. After serving for a time as a chaplain near Calcutta, he returned to England, remarried and obtained a curacy at the parish church of Rothwell in Northamptonshire. Apart from the infant he had left in the West Indies, he appears to have had no living children of his own. He and his wife were still at Rothwell in 1850 when his young nephew and namesake returned from the Antipodes. According to William, his brother Allan was a poor correspondent—almost as bad as Allan Williams—so there was no way of knowing precisely where he was or what he was doing at any particular time. But William had no reason to doubt that his brother was anything other than a respectable local vicar, who would help keep his sometimes wayward son on the straight and narrow and encourage him to be more conscientious in his religious observance.

Aunt Harriot was likewise certain to be a wise and good mentor. During the 1830s and 1840s she had lived with her husband, Lieutenant-Colonel Edmund Craigie, first in the Scottish Lowlands, then in rural Devonshire. Her adopted daughter Isabella, who never married, was her constant companion. Harriot was, as her mother had been, a model of piety and respectability, a staunch defender of traditional forms of worship and upholder of proper forms of behaviour: which is partly why the suddenness and manner of her husband's death came to those who knew her as such a complete shock. One morning in 1850, when she, the Colonel and Isabella were at their home near Exeter, the Colonel was late for breakfast. The maid discovered that the door to his bedroom was bolted; and when the coachman and butler forced it open, they recoiled at the dreadful sight of their master in his nightgown, sitting on the floor in a pool of blood, his arms, thighs and stomach mutilated, and his throat cut from ear to ear. A razor lay on the dressing table and a knife on the wash stand, both covered in blood. Rumours circulated that he had been murdered; but the inquest left no doubt that he had done the deed himself. His reasons remained a mystery; although one of the doctors remarked that he had always been 'a nervous agitated man', while another observed that he had recently suffered from 'depression in the spirits', which might in turn have been caused by liver ailments after nearly thirty years' residence in India. The jury concluded that he had destroyed himself during a fit of temporary insanity.

This was a salutary reminder that even in the most respectable and pious of families things could go terribly wrong. Newspapers across the country reported 'a most appalling act of suicide'. Mercifully there was no mention of the Macpherson name; and over the years the tragedy was expunged from the family's collective memory and almost obliterated, consciously or otherwise, from the family records. In the meantime, William urged his son to be attentive to his aunt in her time of distress, reminding him that, apart from himself and Uncle Allan (and of course forgetting Allan

Williams), he was her closest living relative. He should also remember that her wealth had come chiefly from Allan's grandfather, Colonel Allan, and her first husband, General Macintyre, rather than Colonel Craigie, so that the late Colonel's children by an earlier marriage had no claim on it; and that therefore he could reasonably expect to inherit the bulk of it. Now he should endeavour, by every means in his power, 'not only to keep up the warm affection she has always displayed towards you, but even to increase it'.

Allan took the hint and was duly solicitous. But in truth he needed little encouragement, for he had always regarded his aunt as a warm friend and confidante; and if his affection was increased by the expectation of inheriting her estate, it was nevertheless genuine. So when he and Emma

Aunt Harriot Craigie in 1857 or 1858, when she was aged about seventy, with her nephew Willie Macpherson, eldest son of Allan and Emma. MACPHERSON COLLECTION

decided several years after Colonel Craigie's death to visit Australia, she was the obvious person with whom to leave the baby Willie. She was, he told her, 'almost a parent'; and if he should ever need advice about a problem—a delicate family matter, for example—she would be the person to turn to.

Scarcely had Allan, Emma and little Jessie stepped ashore at Sydney Cove in mid-1856 than Allan was confronted by just such a problem. Never, he told Aunt Harriot, had he been in greater need of advice from 'such a kind and prudent aunt'. What troubled him, indeed infuriated him almost beyond endurance, were his father's domestic arrangements.

At first sight, William was living a life of sober respectability. Now in his early seventies, his thoughts were turning increasingly to the afterlife, and the time when 'it shall please the Almighty Father of us all to remove us from this World of care, and anxiety, and tribulation'. Although his wife had died nearly a decade previously, he prided himself, wrote Allan, as 'a paragon of faithfulness to my Mother's memory', ostentatiously wearing her miniature, dressing in deep mourning, and requiring his housekeeper, Mrs Egan, to do the same.

Here was the problem: the 'infernal housekeeper'. Ellen Egan, as Allan told Aunt Harriot, had emigrated to New South Wales from Ireland about fifteen years earlier. Recently widowed, she had brought with her a young son, Patrick, who was now approaching twenty years. She had immediately been retained as a general servant in the Macpherson household, and had risen steadily in her employers' esteem. According to William, Jessy before she died had urged him to keep Mrs Egan always with him; but surely, added Allan, not in the way that now appeared to be the case. There could be no doubting that she took good care of him, bringing him his morning coffee every day at six before attending mass, seeing him off to work, preparing his meals, and looking after him when he was ill. At the same time, though, she had acquired 'an amount of influence over him' which Allan was determined to reduce, and if possible put an end to.

The enormity of the situation became apparent when William invited his son and daughter-and-law, who were initially staying in lodgings, to a small gathering in their honour. As he entered the dining room Allan was astonished to find 'the *woman in question* seated at the head of my Fathers table and *her Son* at the side of it, both on a footing of perfect equality with my Father and several guests whom he then had at his table'. Mrs Egan rushed up first to Allan, then to Emma, threw her arms around their necks, and kissed them violently, 'following this by performing the same compliments in favour of *my Father*'. Her son followed with 'somewhat more subdued demonstrations', after which they all sat down to a pleasant family cookie shine, or tea party.

Allan assured Aunt Harriot that such behaviour was not out of the ordinary:

> Lest you might think the *kissing* demonstrations as merely a *feu de joie* on the occasion of our arrival I must pause in my narrative to mention that every morning and afternoon on my Father's departure to and return from his office she confers and my Father receives similar favours from her not only *in our presence*, when there, but also in that of every one else who may be there including the workmen who are now painting and papering his house, with this addition to the kissings that she *sprinkles him all over with Holy Water* which she keeps in a bottle for that purpose to the great damage of his clothes in dusty weather.

The morning after this alarming experience, as Allan and his father strolled along Macquarie Street towards the Council chambers, Allan decided that this was as good a time as any to settle matters regarding his father's future. He and Emma, he said, were looking forward to his accompanying them to Scotland just as soon as the colonial properties had been disposed of. To this William agreed cheerfully, as this was exactly what he had always had in mind. Then he added that, while he was keen to come home, he considered that once they had arrived there it would be best if he were not to live with them in Blairgowrie House, but rather to build or rent a small cottage on the estate, 'where *he*—and *his housekeeper* who was used to his ways—and he said *essential to his comfort* could keep house together'.

Needless to say, to this proposition Allan objected most strongly, plainly telling his father that if *he* would not live in Blairgowrie House, nor would they. After further conversation, William expressed a willingness to compromise: he would live with them at the mansion house under two conditions. First, he would require a separate room in the house in which to place his wife's coffin, as he had always intended that Jessy's remains, encased in lead, should be returned to the land of her birth. Second, he expected that Mrs Egan would live with them and that Allan and Emma would receive her at their table on the same footing as he did. Allan replied that, while every room in the house was at his father's command, it would be 'utterly impossible' to allow the housekeeper to sit at their table, lest they be 'entirely *cut* and refused to be visited by the entire circle of our country acquaintances, to the utter ruin of ourselves and our children so far as *society* was concerned'. William instantly relented, conceding that Mrs Egan might keep a separate table, with her own servant girl. Whatever domestic arrangements might eventuate, though, there could be no question that she would accompany him home.

There the matter rested, with William maintaining his dignity and Allan having as little to do with Mrs Egan as possible. After a week or so, William took his son aside and declared, in his 'usual affectionate manner', how much it grieved him that Allan took so little notice of Mrs Egan and so rarely shook hands with her, adding that she was a most reputable woman who had more than once saved his life when he had been ill, and that all his friends in the colony shook hands with her whenever they visited. He was of course aware that many people had spread scandalous stories about him, suggesting that there was a '*criminal intimacy*' between them (the word 'criminal' implying extreme immorality rather than any illegality). But he had no intention of sacrificing such a faithful servant to such tales; and he was sure that his son would give them no credence.

Of course, said Allan: had he for a moment supposed there was a criminal intimacy between his parent and the housekeeper he would not have allowed Emma to enter his father's house. It was hardly surprising, though, that people would draw certain conclusions, given the familiarities he allowed her; and it certainly did not reflect well on his supposed respect for his wife's memory—at which point the conversation was mercifully interrupted and the problem left to simmer.

This was how matters stood when Allan sought his Aunt Harriot's advice. The truth was, he wrote sadly, that while his father was still quite capable of managing his own business affairs, his intellect was '*very* much weakened', proof of which lay in his failure to recognise how his behaviour would be perceived by society, especially back home in

Scotland. Conscious of his 'physical innocence', he had 'no feeling of shame in his lost reputation and no sense of impropriety in virtually *insisting* on his Son and daughter-in law associating with the person in question'. Occasionally there seemed to be a glimmer of understanding: only the other day he had been mortified when Lady Denison, the wife of the new Governor, had 'distinctly refused to see him!!!' Perhaps he should marry the woman—though at the moment such a suggestion would fill him with horror and indignation, owing to his respect for his late wife. There was no question that money was an issue; though William spoke of settling on the woman £100 a year and a small cottage. Just a year ago he had written of bequeathing her £30 a year, with no mention of a cottage: 'if his ideas go on increasing at this rate *where* will he stop?'

Allan did not expect an answer to this question, any more than he expected his aunt to come up with a solution for the larger problem. His purpose in writing was not so much to seek her advice as to forewarn her of troubles ahead, and suggest that she might hint at her brother's 'eccentricities' to some of their closest friends. There was, in any case, a more immediate problem, which he would have to confront long before

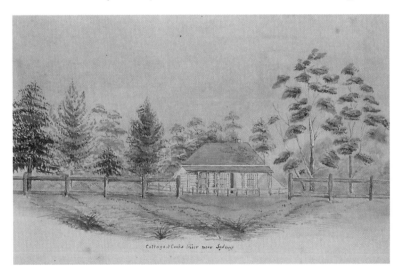

Cottage at Cooks River near Sydney, watercolour by Emma Macpherson, 1856. This is the house that Allan Williams built and his father paid for. Despite the crowded conditions, Emma liked to stay here, 'in the very centre of a wilderness of trees and flowers', and safely distant from her father-in-law's improprieties in town. MITCHELL LIBRARY, STATE LIBRARY OF NEW SOUTH WALES

the fastest mail steamers could deliver to Sydney Aunt Harriot's reply. If Allan were to get a satisfactory price for Keera and Mount Abundance, he would have to ensure they were in the best possible condition for sale. That would require a long and arduous journey, at least as far as Keera. While he was away, perhaps for a year, Emma and little Jessie would have to remain in Sydney. But where would they live? Lodgings were out of the question: apart from the cost, such an arrangement would provide more fodder for the gossips, who might suspect family ructions. The obvious solution was to stay with William; but there Emma would be exposed to 'further insult and annoyance at the hands of the housekeeper' (as well as hurtful asides from the town gossips).

Before undertaking the inland excursion, Allan decided to make a short trip by sea to Melbourne to undertake some business relating to a land grant. During his absence he arranged for Emma and Jessie to stay with Allan Williams and his wife Sophia at their newly built house at Cooks River. The Williams family, notwithstanding their modest circumstances and (except for Sophia) dusky skins, were above moral reproach. Their respectability had been confirmed many years earlier, when Allan Williams had been appointed a magistrate, which entitled him to put the initials 'JP' after his name. There were, however, seven children still living at home, including one in napkins, leaving Emma with scarcely any room to move. So when William urged her to reside with him in town, she readily complied; and it was here that Allan found her when he returned from Melbourne.

There was a scene. One evening, according to Allan, a heated argument took place, during which Mrs Egan used expressions towards himself and Emma that could not have passed from his mother's lips. William was evidently out of the room at the time; and when Allan told him what had happened, he conceded that Mrs Egan was sometimes violent, adding that Allan should not have provoked her. This was the limit! What would Allan's mother have thought if she heard her only son and his wife being 'deliberately insulted by an uneducated Irish Roman Catholic woman of low origin, and in the estimation of the Public (altho' not to that extent in mine) of bad personal character'? Allan put it to his father directly: what would Aunt Harriot and Uncle Allan and Sir William Chalmers say if they heard how his father allowed his housekeeper to behave so abominably? William responded that if Allan told tales to relatives in Scotland 'it would be better for him to remain here and die and never go home'. There the conversation ended, with William declaring that he would never mention Ellen's name again, and Allan and Emma resolving not to venture out of their room unless to leave the house entirely.

That settled the matter of where Emma and Jessie should stay when Allan headed north. As the Williams' house was uncomfortable, and residing with his father and 'the odious creature' inconceivable, there was only one solution. Emma and little Jessie would accompany him on the 400 mile journey to Keera. This was probably as much Emma's decision as Allan's. While she was better able than her husband to live peaceably in her father-in-law's household, an extended stay there was hardly likely to be pleasant. Nor for that matter was a long spell in Sydney. While she was charmed by the beauty of the harbour, and took great pleasure in 'many rambles through the bush', she found little to commend in the town, with its streets 'badly paved—when paved at all—shockingly drained, and indifferently lighted', its architecture inferior to second-rate provincial towns back home, and its society, for her taste, altogether too American. A journey into the bush offered the prospect of escape as well as excitement. She could hardly wait.

There was a complication: she was now five months pregnant. Acquaintances in Sydney warned that the journey would be too much for her. But Emma was adventurous; and having made up her mind to go, nothing would get in her way.

A BUSH JOURNEY

They set out from Sydney early in October 1856. The journey north followed much the same route that Allan had taken more than seventeen years earlier: first by steamer to the Hunter River, then by road along the valley and over the Great Dividing Range, across the Liverpool Plains to Tamworth, and onwards another 90 miles to Keera. The roads and tracks were little better now than they had been then, owing partly to heavy recent rains, but also because there were so many travellers, including miners heading to and from the diggings. Except for the last stretch, there were now plenty of villages and inns along the way. But Allan had come prepared to camp; and after being forced to pay nearly £6 for two nights at Maitland, he and Emma decided to follow his original plan.

They had brought with them from England a dog cart—a two-wheel vehicle with four seats, two facing forwards and two backwards (and so-named because the box beneath the seats had originally been used for carrying hunting dogs). Allan had it built with extra springs to withstand the tough terrain, and a waterproof canvas cover. Stuffing was added to the back of Emma's seat, and she was given a footstool, so that she could travel in reasonable comfort. They also took with them a horse-drawn dray to carry all the baggage and equipment necessary for the journey. The heavier goods and extra supplies they would need at Keera came separately on two bullock drays.

Allan had hoped to achieve 15 miles a day, but Emma, perched high on the dog cart, became nauseated whenever they travelled at more than walking pace, so they were lucky to manage 6. Then there were other delays—fractious horses, torrential rain, swollen rivers, boggy roads—which made their progress agonisingly slow. William, at his desk in Sydney, complained that they were taking too long and spending too much money.

Emma kept a detailed diary, knowing that her adventures were likely to be of interest to family and friends back home. This eventually provided the basis for a book, which she published anonymously as *My Experiences in Australia*, by 'A Lady'. She also took with her a sketchbook, brushes and paint, which she used to capture scenes and events on the way. Somewhere along the Hunter River valley they camped beside a creek, long enough for her to sketch their complete entourage. There are eight members of the party: Allan, Emma and Jessie; a maidservant and nurse, Ellen Cunnison, who had accompanied them from Scotland; a manservant and his wife, whom they had retained in Maitland, and who also have a child; and a lad whom Emma describes as 'the son of a connection of my husband's'. Emma includes herself in the landscape, in broad-brimmed hat, and facing little Jessie—perhaps they have been picking flowers, one of Jessie's favourite amusements. Behind them is a tent of 'very comfortable dimensions', which serves as their bedroom and manages to keep them dry, even during a downpour. Allan, bewhiskered, and holding some tool or utensil, stands at the right besides the baggage cart, which is where the manservant and his wife and child lay their mattresses. The woman, who serves as cook, is probably bending over the fire, while Ellen, standing alongside the saucepan and water jug, looks on. The manservant, whose main responsibility is to drive the cart, is in the background beside the creek. Perhaps he is holding the hand of his child, who is otherwise missing from the picture. In the foreground at the left, seated on a log, is the young lad. This is none other than

Allan Williams' second son and namesake, now aged seventeen, whom Emma says is 'desirous of seeing something of bush life, with the hopes of some day becoming a squatter himself'. His elder brother, William, has lately left his grandfather's home with similar objectives, and now the visitors from Scotland have provided young Allan Williams with the opportunity he has been waiting for. The dog cart is in the background, with the canvas arranged so as to provide a complete cover down to the ground. This is Ellen's sleeping quarters, while Allan Williams throws his oilcloth on the earth beneath. The four horses, a constant source of trouble, graze untethered in the distance.

Emma quickly adapted to life in the bush, where 'the vastness and stillness of these primeval forests formed such a pleasant contrast to the

Encampment in the Bush, watercolour by Emma Macpherson, 1856. Several days into their journey, Emma captured the party as they camp in a clearing alongside a creek flowing into the Hunter River. MITCHELL LIBRARY, STATE LIBRARY OF NEW SOUTH WALES

Keera homestead, watercolour by Emma Macpherson, 1856–57. Perhaps intentionally, Emma has painted their humble bush cottage on notepaper embossed with their mansion house in far away Blairgowrie. MUNRO FAMILY COLLECTION

bustle and petty worries of a town life'. She delighted in waking to the 'chattering and chirping of the birds', extolled the 'wonderful clearness' of the Australian atmosphere, and even conceded that the thickly wooded mountains were more beautiful than the Grampians back in Scotland. 'English eyes', she wrote,

> may miss the bright green foliage of the trees of their own land; but to mine, which had been so long accustomed to the darker hues of our Scottish fir woods, the sombre tints of these trees, which are mostly of the *Eucalyptus* tribe, wore a home-like aspect.

She did *not* like the mosquitoes and swarms of sandflies, nor having to take the reins of the dog cart when Allan was needed to coax the reluctant horses to pull the dray. But overall she enjoyed the open-air life 'exceedingly'. Allan, the old hand, was less enthusiastic. Much to his embarrassment, he suffered from bouts of tic douloureux, a painful nervous disorder that made him more than usually irritable. His main objective was to get what he could for the properties and head for home.

After a month on the road they reached Keera. The rains had transformed the valley, and even Allan had to admit that he had never seen the station in better condition. Emma was rhapsodic: 'A prettier little spot could hardly be imagined'. She had to admit, though, that the cottage where they were to live looked more like a barn than a mansion and was desperately in need of repair. Set just back from the creek, it was typical of its kind—long and low, with a veranda extending from end to end. The four best rooms opened onto the veranda, with three more facing a courtyard at the rear. The kitchen and servants' quarters were, in the usual fashion, separate from the main residence. In front her husband had laid out a garden, with familiar English trees and bushes—conifers, roses, verbenas, geraniums and annuals. The surrounding fence was partly covered with a passion vine, now in flower, while beyond the formal garden there were apricots, peaches, nectarines and melons, all promising a healthy crop. There was a vineyard, too, probably planted by Allan and improved by the elder Allan Williams, who had previously enjoyed some success with wine growing experiments in the Hunter Valley.

By the time they arrived at Keera, Emma was about seven months pregnant. The nearest doctor lived 100 miles away, so he was summoned to be in attendance from a fortnight or so before her expected confinement. A healthy boy was born in mid-January 1857, and in defiance of family tradition was named Alan, with only one letter 'l'. It was now the heat of summer, with the thermometer sometimes reaching 106 degrees in the shade; nevertheless, Emma had no choice but to help out with domestic chores that would have been unthinkable back home, even having to try her hand at cooking and sewing the children's clothes.

These she managed with fortitude, only complaining that they took her away from more appropriate and enjoyable 'intellectual pursuits', such as reading and painting. A greater challenge was to maintain social distinctions that back home were taken for granted. Here it was universally acknowledged that *'the servant* is greater than his lord'; and while she might cling to a refined notion of upstairs and downstairs, it was hard to keep them apart when everyone was obliged to 'muck in'. 'Life in the bush is really a trial for any lady', she reflected; 'yet had the first home of my married life been our wild bush station, I can believe I might have been happy in it, and even become in time a notable housewife.' For the moment she was content to rough it and enjoy the adventure, safe in the knowledge that they would soon be back in their 'home in fair Perthshire'.

Allan, having experienced nearly a decade of roughing it, was less amenable. His affection for New South Wales while he was away from it had disappeared. 'We *hate* this Colony and everything in it so much that we will certainly not remain an hour longer in it than we can help.' As in the past, his main anxieties related to his workers. But where he had once been plagued by men who were fractious and uppity, now the problem was to get any workers at all. What he had not been prepared for when he sailed from Britain was the impact of the gold rushes, which forced squatters to pay what they considered to be outrageous wages even for lowly shepherds. A neighbour and his wife had been forced to look after the sheep themselves.

A month after they reached Keera, the station 'establishment' was eleven men, as well as young Allan Williams and the man and wife from Sydney. One of the eleven was an old man who looked after the garden and vineyard; another was directing the pressing of the wool, as the sheep had just been shorn. The remaining nine were shepherds. As the station was unfenced except for the cottage and vineyard, and a few cattle yards and holding paddocks, their role was indispensable. Together they had charge of about 12,000 sheep.

Four of the shepherds were whites, two Chinese, and three Aboriginal. The Chinese had been attracted to the Australian colonies, like many of their countrymen, by the rush for gold, but had found they could succeed better away from the diggings. Allan paid each shepherd what he thought he was worth and what he could negotiate. One of the Europeans received 30 shillings a week and the other three 20 shillings, in each case with rations added. The two Chinese were paid on average more cash (35 and 28 shillings), but probably looked after their own rations:

> I tried in vain yesterday to induce a sickly Chinaman at the diggings to hire on reasonable terms[,] he asked fifty shillings a week but said as he was sick he would take thirty-five shillings. Of course I did not hire him, but each moment I am in terror of hearing of the loss of a flock by the Blacks.

This did not mean, as it might have done in the past, that he feared the blacks would attack and kill his flocks, but rather that one of his Aboriginal shepherds might abandon his sheep and lose them in the bush.

In the fifteen years since he had first come to Keera, the local Aborigines had been transformed from a threat to his sheep and cattle to an essential

The Blacks' Camp, watercolour by Emma Macpherson, 1856–57. There appear to be thirteen or fourteen people in the painting, including, on the right next to the swamp oak, one or two children. Many contemporary observers remarked that the numbers of children were declining. MUNRO FAMILY COLLECTION

part of his workforce. As well as tending the flocks, they were given jobs searching for lost horses, rounding up stray cattle, and helping in the garden and vineyard. One acted as a stockkeeper, another as what Emma called 'a sort of groom', whose jobs included running errands and taking letters to catch the Sydney mail. Allan paid the Aboriginal shepherds just 10 shillings a week, which he explained by pointing out that they needed twice the rations of the Europeans to feed and clothe their gins. For most of the other jobs they were given food, which, said Emma, was all that they wanted. Occasionally she tried to get two of the black women to do their washing for them, 'but all services, though duly paid for, they looked upon as so many favours conferred'. After her baby was born she trained a young woman to carry him when she went out for a stroll and to walk with him up and down the veranda while she relaxed with a book or wrote in her diary. But she never trusted the girl sufficiently to let the baby out of her sight.

Emma was innately curious. Also, her education and upbringing encouraged a spirit of inquiry in relation to everything exotic and new. So she was 'naturally very anxious' to learn all she could about 'this strange race'. In the evenings, she and Allan visited the Aboriginal camp, where Allan struck up a conversation (in a common vernacular) with 'some of the more sociable individuals' and tried to extract from them any information that would interest his wife; 'but they were very chary', Emma admitted, 'in communicating anything touching their ways and customs'. That did not stop her and Allan from seizing the rare chance to observe a corroboree, though they were sufficiently sensitive of the occasion to keep at 'a respectful distance'. Her observations were often sympathetic, and rarely censorious. Although she shared the common understanding of the time that the Australian Aborigines occupied 'the lowest place among the human race', she fancied that very few of her compatriots 'ever felt more kindly towards the natives than I did'. She even thought of them as friends, a title that she rarely extended to colonists, who were apt to abuse the privilege by becoming excessively familiar.

The blacks' camp was situated about a quarter of a mile from the cottage, though Emma observed that they never stayed in exactly the same place for long. When she arrived, she counted just eight or ten men, women and children 'who belonged to that neighbourhood, or to use their own phrase looked on Keera as their *tourai*, the little domain which belonged to them and they to it'. In other words, they regarded the valleys and mountains where they had lived and roamed from time immemorial as their home. Emma's acknowledgment of this attachment might seem odd, given that her husband had long regarded the property as *his* domain, had named and mapped it, and had spent so many years improving it. But, intentionally or not, she was reflecting the official policy, as enunciated by the Secretary of State for the Colonies in 1848, that the land should be shared: that pastoral leases should not deprive the natives of their traditional rights to hunt or to wander over the lands in search of subsistence 'from the spontaneous produce of the soil', excepting only those lands that were used for cultivation or fenced for that purpose. Squatters and Aborigines were supposed to enjoy 'mutual rights' over the lands they occupied; and the Secretary of State believed a 'distinct understanding' of those rights would assist in maintaining order and forbearance. Emma echoed this view, declaring that it was in the squatter's own interest that he 'cultivate a good understanding with the surrounding tribes'.

The small band who camped near the cottage were soon joined by others, attracted perhaps by the prospect of obtaining food, tobacco and alcohol. Emma concluded that they remembered her husband's generosity in previous years—which might well have been true: for while Allan had been capable of hunting down and shooting those who attacked his sheep and cattle, he was equally likely to act as friend and protector to those whom he regarded as loyal. Before long there were about thirty or forty Aborigines living on the property and participating intermittently in station life.

These were all Kamilaroi people, members of a large language group whose traditional lands stretched west from the Great Dividing Range, covering much of the colony's north. No one knew how numerous they were when Europeans had first invaded their territories in the 1830s; no one doubted, though, that their numbers, like those of Aborigines throughout the colony, had dramatically fallen. Early estimates suggested that they numbered well into the thousands. But in 1851 Richard Bligh, the Crown Lands Commissioner for the Gwydir District, which covered about half the Kamilaroi lands, calculated that there were just 410 individuals living in the whole region. Many of the deaths in earlier years could be put down to violence between blacks and whites. Now the worst violence had moved with the moving frontier beyond the Gwydir District, so that Commissioner Bligh could report that all the tribes in the region were now 'perfectly peaceful and harmless', except for 'a few indomitable spirits' in the far west, who refused to have anything to do with the invaders. Yet the population continued to fall, with many deaths and scarcely any births. Bligh attributed the high mortality to illnesses, including syphilis and inflammation of the lungs, introduced by Europeans. He offered no explanation for the scarcity of births.

The Commissioner reported that the Kamilaroi were divided into 'tribes', each of which was attached to a particular locality. The smallest, which he called the 'Wouraferi', lived near Keera. Perhaps these were the people whom Emma painted in their camp beside the river, seated around their fires and clad in their possum skin cloaks. She did not give a name to the blacks she regarded as her friends, but she knew that they were dying. The evidence was there in the well-maintained burial ground, which she insisted on seeing despite the warnings of her black guide. She assumed their dwindling numbers were due in part to infanticide, as well as to frequent domestic feuds which resulted in violent deaths.

Both she and Allan observed that drink was becoming a problem. Whenever there was a corroboree, they were anxious that something might go wrong; and on one occasion, after a night of carousing, one of the men from the camp entered the cottage. Emma noticed that alcohol often fuelled dissensions in the camp, and that in such cases 'the poor gins come very badly off'. But there was nothing remarkable in this colony about drinking too much, so Emma did not ask herself if intoxication within the blacks' camp might disguise a deeper malaise.

On the face of it, the black and white communities lived together in reasonable harmony, each dependent on the other in different ways. In mid-February Allan summoned all available hands to help with wine making. The old gardener, three blacks and little Jessie were put to work picking grapes; Emma and her servant Ellen removed the bad ones from the bunches; Allan, much to everyone's amusement, took off his shoes and trousers and crushed the grapes in a makeshift vat; and young Allan Williams and a visiting neighbour strained the liquid into the kegs. They made a hogshead and a half in a day, the equivalent of over 600 pint-size bottles, and were delighted when a gentleman who appeared knowledgeable about such matters pronounced their wine the best he had tasted of that year's vintage.

Allan and Emma raised a toast to their achievements. They had plenty to celebrate: an adequate return from the shearing season, abundant crops of grapes and stone fruit, a successful experiment in wine making, the birth of a healthy son and, at last, a prospective buyer for Keera.

WILLIAM DECIDES WHERE HOME IS

Allan had hoped to get at least £10,000 for Keera, including the sheep and cattle. He was eventually offered £8000, which was disappointing; but he was in no position to bargain. For Mount Abundance he hoped for £5000 but was offered a little over £3300. In the end he was relieved just to be rid of it.

The goods and chattels at Keera were to remain there, so Allan and Emma decided to hold an auction. Almost everything was to go: thirty or so horses, a blacksmith's bellows, two anvils and a vice, twelve bullock bows, four old guns, saucepans, garden tools and a wheelbarrow, bottles of pickles, several quarter casks of wine, and the rocking chair that once graced the veranda as a symbol of the squatter's ambitions. They even sold the child's cot and bassinet that they had brought with them from Sydney six months earlier. Twenty bidders came, most or all of them presumably living within a day's ride of Keera, suggesting how much the district had changed since Allan had first settled there. The auction yielded £651/13/9.

A week later they were ready to go. Both were sad leaving a home they would surely never see again. Allan reflected wistfully on what might

have been. Emma regretted leaving 'such a very pretty spot' that had been her baby's birthplace; and 'there was such a weeping and wailing, too, among the tribe of Blacks assembled to witness our departure, that I could not help feeling somewhat sorry to wish them good bye'. Like most of her white contemporaries, she expected that within a few generations the race would be extinct, which added perhaps to the poignancy of her farewells.

They expected to travel fast and light, taking just the dog cart and horses for riding. Allan estimated it would take them ten days but, owing to torrential rains and bad roads, the journey dragged on for six weeks. Instead of retracing their steps, they travelled east to the New England plateau, then south to Tamworth and the Hunter. With a newborn baby there was now no prospect of camping, so they took advantage of the famous bush hospitality and stayed at squatters' homesteads and cottages along the way. This time there were fewer members of the party: Allan, Emma and the children, Emma's Scottish maidservant and a male servant. Young Allan Williams stayed behind, as he had always intended to do, having found employment with Keera's new owner.

As they plodded through the mud, they looked towards Sydney with unbounded enthusiasm; or, at least, it would have been unbounded but for the nagging recollection that certain matters had been left unresolved, especially relating to 'the odious creature', William's housekeeper. Once again, there was the urgent problem of where to lodge. Allan Williams confessed that a long stay in his modest cottage would be something of a trial. But Allan was undeterred, convinced that any discomfort (presumably for Allan Williams and his family a well as themselves) would be a small price to pay for avoiding unpleasantness under his father's roof. So on arrival at Circular Quay they made straight for Cooks River, intending to remain there until all the colonial business was done.

Well before they reached Sydney, William had made a decision. Despite his long-held plan to return to his ancestral home, the difficulties of doing so seemed insurmountable. Apart from his reluctance to undertake the long voyage and then acclimatise to bitter Scottish winters, he had no intention of sacrificing his domestic arrangements; and if Mrs Egan could not be made comfortable in Blairgowrie, then nor could he. Allan, writing to Aunt Harriot, put it bluntly: the only chance of his father coming home was if 'the woman' should die, which was highly unlikely unless she should drink herself to death. This (he implied) was a tantalising possibility, though slight. For the benefit of friends and acquaintances in Scotland, he simply reported that his father had become 'so perfectly wedded to Australian life & habits that I fear there is now but little hope of his accompanying me home'.

At least that matter was resolved, albeit unhappily. Issues relating to property remained. Just as Allan had feared, his father was hinting that he might settle more on Mrs Egan. How much was unclear. William seemed evasive about his colonial assets, including the proceeds of the recent sales of Keera and Mount Abundance. What was more alarming was that he had not transferred the Blairgowrie estate to Allan, and that he was yet to make a will. Allan did not put this down to his father harbouring any ill feeling towards him, but rather to 'the procrastination and inaptitude for business (which I found at Blairgowrie from old correspondence) which so hampered my grandfather in his latter days'. In other words, he feared that history might be repeating itself.

The family remained at Cooks River for over three months. For much of this time Allan was in Melbourne, finding a tenant for the property north of the city, which his father seemed willing to transfer to him.

Crossing the Hunter in a flood, watercolour by Emma Macpherson, 1857. Although the flood waters have receded sufficiently to allow the river to be forded, Allan and Emma and their party make use of the whaleboat that serves at such times as a ferry. Allan appears to be standing, while Emma, her maidservant and the two children sit near the dogcart at the stern. The horses wait on the opposite bank and, further along, a solitary (and probably imaginary) kangaroo sits watching. MITCHELL LIBRARY, STATE LIBRARY OF NEW SOUTH WALES

During his weeks in Sydney he visited William often, always staying clear of the housekeeper and doing his best to avoid discussing controversial topics. Nevertheless, relations between father and son were cooling, especially after Allan Williams reported that William had been seen with Mrs Egan at the theatre. When Allan, Emma and the two children embarked at Circular Quay in mid-September 1857, Allan Williams and William Forster were there to see them off, while Allan's father pointedly stayed at home.

This time they were to travel by steamer to Ceylon and on to Aden, then overland to join another steamer at Port Said for the final voyage home. After leaving Sydney, they paused at Melbourne, which Emma decided was a better place for making fortunes than enjoying them once made, and which gave her cause to reflect that 'there is no place like the old country to form one's home in'. Before heading on to the Indian Ocean, the steamer stopped briefly at the port of Albany in King George's Sound, in the far south-west of the continent, where they seized the chance of a few hours on dry land. 'On the shore', wrote Emma, 'some fifteen or twenty of the original inhabitants were assembled to do us honour, or rather to see what begging could extract from these invaders of their native soil.' She and Allan joined the ship's doctor and two or three other passengers in exploring the surrounding hills, and from the summit of one of them she sketched the town and harbour. The spring wildflowers were in bloom and Emma was enchanted with them. She and another lady picked large bouquets; but Allan, 'less easily satisfied', pulled up many by their roots, intending to add them to their collection of Australian plants and seeds. Of course, the plants never reached home.

14

MATTERS OF PRINCIPLE

WHEN THE MACPHERSON FAMILY—ALLAN, EMMA, LITTLE JESSIE and baby Alan—steamed out of Sydney Cove at the start of their long journey home, they passed a small island that had been known since the colony's beginnings as Pinchgut, after some hungry convicts who had been forced to spend time there. Over the past two years the barren rocky outcrop had been transformed into an impressive fortress, with two 10-inch cannons and a dozen smaller ones positioned so as to defend the inner harbour against enemy intruders. Exactly who those intruders might be was uncertain. In the mid-1850s colonists lived in fear of the Russians, who

Fort Denison, Sydney, sepia wash by Conrad Martens, c 1858, looking down the harbour from Bennelong Point. NATIONAL LIBRARY OF AUSTRALIA

were fighting the British and French in the Crimea; but by the time the guns were ready to fire, the Russians had been beaten, leaving no obvious threat except perhaps the perfidious French and the fickle Americans. Nevertheless, the fortifications remained as a warning to any potential enemy that the inhabitants of Sydney (supported by a garrison of soldiers from the motherland) were ready to stand their ground.

Fort Denison, as the island was soon renamed for the colony's Governor, also served to remind voyagers such as Allan Macpherson that certain things in life had to be stoutly defended. Here, it was a thriving colony, and the rights and liberties of a community of Britons abroad; but other things had to be guarded too, including individual rights of property, and matters of principle. Allan Macpherson was a man of property and principle; and if either were threatened, or both (for they often went hand in hand), he could be relied upon to defend them with all guns blazing.

UNFINISHED BUSINESS

In Allan's view, the immediate threats were obvious: the housekeeper's designs on his rightful inheritance and his father's incapacity, through weakness or senility, to resist them. Property and principle were at issue. The main property was the Blairgowrie estate; but there was also Bernera, a 1000 acre allotment near Liverpool, west of Sydney, which Allan had purchased in 1850 and then mortgaged to William. The overriding principle was the traditional right of an only son (for in such matters Allan Williams, as a natural son, did not count) to inherit his father's estate; and there were other principles relating to morality, propriety and the family's place in society. With so much at stake, there was the potential for a family feud, which could be vicious and costly.

Allan, back home in Blairgowrie, learned from his friend Forster that the old man and his housekeeper had again been seen together at the theatre. There were even rumours, wrote Forster, that the two were privately married. Faced with the prospect of his inheritance slipping away before him, Allan prepared for his father's signature a series of documents intended to remove ambiguity about who owned what, and specifically to ensure that he would have undisputed right to the Blairgowrie estate. In return, he would surrender his claim to Bernera. This had an effect opposite to the one he intended. William was now in his mid-seventies and in rapid physical decline. But, as Forster discovered when he gently broached the subject of Allan's inheritance over coffee in Parliament House, the old man was mentally as sharp as ever. While he might be unsteady on his feet, he was every bit as capable as his son of defending what he considered to be *his* rights and interests. Rather than yielding to Allan's proposals, he delivered an ultimatum that if the Bernera land were not transferred to him unconditionally by a specified date, he would be on the next ship home, with the object of putting Blairgowrie on the market.

It seemed that Allan's worst fears might be realised. Apart from the horror of his father returning with his housekeeper, the estate might be lost to him forever. Blairgowrie was a valuable asset, now worth at least £40,000, and yielding £1700 a year. Whatever might eventuate in negotiations with his father, he would surely get a large share of the proceeds from any sale. But it was not just the money that concerned him. The estate had assumed for him a much larger value, in the same way, he told Emma, that Warren Hastings' ancestral home in Worcestershire had become that great man's ruling passion in his later years. If the estate were sold, 'the *object* of my life would be defeated'.

Some compromise seemed unavoidable. He therefore responded to his father in a tone intended to be conciliatory, stating that he would freely hand over Bernera, provided that William wound up his affairs in New South Wales and returned to Scotland, unaccompanied by the person who had been the real, *if unintentional* cause of so much trouble. This, he told Forster, was as far as he was prepared to go. To carry filial respect any further would be to sacrifice his own responsibilities as a husband and father. If William arrived in Scotland still determined to sell the estate, Allan was prepared to *fight*. 'In other words, I'll throw the whole [dispute] into Chancery in England, Scotland and NSW simultaneously, in various forms.' He was ready 'for a terrible legal warfare—which may outlive me—let alone my Father—but anyway *open war* is better than a truce which I firmly believe would not last six months *if my Father remained under Mrs. Egan's influence'*.

In reality, though, neither party had any taste for prolonged conflict; and the long delay between the despatch and receipt of letters allowed time for tempers to cool. Allan, when he reflected on the situation, realised that he was in no position to bargain. He could hardly continue as laird of Blairgowrie while his father retained the title deeds, and his income from the estate was scarcely sufficient to maintain the trappings and dignity of his station. So when he received from his father a letter which he took to be milder in tone, he decided that reconciliation was possible, on the understanding that he need have nothing to do with 'the odious woman' and that his father would not mention her name in correspondence.

Allan concluded that the only way of settling the differences once and for all was for him to return to Australia. This would mean leaving Emma and the children—now increased to four with the birth of another boy, Charles—behind, and living for a time in voluntary exile. But he might get a job in Sydney, and then the family might follow, and they might make a life together in Australia until his inheritance was secure. So he booked a passage on the next mail steamer, telling no one except Forster that he was coming, so that 'the enemy', Mrs Egan, had no time to prepare her defences.

The strategy worked. Arriving in Sydney in mid-1860, Allan embraced his father affectionately and the two sat down to negotiate arrangements satisfactory to both. Discussions proceeded amicably and quickly, for really there was only one matter at issue: how much should Mrs Egan receive in William's will. William had no hesitation in confirming that the bulk of the estate, including the properties at Blairgowrie and Bernera, should go to Allan. Allan Williams was to receive a legacy of £1000, and each of his children, along with Mrs Egan's son Patrick, £100. Mrs Egan

Allan and Emma Macpherson at Blairgowrie in late 1857 or early 1858, soon after their return from Australia, with Willie, baby Alan and Jessie. MACPHERSON COLLECTION

herself was to receive £200 a year, as well as being entitled to live in William's house during her lifetime and to have absolute possession of all the furniture, 'such', said Allan, 'as it is'.

The provisions for the Williams family seemed to Allan perfectly fair; and indeed, he had promised as much to Allan Williams should their father die intestate. The arrangements for Mrs Egan, though, seemed over-generous. Two hundred a year would have been quite sufficient for 'a person in her position', without the house as well. But as he and his father were now good friends again, he had no intention of upsetting their hard-won harmony. In any case, he had now decided that, as his father had made his money, 'if he likes to make ducks & drakes of it he has some sort of right to do so'. This was an astonishing turnaround, an implicit recognition that other principles needed to be taken into account besides his own. Was he mellowing with age? Or worn down by attrition? 'I really do not know and don't much care about anything more', he told Aunt Harriot.

But, as he well knew, there was need for perpetual vigilance. While his inheritance appeared to be secure, Mrs Egan could still influence William while he was living. There was no telling, said Allan, what his father would do next. 'His infatuation about that wretched woman is perfectly amazing.' When, in his crueller moments, he suspected that his father was senile, his friend Forster consoled him with the observation that:

> conditions of mind may exist, especially in very old men, which render very doubtful their moral responsibility on certain points and within a given sphere of subjects, these being moreover generally such as most affect the interests of their nearest relatives.

Allan's grandfather, the Colonel, had certainly behaved erratically in his later years; and his father's behaviour was confirming Forster's theory. And now, as if more proof were needed, Allan received news from London that his father's brother, the Reverend Mr Allan Macpherson, had behaved in ways that threatened to tarnish irreparably the family's good name.

By the mid-1850s, Uncle Allan had served for two decades as Vicar of Holy Trinity Church in the Parish of Rothwell in Northamptonshire.

Such dedication gave the lie to his parents' worries, when he and William had been in the West Indies, that he might not be steady enough to make his way in the world. Yet now the life of a country curate was starting to pall, especially perhaps after he had lost his second wife and a daughter. Whatever the reason, he discovered that there were other ways of contributing to society (and improving his own situation) than as a servant of God. Improvement was the talk of the age—in manufacturing, agriculture and transport—and people everywhere seemed to be exercising their ingenuity and getting rich. The Vicar of Rothwell decided that he too should keep up with the times.

Around 1853 Uncle Allan evidently sought leave from his Bishop to visit the Continent, where he learned about numerous inventions that were sure to help people in cities live healthier and happier lives. These included devices for purifying gas, improving gas burners and lamps, and disinfecting sewers and drains. Allan recognised that there was money to be made by purchasing certain patents, and then selling them to manufacturers. But as he had no other income beyond his living as a clergyman, he would need to borrow. Fortunately, the local bank of Gotch & Sons at Kettering, a town just a few miles from Rothwell, was willing to help. Old Mr Gotch had died, but the son who ran the bank was especially attracted by the Vicar's determination, enthusiasm and honesty, and promised to support his enterprises. Soon Allan was investing in lead mines and state quarries, and planning schemes such as manufacturing of peat charcoal which, when mixed with nightsoil, would produce over 6 tons of manure and realise a clear profit of £10 a ton.

The ideas flowed and so did the money, but only in one direction. When the Gotch brothers began to worry, he reassured them 'as a gentleman and a clergyman' that all would be well, so long as they continued to meet his requests. Success was always just around the corner. His gas burner patent, for example, had attracted the interest of foreign gentlemen of the highest respectability, including the Marquis of St Armand, a member of the ancient nobility of France with 'very considerable estates', who now occupied his time with improvements of various kinds. 'I feel every day more confident', he told his bankers, 'of the complete success of my undertaking under the continued blessing of Him without whose aid nothing can do well.' In 1855 he retired from his parish and moved to Belgium, desiring the Messrs Gotch to address him now as 'Mons. Macpherson' rather than 'the Reverend Mr Macpherson', as he had not brought his clerical designation with him to Europe and was engaged in secular business.

By 1856 he had broken the bank, having borrowed the enormous sum of £25,000. The Gotch brothers were hauled before the Court of Bankruptcy, where Allan's follies were spelled out in embarrassing detail. The bankrupts could scarcely plead that he had not kept them informed. Over a period of four and a half years he had sent them 495 letters, many of them very detailed. The attorney for the assignees (the managers of the bankrupts' estate) declared what everyone in the courtroom no doubt thought: that 'It was incredible that any sane man could be misled by the rubbish written by this person, who was a scandal to his order'. Among the bank's creditors were sixty-six 'sick clubs' and benefit societies, as well as many individuals who had been reduced from a state of comfort to one of poverty. The Gotch brothers were obviously guilty of gross negligence; but the 'reverend personage' himself, as 'a refugee' living in Brussels, was beyond the pale of the law.

How much brother William and nephew Allan knew of their relative's misconduct and disgrace is not clear. Presumably the younger Allan was not aware of it in 1856, when he was worrying about what his uncle might think about his father's indiscretions with his housekeeper in Sydney. In 1858, though, when he and Emma were back in Britain, they could scarcely miss the excruciating reports from the Court of Bankruptcy that appeared in the London newspapers for all to see. At least Uncle Allan was safely out of sight on the Continent, so they could try to put him out of mind as well.

But there was worse to come. Soon after the younger Allan had arrived back in New South Wales with the object of making peace with his father, he heard the shocking news that his uncle had fathered a child in Rothwell (though there was allegedly some doubt about the child's paternity). Whether this had happened before he left England in 1855, or during some later visit, is not clear. In 1860 Uncle Allan and the child's mother were married and living a hand to mouth existence somewhere in England, presumably surviving inconspicuously on his clergyman's pension of £150 a year and handouts from Aunt Harriot. Unsurprisingly, young Allan was appalled by his uncle's 'inexpressible act of folly' and insisted that Emma should have 'nothing whatever' to do with his wife, 'either directly or indirectly'. Neither he nor his father were able to help out with money. 'I am sorry for my Uncle poor old man', he told her; '—there is a great deal of genuine

Uncle Allan in Paris in 1863, the year before his death.
MACPHERSON COLLECTION

kindness about him—but his utter lack of the smallest fragment of the commonest of common sense makes him in my opinion entirely removed from the list of *responsible* human beings'.

And that ought to have been that. A year later though, Aunt Harriot, having already parted with £1000, decided that she had reached her limit and suggested that her brother and his wife and little boy should emigrate to New South Wales, where William and Allan would be able to look after them. This was out of the question. Allan, having been confronted with the prospect of his father and housekeeper returning to Scotland and putting the family to shame, now had to imagine his uncle committing a comparable or worse offence in the opposite direction. He wrote back quickly, explaining to Aunt Harriot that, owing to Mrs Egan's excessive temper, Uncle Allan and his family would not survive a month under the same roof without violent quarrels, and that a separate residence in New South Wales would be at least as expensive as in any part of Europe. That put an end to the matter.

In the last recorded meeting between Aunt Harriot and her brother Allan in March 1862, he scarcely had any clothes to wear. It was melancholy, she said, to see a brother in such a pitiable state. But he had broken the rules and had to pay the consequences.

> I spoke openly and plainly to him about his wife! He *assured* me all was right as to virtue & *respectability* of Character—I told him I was glad to hear that, & I hoped she would in every respect make him an affec^te & attentive wife—but that she

could not expect me, or any of his Relatives to meet her or associate with her …

He talked of going to the Continent to live more cheaply. Harriot gave him six shirts and £5, and expected never to see him again. He died in Paris in 1864, aged in his mid-seventies.

Young Allan, when he heard the news of his uncle's death, was still in Australia. Having achieved a reconciliation with his father, he was not about to risk his inheritance by returning to Scotland. A short trip to Melbourne in 1860 to attend to his properties there reminded him of what could go wrong. While he was away, 'the enemy' had been at work, 'making the house unusually hideous by her howlings at my Fathers horrible inhumanity on having only allowed her the house and [a] poor £200 a year'. Back in Sydney, he reported that the woman was still trying to cause trouble, which he mostly avoided by refusing to have anything to do with her; and although the occasional meeting was inevitable, he assured Emma that '*nothing earthly will induce me to shake hands with her or her son*'. William complained about his son's superciliousness, but Allan stood his ground.

Resigning himself to a long period of 'banishment', Allan prepared himself to make the best of it. First he had to decide how and where to live. Gone were the days of extravagance. As a family man, he was determined to live frugally and avoid borrowing against his future inheritance. To save money he decided to set up house at Bernera, which was now within easy reach of the metropolis by train: the journey to Liverpool took an hour and a half, travelling 'cheap and nasty always 3rd class', and was followed by a brisk 3-mile walk. This seemed just the right distance—close enough to town to allow him to monitor the housekeeper's scheming, but far enough away to limit the chance of unpleasant encounters. The property was well watered and suitable for cultivating fruit and vegetables and dairy farming, promising a sufficient, if far from lavish income; and there was already a small cottage there, with a bedroom, sitting room and storerooms. There was no ceiling, the shingle roof leaked, and the kitchen had an earthen floor. Nevertheless, Allan persuaded himself that he could live there in comfort; and, though not in so many words, he made it clear to Mrs Egan that she had as much chance of stepping onto his veranda as of passing through the front door of Buckingham Palace.

He was missing Emma and the children terribly. Fortunately for him, Emma was missing him equally, and when he begged her to come she was quick to follow, bringing with her this time all four children, as well as a cook and maidservant. In preparation for their arrival, he embarked on major renovations and extensions to the cottage, which was soon transformed into a sixteen-room timber residence, with a long veranda and a corrugated iron roof. Although it was nothing to compare with the grandeur of Blairgowrie, it was a reasonable colonial substitute, where Allan could maintain a respectable lifestyle as a gentleman farmer, keep a carriage and dog cart, and resume his customary role as local dignitary. He planted several acres of oranges and other fruit trees, with potatoes, pumpkins and melons in between, and a quarter of an acre of grapes. By 1862 the family was happily settled there, and prepared to stay for all of William's remaining years.

William, who was now approaching eighty, had only recently retired as Clerk of the Legislative Council, an office he had held for over two

Bernera Cottage, near Liverpool, west of Sydney. Allan Macpherson designed and built the residence in 1861 to accommodate Emma and the children. One of the wings at the rear was probably the original cottage. Emma painted this watercolour before she left the colony in 1868. MITCHELL LIBRARY, STATE LIBRARY OF NEW SOUTH WALES

decades. In 1856, when the colonists were granted a new constitution that gave them more power to govern themselves, he feared that he might lose his job; but old friends came to the rescue and he survived the transition. By 1860, though, there was evidently a feeling that it was time for him to go, and when the President of the Council tapped him on the shoulder, he promptly (if somewhat indignantly) resigned. The Council passed a resolution commending his distinguished and exemplary service, and friends commissioned the half-length portrait reproduced in the first chapter of this book.

In retirement, as in his working life, he remained a man of routine. Each morning he rose at five in summer and six in winter, and spent the day reading, writing letters or attending to business matters. He never seemed short of things to do. Apart from Mrs Egan there were two other members of the household: his grandson Henry, the third boy in Allan Williams' large family, who lived with him until he reached the age of seventeen in 1861, when he followed his two older brothers into the bush; and Mrs Egan's son Patrick, now in his mid-twenties, who was working as a clerk in a solicitor's office. During the week William often visited or received old friends, including his medical man Dr Macfarlane, the Postmaster-General Major Christie and Canon Allwood, the rector of St James' Church. On Saturdays he took an excursion by train or omnibus to places in and around Sydney; and on Sundays he invariably attended divine service in the morning and afternoon at nearby St James', where Canon Allwood upheld the traditional forms of sacramental worship that William favoured, against the evangelical leanings of the day.

At the age of seventy-seven his health, in his own estimation, was very good, though a 'scorbutic eruption' on his left leg refused to go away, and could be treated only by having it constantly wrapped in a poultice of bread and water. He also suffered from severe bouts of lumbago, which he attributed in part to lifting heavy weights as a young man in Berbice. This was the only time in the surviving letters from his years in Australia that he referred to the West Indies, though the presence of Allan Williams and his family ensured that his past life was always with him. His main infirmity was dropsy. This was kept in check by the devoted ministrations of Mrs Egan, who massaged his feet and ankles every evening for two or three hours before he retired to bed, a remedy suggested by another close friend, the Catholic Archbishop, John Polding. Neither the Archbishop nor the Canon nor any of his other friends seemed to be much concerned about his relationship with his housekeeper, suggesting that while his attendance at the theatre or excursions on the railway with Mrs Egan might set tongues wagging, they did little or no harm to his reputation among those who knew him.

Every second or third Saturday William caught the morning train to Liverpool station, where Allan and the children met him in the carriage and drove him out to Bernera, returning in time to catch the two o'clock train. Relations between father and son remained harmonious, so long as Mrs Egan stayed out of the way. Allan was certain that she had bewitched his father; but 'great as was her influence she could not persuade him to take the step of marrying her'. Increasingly, said Allan, she neglected and abused him, even beating him in a public street.

Eventually Allan persuaded William to come and live with the family at Bernera, of course leaving Mrs Egan behind. In the final months of his life, he spoke often of the pleasure he had in being there, and the indignities that Mrs Egan had subjected him to in the past. That, at least, is how Allan told the story.

William died at Bernera in 1866 at the age of eighty-two. His friend Deas Thomson, the Colonial Secretary under the former regime, told the Legislative Council that during the thirty years from Mr Macpherson's arrival in the colony until his death 'he believed there had not been any public servant more universally or deservedly respected', which was probably truer than the usual run of tributes on such occasions. As expected, his will left everything to Allan, excepting the legacies that had already been provided for.

But Allan's war was not over yet. Mrs Egan insisted that he was trying to deprive her of her due and took out an affidavit against him; and her son Patrick laid claim to a piano and music stand that he insisted the old man had promised him. This was the limit. Allan was not about to yield to a former cook and a young man who had once blacked the shoes in his father's household. In the event, the dispute was settled out of court, but only after Allan had enlisted his friend the Attorney-General and prepared for a long battle. After all, there were important principles at stake.

POLITICS

Many years earlier, when Allan Macpherson and his friend William Forster had been living lonely lives in separate parts of the Australian bush, Forster

William Macpherson, about the time of his retirement as Clerk of the Legislative Council in 1860, by an unknown photographer. NEW SOUTH WALES PARLIAMENTARY ARCHIVES

had prophesied that 'the destiny of both of us must be literary or political'. If this were to happen, their old schoolmaster, Mr Cape, must receive much of the credit. He had always encouraged his boys to be 'scribbling', as Forster put it; and through a 'school parliament', he had introduced them to the glories and subtleties of the British Constitution and the great political issues of the day. Those issues, in the mid-1830s, included the Constitution itself. Only recently the great *Reform Act* had broadened the franchise beyond the aristocracy and landed gentry, and removed some of the worst abuses of the old regime.

But these reforms had not dispelled the notion that Parliament was the province of gentlemen and, conversely, that gentlemen of property (property being a chief qualification for being a gentleman) should play a role in politics, and perhaps aspire to become members of parliament. Even young gentlemen such as Allan Macpherson and William Forster, located in some of the remotest corners of the empire, could properly look forward to a political career; and while the lofty heights of the House of Commons might be too much to hope for, at least they could reasonably expect to cut a figure on the colonial stage.

If their upbringing gave them the right, the disputes over squatting in the 1840s gave them a cause. Here the 'enemy' was the imperial government and their local representative, the colonial Governor, who were making life hard for them on the land. The squatters, seeing themselves as underdogs, argued their case (and honed their political skills) in newspapers and submissions to the local legislature. By the late 1850s, though, the political landscape had entirely changed. Now the colonists were chiefly responsible for their own affairs, including control over the land. If there was to be an enemy, it was likely to come from within. The new Parliament, as it was now called, was roughly modelled on Westminster, with an upper house (the Legislative Council) nominated by the Governor, and a lower house (the Legislative Assembly) elected on a generous franchise. As in the British Parliament, the leader of the government (styled Premier or Prime Minister and, for a time, Colonial Secretary) was chosen by a majority vote in the Legislative Assembly (modelled on the House of Commons) and was responsible or accountable to that house for the effective conduct of government: hence the system was termed 'responsible government'. Elections for the Assembly were based on a property qualification broad enough to include a majority of men in the colony, but giving voters in the country more influence than those in the city and towns.

The old guard who had drawn up the Constitution had intended that men of property, especially pastoral landholders, should be strong enough to keep democratic tendencies at bay. Within a few years, though, their opponents had won an election and extended the franchise to almost every man in the colony, regardless of what he might own or earn, reduced the weighting given to the pastoral interest, and introduced the secret ballot, so that servants would not be obliged to vote as their masters directed. In a word, the colonists created a democracy; or more precisely, they introduced democratic institutions far more radical than anything yet seen in the old country. All this happened peacefully, though there was no shortage of heated debate and verbal abuse.

Allan Macpherson missed most of the turbulence of these years. When the new Parliament opened in mid-1856, he and Emma were still on the high seas headed on their first voyage together to Sydney; and when they arrived, he was preoccupied with his father's improprieties and disposing of Keera and Mount Abundance. Nevertheless, there was no escaping talk about politics. As Emma soon discovered, apart from interminable discussions about sheep, politics dominated conversation. Everyone seemed to be knowledgeable and everyone had an opinion, including even the ladies (though there was scarcely any talk at this stage of giving them the vote). William Forster was in the thick of it. Now settled at Brush Farm, he had won a seat in the colony's first parliament and was quickly gaining a reputation for speaking his mind. When Allan and the family returned to Scotland after their sojourn in the bush, Forster kept him informed about who was in and who was out, remembering perhaps that politics was Allan's destiny as well as his own, and anticipating that his friend might one day join the fray.

Back in Blairgowrie, Allan had resumed his role as laird, taking an interest in the welfare of the community, supporting worthy causes and acting as patron to various societies, just as his father and grandfather had done before him. Could this be described as politics? Certainly he was winning friends. According to Blairgowrie's newly established newspaper (further evidence that the town had come of age), Mr Macpherson was well known for acts of kindness and goodwill towards the town, such as donating land for a town hall and agreeing to serve as President of the Mechanics' Institution.

Early in 1859 he invited all the members of the local Curling Club to a sumptuous dinner at Blairgowrie House, where he dilated, with the customary balance of wit and earnestness, on the 'moral and social advantages of curling associations'. 'It is a well known fact', he declared, 'that more than half the quarrels and ill-blood which exist in this world, whether between classes or individuals, arise from the fact of these classes and individuals knowing very little of each other.' Curling associations helped bring the classes into 'frequent, kindly, and easy intercourse with each other' and removed the 'unkindly prejudice of class against class'. (This was not meant to imply that the various ranks should be done away with, only that there should be better understanding between them.) He concluded by proposing a toast to 'The Grand Caledonian Curling Club', which was received with 'great enthusiasm'. Then, after further toasts interspersed by a band playing 'appropriate airs', Allan was asked if he and Mrs Macpherson (who of course was not present) would consent to becoming Patron and Patroness of the Blairgowrie Curling Club, to which Allan wittily responded that poor curlers, like himself, were rather like poor politicians who might find themselves elevated to the House of Lords; and as politics had fortuitously been mentioned, he took the opportunity to remark that, while it was considered a high honour to be a member of parliament, municipal authorities could in fact do more good for their fellow men than most legislators. After further mutual compliments, the proceedings concluded with 'Auld Lang Syne' and a final toast to the host and his family. The fifty curlers, well fed and lubricated, poured out of Blairgowrie House a few minutes before midnight, thinking perhaps that, should Mr Macpherson chance to offer himself for the House of Commons as their local member, they would (if they were qualified as electors) be happy to give him their vote.

Allan sent Forster an effusive account of the dinner that appeared in the *Blairgowrie Advertiser*. You'll see, he wrote, that I've been making friends 'if not with the unwashed, with the semi-washed'. 'I sincerely believe all I said'. But if cultivating the curlers had any particular objective, it would have to wait, for a year later he was about to leave for Australia to try to pull his father into line.

When Allan arrived in Sydney in mid-1860 the colony was in political turmoil. There was nothing remarkable about this: indeed, it seemed to have become its usual condition. While the introduction of responsible government had proceeded peacefully, it could scarcely be said to have gone smoothly. Cynics such as Governor Denison had expected the worst from the outset: 'Responsibility', he wrote, 'is in fact a name, a claptrap, meaning nothing but the right of the majority to make fools of themselves to their hearts content'. Within five years of the opening of Parliament the colony had four Premiers and five changes of government. Emulating the way things worked in Westminster, members allied themselves from time to time with the Government or Opposition and often saw themselves as representing conservative or liberal interests. But there was little in the way of party discipline nor, for that matter, any sort of discipline. As a result, parliamentary exchanges were often disorderly and sometimes uproarious.

William Forster told Allan of his 'growing disgust at the hollowness and inefficacy of our present politics'. This was in 1858, when Charles

Cowper, universally known as 'Slippery Charlie', was serving for a second time as Premier and Colonial Secretary. The son of a Church of England clergyman, Cowper was a moderate landholder whom conservatives saw as having betrayed the squatting cause by failing to uphold the rights of property. Now he was the most prominent liberal, popular among the electorate and adept at winning and retaining support in the Assembly. Forster castigated him and his followers as 'wretched mountebanks and charlatans', 'utterly without political principles or at all events devoid of earnest purpose'. In 1859, though, Cowper's numbers turned against him, and the Governor, running out of people to turn to, asked Forster to form a ministry. 'I am Colonial Secretary', he told Allan; but he did not expect to be there long. He prided himself on his principles and independence, choosing as ministers both liberals and conservatives. What he needed, though, were followers; and when the colleagues he had mustered fell away, he resigned, almost enthusiastically, after just four months in office.

Allan had predicted that Forster would one day become Premier, so when he heard in Blairgowrie of his friend's elevation he was not surprised. He arrived in Sydney hoping to find him in office. Perhaps the government would offer him a job; he might even replace his father as Clerk of the Legislative Council. But his timing was bad. Now a new ministry, led by another of Mr Cape's boys, John Robertson, was in power, planning radical reforms that threatened the pastoralists' hold on the land. Colonial politics were thrown into convulsions yet again. The Assembly was dissolved, and towards the end of 1860 voters prepared themselves wearily for another election, the fourth in less than six years.

The opponents of Cowper, now loosely described as 'the conservative party', needed all the help they could get. No sooner had Allan arrived than he was being 'harassed and besieged' by Forster and other old friends to join them. At first he resisted; but the pressures were great, and the attractions of being in government strong. If his party were elected, he would surely be offered a ministry, which would be much more exciting and lucrative than farming at Bernera. So Allan agreed to stand for the seat of Central Cumberland west of Sydney, where Bernera was located, and as soon as the election was called, threw himself into the business of drumming up votes.

This was a brave move. Central Cumberland, as Allan described it, was 'one of the most radical & destructive constituencies in NSW'; and within the electorate, Liverpool was 'the enemy's stronghold'. Five candidates were standing for two seats and Allan was prepared for anything to happen: he might come first or last. As he had been so long out of the colony, and before that resident far from the metropolis, he was little known in the electorate. To have any chance of winning a seat he would have to present himself as often as possible at the hustings and tell voters what he stood for.

If ever he doubted that politics in New South Wales and rural Scotland were worlds apart, his first campaign appearance must have set him straight. When in the previous year he had entertained the Blairgowrie Curling Club, his audience had responded with 'hear, hears' and 'great enthusiasm'. Granted, the curlers were a select group responding to their host's generosity and bonhomie; but had he appeared on the hustings in his home town he might reasonably have expected to be listened to with the respect due to the laird, even by listeners who did not share his opinions. How differently people behaved in New South Wales. As one of the colony's most pungent satirists put it, 'You have no idea … what ferocious savages in handling a gentleman the Natives are in that part of the world'. At a gathering in Parramatta courthouse, some of Allan's remarks were met with 'a storm of hisses and groans' so loud at times that he could not be heard. And when he ventured an opinion on the cost of surveying land, someone from the audience rudely called out, 'What do you know about it?' which led to 'cheers, laughter, and confusion'. In short, the unwashed of New South Wales were a disrespectful and rowdy mob. Unfortunately for the conservatives, almost all of them had the vote.

Allan, though, was not one to quail before the masses. More speeches were to come—fifteen in all during the campaign. Rallying his friends, he organised his own meeting at the Parramatta courthouse. 'I stand before you on principle', he declaimed. 'If you send me into the Assembly I shall give my votes for measures that I approve of and not men.' The immediate issue on which the election was being fought was who should control the land. John Robertson's liberal ministry wanted to allow small farmers to take plots from the vast acreages currently held by the squatters, on the principle of 'free selection before survey'. The conservatives insisted that the future of the pastoral industry depended on the squatters having security of tenure. 'Free selection before survey', Allan declared, 'is the golden image we are commanded to fall down before and worship.' Just as Nebuchadnezzar, the King of Babylon, had cast out all who refused to worship at his idol, so Robertson had already condemned many to the fiery flames. 'But I for one,' said Allan, 'standing on the edge of the gulf—relying on my own conscious honesty and integrity of purpose—appeal from the sentence of Nebuchadnezzar to the intelligence, the justice, and the majesty of the people.'

'Loud and long-continued cheering' followed, after which one of his supporters (whose name also happened to be Macpherson) rose to say that this was the best of the many speeches he had heard in the courthouse. 'There was a *gentleman* before them', he declared; and then proposed: 'That Mr. Allan Macpherson is a fit and proper person to represent the electors of Central Cumberland in the coming Parliament of New South Wales'. The motion was passed with just one hand raised in opposition.

But it was all in vain. When the final votes were counted, Allan came last. It was an ignominious defeat, but he did not take it personally. Across the colony the conservatives had been routed. John Hay, the leader of the party, had managed to retain his seat, but even he had been challenged—by a grave digger! It was a victory, said Allan, for 'insane democracy'. Now the woolgrowers, on whom the prosperity of the colony depended, were at the mercy of the mobs of Sydney. The 'intelligence and respectability

At the hustings. Although this depicts a city electorate a year after Allan Macpherson had left New South Wales, the sketch captures something of the turbulence and enthusiasm that attended elections for the colonial assembly. *Illustrated Sydney News*, 23 December 1869.

of the country' had been overthrown by the 'the lowest and most ignorant body of men who have ever been called together as a legislative body either in New South Wales or in any other British Colony'. 'Such are the results of Universal Suffrage and vote by Ballot—God preserve Great Britain from either the cause or the results.' To make matters worse, the venture had cost him £300, which he was obliged to draw against the Blairgowrie estate. But at least his candidature had brought him to public notice, which would be valuable if he stood again.

His next chance came at a by-election for a Central Cumberland seat in mid-1863, precipitated by the bankruptcy of the sitting member. This time Allan was well prepared. He travelled through the electorate and, with the help of supporters, set up a dozen or so committees to promote his candidature. He paid for advertisements that exalted his own claims and dismissed those of the other candidate. He expounded his principles, chief of which—after the land question had been settled—was the need to restore state aid for religion, which the legislature had lately abolished. This was not a popular cause; but Allan stood his ground against groans of disapproval and 'grotesque clamour'. Despite all his efforts, the vote was close. On the show of hands, his opponent carried the day, forcing Allan to demand a secret ballot. This must have been galling, given his view that secret voting was 'non-Anglo-Saxon'. But the sacrifice of principle was evidently worth it, as the poll was in his favour, allowing him to enter parliament as Member for Central Cumberland.

So Allan joined the Assembly, and quickly adapted to its rumbustious ways. Never lost for words, he proved to be one of its most forceful speakers. In his first contribution (which followed immediately upon one member accusing another of being 'pot-valiant tonight', and the other responding that his accuser was drunk *every* night), he launched an assault on 'the abominable state of the Commission of the Peace', meaning the unpaid magistrates of the colony, some of whom, he said, were so appalling that they would not have been tolerated on the benches of the Southern States of the American Union. This was a familiar subject, as it was widely accepted that successive governments used appointments to the magistracy to bolster their political support, and that many appointees were totally unqualified to sit on local benches. Allan did not mince words:

> A body of men more unfit to fill the offices they hold—a body
> of men more entirely the instruments of the Government

of the day—a body of men more utterly depraved—more utterly corrupt—more utterly ignorant and unfit, do not exist in the world.

(Cries of 'Oh, oh!' and 'scandal!'.)

Here, for Allan, was an issue that symbolised all that was wrong with colonial society. How could justice be fairly administered when a servant could be taken out of livery and made a JP? In another case, a scavenger was appointed to the bench. In his own electorate, a magistrate borrowed half a crown from a poor woman to buy some mutton chops, and when she abused him for not paying her back, he and a brother magistrate had her thrown into Parramatta gaol for thirty days. But what could you expect when magistrates were appointed for political reasons, without any attempt to discover whether they had sufficient means to occupy a position of trust? Allan believed that anyone responsible for administering justice should possess 'a stake in the country'. The same applied to members of parliament. Politics should be left to 'the intelligence and respectability' of society, men of sufficient means to remain independent of party and free of personal interest, men who could be relied on to weigh the great issues of the day with honesty and integrity. In a word, gentlemen.

The problem for Allan was that his own qualifications as a gentleman were fragile (which is partly why his father's indiscretions caused him such anguish). Thankfully, after the reconciliation with William in relation to the inheritance, his credentials as a man of property were secure. His address, 'Bernera, near Liverpool', was sufficient evidence of his stake in the country. But money had always been a concern, and even now he had to be frugal. True gentlemen should have enough money not to have to worry about possessing or desiring it. Forster, in Allan's view, was a true gentleman: a man of rare honesty and integrity, with a 'superb disregard for pecuniary gain'. He knew the value of money and sought sufficient for himself and his family, but had no interest in wealth for its own sake, deliberately leaving the pursuit of money to 'men of lower aspirations', such (Allan did not need to add) as himself.

Fortunately, few people in the colony knew of Allan's vulgar but compelling desire to make money. On the other hand, few could *not* have noticed that his behaviour inside and outside the house was often ungentlemanly. During the first two elections he contested, he drew unfortunate attention to himself by taking issue with the returning officers, on one occasion provoking a liberal newspaper to refer to his 'hectoring impertinence'. In the Legislative Assembly he distinguished himself for his excessive language. One of his fellow members, after listening to yet another of his diatribes against the magistracy, pointedly remarked that the bench was 'not the only place where ignorant and improper men were to be found'. Before long, Allan Macpherson was as well known in the colony for his pugnacity as for his principles.

Allan survived another election in 1864 and remained in Parliament for over five years in all. Throughout this period he sat on the Opposition benches, in varying degrees of discomfort, as the office

William Forster, Allan Macpherson's closest friend, by an unknown photographer, probably taken during his four months as Premier and Colonial Secretary in 1859–1860. After examining his physiognomy, a phrenologist told him that he was 'deficient in self esteem and self reliance'. Forster did not set much store by phrenology, but he certainly did not see himself suited to 'the details of official life and the constant vigilance over small matters—the necessity for small tactics and contrivances—the perpetual caution'. MITCHELL LIBRARY, STATE LIBRARY OF NEW SOUTH WALES

James Martin, 'the bitterest enemy I have in the world'. Engraving after a photograph by Frith, 1867. STATE LIBRARY OF VICTORIA

of Premier alternated between Cowper, whom Allan regarded with disdain, and James Martin, whom he loathed. Martin, another of Mr Cape's boys, combined humble origins with patrician airs. His father had been a steward at a castle in Ireland before coming to Australia with his wife and the infant James, to serve as a groom at the Governor's country residence at Parramatta. At school he had been an exceptional student—perhaps Allan's animosity towards him began there. Like Allan, he had joined a law firm; but where Allan had eagerly abandoned the law for squatting, Martin had persisted, shining and making money in the courts and winning a name for himself as a journalist and politician. On certain matters, such as manhood suffrage and the secret ballot, the two men were as one; on others, such as free trade and protection, they were strongly opposed. It was a principle on which they agreed that drove the final wedge between them. In 1866 Martin claimed to support Allan's campaign to restore state aid for religion. But when the issue came to a vote in the Assembly, he failed to say the words that might have won the day. Thereafter Allan denounced him as a traitor, pursuing him, as a liberal newspaper put it, 'with the bitterness and pertinacity of contemptuous and inexorable hatred'.

With either enemy in power—one, Cowper, political; the other, Martin, both political and personal—there was little prospect of Allan joining a ministry. When he retired in 1868 it seemed that his career as a legislator would sink into the oblivion that attends most ventures into politics. And so it would have done, but for one sensational incident.

A HORSEWHIPPING IN PARLIAMENT HOUSE

By the beginning of 1868 Allan and Emma had stayed longer in the colony than they had originally intended. Now that William was gone there was nothing to detain them, apart from Allan's political prospects (for politics are almost invariably associated with prospects) and the need to ensure that property matters were all in order. On the other hand, they had decided that their sons should receive an English education; and now that Willie, the eldest, was approaching thirteen, it was time to leave for home. They therefore decided that Emma and the children should go on ahead, with Allan to follow later in the year.

Perhaps the loss of his domestic anchor contributed to what happened next. One afternoon towards the end of February, seven weeks after his family had left the colony, Allan was seated at his usual place on the Opposition benches during a typically turbulent session. A minister in Martin's government, Henry Parkes, had just moved that certain papers relating to inspectors of schools be printed and was proceeding to say a few words on the subject. This, as Parkes conceded, was an unusual course (as standing orders prohibited discussion without prior notice); but it was his duty, he said, not to allow misstatements to go forth into the world.

As the house had a Pickwickian concern for obedience to procedures, this deviation from standing orders clearly would not do. Several Opposition members rose to order. The Speaker ruled in favour of the Colonial Secretary—the Opposition members held their ground; the Speaker held his. With the house descending into familiar disarray, the Member for Central Cumberland, having presumably been collecting his thoughts, rose to speak on the point of order. The Speaker responded that there was no point of order, but Allan remained on his feet, insisting that he be heard. Government members called out 'Chair', 'Chair', 'Sit down', and 'You're out of order'—to which Allan responded: 'What else can you expect from the paltry hangers-on of a moribund Government?' A voice was then heard to say: 'Blackguard!' Forster rose and demanded: 'Who says blackguard?' The Member for West Maitland, Benjamin Lee, a successful squatter and merchant, called out, 'I do', and as he spoke leapt to his feet and strode across the chamber towards Allan. John Robertson, anticipating mischief, tried to come between them, crying out, 'None of this; for God's sake, none of this'; but Lee pushed him aside with his left hand, at the same time applying his right fist to Allan's face.

Not so long ago there had been a ready remedy for gentlemen who considered themselves slighted, let alone, as in this case, assaulted. Duelling, however, was no longer in vogue. The last known duel in New South Wales was in 1851, when the irascible Surveyor-General, Sir Thomas Mitchell, and Stuart Donaldson, soon to become the colony's first Premier under responsible government, came close to killing one or other on Sydney's outskirts. Now, when Lee punched Allan in the face, there was no script to dictate what happened next. Allan, evidently caught by surprise, missed the chance to land on his assailant a similar blow. As Lee was led away, Allan resumed his seat, and after a short while left the chamber, nursing his sore nose and muttering something to the effect that he would murder his assailant or at least give him 'a good hammering'.

Stepping out of Parliament House, he crossed Macquarie Street and marched several blocks down the hill to George Street, where he entered a saddlery and purchased a horsewhip, which the shopkeeper wrapped for him. He then charged back up the hill to the legislature, where he secreted his purchase in an anteroom and resumed his seat in the chamber. Members were now engaged in heated debate about what was to be done. In Allan's absence, Benjamin Lee (who it was said had 'got a little grog in') had already offered several abject apologies to the house for affronting its dignity; but Allan, joining the discussion, declared that, while the house 'might guard its own dignity', he was well able outside the chamber to look after his own; and that 'Whalebone and whipcord, used with skill and determination, were a very effectual reply to any insult of the kind he had received'. He then stepped into the adjacent library to wait on Lee's withdrawal from the chamber; and the moment his assailant appeared, struck him across the face with the whip and seized him by the throat. 'The scene that now ensued', wrote an eager reporter, 'was far more exciting than anything that had ever before taken place in the Parliament of New South Wales.' Lee rushed at Macpherson, Macpherson grabbed again at his throat, and the two fell to the floor. Other members from both sides of the house came rushing out of the chamber, and soon were engaged in a general melee, with the Sergeant at Arms struggling valiantly but ineffectually to assert some control. Eventually the two main

PARLIAMENTARY "PURE PUPS;" OR, PUG *v.* POODLE.

A dog fight in the Legislative Assembly. Pug is probably Allan Macpherson the pugilist, while Benjamin Lee is seen as the ministry's poodle. *Sydney Punch*, 7 March 1868.

combatants were separated. Lee was escorted from Parliament House by the front door and Macpherson by the back.

Over the next few days, the altercation was the talk of the town. The Australian colonies were currently hosting their first royal visitor, Prince Alfred the Duke of Edinburgh, Queen Victoria's second son. Fortunately, he had lately left Sydney for a short trip north to the new colony of Queensland—otherwise, what would he think? The liberal *Empire* newspaper referred to 'the most disgraceful scenes that had ever yet been witnessed in the Legislature of this colony'. The conservative *Sydney Morning Herald* lamented that 'the country will see the fatal effects of this contempt for the decencies of social life and public order'. The satirical *Sydney Punch* had a field day. Everyone agreed that matters had got out of hand, and many wondered why. John West, Congregational minister and editor of the *Herald*, put it down to the vanity and vulgarity of the native-born legislators, 'the tall, bright, fresh, noble, and aspiring youth of Australia!', among them Allan Macpherson and the Premier, James Martin. West pointed his censorious finger at 'the Australian schoolmaster', having in mind perhaps that several of 'the native legislators' had been students of Mr Cape. Allan, of course, had not been born in the colony, and nor had Martin and several others on the *Herald*'s list of offenders. But in West's eyes the attributes he displayed on the floor of the house were distinctively and offensively Australian.

Inside the Assembly, members remained divided more or less on party lines, one describing Allan's conduct as 'the cold-blooded malignity of a dastardly assassin', another as 'everything that could be expected from a gentleman'. A third declared that 'any man who received a blow and did not resent it was a coward', though conceding that Allan should really have waited until he was outside the Parliament entirely. After long and impassioned debate, the House passed a vote asserting that the members for West Maitland and Central Cumberland had been 'guilty of a high offence against the dignity of this House', and directing the Attorney-General to prosecute them. Lee threw himself at the mercy of the House and declared that he would accept whatever punishment was meted out to him. Allan expressed 'a large amount of regret' at what had occurred, but stated in effect that incidents outside the chamber were none of its business. In any case, was it just that he should be called to account by the Attorney-General, who happened to be James Martin, 'the bitterest enemy that I have in the world'? The stage was set for a mighty battle.

Who would have thought, wrote the *Empire* several weeks later, that 'this trifling affair would become a celebrated cause in the annals of Australian legislation and jurisprudence? But of such small events the history of the world is made up'. For the moment, though, colonists were distracted by an event of far greater import: Prince Alfred, back from Queensland, was attending a charity picnic by the harbour when a man with a revolver stepped forward and shot him in the back. Thick rubber braces and a sturdy constitution probably saved the Prince's life. But until his safety was assured, the colony was in anguish, and then in turmoil over whether the attempt was part of a Fenian plot. By comparison, Allan's offence was minor. It was nevertheless a breach of decorum in a society attempting to present itself favourably to the world.

Obediently to the resolution of the House, the Attorney-General charged Allan with assaulting his fellow member, violating the dignity of the House, and obstructing its business. Allan's training as a lawyer had ended nearly thirty years earlier when he had thrown in his job at the solicitor's practice and headed for the bush. Nevertheless, confident as ever that right was on his side, he prepared to mount his own defence. Martin himself appeared for the prosecution. Allan, when asked whether he was guilty or not guilty, declined to plead and entered instead a demurrer, or legal objection, arguing that the alleged offence of violating the dignity of the Assembly and obstructing its business was unknown in common law or the statutes of the colony. Accordingly, he asserted, there was no case to answer. The two judges differed, and referred the matter to a sitting of three judges, whom Allan addressed with rhetoric appropriate to the occasion. His duty, he said, in standing before them was not to indulge any sense of self-justification or retaliation, but rather to protect independent views in Parliament, the liberties of the press and the liberties of the public at large. Whether or not they were swayed by his eloquence, the judges decided in his favour, two to one, and Allan walked out of the court triumphant. The decision, according to one enthusiastic reporter, was a vindication of the great constitutional principle that no man shall be found to answer for an offence unknown to the laws of the land.

But for Allan it was a Pyrrhic victory. Despite his characteristic bravado, he had been wounded by some of the things that appeared in the press. John West in the *Herald* had been particularly offensive. 'Of Mr. MACPHERSON,' he wrote on the day after the collision in the house, 'it is useless to say a word. It is difficult to believe that he is a man of sound mind. Neither private differences nor political animosity can account for his behaviour'. And there was worse to come: 'Mr. MACPHERSON is the son of a gentleman; it is said a man of estate'. But who could compare him without sadness with the fine old gentleman who had lately disappeared from the legislature?

> No! We have had in our Assembly men from the plough, from the mine, and from the mechanics' bench, of imperfect education; but we never remember to have seen one of them behave or employ the language we have seen and heard from men having from birth, fortune, education, and professional standing the conventional title of the name of gentlemen.

Allan responded with feeling in the Assembly. 'Every man in this world has some end,' he declared:

The family at Bernera in about 1867. Allan relaxes with his newspaper in the deck chair while Emma is seated in the carriage with baby Ewan, then aged two or three years. Jessie, aged about thirteen, is astride the horse being held by Willie (eleven), while his brother Alan (ten) holds onto the carriage horse. The boy playing near the water tank might be either Charlie (nine) or George (six), as one of the brothers appears to be missing. Intentionally or not, the image of most of the family being about to go somewhere is apt, as Emma and the boys will soon return to Britain, leaving Allan behind. MACPHERSON COLLECTION

some aim, which it is painful to have in a moment crushed and destroyed. I feel more for the effect which that article and those statements [in the *Herald*] are likely to have against me in Great Britain—I feel more sorrow on this account than dread of the vengeance that my greatest political enemy, Mr. Martin, can inflict upon me.

What was this aim, so cruelly crushed and destroyed? Was it a desire to live up to his father's expectations? Or perhaps an ambition to enter British politics? Either way, the wound to his feelings healed quickly, helped along by his victory in the courts, and it soon disappeared entirely, along with a slight bruising to his nose.

Even when feeling at his lowest, he knew that he could rely on Emma for support. She heard about the altercation soon after she and the children had arrived in London, and wrote immediately to console him. 'As far as I can judge you could hardly have acted differently though of course it has given me great pain to think of.' Whatever should happen, she would not blame him; after all, he was probably the victim of a government conspiracy. Nevertheless, it was best, she told him, to say nothing about the case in Britain. People would not understand.

It was time to go. Although some of his political friends tried to persuade him to stay, Emma was adamant that she and the children needed him more than they did. In his last speech to the Assembly, delivered by chance as the ministry led by his enemies Henry Parkes and James Martin crumbled and his friends Robertson and Forster took charge, he offered the new ministers some advice on how they might govern better, before concluding in an unfamiliar tone of contrition. 'I suppose that I, as much as any other member of the House, whether from temperament or any other cause, have, perhaps, offered offence to a considerable number of hon. Members.' For all those breaches of decorum, he now apologised, departing the chamber in the spirit of charity and forgiveness, and seeking the Assembly's charity and forgiveness in return. Forster and Robertson organised a farewell dinner in his honour. Parkes, Martin and Cowper appear to have stayed away. The next day, he was headed for home.

One evening a year later, a much grander banquet in his honour—initiated by the Blairgowrie Town Council and the local Curling Club—took place in the new Blairgowrie Town Hall, built on land that he had donated to the community. Everybody who was anybody attended, including even the ladies, who were seated at tables behind the platform and around the sides of the hall, a sign of changing times. The venue (according to a newspaper report) was splendidly but tastefully decorated, with 'a profusion of evergreens' festooned around the walls. Allan sat at the centre of the podium. Suspended from a beam above him was a gigantic monogram, composed of holly, laurel, fir, rowan berries and flowers neatly twisted together into the initials 'A.M.'. In proposing the toast to the guest of honour, the Bailie, or Chief Magistrate of Blairgowrie, referred to the community's 'genuine feelings of esteem and regard' for their returning laird ('applause'); praised his innate kindness of disposition ('applause'), his desire to advance the improvement of the town ('applause'), his charity towards the poor and needy ('applause'); and affectionately recalled the hearty meeting of the Blairgowrie Curlers at 'his own hospitable mansion' ('applause'). The audience then responded to the toast 'with great enthusiasm'.

Allan, rising to reply, was received with 'loud and continued applause'. While a man, he opined, cannot have two wives (except in parts of the United States) and should not serve two masters, it was possible for him to love two countries. He confessed to a deep affection for Australia, where he had lived most of his life and had many dear friends; but Scotland was the land of his birth and his forefathers, and within Scotland, there was no place dearer to him than Blairgowrie, where he intended to spend the rest of his days. Throughout the speech there was frequent applause, until he resumed his seat 'amidst loud and continued cheering'.

Then came a succession of toasts: to the 'The Town and Trade of Blairgowrie', the manufacturing and agricultural interests, the banking and legal interests, the clergy of all denominations (somewhat undermined by the proposer regretting the 'latitudinarian spirit of the present day' and hoping that Scotland would yet return to its old faith), the Bailie and Council, the Curling and Bowling Clubs, the tenantry and vassals, the ladies, the strangers (or visitors to the town)—in other words, to everyone, with each toast followed by music performed by a quadrille band.

Together they were celebrating not just the return of the laird, but the welfare and prosperity of a community in which, as one speaker put it, 'Laird and tenant, trader and farmer, manufacturer and merchant, are all bound together by common interests and common sympathies'; which Allan and perhaps everyone else present that evening believed was just as the world should be.

15

MAKING FAMILIES

SHORTLY BEFORE SETTING OUT FROM SYDNEY FOR HOME at the end of October 1868, Allan Macpherson celebrated his fiftieth birthday. If he chose to reflect on his life so far, there was certainly much to contemplate, not all of it encouraging. Just as he had abandoned his squatting career with little to show for it, his political career over the past five years had been at best a mixed success. But Allan was not one to dwell on the past. As he sailed north, he looked forward to resuming his role as laird of Blairgowrie and even to winning a seat in the British Parliament. This was a distinct possibility. W.E. Gladstone's Liberal Party was in the ascendant; and while Allan in New South Wales was happy to be described as a conservative, in Britain he was sympathetic to the Liberals' policies, especially those relating to religion and taxes. Although he had been out of Britain for many years, he was still well enough known to win nomination as a Liberal candidate.

Bad luck, though, destroyed his chances. When the election was called he was still at sea. He arrived home to find the Liberals swept into power, and the local seat of Perthshire won by a Liberal sent up by Gladstone from London. This was the prize he had most coveted, and had he been on the spot he would surely have won it. Now, all he could do was hope for better luck next time.

With that prospect sadly closed, at least for the moment, Allan set his heart on another. Before he had left New South Wales, his friends William Forster and John Robertson had promised him (or so he thought) the position of Agent-General for the colony, if they were still in power when it fell vacant. This was a paid appointment, based in London and responsible for promoting the colony's political and commercial interests. But when the vacancy occurred, he heard from Forster that he was unlikely to be chosen after all and that Charlie Cowper, of all people, would be appointed in his place.

This was a terrible blow. Allan immediately concluded that Forster, his oldest and dearest friend, had betrayed him. He did not spare the whip in letting Forster know, telling him that he had left New South Wales convinced that his two friends had 'absolutely pledged' to offer him the agency. Now it appeared that Forster's support had been at best lukewarm, and that he might even have intended the job for himself. This was the most 'bitter mortification' that he had ever experienced, a product of his 'misplaced reliance' in his trusted friend. All he wished to do now was to put out of his mind the memory of politics and politicians in New South Wales, 'to which there is not the most remote probability of my ever returning'.

Forster gave as good as he got: there had never been, nor could there have been, any pledge; and if Allan thought there had been, he must have been labouring under 'some strange hallucination'. 'That you have believed me capable of such deceit and treachery is enough for me.' And with a final signing off:

> I now remain
>> for the last time
>>> your old and still sincere friend

their forty-year friendship appeared to be at an end.

For Allan, New South Wales had become an annoyance. His enemy James Martin, having suffered a humiliating loss over the assault case in the colonial courts, took the matter to the Privy Council. Allan was not required to attend the hearing, which took place in London in mid-1870, shortly after the falling out with Forster. The Law Lords overturned the decision of the Supreme Court in Sydney and ruled that Allan did have a case to answer. Fortunately for him, the government in New South Wales had twice changed, he had left the colony, and Martin, having won a moral victory, had better things to do than pursue an issue that everyone was weary of. Allan read the newspaper reports of the judgment and threw them onto the fire. 'The decision in New South Wales answered my purpose and beyond this I must admit to having long ceased to feel any interest in the matter.'

With colonial affairs behind him and his ambition for a seat in the Commons thwarted, Allan turned to his family, just as his grandfather and namesake Colonel Macpherson had done many decades earlier when he had returned from India and realised that James 'Ossian' Macpherson was a villain in disguise. Families had to stand together in times of need. In good times a strong and cohesive family provided the surest protection for each and all of its members against accident and misfortune, confirmed their status in society, helped fulfil their individual ambitions, and laid solid foundations for future generations. But Allan, reflecting perhaps on the mixed fortunes of his own forbears, knew that families such as this did not simply happen: they had to be created and nurtured. He had set his course a decade earlier, when he told Emma of his 'fixed determination to make a *family*—and who knows perhaps *two*, one at each end of the Antipodes'. Now that Australia had ceased to interest him, the family in Scotland became his ruling passion.

A TUNDING AT WINCHESTER

Allan and Emma now had six children: the eldest, Jessie, and five boys. Another child, a girl, was born in 1874, twenty years after Jessie and ten after the youngest boy. The girls' future was clear: they would follow the usual course available to young Victorian ladies by attending good schools (including, in Jessie's case, a finishing school in Paris), making advantageous matches, and having children of their own. The boys had more opportunities open to them. Remembering how he had begged to escape the drudgery of a legal office for life in the bush, Allan was determined to let them decide their own futures. A father's responsibility, as he saw it, was to see that they were well placed to follow whatever course appealed to them, taking advantage of whatever offered. '[M]y one all absorbing idea', he wrote, 'is how best to start my boys in life.

> I feel what a poor [fist?] I made of my own early days in the way of providing me a decent competency—and that I would have been literally little more than a hewer of wood and a drawer of water in my old age if I had not had this property [Blairgowrie] to fall back upon. And therefore I feel it all the more incumbent on me to give all the boys both the opportunity and the inducement to try to get a little above the level of the Common herd.

The surest way of doing this, he decided, was to give them 'the very best education that Great Britain will afford', by sending them to an English public school, preferably one of the 'great public schools'—Winchester, Eton, Westminster, Harrow, Rugby and several newcomers—whose influence in preparing boys for leading roles in government, business and the professions was universally acknowledged. Allan chose Winchester, perhaps for its academic renown, perhaps on the advice of his friend Charles Wordsworth, Bishop of St Andrews, who had taught there. Steeped in antiquity and tradition, Winchester offered the perfect counter to Allan's own colonial upbringing and the years his boys had spent in the Australian bush. Founded nearly five centuries earlier by William of Wykeham, in the time of Richard II, the college had nurtured kings and educated sons of the nobility. But whether a boy entered as the son of a nobleman, a merchant or a clergyman, he would leave as a Wykehamist, elevated not just a little, but far above the common herd. The fees were enormous, but Emma's parents helped, and Allan had no doubt that the sacrifice—his and theirs—was worth it.

William Charles Macpherson—Willie—was admitted to Winchester early in 1870, aged fourteen. His brother Alan (the one born at Keera, and his junior by eighteen months) followed later in the year. Willie was a thoughtful and determined lad, dutiful to his parents, well built like his father and a keen sportsman, which helped him withstand the rigours of college life. During his first few terms he learned what was expected of him in the classroom and living quarters. As in other public schools, Classics dominated the curriculum, the assumption being, in the words of an old Etonian, that 'every gentleman must understand Greek and Latin'. At first Willie, like many new boys, appeared to be struggling: his initial report placed him near the bottom of the class. His Classics master described him as 'puzzled and nervous', though he expected him to do better as he became more confident. Eighteen months later he had climbed halfway up the ladder, but the Head Master (also known at Winchester as the Informator) was still disappointed. Young Macpherson was 'lazy and hesitating', though he expected his abilities to come out soon. These early predictions proved correct. After four years he had risen in the Classics class to second out of twenty-five, his master reporting: 'Has worked excellently during the term. Examination very good. His book papers show clear-headedness & a considerable power of translation'.

Winchester was no place for weaklings. One of Willie's near contemporaries later reflected that his own first month there was 'pure misery'—the food insufficient and unpalatable, and the system of fagging, in which the seniors lorded it over the juniors, 'a perfect nightmare of thoughtless cruelty'. Readers of *Tom Brown's Schooldays*, first published in 1857, might well have assumed that public school brutality was a thing of the past and that justice and decency prevailed. A royal commission several years later issued a glowing report on the system, praising the schools for 'their capacity to govern others and control themselves, their aptitude for combining freedom with order, their public spirit, their vigour and manliness of character', and so on. At Winchester, though, 'praefects' continued to exercise near absolute power over 'inferiors', with frequent and often arbitrary recourse to corporal punishment, so that few junior boys managed to escape a flogging. Although the college motto was 'Manners Makyth Man', manliness was also seen as resulting from liberal use of the stick; several months before Willie Macpherson enrolled there, the satirical magazine *Punch* suggested that William of Wykeham might better be known as 'William of Whack'em'. As another, slightly older contemporary of Willie later put it, 'it would have required a boy with a spirit of Luther to have stood out against the system'.

The Head Master, the Reverend George Ridding, was a Wykehamist through and through. His father had been a master there, he had been born and educated there, he had married the daughter of the previous Head Master, and he had taught there for several years before being appointed Head Master in 1867. Ridding was an imposing and much admired figure, with jet black hair and piercing eyes. He was also a builder—he later became known as the school's 'second founder'. During his early years as Head Master the numbers of pupils grew significantly, and he created a new system of 'Houses' to accommodate them. But changes to the size and structure of the school did not suggest to him that other things had to change. In Ridding's view, the old ways had served the school well, and he was prepared to defend them at almost any cost.

In October 1872, as he neared the end of his third year in college, Willie started a letter to his mother with some alarming news. 'Dear Mamma,' he wrote, 'I have had a remarkable and not altogether pleasant adventure.' A few days previously, the Senior Commoner Praefect, Whyte, had summoned him and other boys in his House to take an examination in 'notions', the extensive vocabulary of words and expressions unique to the school. While other public schools had their own arcane usages, Winchester's 'notions' were a sacred tradition. Some had been in use for centuries, others were freshly coined; some were corruptions of Latin, Greek or English words, others more or less ingenious inventions; some referred to customs, others to people, places and objects. 'Brum' meant impecunious; 'to prose' was to make a long-winded speech; 'toys' were the small bookcase and desk that each boy had beside his bed; and a 'tunding' was a thrashing with a ground ash, a sapling prolific within the school grounds. Whatever they had once been intended to do, the notions now served as a means of binding the school together, imposing uniformity, excluding outsiders, vetting newcomers, and maintaining the authority of the old boys over the new. As soon as a boy arrived in the college, he was instructed in the language by one of the older boys; and if, at a subsequent examination, his proficiency was found wanting, both he and his mentor were likely to feel the sting of the praefect's ground ash. Now the praefect Whyte, having observed that the House where Macpherson boarded was fractious and disorderly, took it upon himself to bring its occupants into line by giving them an examination in notions.

Willie Macpherson knew his notions. He was also, according to a schoolfellow, 'a person with strong views as to precedent and legality' (a trait that would scarcely have surprised anyone who knew his father). As the senior boy in his House, and soon himself to become a praefect, he had no intention of being subjected to an examination by a praefect from another House. When summoned, he claimed exemption and refused to attend.

This resistance was tantamount to mutiny. The case came before the Head Master who, having studied the book of rules and customs, concluded that Macpherson had no claim for exemption, though as the case was a thorny one, it was best not pursued. But rather than undermine the authority of the praefects, he referred the issue back to them; and they, rather than submit to what was clearly an instance of flagrant disobedience, determined by a majority vote that the offender must be punished.

By now the whole school knew of Willie Macpherson's defiance and was watching intently to see what happened next. Summoned to meet his fate, he appeared before Whyte, who asked him to admit his guilt. Macpherson responded that he 'had come to be licked, not to talk', and refused to give an inch. Whyte then said he would give him a 'spanking'

Mr Turner's House, where Willie Macpherson boarded, in 1873, shortly after the tunding row. While none of the boys are named, Willie is most probably the boy wearing white trousers on the right. In the absence of a school uniform, the requirement that every boy learn his 'notions' helped impose uniformity. WINCHESTER COLLEGE

on the buttocks; but as this was a punishment normally applied to 'very small boys', Macpherson perversely insisted on the normal treatment administered to seniors. This left Whyte with no alternative but to give the recalcitrant what he had asked for. With the whole of the executioner's House watching, he subjected Macpherson to a vigorous tunding across the shoulders, wielding the ground ash thirty times, breaking five of them in the process, and leaving his victim's back, as Willie told his mother, 'in rather a lively state of bruises'. Mercifully, he wore his jacket throughout the ordeal. According to Willie, Whyte had lost his temper. Whyte himself claimed he was 'not in a passion, but decidedly irritated'.

Willie was quite proud of his achievement. Singlehandedly, he appeared to have put an end to a 'reign of terror' that had seen over a hundred thrashings during the preceding six weeks. Among his peers and the younger boys, he was exalted as 'a regular hero', and for a time at least conditions for the juniors definitely improved. The Head Master told Whyte that his punishment had been excessive and instructed the praefects not to administer more than a dozen cuts on any one occasion. Whyte privately apologised, telling Willie that he had been obliged to 'lick' him because, had he not done so, 'not only his own dignity but also that of all the Praefects would have suffered'. The apology was accepted, the two lads became 'perfect friends', and were seen walking about arm in arm.

Having been thoroughly vindicated, Willie would happily have let the matter rest. Back in Blairgowrie, though, the letters to his mother set his father fuming. He immediately wrote to Willie, to ensure that he was not at fault, and to the Head Master, suggesting that if his son's version of events was discovered to be correct, the Senior Commoner Praefect should publicly apologise, and 'the authority he has greatly abused' should be withdrawn. Ridding responded by conceding that Whyte had indeed committed 'a very grave error of judgement', and regretting that 'so good and gentle a boy as he should have allowed his zeal for discipline to have so far outrun his discretion'. He was especially sorry that the punishment:

> should have fallen on your son of all boys, for though he is no doubt obstinate and in this matter was in the wrong, he is so good and nice a boy that I am doubly sorry that it should have been he.

This merely increased Allan's fury. After enlisting the support of his friend Bishop Wordsworth, who was strongly opposed to excessive flogging, he told Ridding that if he did not insist on Whyte formally apologising, he would take legal action or some other steps that would make the matter public. After a further exchange of letters, in which Ridding unwisely implied that Allan was at fault for not letting the matter rest, Allan wrote a strong letter to the *Times*, accusing Ridding of a lack of moral courage, suggesting that he had 'hushed up' many similar cases, and hinting none too subtly that he should find other employment.

In the meantime, stories about the tunding had drifted far beyond the college grounds and into the press. The first letter appeared in the *Daily Telegraph*, followed by others under the headline 'Public School Brutality'. Then a former Wykehamist, probably a friend of Allan, raised the matter in the *Times*, describing the powers possessed by the praefects as 'licensed tyranny'. Other old public schoolboys followed, some offering specific examples of tundings they had experienced or witnessed, most agreeing that it was 'an indefensible and barbarous practice', a few defending the system as generally 'wholesome and effective'. Willie, signing himself 'The Victim', sent his own letter to the *Times*, making light of the incident, declaring that ground ashes were not as tough as they were made out to be and that the praefect had made an honest mistake. This won him compliments from some who saw in him 'the genuine spirit of "Tom Brown"'. But it did not stop the flow of correspondence. Allan fired his broadside, Ridding ducked and weaved, the assistant masters came to his defence, and Allan fired another round, publishing four of Willie's private letters as proof that his son had suffered a great wrong.

Willie was learning a lesson that had long escaped his father: that certain actions can have unintended consequences. All he wanted now was for the affair to go away. His complaint had not been about the system, but merely the way in which it had been administered in one instance. He did not object to examinations for notions, fagging or even tunding. All that had concerned him was the affront to his dignity by praefects who were exceeding their powers and breaking the rules. Unwittingly, though, he had raised issues that not only questioned Winchester traditions, but struck at the heart of the English public school system. The tradition of examinations for notions was held up to criticism and ridicule. Even the austere *Times* commented with heavy irony on 'what a priceless advantage it must be in after life to have had such elegant and useful learning kicked and cudgelled into one at school'.

The larger issues, which extended beyond Winchester to the other great public schools, related to corporal punishment and the tradition of boys governing themselves, with little or no superintendence by the masters. 'Boy government', as it was sometimes called, was a tradition jealously guarded by those who practised it. Its advocates credited the practice with erasing the arrogance of youth, introducing boys to the realities of life and, in the words of one correspondent, leading to 'that indefinable something which is our idea of a Christian English gentleman'. Ridding himself upheld it with almost religious zeal, which explains his reluctance to overrule his praefects, even when he suspected that they were acting unjustly. Corporal punishment was often defended as a means of making men out of boys. But now the *Times* was doubting whether lads of eighteen should be entrusted with such powers over their juniors. Attitudes to education were evidently changing, as people of influence began to talk of moulding boys rather than leaving them to their own devices. What was at stake, as 'An Old Eton Boy' explained, was 'the training and formation of the moral character of those youths who are hereafter to constitute the life-blood of England'. Little wonder so many people had something to say.

When the row spilled over into the popular press, the tone became subversive. A newspaper in the industrial midlands remarked that 'A little boy who has been much flogged will almost certainly be a great flogger when he is big', and proceeded to argue that brutality in the great public schools chiefly explained why upper class sports, such as pigeon-slaying and battue-shooting, were often so cruel. *Punch* published 'A letter from an artisan', in which an imaginary figure signing himself 'A Father' presumed 'This is the Way wich yung Swells lurn sweatness and Lite which Make Them so clever and Brave to Make us heat umble Py wen They grow into the guvning Classs'.

Clearly the discussion had got out of hand. In castigating the praefect and then the Head Master, Allan Macpherson had inadvertently exposed the system to ridicule. This was not at all what he had intended. Had he attended a public school himself, and properly appreciated its traditions, he might have been more inclined to tolerate its excesses. As a brash colonial, he was unfamiliar with how things were done; although that, of course, was the last thing he would want said of him. Fortunately, none of the newspaper editors or letter writers seemed to notice that he had been educated at Mr Cape's school in Sydney, alongside the sons of convicts. Nor did they mention, though some must have known, that he was famous in some quarters for wielding a horsewhip.

Allan failed to take the Head Master's scalp. However, the Second (or deputy) Master, who had not noticed an epidemic of tunding before his eyes, 'went away to a canonry somewhere'. Ridding referred the incident to Winchester's Governing Body, which warmly praised his running of the school, but formalised limits on corporal punishment and insisted that the masters retain ultimate control. Allan could reasonably claim a victory, having forced those in authority to acknowledge that his son had been unjustly treated, as well, presumably, as having caused the Head Master and offending praefect some sleepless nights.

Whether Willie eventually regarded the affair as a victory is another matter. While he had no reason to fear another tunding, his position in the school as one who had bucked the system was certainly uncomfortable. In any case, he had decided to try for a career in the Indian Civil Service, for which the best starting point was a private school in London. He remained at Winchester another six months or so until mid-1873, leaving before completing his final year. During this time he was invariably known as 'Tunded Macpherson'. Later, his fame or infamy followed him to India. The English establishment had long memories.

THE FAMILY TREE

When the elder William Macpherson had died in New South Wales in 1866, his son Allan regretted that he had never questioned him about the family's ancestry. He knew that there was a special relationship with the Macphersons of Cluny, the hereditary Chiefs of the Clan. But beyond that, his information was sketchy. Fortunately Aunt Harriot was still living, so two months after his father's death Allan sat down at his writing desk at Bernera and addressed a series of questions to her. Did she know anything about her maternal grandmother? How was Colonel Allan related to James 'Ossian' Macpherson and to her first husband, General John Macintyre? and so on. Harriot, now in her eighty-first year, was able to answer some questions, but knew little about her grandparents, other than that her paternal grandfather had been born in Inverness-shire, and had died at the Battle of Falkirk in 1746. Before that date, the family seemed to have no history at all.

Returning to Blairgowrie, Allan resolved to set matters right by compiling a family tree. This was no mere exercise in self-indulgence. He believed that, just as a family was bound together by affection and mutual respect, it could also be sustained and strengthened by mapping its ancestral roots and branches. His children should know who they were and where they came from. Furthermore, a long pedigree could lift a family's status in the eyes of the world.

Supercilious Sassenachs sometimes teased the Scots for being too much concerned with their supposed pedigrees. In 1802 Eliza Macpherson came out of a farce at Covent Garden complaining that it was not very amusing, 'being a severe ridicule upon the Scotch pride of genealogy'. But there was no denying that her kinsmen and women were intrigued by the ties that bound them into families and clans. Dr Johnson, during his celebrated trip to the Western Isles in 1773, observed how:

> Men in a small district necessarily mingle blood by inter-
> marriages, and combine at last into one family, with a common
> interest in the honour and disgrace of every individual.
> Then begins that union of affections, and co-operation of
> endeavours, that constitute a Clan.

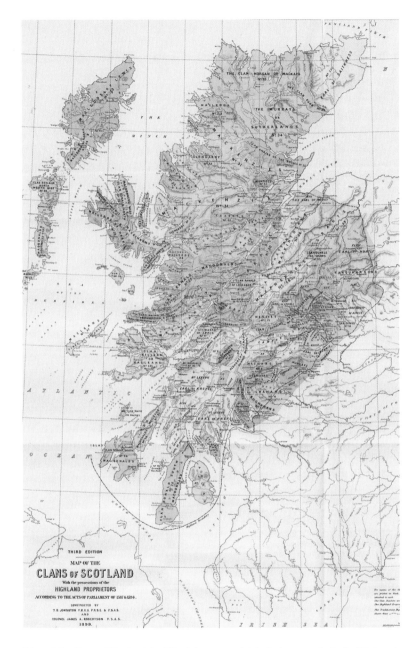

Map of the Clans of Scotland, by T.B. Johnston and J.A. Robertson, 2nd ed., Edinburgh, 1873. MACPHERSON COLLECTION

Each family and Clan had its own *seanachaidh*, who recited stories of long-gone ancestors and passed on genealogies from one generation to the next. These served practical as well as sentimental purposes, documenting the usual practice of marrying within the Clan. Such marriages provided the cohesion necessary for Clans to retain their ancient rights of possession. Marriage outside the Clan was generally restricted to the leading men of each lineage, in order to strengthen the Clan by alliances.

The Macphersons had been well served by their seanachaidhs who, during the three centuries between 1400 and 1700, had helped confirm the Clan as the dominant group in Badenoch. The Clan was the first in the Highlands to have its genealogy committed to paper, when around 1700 a respected elder, Sir Aeneas Macpherson of Invereshie, applied himself to what he called this 'useful and ingenious science'; and after consulting with many Highlanders of 'sense and reputation', produced a manuscript which traced the Clan's descent from the mid-fourteenth century. Allan Macpherson obtained a copy of this manuscript and made it the basis for his own genealogical research.

Allan was not one to do things by halves. After many months perusing every relevant document he could lay his hands on and making inquiries of Clan members with long memories, he produced a parchment scroll some 35 feet long and 3 feet wide, and incorporating hundreds of names. Following Sir Aeneas, he traced the Macphersons back to one Muriach or Muireach, the lay parson of the parish of Kingussie in Badenoch around the middle of the twelfth century. This parson, or Phearsain, had a son called Evan Bàn, the fair-haired one, from whom three branches descended, each with its own name, but all recognised as Mac a' Phearsain, or 'son of the parson'. In later generations different families were spelt M'Pherson, McPherson, MacPherson or Macpherson—but whatever they chose to call themselves, they were all said to be descended from Muriach, the parson of Kingussie, and were seen as the 'Posterity of the Three Brethren', or Clan Muriach.

By the 1870s, when Allan was preparing the family tree, just one branch extended from the parson of Kingussie to the present in a continuing male line. This branch was known as Macpherson of Cluny, and ever since Evan Bàn it had provided the Chiefs of the Clan. So far there had been twenty-two Chiefs, including the Cluny Macpherson who had evaded capture by the Hanoverian forces after the Battle of Culloden. Allan's tree showed a close relationship between his own family—the Macphersons of Blairgowrie—and that of the Chief: his own great-great-grandfather Andrew, the father of William Macpherson who had died at the Battle of Falkirk in 1746, was the brother of Lachlan Macpherson, the then Chief of the Clan. So Allan and the children of the current Chief were fourth cousins. As there were few branches to get in the way, this placed the Macphersons of Blairgowrie in close proximity to the Macphersons of Cluny.

When, after three or four years intermittent work, 'the great tree' was finished, Allan enlisted the services of an amanuensis and prepared two copies of a condensed version, one of which he presented to the Clan Chief, Ewan Macpherson of Cluny, and the other he hung in Blairgowrie House. In retrospect he had mixed feelings about the results. In recent years the Cluny branch had seemed to wither, and it was sad to see the decline of a family 'who had so large a share in almost changing a dynasty' (through the Jacobite rebellion). On the other hand, it was pleasing to see how his own family related to Cluny; and later generations would no doubt be reassured to know that they descended from an ancient lineage. He finished the tree in 1874, perhaps just in time to show it to Aunt Harriot, who died in that year at the age of eighty-eight.

One person missing from Allan Macpherson's tree was his half-brother Allan Williams. This was scarcely surprising. If a family tree was intended in part to enhance a family's status, there was no place for illegitimate branches, let alone those of colour. Had Allan Macpherson wondered about whether or not to include his half-brother's family, his grandmother Eliza's insistence more than half a century earlier that the 'moonlight shades' should not be called Macpherson might have made it easier to ignore the Williams line. More probably, though, the thought of including him in the tree never crossed his mind.

In other ways, though, the links between the half-brothers remained close. In conduct and character the two were far apart. Where Allan Macpherson was ambitious, assertive and determined to get his way, Allan Williams, eight years his elder, was quiet, unassuming and ready to yield (except on the rare occasion when his father's hectoring became too much to bear). Perhaps their shared experience of having to oblige an affectionate but demanding parent had helped bring them closer. Later it helped that their wives, Sophia and Emma, got on well. Whatever the cause, they remained friends throughout their shared lifetimes. Allan Macpherson regarded his elder half-brother with fraternal affection, forgiving the lassitude that had caused their father so much annoyance. Allan Williams reciprocated with respect and gentle tolerance of his younger half-brother's excesses. Around 1870 their letters concluded, typically, 'very affectionately yours' (from Allan Williams), and 'with our united kind love to you all' (from Allan Macpherson).

Allan Macpherson had plenty to thank Allan Williams for. When he had left Keera for Mount Abundance in 1847 and later returned to Scotland, his brother had taken over the running of the station. Twenty years later, when Allan Macpherson had resigned from the New South Wales Parliament, Allan Williams acted as his agent, taking charge of his colonial properties. This was a thankless task, as the land near Melbourne proved a poor investment and Bernera yielded little each year beyond a few casks of wine, of sometimes dubious quality. Soon the job of agent became too much for him, but he remained for his brother someone in the colony he could trust.

Allan Williams had problems of his own. He complained of headaches—William Forster thought he was suffering from 'a softening of the brain'—and he was constantly anxious about money. In 1870, at the age of sixty, he was forced to retire from the Surveyor-General's office, only to find that the government had run out of funds to pay its pensioners. With several children still at home—the youngest, Lucy, was just twelve—he and Sophia struggled to make ends meet. 'Nothing benefits me but perfect rest & quiet', he told his half-brother—but he seemed to get little of it.

Most of his eleven children left scarcely any record of their lives. Only two of them, both boys, married, well short of the colonial average, and suggesting perhaps that in late nineteenth century Australia it paid to be white. Only one, through his children, left some account of his comings and goings. This was Allan Williams' second son and namesake, who in 1857, at the age of seventeen, had accompanied Allan and Emma Macpherson on their trip to Keera. When the Macphersons had saddled up their horses and loaded the dog cart for the return trip to Sydney, young Allan had remained as servant (he would later have been called a jackeroo) in the employ of Keera's new owners. After three years learning to become a sheep and cattle man, he headed north with one of

The second Allan Williams 1840–1931, photograph by E.B. Cardell, about 1890.
ELSIE HOMER WILLIAMS COLLECTION

his employers to Curriwillinghi station, just across the border between New South Wales and the new colony of Queensland, and over 200 miles short of Mount Abundance. There he remained for the next seventeen years, evidently still as an employee, but (perhaps with the help of his grandfather William Macpherson's legacy of £100) acquiring an interest in other properties, including one in the Hunter Valley, not far from where he was born. Around 1880 he moved another 600 miles north towards the coastal town of Mackay. Here, in the gently undulating hinterland around the village of Nebo, he managed cattle stations, steadily increasing his wealth and social standing. In 1894 he settled on his own station, known as Burrenbring, where he continued to prosper.

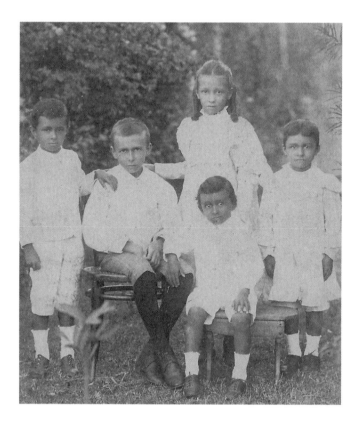

The second Allan Williams' children in the mid-1890s: left to right, Allan Crowther (born 1889), Edward Homer (1885), Edith Sophia (1886), Henry Stewart Homer (1892) and Elsie Homer (1891). ELSIE HOMER WILLIAMS COLLECTION

Some time around 1890, when he was aged about fifty, he had his photograph taken. The photographer, who happened to be based in Roma, captured a smartly dressed gentleman with fine features, high cheek bones, gentle eyes and perhaps the strong Macpherson nose. His skin might have been no darker than that of most men who lived under the harsh Queensland sun, but in other ways his portrait does not fit the image of the typical outback bushman. Some people probably knew of his background. Others who did not might have wondered and gossiped. Either way, his mixed descent did not prevent him becoming prominent in the Nebo district, where he was Chairman of the local board, President of the jockey club, and one of the community's most respected citizens.

Nebo was a long way from Sydney—several days by coastal steamer from the port at Mackay—so it is unlikely that the younger Allan Williams saw his parents often. He certainly travelled south in 1884, for in that year he married in Sydney an old family friend, Harriet Homer, whose father had served for a few years as agent for Allan Macpherson. He was presumably at Nebo when his parents died, five years apart, at their home in Ashfield. His mother, Sophia, died in 1891 at the age of seventy-five. His father, the son of William Macpherson and his black mistress Countess, defied much earlier predictions of senility and succumbed to kidney disease in 1896, at the age of eighty-six. He had lived long enough to hear of the birth of five grandchildren to Allan and Harriet—three boys and two girls—and perhaps even to have seen them. He might just have lived long enough to have seen their photograph.

Many years earlier, Allan Macpherson had dreamed of making two families, 'one at each end of the Antipodes'. That was not to be. But perhaps ironically, his half-brother made sure the Macpherson line would continue in Australia, albeit under a different name.

RETIREMENT

Although compiling the family tree proved to be an engrossing occupation, Allan Macpherson did not adapt easily to having time on his hands. For several years after returning from Australia he busied himself looking after his boys' futures. By the mid-1870s, though, they had all left home, leaving only Jessie, who married in 1885, and the baby Frances, who was chiefly Emma's concern. He worked hard improving the estate, planting ornamental trees around the grounds of Blairgowrie House and attending to the home farm. Each day he walked into town to the post office, and then to the reading room, where he perused the daily papers and talked with friends. Emma maintained her literary interests, reading widely and writing occasional romantic and metaphysical verse with titles such as 'Flowers on a grave', 'Lines on the death of an amiable young lady friend at an early age', 'Song of a band of beautiful Russian ladies in honour of the new spring', and 'What should a woman be?' (the answer to which was 'Chaste, bright, and shadowless, illuming / What comes within her sphere …').

The House of Commons remained beyond Allan's reach. But there was plenty to do in the county and parish and, as laird, much was expected of him. He was appointed a Deputy Lieutenant for the county (as his father and grandfather had been before him), responsible for raising militia should the need arise. He was Chairman of the Blairgowrie School Board, the Parochial Board (which distributed money to the needy), and the Water Commission (which built and controlled the town's first communal water supply). In each of these roles, as the local newspaper put it, 'He expressed his views with clearness and vigour, and gave his opinion or vote with unflinching courage for the course he deemed right, whether it might happen to be popular or otherwise'.

Needless to say, such clarity and vigour led to heated debates, as they had done in New South Wales—always on some matter of principle. He engaged the School Board in a pitched battle relating to the teaching of religion; he took on the local sheriff on an improbable issue relating to the testing of weighing machines used by the railways. As had happened in the past, the weighing machine controversy got out of control, becoming a contest between the unpaid magistrates (such as himself) and the paid representatives of justice. 'If Mr Macpherson was not so earnest a man,' wrote the *Perthshire Advertiser*, 'we might be inclined to look upon the whole mad proceedings as a gigantic joke.' Unhappily for Allan, the editor had got his measure, as 'one of those irrepressible persons who cannot be long without a grievance'.

One painful scar at least was healed. In 1874 he swallowed his pride and wrote to his old friend William Forster in the hope of restoring their former intimacy. After a long and, for Allan, no doubt painful delay, Forster wrote back to say that he was equally keen to renew their old friendship. But first he wanted to hear Allan acknowledge the mistake he had made in supposing that Forster had sought the post of New South Wales Agent-General for himself. There was too much at stake for Allan to quibble, so he responded by acknowledging 'a great error of judgment on my part'. This declaration, Forster replied, was all he could have wished for. No more was said on the matter, and thereafter scarcely a harsh word passed between them.

They had plenty of harsh words, though, for others, especially the 'political mountebanks' who were degrading politics in both New South Wales and England. In Sydney, Forster fulminated against the triumph of the mob, their contempt for education and independence of principle, and their indifference to truth and honesty in politics (which had led to the triumph of 'the vain puffed up democratic monster', Henry Parkes).

Family man: Allan Macpherson at Blairgowrie House in 1884, surrounded by family, friends and dogs. Seated to Allan's right are Emma (with dog), Alan, Ewan and Willie's future bride, Ella Kinloch. Frances, Allan and Emma's youngest child, is seated on the ground to their right. MACPHERSON COLLECTION

'This state of things', he warned Allan, 'will be fully paralleled in England before long, only the rottenness will be better painted and plastered over.' In Blairgowrie Allan lamented the decline of respect for vested interests, and the abandonment by Gladstone's Liberal Party of what he saw as genuine Liberalism. Gradually he came to see the Conservative Party as the only hope for the future.

In 1875 Forster visited England and was soon appointed colonial Agent-General. Although Allan probably still coveted the position, he had no intention now of upsetting the hard-won harmony between them. Over the next few years Forster and his young family visited Blairgowrie at least once for an extended stay, joining his old friend in railing against the decaying state of the world. Forster's appointment as Agent-General was not a success. Once out of Australia he seems to have become more aggressively Australian, offending polite society by exercising his democratic right to wear bushmen's clothes. (He refused to attend the opening of the House of Lords because he would be obliged to wear court dress, though he did so when his wife was presented to the Queen.) He infuriated Henry Parkes and the colonial ministers who had appointed him by publicly expressing opinions on colonial affairs, such as the prospect of the Australian colonies joining in a federation, without any concern for whether his own views complied with government policy. Reversing their usual roles, Allan advised caution, suggesting that while the colonial agent was free to comment on English politics, on Australian matters he should hold his tongue. But Forster offended once too often and was recalled at the end of 1879. This was the last Allan saw of him. Returning to New South Wales, he resumed his political career but died in 1882, at the age of sixty-four, widely mourned as a politician of rare intelligence and integrity. In Blairgowrie Allan grieved for the loss of a soulmate.

By now, Allan had little interest in colonial affairs. He wrote his booklet on Mount Abundance, spoke occasionally to potential emigrants (telling those who were strong and energetic that they might well improve themselves in the colony, but if they were already well off they should stay at home), and he fretted about his colonial properties. Every letter from New South Wales or Victoria provoked in him a 'hatred of human nature in general', as it seemed always to report 'some rascality on the part of a tenant' which he was powerless to avert or avenge. In 1884 he made a final visit to the colonies, when he arranged to sell Bernera and the Melbourne properties, but could not resist acquiring more. None of the colonial lands yielded large profits. Like his father and grandfather, he had a knack of buying and selling the wrong properties at the wrong times.

Blairgowrie remained the family's financial mainstay. On the face of it, Allan and Emma lived well, sending their children to the best schools, entertaining large groups of relatives and friends, giving generously to community causes and helping out individual families in need. But appearances could be deceptive: the property was running into heavy debt. In the 1870s Allan threw his still considerable energies into growing strawberries and manufacturing jam, industries for which the region was becoming famous. This kept him busy. Whether it did much to improve the family's finances was another matter.

Allan was still hard at work managing the strawberry farm and attending to local affairs when Willie and Ella visited from India in 1891. Now there were two children, Alan and Sheila; a third, Isla, was born during their visit. They set out on the return voyage to Calcutta towards the end of the year and were still at sea when they received a telegram to say that Allan had died, from complications arising from a bout of influenza. Aged seventy-three, he predeceased his half-brother Allan Williams by five years and his wife Emma by twenty-four. He left a family strong in itself, with each of his children well equipped to make the best of what life had to offer. He also left enormous debts.

A local newspaper offered a gently understated epitaph:

> As a landlord Mr Macpherson maintained with scrupulous exactness his legal rights, believing that a bargain deliberately entered into was not to be lightly broken; but he was equally scrupulous of the legal rights of others; and when he saw real hardship that he could alleviate, he spared neither his sympathy nor his purse. While he was constitutionally somewhat irritable under provocation, he had a kindly heart beneath it all.

16

DUTY

*D*URING HIS TUMULTUOUS DAYS AT WINCHESTER IN THE early 1870s, Willie Macpherson's thoughts often turned to India. This was not the preferred destination for Wykehamists, who were more likely to pursue careers in the military, business, the law or the church. It was hardly surprising, though, that Willie set his heart on going there. On both the Blake and Macpherson sides of the family the links were strong. He had lived much of his life in a house decorated with artefacts that his paternal great-grandparents had brought back with them from Bengal. And his father would have become an Indian civil servant rather than an Australian squatter, had he had the chance. It was as though India was in Willie Macpherson's blood (as indeed it was, through his mother, though he might not yet have been aware of it).

Britain's relationship with India in the 1870s was very different from the relationship of a century—or even two decades—earlier. Willie's parents had witnessed a moment when the relationship changed. Passing through Ceylon on their way home in 1857, they heard news of what Emma called 'the terrible Sepoy mutiny'. This had occasioned 'very painful excitement' among their fellow passengers, though they had all taken comfort in the sight of a P&O steamer conveying troops to put the rebellion down. Disturbing reports of the uprising—in reality a revolt that spread across northern India and challenged the legitimacy of British rule—continued for many months after they reached home. The uprising was ruthlessly suppressed, leaving a legacy of mutual mistrust, and a determination on the part of the British to maintain absolute control over their Indian possessions. The Mughal dynasty was cast aside, the old system of administration by the East India Company abandoned, and the British Crown assumed formal sovereignty. Nearly two decades later, in 1876, Queen Victoria was proclaimed Empress of India, confirming imperial dominance of what was now widely known as the British Raj. Towards the end of 1877 William Charles (Willie) Macpherson set out for Calcutta as an officer in the Indian Civil Service.

SERVING THE RAJ

Over a century earlier Willie's great-grandfather, the 'first' Allan Macpherson, had sailed for Calcutta in the hope of making his fortune. But times had changed. Although there were still fortunes to be made there, many young men now travelled to India with the object of pursuing a career. This was a more precise ambition than the old notion of following a particular 'line of life'; and it required significant preparation. Gone were the days when the directors of the East India Company each controlled their own little empire of patronage. Now candidates for the Indian Civil Service had to pass competitive examinations (introduced for India long before they were required for entry into the civil service at home). Once admitted, they were expected to spend a total of twenty-five years in the service, including up to two years receiving specific training in Britain and up to three years furlough.

So Willie became what supporters of the old system disparagingly referred to as a 'competition wallah'. On leaving Winchester in 1873, he enrolled at Walter Wren's private school in London, which specialised in preparing young men for the Indian Civil Service examinations. According to another Winchester boy, 'No greater contrast to the gentlemanly unpractical Winchester could be conceived'. The school was located in a depressed area of London, near brickfields and turnip patches, with Mr Wren's chickens running freely outside. Wren himself, like George Ridding, was 'a character', 'a genial, loud-voiced man with no nonsense about him' who was unable to walk without a stick in each hand, a result he said of rough treatment as a child by a school bully. Active on the radical wing of Liberal politics, he was always ready to hold forth on subjects relating to aristocratic pretensions and privileges, such as the game laws, primogeniture and the House of Lords. Although he did not like to be called a crammer, his candid purpose was to get his students through the examination, and that meant stuffing them with information in subject areas nominated each year by the Civil Service Commissioners. Candidates were required to pass four or five papers in fields such as English language and literature; the language, literature and history of Greece, Rome, France, Germany and Italy; mathematics and the natural sciences; the moral sciences (philosophy); and Sanskrit and Arabic languages and literature. He achieved remarkable results. In the eleven years after 1867, his school accounted for some 40 per cent of successful candidates.

At his first attempt, though, Willie failed. Mr Wren, in preparation for the English history paper, had crammed his students with constitutional history. But the examiners, perhaps to spite the crammers, set a paper on the broad facts of English history, for which Willie was quite unprepared. Allan was annoyed with Wren and thought his son was wasting his time at the college. But Willie was determined, and after another year of cramming, subjected himself again to 'the dreadful examination'. This time he passed, becoming one of thirty-seven successful candidates in a field of nearly 200. His parents were delighted. He was immensely relieved.

But the ordeal was not over yet. During the next eighteen months he was on probation, studying and being examined in subjects intended to prepare him to perform his duties in India. 'The Commissioner gives us a most awful lot to do', he told his parents. In the course of a year they were expected to master:

> the whole of Smith's *Wealth of Nations* in Political Economy, all Indian History down to the end of the last century, all Blackstone, & a tremendous deal of law English & Indian, those subjects of course being entirely new, not to mention languages.

When he was not studying he was attending various courts in London to see for himself how justice was administered. By late 1877 he had passed every test; and, equipped with the amalgam of knowledge, skills, values and attitudes he had acquired at Winchester, Mr Wren's coaching college and under the eyes of the Civil Service Commissioners, he prepared to embark on his lifetime career.

While Willie had been training for India, his brother Alan, having completed his studies at Winchester, went up to Oxford to prepare for a career in the law. Their two younger brothers, George and Ewan, evidently undeterred by the tunding row, or confident perhaps that Willie's noble stand would make life easier for them, urged their father to send them to Winchester. At the end of their time there, George joined the army and Ewan went up to Oxford to read law. The remaining brother, Charlie, who was three years younger than Willie, also set his sights on India; but he was no scholar. Instead of following his brothers to Winchester, he decided to accompany Willie to India and try his hand as a tea planter.

So in 1877 Willie and Charlie boarded the SS *Viceroy* bound for Calcutta, a voyage that had taken his great-grandmother Eliza eight months but which now, by steamer through the Suez Canal, took just one. Willie spent much of the journey improving his Hindustani and reading books that would equip him for his official duties, including John Stuart Mill's *A System of Logic*, which proclaimed the superiority of reason over intuition. Charlie spent his time enjoying himself, including admiring two sisters who were just out of school in Paris and who were, according to Willie, 'decidedly fast'. Charlie talked to one of them 'with a view to dancing', but Willie, having noticed that two other young men had already claimed their attentions, kept his distance. Other passengers included 'a horribly affected young dissenting missionary' who read the Church of England service (the only one the ship's captain would allow) in a tone of protest; several army officers, who joined Willie and other civil officers— or 'Civilians', as they were called—in a game of cricket against 'the world', which presumably included Charlie and other fortune seekers; and a Mr Hancock, a young lawyer who forced Willie into a spirited defence of Gladstone and Liberal politics. Politics aside, Hancock was an annoyance, chaffing Willie about his tunding and telling him that his father's letters to the *Times* had caused much amusement in his office.

Willie's reputation had also reached Calcutta, where one of the under-secretaries greeted him with the comment: 'You were at Winchester weren't you … we heard a good deal about you some years ago'. But the reception was friendly. As a new recruit, he expected to be appointed to a junior position in one of the districts, and soon he was on his way to the ancient city of Patna, nearly 400 miles to the north-west on the banks of the Ganges. Within a year he was transferred to a vastly different environment near Sylhet, where the paddy fields of eastern Bengal yielded to the forests and tea gardens of Assam. Most Civilians avoided Assam as remote and dangerous, but Willie preferred it to the plains of western Bengal.

Old Court House Street, Calcutta, sketched about two years before Willie Macpherson arrived there. This view looks towards St Andrew's Church and the point where Thomas Daniell sketched a similar scene in Colonel Allan Macpherson's time, depicted at the beginning of chapter 2. St Andrew's was built in 1818 on the site of the Old Court House. *The Graphic,* 20 October 1875. NATIONAL LIBRARY OF AUSTRALIA

As a member of the Indian Civil Service, William Charles Macpherson was one of fewer than a thousand men who ruled a population exceeding 250 million. Their responsibilities were vast, covering almost everything relating to the administration of justice and the collection and distribution of revenues. The individual Civilian could wield immense powers, but not before he was qualified to do so. A new recruit had to pass frequent examinations, including translating to and from appropriate languages, before he was allowed to perform specific functions. Willie became so inured to the routine of examinations that he claimed to miss them when he no longer had to sit for them.

Once fully qualified as an Assistant Magistrate and Justice of the Peace, he threw himself into 'district work'. Much of his time was spent travelling by horse and boat around the subdivision, and camping in isolated villages, where he heard minor criminal cases and administered summary justice. Most of the cases involved misdemeanours, such as allowing cattle to stray onto a neighbouring property, or domestic or local feuds. There was always a risk of violence between communities, so the diligent magistrate had to be on his guard. One of the more difficult tasks in the region was to protect 'coolies' against tyrannical tea and indigo planters. According to another Civilian, the planters were a 'rough, rowdy bachelor lot', truculent and hard drinking. They, like Allan Macpherson on the Australian frontier in years past, had come to make a fortune, and were not going to let authority get in their way. Willie's brother Charlie was one of the planters, first of tea, then of indigo, without apparently achieving much success in either. Given that their reasons for being in India were so different, it is hardly surprising that the brothers often failed to see eye to eye.

District work could be tiresome and frustrating, especially when a case was impenetrable to an outsider or, as sometimes happened, the magistrate discovered he was being used in some vendetta. Willie preferred more substantial jobs, such as organising the census or setting up, on his own initiative, a local dispensary. He was often lonely and homesick, the cure for which was hard work. 'People say sometimes ... that I work harder than any sahib', he told his mother. She had just sent him a copy of his father's pamphlet on Mount Abundance, which set him thinking how much he owed him. His propensity for hard work, he was sure, must have been inherited. 'I think I never read such a record of taking pains as Mount Abundance.'

After several years of district work, Willie transferred to the provincial headquarters at Shillong, high in the hills of Assam. This was 'a delightful station with a good climate', green for much of the year, with a mass of azaleas and rhododendrons. Here too the work was demanding, as he came to terms with 'the despotism of despatch boxes by which India is governed'. But there was more time for relaxation than when constantly moving from one campsite to the next. He built an orchid house, intending to have the best collection on the station. And he participated in a constant round of entertainments. In 1883 the European population was about seventy, including a dozen or so wives and daughters, sufficient to organise regular dinners and dances (from which Indians were generally excluded). Willie told his mother that he and a chum called Willson had given a dance, which nearly everyone at the station had attended. They decorated the ballroom with orchids and organised everything strictly in accordance with the essential protocols, so that Willie, as the more junior in his chummery, escorted the wife of the senior military officer, while Willson offered his hand to the wife of the Chief Commissioner.

> I am aware that this proceeding reads to you as rather frivolous
> and indicates a state of things hardly compatible with the

account which I am always giving you of my hard work, but it is not really incompatible. Bachelors have to give some return for hospitality, & Willson and I came to the conclusion it would be a smaller waste of time to give a dance than to have several dinner parties.

The next morning—Sunday—he was back at work, and the following day in his usual routine of working from seven in the morning until seven at night.

Shillong, Willie told his father, was a 'really pleasant berth', but it was an easy place to fade into obscurity. He knew that if he wanted to become 'a distinguished Indian official' he would have to go back to Bengal. So after nearly six years in Assam he returned to district work in the more densely populated plains of Bengal and Oudh, criss-crossing territory that his great-grandfather had frequented more than a century earlier. Now it was possible to make long journeys—from Calcutta to Patna, for example—by train. But when he travelled between isolated villages, the means of transportation was horse, boat or palanquin, as it had been in Colonel Allan Macpherson's day. On one good day's journey he travelled 28 miles by palanquin, transported by sixteen bearers, four at a time, jogging along to the monotonous rhythm of

The Collector's bungalow at Shillong, Assam. Willie Macpherson probably shared this house with his chum, Willson. MACPHERSON COLLECTION

'Mac-pher-son' and pleased, he gathered, with his long name. The trip took seven hours.

These were 'very laborious and cheerless days'. Having spent so many years in the green hills of Assam, he was shocked by the desolate landscape. Much of the region was in famine. He told his diary: 'I have seen no such poverty elsewhere in India as there is in some of the villages of this subdivision'. South of Patna he watched as four women scraped a field to collect grass seeds to eat. They told him that after six hours they would each have about a pound of grass, sufficient to make a kind of bread. At the small village of Arhanpur, not far from the spot where the Battle of Buxar had been fought in 1764, six small children came to his camp to beg for food. He invited them in for breakfast and dinner for the duration of his stay there, telling their fathers that they must look after their children and that he would hold them responsible for their welfare. But it was all very well to offer paternal advice: Willie knew how difficult it was to get work. His own responsibilities included building dams and repairing roads, partly as a form of unemployment relief. But the relief was not enough, and with the problems of having funding approved and then getting the work done, 'I have an anxious time'. Again he remembered his inheritance:

> I think I resemble my Father in making myself unhappy over details with the desire to do things thoroughly & in refusing to blink at wickednesses small & great in high & low places; but life is too short for one to be able to reform everything & one only breaks one's own back with much trying.

Even during moments of relaxation it was hard for him to forget the grinding poverty. As Christmas approached in 1884, a local maharani asked all the European officers within reach to spend the short break on her estate, promising gay entertainments and prizes, such as a gold bracelet for the winner of a tennis tournament. 'She wd do much better to spend the money in relieving some of the distress', Willie told his mother, 'but if we could forget this we should have a pleasant time.'

'THE PRIZES & THE HONOURS OF THE SERVICE'

If the work was so disheartening, what was it all for? Certainly the pay was good: higher than for the civil service at home. As a young official in the 1870s, Willie received a salary that was ample to live on; and he could look forward to earning £2000 to £3000 a year by the end of his career, or much more if he rose to the highest ranks in the service. At the end of twenty-five years he was assured of an annual pension of £1000, regardless of his rank. The provisions for furlough and 'privilege leave' (one month's holiday each year, which could be accumulated over three years) were generous; and there were other perquisites, including retreating to the hills during the hot season (though this was not guaranteed), and an abundant supply of servants (though nothing to compare with the army who waited on his great-grandparents a century earlier). But surely none of this was sufficient to compensate for the long hours, the dreary routines, the oppressive heat of Calcutta, the shivering nights in his tent on the plains of Bengal, the constant risk of disease—above all, the long periods of deprivation of family and home.

The chance of honours provided some incentive. Two orders of chivalry were created specifically for service in India: the Order of the Star of India, created several years after the 'Mutiny', and the Order of the Indian Empire, established in 1878, soon after Willie had first arrived in Calcutta. A Civilian who distinguished himself through long and faithful service could reasonably expect some form of recognition, perhaps even a knighthood. Willie described himself as ambitious, and certainly he valued recognition; but he was not one to seek honours if he did not think them deserved, nor to devote much of his life to work that had no higher purpose.

What was that higher purpose? From his private letters home it seemed that Willie was impelled by a sense of duty. Duty could mean many things. His ancestors had invariably acknowledged their duty to God; often they had spoken of the duty they owed themselves and their families; his great-grandfather had urged his son, as he was about to sail for the West Indies, to remember above all his duty to his employer. Soldiers pledged themselves to serve king (or queen) and country. Now Willie, and many others like him in the Indian Civil Service, recognised the duty they owed to the Empire and what they understood to be Britain's imperial mission.

And what was that mission? Queen Victoria herself helped focus attention on what purpose her Indian possessions were intended to serve. She had eagerly sought the title Empress of India, and her Prime Minister, Benjamin Disraeli, had been keen to oblige her. The Liberal Opposition, though, recoiled from a change that might link Britain symbolically with the hated empires of Germany and, until recently, France. One of the most strenuous critics of the Royal Titles Bill was Robert Lowe, who had made a name for himself in New South Wales in the 1840s and was now a luminary in the House of Commons. Lowe urged his fellow parliamentarians to discourage any comparison with the Mughal Emperors, who were infamous for their violence and debauchery.

> Would it not be better for us to teach the Natives of India that
> those men reigned for their own pleasure and gratification ...
> and that our object, on the contrary, is simply to do as much
> good as possible?

Lowe's call resonated with young Willie, just as he was immersed in Indian law, history and languages during his months in London as a probationer. The young man concluded that Lowe, whom his father had known and much admired in New South Wales, was right: Britain's imperial rule had to

In 1875, during the Prince of Wales' visit to India and when memories of 'the mutiny' are fading, *The Graphic*, published in London, offers its readers a reassuring message.
NATIONAL LIBRARY OF AUSTRALIA

be 'wise and beneficent'. Willie took the lesson with him to India, throwing himself into learning Bengali so that he might perform his duties better, and looking for ways that he might improve the lot of the people over whom he had charge. After several years in the Service, having witnessed at first hand the devastating impact of famine, he determined to use part of his furlough to increase his own knowledge of agricultural science and to make that branch the focus of his future career.

This sense of responsibility was accompanied by a sense of entitlement to rule, shared by all but a few of his contemporaries in the Service. As products of English public schools it was hardly surprising that they considered themselves born to rule, at home and abroad. And although Mr Wren espoused liberal opinions, nothing in Willie's education challenged the prevailing view that Britons were better placed than Indians to govern India. But if he and his colleagues accepted implicitly their right to rule, they also knew they had to rule wisely and well.

Similarly, he assumed that British magistrates were better able than Indians to administer justice fairly. This became an issue in 1883, when the government in Calcutta proposed to remove a legislative anomaly which discriminated against Indian magistrates by preventing them from trying Europeans in criminal cases outside the major cities. Many Europeans were outraged, especially the tea planters of Assam, who were accustomed to beating their 'coolies' and getting off lightly. Willie, along with almost every other European in Assam, believed that the proposal was 'foolish and unnecessary', and dangerous in principle. As he explained to his father, native magistrates were 'rarely as thorough and painstaking' as their European counterparts, and their judgments were 'never as conscientious and as logical' as those of Europeans. In any case, 'I think an accused person has a right to be tried by a countryman if he desires it'. Presumably this applied only if the accused was British.

In Willie's view, shared by nearly everyone in the Indian Civil Service, Britain had an undoubted right and responsibility to rule India. Beyond India, however, he recognised limits to imperial power. Afghanistan was clearly beyond those limits. In the late 1870s, the Afghan king, or Amir, Sher Ali, was caught up in the 'Great Game' between the British and the Russians for ascendancy in central Asia. The British had long regarded his country as a buffer state, serving a similar purpose to Oudh a century earlier in protecting British India against hostile powers. When a Russian diplomatic mission imposed itself on the Afghan court in 1878, Her

Majesty's government in Calcutta responded by sending its own mission. Sher Ali, unable to do much else, turned back the British at the Indian border. In London, Disraeli's government interpreted this as a hostile act and resolved to replace the Amir with a more pliant ruler.

Willie watched with dismay as events unfolded. 'There seems to be no doubt about our going in at the Amir now', he told his brother George, who was then at Winchester. 'I think we are trying to bully him in a most unjustifiable manner.' If the matter should come up for debate at Winchester, George should denounce the Viceroy, Lord Lytton, who was agitating for war, and the 'unspeakable Jingos' (a term just coined) back home who supported him. Once British troops were at war, 'everyone will want to smash up the unfortunate Amir'.

These predictions proved well founded. The Viceroy issued an ultimatum, and when it was ignored sent into Afghanistan an army of over 35,000 men, most of them sepoys. The Afghans, who were numerically superior, sustained heavy losses, and Sher Ali, who had called for a holy war against the invaders, was forced to flee into Russia, and died soon after. As reports of the fighting reached Willie's station in far away Sylhet, he wrote to his mother:

> Is it not a distressing state of things in Afghanistan[?]. I wish we
> had never crossed the border to go to that miserable country.
> It is absurd how we seem to have said that it was only the old
> Amir that we should have to fight against and that the people
> were ready to welcome us. They hate us as a nation.

He concluded that there was now no choice but to annex the country: 'we can't with any remains of dignity do what some of the liberal party want to be done—just give the Afghans a good thrashing and then clear out'.

As it happened, Britain—with Gladstone now Prime Minister—stopped short of annexation. After nearly two years of intermittent but bloody warfare, the Queen's soldiers withdrew from Afghanistan in 1881, with little to show for the bloodshed except an extension of British territories along the border regions and an addition to the legacy of hatred that Afghans passed on from one generation to the next.

Growing up in India. Sheila and Isla Macpherson and bearers. MACPHERSON COLLECTION

As a young Civilian, Willie Macpherson expected to remain unmarried for some time. Wives were generally regarded as an encumbrance, restricting mobility, limiting opportunities for service in remote regions, and therefore getting in the way of promotion. A few young men married the daughters of senior officials, but it was more usual to wait eight years until they came home on their first furlough. In the meantime, most lived chaste and lonely lives. Even before the 'Mutiny' the days of taking a *bibi* had passed, and now any relationship with an Indian woman was frowned upon and could interfere with career prospects.

Willie visited Scotland on privilege leave twice in the early 1880s. But, obediently to custom, it was not until his furlough that he looked for and found a wife. In 1886 he married Isabella Mary Kinloch, the third daughter of the late Colonel David Kinloch of Gourdie and his widow, from an estate less than an hour's ride from Blairgowrie. The wedding was another grand occasion for the district, reminding Willie that his Indian exile, while of long duration, was temporary, and that one day he would be welcomed back as the local laird. Shortly afterwards, the couple headed south to board the boat for India.

Ella, as she was known to family and friends, adapted quickly to life in Calcutta while Willie, promoted to the office of Undersecretary, threw himself into working as hard as ever. They took a house fronting the river

and soon were 'fairly launched', as Willie put it, 'in the small vortex of
Calcutta society'. Charlie, passing through Calcutta on the way to his
plantation, gave Ella a pony as a wedding present, and the newlyweds
rode together around the maidan, just as Colonel Allan and Eliza had
paraded in their carriage a century earlier.

'I believe we are as happy as it is possible to be', Willie told his mother.
Their first child, a boy, was born in September 1887. There was no
question that he should be called Allan; but should he be spelled with
a single 'l', like Willie's elder brother, or in the traditional Scottish way,
with two? After careful thought, Willie and Ella introduced Alan David
Macpherson into the world with just one 'l'. A daughter, Sheila, was born
in 1889, and she was followed by two more daughters, Isla and Jean, and
a second son, David.

Willie soon wearied of being tied to his desk in Calcutta; and
seeing few opportunities for further promotion if he stayed where he

Family man: Willie, Ella, Sheila and Isla in the mid-1890s. MACPHERSON COLLECTION

was, he accepted an appointment as a district officer in Mozufferpore, north-west of Calcutta on a tributary of the Ganges. From there he moved on to serve in other towns, mostly in the province of Bihar. The District Officer—otherwise known as District Magistrate and Collector—was the cornerstone of British administration, responsible for collecting revenue, administering justice and generally looking after the welfare of the people. At Mozufferpore in 1889 Ella noted in her diary that Willie left at six o'clock, came home exhausted in the afternoon, often not until 2.00, then sometimes returned to the office for three of four hours in the evening. While the job entailed specific duties, it was also defined by what individual officers made of it. As there was no guide to the innumerable rules and regulations that officers were expected to administer, Willie set about making one. His 'Aid to revenue and magisterial duties in the Lower Provinces of Bengal' covered everything a district officer needed to know, from 'gun licences' and 'treasure troves' to 'ferries' and 'bad characters'. It quickly became a standard reference work for Bengal civil servants, and was later transformed into an official publication.

In 1891, just as Willie was finishing his guide for district officers, the Lieutenant-Governor, Sir Charles Elliott, recruited him to survey the relationship between land ownership and revenue in Bihar. This grew into a massive undertaking, extending far beyond Bihar and keeping him busy for more than six years. His job was to implement recent legislation designed to determine who owned the land (and hence who should pay the taxes) and to ensure that tenant rights were adequately protected. As well as formulating the principles of land settlement, he had to see that they were being fairly applied. In the eyes of its proponents, the survey promised to improve the condition of the peasants, increase cultivation, and reduce the likelihood of devastating famine. It was exactly the sort of task Willie enjoyed and considered worthwhile.

It was also physically exhausting. One tour early in 1894 had him leaving Calcutta by the 5.54 am train, travelling halfway across India, and arriving at Nagpur, capital of the Central Provinces, at 7.35 pm the next day, a journey of 760 miles and more than thirty-seven hours. During the next nine days he visited villages throughout the district, travelling by pony or bullock cart, on horseback or by foot, in each location interviewing the settlement officer—who was responsible for district surveys—and inspecting the land records to see that they were being correctly maintained. Then he set out immediately for home. In later years his children remembered how the familiar jingle of his watch chain as he walked up the stairs told them that he had returned from yet another long journey.

The survey was a task of labyrinthine complexity, fraught with difficulty at every turn. The *zamindars*, or landlords, resisted any reduction of their privileges. The *raiyats*, or peasants, demanded that their newly defined rights as tenants be recognised. Between the two was a new class of small-scale proprietors, or *maliks*, who had no traditional rights to the soil. There was no way of keeping everyone happy. The Chief Secretary of Bengal remarked that the Bihar survey was 'exciting a great deal of interest and irritation' among *zamindars* and *raiyats* alike, and forecast that it would become a fiasco. That did not happen, owing in part to Willie's hard work; but whether in the long term the survey achieved its aims was another matter.

By the time he had finished his own contribution, Willie was an acknowledged expert on land and revenue, earning him the nickname *Tauzi*, meaning Revenue. Sir Charles Elliott described him as his right-hand man and put his name forward for a decoration. But Elliott was

Men of the Raj: 'Settlement Officers in North Behar, 1895–96'. Willie Macpherson is seated at right. MACPHERSON COLLECTION

no longer Lieutenant-Governor, and recommendations in favour of others took precedence. Although Willie acted from time to time as a Commissioner, with responsibility for up to three districts, further promotion seemed to elude him. Always self-effacing, he assumed that hard work would bring its own rewards. By 1898, though, when it appeared that another officer with less experience in revenue matters would be appointed to act in a position he aspired to, he decided the time had come to press his claims. By then he had served in India more than twenty years. He told the Chief Secretary that while he would give his best in whatever capacity the government chose to employ him, he was 'not content to be forgotten & to drop out of the running for the

Emma Macpherson in widow's weeds. Oil by Sydney W. White.
MACPHERSON COLLECTION

prizes & the honours of the service'. The Lieutenant-Governor responded that he would keep him in mind.

Nothing happened for four years. Then, in 1902, he was finally appointed to the office he so much wanted: that of Revenue Secretary. Further promotions came in quick succession: first to the office of Commissioner at Patna, the most populous district in India; followed by the role of Chief Secretary to the government of Bengal. In the meantime, at the Coronation Durbar in January 1903, when a vast assemblage gathered in Delhi to celebrate the British Raj, he was admitted as a Companion of the Order of the Star of India, the long-awaited honour that allowed him to put the letters 'CSI' after his name.

Willie spent another eight years in India. During a period of extended leave in Scotland in 1905 he contemplated retiring, having passed the twenty-five years that qualified him for a pension. But his mother Emma, now an imperious lady in her early seventies living at Blairgowrie House with her younger daughter Frances, seemed to be quite capable of managing the estate without him. She also had the help of her fourth son, George, who had been wounded in the South African War and, after several more years military service, had retired to Blairgowrie. This left Willie with the problem so often faced by Indian Civil Servants of what to do when they came home. The Lieutenant-Governor, now Sir Andrew Fraser, urged him not to retire; and as the news from Bengal reminded him of 'how much of my heart is left there', he decided to stay on. Returning from leave in 1906, he resumed his former office of Chief Secretary and took up appointments to the influential Revenue Board and the Corporation of Calcutta.

Those final years in Bengal were unhappy ones. In 1905 the Indian government realigned the boundaries of the province, effectively dividing it into two. This led to an outbreak of terrorism and communal violence, with the Hindu majority in the west set against the Muslim majority in the east. Willie Macpherson kept his head down through the troubles, no doubt hoping and expecting they would go away. But with attempts on the life of the Lieutenant-Governor, judges and civil servants murdered, and Calcutta intellectuals calling for revolution, it was hard to ignore the growing resentment of British rule.

His personal unhappiness, though, had more to do with the appointment in 1908 of a new Lieutenant-Governor, Sir Edward Baker. Baker had joined the Indian Civil Service a year after Willie and had followed a similar career; and now he was charged with reversing the partition that had caused so much unrest. According to Willie, he was too eager to curry favour with young Indian nationalists, as shown by his proposal to use the money collected in 1910 in memory of Edward VII to build a student hostel in Calcutta. Willie put forward an alternative proposal to fund a school of tropical medicine, which he said would benefit the whole of India. This suggestion won the day (though in the event most of the money went towards erecting a statue of the late King). After this, Willie believed Baker never forgave him nor missed an opportunity to put him down.

In 1911 Willie, now in his mid-fifties, resigned abruptly, convinced that the government had treated him shabbily. What pained him most was that since 1903, when he had been awarded the CSI, he had been offered scarcely a word of public recognition apart from routine annual acknowledgments. He had watched as others junior to himself, and less hard-working, had been awarded knighthoods. 'From Sir Edward Baker, I never received one line to soften disappointment or convey thanks.'

Nevertheless, there were many consolations. The Maharajah of Cooch Behar, one of the principalities that had maintained its nominal independence from the Raj, urged him to accept appointment as Superintendent of his small state: Willie said he would have done so had he been younger. The English language newspapers effused about his contribution. One called him, before his retirement, 'the ablest and most experienced officer in Bengal'. Another, when he left, referred to his 'almost painful conscientiousness, ... his unswerving devotion to duty, his kindly disposition, and the unvarying gentleness and courtesy with which he fronted to the world'. It was said that among the Indian community 'no British officer could have been more highly respected than he was'.

Such praise warmed his heart. And yet, as he reflected on his career of thirty-four years, he felt that something was lacking.

CONSOLATIONS

Just as his father had done in 1870 when he returned from Australia sensing that he had not achieved all he had hoped for, Willie now found consolation in his family. All his and Ella's five children had been born in India; and all had followed the usual pattern of 'Anglo-Indian' families by travelling to Britain at an early age to complete their education. They would all spend periods of their later lives in distant parts of the empire.

The future doctor, Sheila Macpherson and the young officer, Alan Macpherson.
MACPHERSON COLLECTION

By the time Willie resigned from the Indian Civil Service in 1911, Alan, the eldest child, then in his mid-twenties, was an army officer based with his regiment in Ireland. On leaving Winchester, he had been accepted into the Royal Military Academy at Woolwich, graduating into the Royal Field Artillery. Early in 1914, he was on his way to India, and looking forward to visiting some of the places frequented by his parents. Within months, though, his division was recalled to fight in France. He remained there for the next four years, serving on some of the bloodiest battlefields on the Western Front. Although he never boasted of his military achievements, they were considerable: mentioned three times in despatches, Military Cross in 1917 and Distinguished Service Order in 1918.

Between the wars Alan travelled widely. In 1919 he was stationed on India's north-west frontier, where British forces were locked in fierce (and largely futile) battle with Waziri tribesmen. Back in Blairgowrie in 1922, he married Catharine Hill, the daughter of a long-term resident of the district who had been involved in trade with China. A week after the wedding the couple were headed for India. They were again in Britain when their first child, Catriona, was born in 1923. Their second, a boy, arrived in 1926. This was William Alan Macpherson, later Sir William Macpherson of Cluny and Blairgowrie, with whom this story began. A third child, Sheila, followed two years later, when Alan was stationed in Malta. Then, after more home service, he was given command of a regiment in Singapore before returning to Scotland on the eve of war in 1939. Promoted to the rank of Brigadier, his last active service was in India. He retired in 1942, trading his Brigadier's insignia for the single 'pip' of a Second Lieutenant in the Home Guard.

Willie did his best to guide his children through life, as his father and grandfather had done before him. From him they gained a sense of Britain's imperial mission. In 1929, Alan asked him what he thought about the current situation in Palestine, which was then governed by the British under a League of Nations Mandate—an incident at the Western Wall in Jerusalem had been followed by bloody communal violence across the territory. The position, wrote Willie, 'is a most difficult one—similar to, but more difficult than, keeping the peace between Hindu & Muhammadan in India'. Both sides, he said, had reasonable claims relating to the wall and the adjacent mosque.

> It is for the Christian to determine what can reasonably be declared to be the respective rights by the Wall in these circumstances, if Jew & Muhammadan cannot agree; & having decided the matter the Christian must have his decision respected unless & until an agreement to the contrary be arrived at ... I would not ... contemplate giving up our Mandate in Palestine. We are not Americans.

Willie's three daughters—Sheila, Isla and Jean—contributed to the empire in other ways. During the Great War they all served with the V.A.D.—the Volunteer Aid Detachment—nursing wounded soldiers in a makeshift hospital in Perth near Blairgowrie. Perhaps it was there that Sheila decided she wanted to become a doctor. Given the strong prejudices against women doctors, this was hard. Her father, though, supported her from the outset, paying her fees at the University of Edinburgh and encouraging her every achievement. When she graduated in 1925, she wrote to thank her 'darling Daddy ... with all my heart because it was your faith in me that brought it all about from the beginning'.

Sheila never married. Isla had an understanding with Alastair Buchan, brother of John Buchan, famous as the author of *Prester John* and *The Thirty-nine Steps*. But before their engagement was announced Alastair was killed in action on the Western Front in 1917. Isla remained unmarried, becoming instead Sheila's life companion. With their father's encouragement, they looked to India, as generations of their family had done before them. Not long after graduating, Sheila accepted the post of medical officer at St Andrew's Colonial Homes at Kalimpong, near the Bengal hill station of Darjeeling. Isla accompanied her as housekeeper, and the two remained there until early 1929.

The St Andrew's Homes had been established in 1900 by an energetic missionary, Dr John Graham, as a partial solution to what was referred to as 'the Anglo-Indian problem' or 'the Eurasian problem' (though the term Eurasian was then going out of fashion). These were the mixed race children of British India, many of whom lived on tea plantations or in the slums of Calcutta, neglected and despised by British and Indian alike. Graham's solution was to provide them with education and industrial training so that some, at least, would be acceptable in the colonies of white settlement. He served as Honorary Superintendent for over forty years, building the Homes into a thriving organisation with accommodation for over 600 children. Willie Macpherson, perhaps remembering his own Indian ancestry, was one of his warmest supporters, serving for many years as an honorary vice-president. No doubt his influence inspired the girls to join Dr Graham's mission.

Sheila and Isla spent two years in Kalimpong, with Sheila treating the sick in the local community and attending to out-patients from miles around. When they left, Dr Graham told her proud father that 'Her patients loved her', and that Isla, as well as looking after Sheila, had contributed much to community life. Returning to Scotland, Sheila practised first in a town in Perthshire, then in a mixed suburb of Edinburgh, where she attended mostly to the poor, with Isla always by her side.

Willie's third daughter Jean, another child of the Raj, had a more conventional career, much of it spent in India. In 1921 she married an old family friend and up-and-coming Indian Civil Servant, James Anderson. As James rose high in his profession, becoming Financial Commissioner for the Punjab and winning a knighthood, she served as a dutiful wife and as mother to their four children.

Alan, Sheila, Isla and Jean appeared to inherit the strong sense of duty that had impelled their father throughout his Indian career. Their brother David, the youngest in the family, had a more robust view of empire as a place for making fortunes. He followed his brother into the army, just missed the Great War, served in Africa and India and resigned his commission in 1926. Returning to Africa he settled as a farmer in Nyasaland. Later, in Portuguese East Africa, he shot 'jumbo' and poached ivory for a living, and stuffed birds for a hobby, achieving some distinction as an amateur ornithologist. Some admired his adventurous spirit and indomitable courage. Others, including some in his own family, were not so sure.

Apart from doing his best to guide his children through life, Willie's duty, as the head of the family, was to maintain the family estate. This was an enormous challenge. When his father died in 1891, he bequeathed debts exceeding £28,000. While his mother, Emma, had managed affairs capably during the following twenty years, the total debt appears to have remained much the same. She died in 1915, a few days after hearing that her fourth son, George, who had rejoined the army soon after the declaration of war, had been killed in Flanders at the ripe age of fifty-three. Now the task of rescuing the family's finances was Willie's alone. He worked hard, as his father had done, to make a success of fruit growing. But a good return from raspberries (substituting for strawberries) scarcely balanced the losses from rental income that confronted all landed proprietors after the war. As he watched other large estates shrinking, Willie recognised that the only way to save the property was to let much of it go. By doing that, he managed in the seven years after the war to reduce the debt by £19,000. By 1926, it seems safe to say that less was owing on the estate than at any time since Colonel Allan had acquired it in the late 1770s.

Willie consoled himself with the philosophy that 'land is a rich man's plaything'. What choice did he have? His son Alan, who stood to inherit the property, reassured him: 'The total burdens were so heavy that I think most men would have thrown in their hands right away & left it to the lawyers to make what they could of a bad job'. There was worse to come. In 1927 Willie concluded, on Alan's advice, that he must sell Blairgowrie House and much of the remaining estate. For a moment it seemed that they would leave Blairgowrie entirely, perhaps purchasing a cottage in St Andrews or returning to the family's ancestral roots in Badenoch. But after many hours agonising over the books, Willie decided they could move across the estate to Newton, the ancient castle on the side of the hill that his great-grandparents, Colonel Allan and Eliza, had occupied on their return from India in 1787. Sheila, still in India, wrote comfortingly that she and Isla knew that 'whatever you have decided has been right & we are proud & thankful for your courage & wisdom'.

This was a painful time. Willie sadly acknowledged that he 'must go down in history as the man who greatly diminished the estate'. From over 700 acres before the war, the family's property had shrunk to just 200. In leaving Blairgowrie House it seemed that they were not just losing the family home of 130 years but sacrificing much of the family's heritage. A nephew by marriage wrote, rather tactlessly, to suggest that he should ask the editors of Burke's *Peerage and Baronetage* to include in their next edition a note about 'the Macphersons late of Blairgowrie'. But that, Willie responded, was surely going too far. Newton, after all, was still formally described as 'the principal mansion house' on the estate, although it was not so grand or comfortable as the home they had sold. In any case, 'I think that in the minds of those here who understand the position there are still Macphersons of Blairgowrie though not of Blairgowrie House'.

The evidence of that was in Willie's contribution to the local community. He served tirelessly, often as chairman, on this and that committee: the parish council, the hospital management committee, the district fruit growers federation, the war memorial committee, the local branch of the League of Nations, and so on. These duties were onerous and sometimes expensive. But Willie knew that being a laird had always cost money.

During retirement he assumed the role of 'family annalist', the office he had proposed to his father many decades earlier. Following his father, he pursued genealogical connections. He unearthed references to Colonel Allan's sister Isobel, who apparently died unmarried in the 1760s. He conducted research into his mother's side of the family. He searched *Who's Who* for possible relatives. He even tried (unsuccessfully) to locate a descendant of his miscreant great-uncle, the former Reverend Allan Macpherson, who had died in Paris after breaking an English bank.

His main task, though, was to organise the Indian journals of his great-grandfather, Colonel Allan Macpherson, and the Colonel's brother, 'honest John'. This was a laborious undertaking, involving deciphering, transcribing and typing documents that were sometimes barely legible, some of them written by his ancestors, others by various *munshis* who copied words without understanding their meaning. His initial intention, as he explained in the Introduction, was to compile family annals only, 'in fulfilment of a pious duty to those who have gone before and who come after'. But after consulting with the historiographer in the India Office in London and old India hands, he decided that the journals might be of interest to general readers 'as throwing light on the life of soldiers' serving in India during the 1770s and 1780s. Long extracts were published in 1928 in a volume of 400 pages entitled *Soldiering in India*, on which the third chapter of *this* book is partly based.

Willie Macpherson recognised a duty to tell future generations about the past. He did not, however, tell his readers what they might learn from it.

17

....

REMEMBERING AND
FORGETTING

*I*N DEATH, ALLAN MACPHERSON, AUSTRALIAN SQUATTER and Scottish laird, was given a grand send-off. At two o'clock on a fine autumn afternoon in 1891 several of the strongest men employed on the estate emerged from Blairgowrie House bearing his coffin on their shoulders. They carried it to the waiting hearse at the front gate, where a large crowd had already assembled. The local police inspector marshalled the cortege, which then set out in the following order: the hearse, drawn by four black Belgian horses with plumes; the empty carriage of the deceased; Emma Macpherson and other members of the family in mourning coaches; the men of the Panton family, who had served the Macphersons as factors for many decades; the magistrates, town clerk, parochial board and members of other committees with which Allan had been so closely involved; the servants of Blairgowrie House and the estate; school children; members of the general public; and finally the private carriages of friends and dignitaries of the parish and nearby parts of Perthshire. As the procession passed mournfully through the town, its numbers increased as 'people of all ranks and classes' came out to pay their respects to their late laird and his grieving family. The muffled peals of church bells added to the solemnity of the occasion.

Allan's last journey took him past Emma Street and Harriet Row (both leading on to Jessie Street), and William Street, reminders of his family's long association with the town. Proceeding up the hill and along High Street, the cortège halted at St Catharine's Church, where the coffin was placed before the altar and where the minister, before a packed congregation, conducted the first part of the service. The coffin was then returned to the hearse and the cortege set out again, along Upper Allan Street (named presumably after Colonel Allan Macpherson) and around

Kirk Wynd to the family burial ground. There the minister performed the second part of the service and the pallbearers—who included Alan, George and Ewan, the three of Allan's five sons who were in the country—lowered the coffin into a vault constructed of white glazed brick and lined with moss and evergreens, that had been prepared to receive it.

MONUMENTS

Thus Allan joined his grandfather and grandmother in the plot of earth that they had set aside for their own and later generations, proof of their intention to create a family dynasty long before the younger Allan had the same idea. The marble monument to Colonel Allan and Eliza still stands, and the simple inscription is still legible; but it misspells Eliza as 'Elisa' and gives the Colonel's death as a year later than it actually was, in 1816, confirming that the headstone was carved after their son William had left for Australia. Monuments cannot be relied on to tell the truth about the past.

The Macpherson burial ground was and is a private place, for remembering within the family. Other monuments speak to the wider world. When Colonel Alexander Champion, Allan Macpherson's commanding officer during the Rohilla campaign, died at his home in Bath in 1793, his wife ensured that he would be remembered forever by the public at large. Acting perhaps in accordance with her late husband's wishes, she arranged for a sculpture to be mounted in Bath

In the family graveyard at Blairgowrie.

Abbey, regarded then and now as one of the finest medieval churches in Britain. The monument stands imposingly, two and a half metres high, at the rear of the church. The sculptor, Joseph Nollekens, once referred to as 'the *Emperor* of bust-chisellers', created a masterpiece: Champion's bust, portrayed on an oval base, is protected by the angelic figure of Fame with weapons of war at her feet. 'His Memory remains!', the inscription proclaims:

> Not less adorned exalted and endeared by domestic Virtues,
> than by professional Abilities.
> He rose, in the Course of twenty Years active Service in *India*,
> [To] the CHIEF COMMAND of the *Company's* Troops in BENGAL:
> And in the various Situations wherein he held that Honor
> his Zeal, his Courage, and Success, were ever tempered
> by Humanity.

There is more, none of which bears much resemblance to the man who, as his aide-de-camp Allan Macpherson reported, ordered three sepoys to have their ears cut off for stealing palm sugar, and deserters to cast a dice to determine which of them should be shot. The sculpture no doubt cost a lot, albeit just a fraction of Champion's share of the £10,000 he received as his part of the 'Rohilla donation'.

Much of the empire is written around the walls of the Abbey. The story it tells depends on how you read it.

Another of Colonel Allan Macpherson's friends who was determined not to be forgotten was his cousin James Macpherson (whom we came to know as Ossian). As well as arranging to be interred at Westminster Abbey, he set aside in his will a generous sum for construction of a memorial in Badenoch, in the grounds of his Belleville estate. As joint executor, Allan Macpherson was therefore assigned the disagreeable task of erecting a monument to the man who had defrauded him, on land that might otherwise have been his. To make matters worse, the project did not go smoothly. The marble turned out to be of poor quality and, through some misunderstanding, the sculptor in Edinburgh made mistakes with the design of the family crest, which of course had to be corrected. Nevertheless, the memorial was eventually completed, transported and installed at Belleville. There it stands to this day, separated from the mansion by the main road that runs from south to north through the

Monument to James 'Ossian'
Macpherson, at Balavil, with
nose restored.

Colonel Alexander Champion,
memorial sculpture by Joseph
Nollekens. BATH ABBEY

Highlands. The monument takes the form of an obelisk, ornately carved with allusions to Macpherson's literary works, and a bust of James himself, worn by time and defaced by a broken nose. In recent decades, the nose has been restored, although clear evidence of the break remains—which is probably as many of his contemporaries would have wished. The grand edifice of Belleville House, now known as Balavil, might have served as a more lasting monument, had not its associations with Ossian been overshadowed by greater fame as one of the mansion houses in a long-running television series *Monarch of the Glen*.

Allan Macpherson's friend and son-in-law, Colonel (and later Lieutenant-General) John Macintyre, was likewise commemorated in Badenoch. Following his death in Sussex in 1828, his wife Harriot erected a marble tablet in the parish church at Kingussie, near his birthplace. Although he had spent little time in Badenoch after setting out for India as a young man, this was evidently where he wished to be remembered, and where he thought he would best be remembered by his relatives and friends. But the tablet fared still worse than Ossian's: it was evidently destroyed when the church was razed by fire in 1924.

The next generation of Macphersons, William and his wife Jessy, were buried in Australia. For nearly twenty years after her death in 1847 Jessy lay entombed in her lead-lined coffin, waiting for William to take her home to Scotland. But William, as we know, never left Australia;

and after he died at Bernera in 1866, his and her final journey was to the Devonshire Street Cemetery, which served at the time as Sydney's main burial ground. In 1901 the land was resumed to make way for the city's new Central railway station. Through newspaper advertisements, the government invited relatives and friends of the deceased who were buried there to come forward if they required their ancestors' remains to be moved to some other cemetery, at the public expense. But the descendants of William and Jessy were then in India and Scotland, so the notices probably never reached them. Without anyone to claim them, the headstones were destroyed and the remains left undisturbed, except by the rumbling of railway trains on the ground above.

William was better served by a public memorial. At the time of his death, work was nearing completion on Sydney's long delayed Church of England cathedral, to be known as St Andrew's. Probably drawing on the proceeds of the will, his son Allan arranged for a stained glass window to be erected in his memory, at the considerable cost of £64. Manufactured by one of London's finest stained glass makers, it arrived just in time for the cathedral's consecration late in 1868. Although Allan probably saw the window safely installed, he did not wait for the consecration. Several weeks earlier he had left for Britain, expecting never to return. He had done his duty by his father—perhaps he was fulfilling his wishes. Perhaps he was also anxious to preserve his father's memory in the colony to which he had given so much; perhaps by this last act of piety he hoped to absolve himself from blame for sometimes thinking and speaking ill of his parent; or perhaps he was showing colonists that he was a dutiful son and, contrary to what some might think, a worthy successor to the family name. Monuments often serve purposes we can only guess at.

The window, located high above the pulpit in the cathedral's northern transept, appears at its best when illuminated by the late morning sun. But the inscription—'In Memory of William Macpherson Esq of Blairgowrie in Scotland who died in this Colony 11 March MDCCCLXVI Aged 81 years'—is so small as to be almost invisible from the floor below, and there is no plaque at eye level to say whom it commemorates. Nor is there any acknowledgment in parish leaflets. Once, it served as a public celebration of a man's life and career; now, it tells a story only to members of the family and a few others who know it is there.

The younger Allan and his wife Emma share a grave and a monument in the Macphersons' burial ground at Blairgowrie. Although their headstone was inscribed many decades after the Colonel and Eliza's monument, its dedication is now much harder to read. The marble used in the later monument may have been of poorer quality, or the mason less skilled. But there is no doubt who lies beneath; and nor will there ever be so long as the Macphersons of Blairgowrie continue to be buried in the family plot and remembered by their surviving kin. Allan, like his father, also has a public memorial. A new pulpit, inscribed to his memory, was installed a year after he died in the church where he and his family had regularly worshipped.

Allan Macpherson fared better than his half brother Allan Williams, the son of William and his slave Countess. When he died in 1896 Allan Williams joined his wife Sophia in the burial ground of the Church of England at Ashfield, just a few blocks from his family home. Two decades later parishioners were complaining that the graveyard was in disrepair. First it was invaded by goats, then horses and cattle took over, disturbing tombstones and trampling on the graves. If Allan and Sophia Williams ever had a headstone, it has now disappeared, along with any record of where exactly they lie.

Monuments to individuals, whatever their original purpose, sometimes represent or celebrate much more than individual lives. After the death of Professor Dugald Stewart in 1828, a number of Edinburgh's most prominent citizens decided to erect a statue in his memory. Stewart, whose lectures in moral philosophy young William Macpherson had attended before setting out for the West Indies in 1801, was widely regarded, in the words of one of his admirers, as 'the pride and ornament ... of Scotland'. His monument, a small circular edifice modelled loosely on a temple built in Athens in the fourth century BC, still stands on Calton Hill, where it offers photographers an instantly identifiable foreground to views across the city towards Edinburgh Castle. While it was intended as a memorial to just one remarkable man, it may also be seen as a larger monument to the ideas and values of the Scottish Enlightenment, including the spirit of open inquiry, that had so great an impact on the rest of the world.

On the other side of the globe, nearly seventy years after his death, Allan Macpherson, the pioneer of Keera and Mount Abundance, was acknowledged in a monument deep in the Australian bush. In the late 1950s, Gordon Munro, whose family had acquired Keera a year or two after Allan and Emma had left there, decided 'to perpetuate and express appreciation to the former pioneers of this area', chiefly members of his own family, but also those who had come before. On a hill overlooking the homestead, in a spot commanding fine views in every direction, he arranged for three large blocks of local granite to be placed on top of one another so as to build a structure 10 feet high. There was talk at the time that the Gwydir River might be dammed downstream, in which case the valley would be flooded and the homestead and all around it submerged. Gordon Munro's monument would stand forever on an island in permanent tribute to his forefathers.

The structure was unveiled by the local member of state parliament early in 1960 in a ceremony open to all and attended by several hundred neighbours and visitors from stations and towns in the surrounding region. According to a booklet produced for the occasion, the granite was of the 'bright, light silver type ... such as used in Aberdeen, Scotland'. Copper plaques on two sides honoured the men and women

Monument to Dugald Stewart, Calton Hill, Edinburgh.

of the Munro family. A third was to recognise 'those men and women who pioneered this area and to record the occupation of Keera by the Munros since 1858'. The fourth, facing northwards, was 'in memory of Allan Macpherson of Blairgowrie', with mention of how the station passed into Munro hands. The monument still stands, though not on an island, as the dam was built far upstream. To all except locals it is now lost in the bush.

As well as paying tribute to 'the pioneers', Gordon Munro was honouring his Scottish ancestry. His booklet begins:

> We are Scots, and whatever our social position
> Whether high-born or lowly, one wish thrills our breast
> To keep unsullied our Nation's tradition
> And give to the wide world our noblest and best.

Then there are extracts from Robert Burns—'A man's a man for a' that'—and from the Scottish-Australian poet Will Ogilvie, whose ballads expressed his love of the Australian bush and the yearnings of Scots abroad:

> We have sung it in our exile till the heartleap and the croon
> Brought us back the brown hills' whisper and the nodding
> blue-bells' tune;
> And the old, old loves are toasted in our cups of brimming wine
> While our hearts beat out the music to the words of Auld
> Lang Syne.

Visitors on the day of the monument's unveiling were invited to explore the property and inspect nearly fifty 'features of interest', including the remains of Allan Macpherson's orchard, the old blacksmith's shop, the jackaroos' quarters, and a carved stump indicating the site of 'the blackfellows' burial ground' (which Emma Macpherson had painted in the 1850s). There was also a basalt sharpening stone and a neck plate inscribed 'Brady King of Bingara', of the kind given to Aboriginal men who had proven themselves useful to Europeans. These were the only references to Keera's first inhabitants. The monument itself did not mention them at all, contributing to a phenomenon that an anthropologist, eight years after the unveiling, famously called the 'Great Australian Silence'.

Monument at Keera, New South Wales.

PLACES

Except for Blairgowrie, where the family is remembered even in the street names, places carry few obvious memories that the Macphersons once lived there. But the Macpherson name still echoes around the mountains and valleys of Badenoch. It is easy to imagine where young Allan Macpherson, around 1750, might have walked from one set of kinsfolk to the next, and to locate the foundations of Cluny House where he threw stones at the redcoats after Culloden. But Badenoch is the spiritual home of the whole Clan—there is a Clan museum and a cairn where clansfolk from around the world come together during their annual gathering—so that memories of the Macphersons of Blairgowrie are subsumed by the claims of the larger tribe.

Nothing remains to remind us of Colonel Allan's presence in India, though we can identify places he visited and imagine landscapes he might have seen. Probably his great-grandson Willie traced his movements through Bengal when he was stationed there a century later. Surprisingly, it is still possible to find, within a hundred metres or so, the location of the house in Calcutta where Allan Macpherson and his friend Captain Macintyre lived in their 'chummery', before Allan married Eliza Dell Fraser in 1781. A few years later work began just across the road on a new Church of England, to be known as St John's. It was consecrated in mid-1787, shortly after Allan and Eliza left for Scotland. St John's survives today as a vestige of the British presence in eighteenth century Calcutta.

Almost nothing remains of the built environment of Berbice two centuries ago, except perhaps a few canal works built by the Dutch and now lost in the jungle. When William Macpherson was there between 1801 and 1813, the landscape was already changing, as cotton and sugar plantations, once the source of great riches for usually absentee owners, succumbed to overcropping and one disastrous season after another. Now ramshackle villages line the potholed road from Georgetown to New Amsterdam, with place names—Eldorado, Belladrum, Paradise, Golden Fleece, Hope, Union—the only echoes of another age. William's Rising Sun plantation is remembered in the names of a rudimentary turf club and a small abattoir and beef processing plant.

In Sydney, many of the places frequented by the family still stand, though most of them are greatly changed: Hyde Park, which served as a playground for the boys of Mr Cape's school; St James' Church, where William and Jessy took the holy sacrament and wished that young Allan would join them; Parliament House, including the Legislative Council chamber, where William wrote letters chastising his son for extravagance, and the anteroom where Allan took to his fellow member of parliament with a horsewhip. The houses where they lived, though, gave way long ago to skyscrapers.

In the bush, the landscape of Keera is much as it was when Allan was last there in the mid-1850s; and with the notable absence of the Aboriginal group who camped alongside the creek, the number of people living on the original squatting run is probably about the same now as it was then. The cottage that Emma painted is gone, washed away by a flood several years after they had left. Bernera, on the other hand, their cottage west of Sydney, remained until it was destroyed by fire in 1986. It survived long enough to be included in a register of the national estate, where it was described as a 'well-designed early vernacular homestead'. Much of the original Bernera property is now taken over by light industry, near a complex junction of motorways. Around Mount Abundance, the

Blairgowrie House about 1930. Watercolour by E. Rose Black. MACPHERSON COLLECTION

landscape has probably changed little, though the town of Roma occupies part of Allan Macpherson's run. There is still a homestead called Mount Abundance, but it is some 30 kilometres distant from Allan's original head station.

Only Blairgowrie suggests continuity. Wherever family members lived—in the West Indies, Australia or India—Blairgowrie remained, literally and figuratively, the main repository of their memories. But not Blairgowrie House. Some years after Willie and Ella moved reluctantly to Newton Castle in 1928, the 'dear old home' burned to the ground.

PAPER

Monuments and places help us to remember. But they are unreliable guides to the past. Places can be washed away or reduced to ashes. Monuments can crumble and fade. Even when structures survive in or near their original condition, they often disguise as much as they reveal. What can sustain their meaning is the written record. Correspondence breathes life into stone. Documents locate people in places that now bear little resemblance to when they lived there. When monuments lie and places mislead, surely surviving papers can lead us to the truth.

Thanks to the first Allan Macpherson's habit of collecting, acquired about 1770 when he was appointed aide-de-camp to Colonel Alexander Champion, and the readiness of his descendants to follow his lead, we have been able to trace the family's movements through the nineteenth century and locate them in the times in which they lived. *Collecting* is perhaps the wrong word, because it suggests some conscious intention to maintain a record of the past. In the first instance Colonel Allan simply *retained* his papers. Sometimes his reasons are obvious: he kept a record of his financial transactions with Ossian in expectation of settling matters when he returned to Scotland (much good did they do him!); he retained his courtship letters to his beloved Eliza because he could not imagine letting them go. His reasons for keeping official papers are harder to guess at. Did he see it as his duty in his various military roles to do so? Did he realise he was living through and contributing to events that would one day be seen as historically significant? Did he think his letters and documents might be of interest to his children or even to a wider readership? Sometimes his reasons are a mystery. Why, for example, did he keep his order to the saddlemaker in 1770 for 'a pair of Handsome Spurrs'?

Neither Colonel Allan nor any of his descendants set out reasons for retaining records; but the habit, once formed, was evidently easy to maintain. So long as Blairgowrie House and, later, Newton Castle, remained the family home, there was plenty of space to store them; and Scotland's climate afforded good conditions for their preservation. The longer they were kept, the more interesting they became as a window into other worlds, and the harder it became to throw anything away. Not that every piece of paper survived. Some letters were evidently destroyed soon after their receipt. Others were simply mislaid. As we speculated earlier, someone—possibly Allan Macpherson himself—removed the diary dealing with his 'war with the blacks', leaving behind a sanitised published version. Willie excised two large files relating to his father's activities as a strawberry grower, keeping just a few letters and accounts 'to show with what amazing energy and industry my father sold his fruit in the last year of his life'. From a much earlier period, he destroyed a bundle of letters from Colonel Macintyre, who insisted that his impoverished friend and father-in-law, Colonel Allan, should pay the full marriage settlement that he had supposedly agreed to. Colonel Allan's wife Eliza had marked these 'unkind letters'. In contrast, Willie retained the heated exchanges between his father and grandfather relating to the housekeeper Mrs Egan, thinking that they might one day be of interest to members of the family.

Caring for the records became part of the process of making a family, akin to compiling the family tree. The bundles of papers, probably stored in the chests that the Colonel and Eliza brought back with them from India, became part of the family's inheritance. Emma and Allan thought their Australian adventures might be of interest to outsiders, but they did not anticipate many readers. There were five hundred copies published of *My experiences in Australia* by 'A Lady', and just one hundred of Allan's *Mount Abundance*, most of which he gave away to family and friends. Except for these accounts of experiences in one part of the world, the record of the family's story seemed disorderly, made up of numerous bundles, interesting in themselves but bearing no obvious relationship to one another. Thanks to Allan's diligence in the 1870s, the genealogy was clear; but so far the family had no history, apart from what might be gleaned from dipping into the bundles and from stories passed from one generation to the next.

In mid-1888 Willie was stationed at Mozufferpore, north-west of Calcutta on a tributary of the Ganges, missing his family, who had lately escaped to Simla to avoid the worst of the hot season, and thinking of home. He had a plan for his next furlough: he would write 'the Annals of the Macphersons of Blairgowrie'. 'I think every family ought to have a book of Annals', he told his mother, '& there should be an Annalist always in office.' The book should record significant matters for posterity and regularly be kept up to date. It should be printed 'for family use only'. 'Will my father begin[?]. No one could bring us from Badenoch to Blairgowrie, Australia and back to Blairgowrie as well as he could.'

But Allan was busy growing and selling strawberries, so the task was left to Willie, who started work on the project during a later furlough, after his father had died. He organised his notes biographically, explaining the family's ancestry, tracing the lives and careers of his great-grandfather and grandfather (his father would have to wait), and briefly recounting a few of the stories that his father had told him, including the stone-throwing incident at Cluny House shortly after the Battle of Culloden. The Colonel's brother 'honest John', who died in 1784, received a mention, as did William's sister Harriot and brother Allan (without hint of his disreputable later years). So did all their wives, and Harriot's two husbands, General Macintyre and Colonel Craigie (with no reference to the Colonel's tragic death). Then, as if there was nothing more to say, he described the portraits of his ancestors hanging in Blairgowrie House, with particular attention to what they were wearing. The text was spare. These, after all, were annals, the chief purpose of which was to record the facts, with minimal embellishment, for future generations.

Emma then arranged to have a few copies printed and bound. The text ran to just fifteen short pages, leaving over fifty pages blank for later additions. The printed version turned out to be full of errors and omissions, which Willie meticulously corrected during a later furlough, adding an affectionate account of his father's career in Australia and Scotland. One amendment was especially revealing. After noting that William had married Jessy in 1815, the typescript stated that 'His only child was Allan Macpherson, afterwards of Blairgowrie'. Willie knew this was wrong. He therefore crossed out the word 'His' and substituted 'Their'.

Through this subtle change the annals allowed for the possibility that grandfather William might have had more than one child. Otherwise, as in the family tree, there was no hint that the 'moonlight shades' ever existed, nor that numerous blood relations might yet be living on the other side of the world.

The first Allan Williams, as we know from his father's complaints, was no letter writer. And if any of his children or grandchildren wrote many letters, neither they nor their descendants appear to have kept them. Their story survives, as it does in most families, through a few letters and documents, and fragments of information passed down by word of mouth from one generation to the next. It was also sustained by a conscious decision around the time of the Great War that their story deserved to be shared.

When the war began, the Williams family was prospering. The second Allan Williams and his wife Harriet, helped by their three sons and two daughters, had built Burrenbring into a thriving cattle and sheep station. Their skill as horse breeders and passion for amateur horseracing were known well beyond the Nebo district. War changed their lives, as it did the lives of so many Australian families. When Australia committed itself to the Mother Country 'to our last man and our last shilling', the eldest son, Edward Homer Williams, was the district's first volunteer. In late 1914, aged twenty-nine and unmarried, he was on his way to Cairo, and then to Gallipoli to join the campaign against the Turks. During his time as a soldier he kept in his pocket a daily diary, which eventually found its way back to Nebo. His entries were succinct:

> 25 June 1915 'Got letters & papers from home. good account
> of races.'
> 26 June 'In firing line. very hot.'
> 27 June 'Digging trenches. very hot.'

The next day his regiment participated in a 'demonstration', or diversionary attack on the Turkish trenches, during which the Australian forces came under heavy machine gun fire, as well as friendly fire from a destroyer whose commander had not been told that they would be there. One way or another, he was killed in action. He was buried with six other troopers in a grave 100 yards from the shore. After the war his remains were exhumed and reburied in a cemetery at the top of a cliff, with fine views of the sea.

The Williams family, about 1910: left to right, standing, Edith, Edward, Allan Crowther and Elsie; seated, a family friend, Harriet and Allan; on the ground, Henry Stuart. ELSIE HOMER WILLIAMS COLLECTION

Local dignitaries expressed their esteem for the second Allan Williams when he and his wife Harriet left the Nebo district for Sydney in 1920. ELSIE HOMER WILLIAMS COLLECTION

Allan and Harriet Williams' youngest son, Henry Stuart Homer (always known as Stuart), followed his brother to war early in 1917. He was then approaching twenty-five years of age and was, as Edward had been, unmarried. He gave his occupation as stockman. After training in Australia to join the artillery he embarked for Britain, and then France, where he transferred to the infantry in response to an urgent call for volunteers. In early April 1918, during a day of fierce fighting in the fields near the village of Villers-Bretonneux, he received a gunshot wound to the head. He died two days later and was buried at the British cemetery at Namps-au-Val. He left behind a wallet, photographs, letters, cards, one coin, a notebook, a damaged mirror and a metal chain, which were carefully packed and addressed to his parents at Nebo. On the way home the ship carrying them was sunk by enemy action.

At the end of the war, in recognition of their losses, Allan and Harriet Williams received, for each of their sons, a British War Medal, a Victory Medal, a Memorial Plaque, 'one Memorial Scroll and King's Message' and a copy of the pamphlet *Where Australians Rest*. Allan Williams was disappointed to find that the name on Stuart's plaque read 'Horner' rather than 'Homer' and, although he was warned that it would involve a long wait, asked for a new version to be issued. As the plaque was to be 'a lasting memento', it was important to get such things right.

As was the custom, one son in the family did not enlist and so was spared the fate of his brothers. This was Allan Crowther Williams, born in 1889 and known always by the middle name he had inherited from his paternal grandmother. He married in 1915, took charge of the Homevale property, acquired more land, and maintained his father's enthusiasm for horseracing. By 1920, when Allan senior, now aged eighty, and Harriet, approaching seventy, decided to leave the region where they had spent most of their lives and retired to Sydney, young Crowther took control of the family's extensive pastoral interests.

The family's story of pastoral achievement and wartime sacrifice was surely worth telling. So when Crowther Williams was approached by an editor with a proposal that his name appear in a forthcoming series of books on the history and development of Queensland, he naturally agreed to purchase a subscription and provide the editor with information sufficient to prepare an entry about himself and his family. The entry appeared in the third and final volume, published in 1923. It explained that Allan Crowther Williams was the son of Allan Williams, a well known pastoral landowner now living in Sydney, and the grandson of Allan Williams, who for many years was 'Chief Accountant of the Survey Department' in New South Wales. It then traced the second Allan Williams' progress from Keera to Nebo, showing how his career was 'closely interwoven with the great industry which is the backbone of the land's prosperity'; and it recorded the tragic sacrifice of his two elder sons. Finally it showed how Crowther Williams was continuing the work of his pioneering father and contributing to the welfare and prosperity of the region.

Like Willie Macpherson's annals (prepared in his case for family use), the entry was intended to be the official history of the Williams family; and like the annals, it was interesting as much for what it did *not* say as for what it did. The family's story mentioned the first Allan Williams, but focused on the second, the pastoral pioneer (his being the type of story

that readers would expect to see). Crowther's great-grandfather, William
Macpherson, had no place in the narrative.

But that omission had been decided many years earlier. When the first
Allan Williams, the son of William Macpherson and Countess, had died
in 1896, his ninth son Edward had provided the following information for
his death certificate:

Name and occupation of father Name and maiden name of mother	Where born
(1) William Williams (2) Unknown	Blairgowrie Scotland

Just as Eliza Macpherson in 1816 had been determined that her son's
'moonlight shades' should not be called Macpherson, now the Williams
family expunged the name Macpherson from their own family's origins.
Evidently, official documents, like family histories and monuments, could
be used to disguise the past.

....
EPILOGUE

$\mathcal{E}$ARLY IN 2008, AS THIS BOOK WAS NEARING COMPLETION, Sir William Macpherson recalled that it was 250 years since his great-great-great-grandfather, then a mere Private but later to become Colonel Allan Macpherson, crossed the Atlantic with the Black Watch to help defend Britain's North American possessions. This was the beginning of the family's relationship with the Empire. Henceforth the Colonel's life and the lives of his descendants would be shaped, in different ways, by Britain's imperial ventures.

Sir William, with his ancestors looking over his shoulder, poured himself his customary Manhattan and raised a glass in the Colonel's honour. This was the only celebration of the anniversary. It was, after all, an occasion for private reflection, marking the beginning of what I have called the family's 'private empire', and bearing no special significance for people outside their circle. There were many other 'imperial families', especially among the Scots; and while few are likely to have followed the Macphersons' journey from Scotland to the Americas, India, the West Indies, Australia and back to India again, or experienced a similar range of adventures and misadventures, other families were no doubt equally peripatetic and equally influenced by events and circumstances in the wider world.

What makes the Macphersons singular is the care with which they preserved the record of their lives, thoughts, achievements and disappointments. The Colonel and his descendants left an unbroken story for successive generations within the family to reflect upon, showing implicitly how each generation influenced the next. And for those outside the family they provided, unintentionally, an intimate view of the Empire. Few families reflect more faithfully through their experiences the diversity of the Empire; and few offer more opportunities for reflection on Britain's imperial past.

The Empire disintegrated, but its legacies remained. Among those legacies was the arrival in Britain of tens of thousands of immigrants from former colonies in the West Indies, South Asia and Africa. Their arrival was followed by frequent episodes of racially motivated violence. As a barrister and High Court judge, Sir William Macpherson was familiar with racial conflict; and in retirement he helped reveal how deeply racism was ingrained within British society.

Sir William submitted to the government his report on the death of Stephen Lawrence in February 1999. Its conclusions had been widely anticipated. During the inquiry, a succession of police witnesses had condemned themselves in their own words and unwittingly pointed to catastrophic failures in the system. Stephen's parents, having struggled for justice over the previous six years, were widely admired for their courage and determination. They had buried Stephen in Jamaica. 'I feel that he is at home,' his father told the inquiry, 'and I can be assured that nobody is going to violate his grave.' The murderers, declared as such on the front page of the *Daily Mail*, were still free.

Yet while it was generally assumed that the report would have an impact on the future of race relations in Britain, few observers expected its findings to be so forthright and its recommendations so far-reaching. As well as cataloguing the ineptitude of individual police officers and the failings of the system at large, Sir William and his three colleagues charged the Metropolitan Police with 'institutional racism'. This expression had been used nearly twenty years earlier in a report by Lord Scarman on race riots in the London suburb of Brixton; but now the Macpherson Report defined it more widely as racism deeply embedded within the culture of an institution, and evident in 'processes, attitudes and behaviour, which amount to discrimination through unwitting prejudice, ignorance, thoughtlessness, and racist stereotyping which disadvantage minority people'.

Some welcomed this as a long overdue statement of the obvious. Others denied it absolutely, arguing that it would serve only to undermine police morale. Still others suggested that the report, by labelling the whole force institutionally racist, would absolve individual officers from blame. As two senior police officers (one of them a Deputy Assistant Commissioner of the Metropolitan Police) wrote in 2000, 'In Britain after Stephen Lawrence, every individual and institution has a responsibility to examine their behaviour, perception and prejudices. The defence of unwitting racism is closed'. Implicitly, the report invited the nation to hold up a mirror to itself. Many Britons refused to do so. Those who did were often disturbed by what they saw. This much was certain: after the Macpherson Report, race relations in Britain would never be the same again.

The arguments were still raging when Sir William and Lady Macpherson, fulfilling a long-held ambition, travelled to Australia early in 2000. There they visited 'cousins', attended tourist attractions, and officiated at numerous Clan gatherings. From Brisbane they drove to Sydney, taking a long detour west to Roma, the site of the old Mount Abundance station, then south to Keera, where they met descendants of Donald Munro, who had purchased the property in the late 1850s. Continuing south to Sydney, they visited the legislative chambers where great-great-grandfather William had served as clerk for more than twenty years and Allan had wielded his horsewhip, and called in at the Mitchell Library to see great-grandmother Emma's watercolours, some of which appear in this book. Towards the end of the journey they attended the annual Highland gathering at Bundanoon, in the Southern Highlands of New South Wales, where 20,000 descendants and friends of Scotland, many of them clad in tartan, kept traditions alive with haggis, blood pudding, Highland reels, caber tossing and eighteen pipe bands.

Bill wondered about the Williams family. Probably the last time the two families had been in touch was in 1896, when Willie Macpherson, on leave from India, had visited Sydney to inspect properties (inevitably unprofitable) that his father had purchased on the other side of the Hawkesbury River, north of the city. Yet the story of the 'moonlight shades' remained vivid in his memory, refreshed by occasional re-readings of William's letters home from Berbice.

The Williams family, on the other hand, forgot—or deliberately disremembered—their links with the Macphersons. While kinship with the Macpherson Clan might be something to be proud of, it was hard to admit such a relationship without explaining its origins on the muddy plantations of Guyana. In rural Queensland during the long heyday of White Australia, the less said about such matters, the better.

In any case, the Williams family developed its own strong traditions. Allan Crowther Williams, the only surviving son of the second Allan Williams, remained in the Nebo district, adding to the family's wealth and winning renown as a breeder of cattle and horses, including pure bred Hereford cattle, racehorses and draught horses. At one stage between the wars, the family was grazing 12,000 cattle and 2000 horses on seven properties totalling over 400,000 acres, a much larger area than Allan Macpherson had claimed at Mount Abundance. Crowther and his wife Bessie had six children, the first of whom, Allan Homer Williams, was born six months after his uncle Edward had died at Gallipoli. This Allan Williams, the fourth to bear that name, inherited from his father, as a local newspaper put it, 'that instinctive understanding of even the wildest rogues which told him just how each horse should be handled'.

Allan Homer Williams fathered two children, a daughter Pamela, born in 1945, and a son, the fifth Allan Williams, born in 1949. By this time, any connection with the Macphersons had been almost expunged from the family's collective memory. Almost, but not quite: Pam's aunts had sometimes spoken of a Macpherson connection, and having made her own genealogical inquiries, Pam had long wondered about the family's origins. Bill and Sheila Macpherson's visit to Keera provided the necessary clue. She telephoned Bill in Blairgowrie. 'I think we're related', she began.

In 2005, five years and several long telephone calls later, Pam Webster, formerly Williams, met Bill in Scotland. Bill showed her the portraits of her ancestors, Colonel Allan and William, and documents from William's time in Berbice, including the bill of sale by which he purchased Countess from James Fraser, and the certificate of manumission for Countess and the three children. Together they reflected on chance and connections, and on what it is like to know and not to know about the past.

Pam's brother Allan had never paid much attention to his family's history. Certainly, as the fifth Allan Williams, it was comforting to be part of a 'dynasty'. Now living at Riverside, one of the stations acquired by his great-grandfather, he was proud of his ancestors' long association with the land and the inheritance that had made the family name one of the best known and most respected in Queensland agricultural circles. The family's properties, though, were shrinking. In the 1960s the ground beneath Riverside and for many kilometres around was discovered to be rich in coal. Allan's father signed a lease to a mining company, and in so doing signed away a fortune. By the first decade of the twenty-first century, the station was almost surrounded by open-cut mines, feeding the world's seemingly insatiable demand for coal, and incidentally destroying the silence and darkness of the bush.

In 2007 I visited Allan Williams at Riverside, nearly 2000 kilometres north of my Canberra home. Smiling beneath his broad-brimmed Akubra, he listened, intent and bemused, to a much abbreviated account of his distant origins. He had little to say. He is a man of few words, a trait inherited perhaps from his four eponymous ancestors. Then again, he was probably more concerned with the present than the past, and the relentless challenge to his family's future on the land.

As Eliza Macpherson might have put it two centuries earlier, fate had delivered the Williams family a cruel blow. Chance seems to have been as much a theme in the history of the Williams family as it was in that of the Macphersons and probably, if the records were there to tell us, of any family. Perhaps what makes the story of the Macphersons most remarkable is its familiarity. While members of the family were often swept along by grand events and movements in history, and sometimes contributed to them, the themes that stand out might recur in the story of any family who had some say in their own destiny: ambition and frustration, friendship and betrayal, wisdom and folly, passion and restraint, pride and shame, an attachment to place, an eagerness to conform to the standards of the day, the tensions between parent and child, a sense of adventure, an affection for kin; above all, perhaps, for Colonel Allan and Eliza and their descendants, an unshakeable loyalty to the family and a determination to secure its welfare in the present and future. As with most families, the story of the Macphersons contains elements of comedy and tragedy: but which is one and which the other—who is to say?

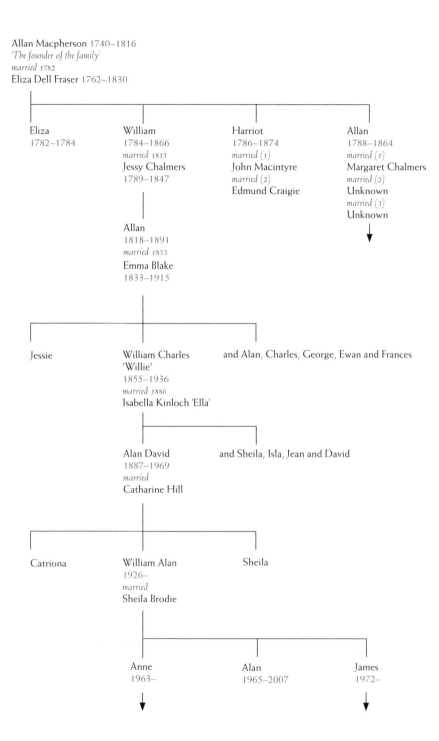

Allan Macpherson 1740–1816
'The founder of the family'
married 1782
Eliza Dell Fraser 1762–1830

Eliza
1782–1784

William
1784–1866
married 1815
Jessy Chalmers
1789–1847

Harriot
1786–1874
married (1)
John Macintyre
married (2)
Edmund Craigie

Allan
1788–1864
married (1)
Margaret Chalmers
married (2)
Unknown
married (3)
Unknown

Allan
1818–1891
married 1853
Emma Blake
1833–1915

Jessie

William Charles
'Willie'
1855–1936
married 1886
Isabella Kinloch 'Ella'

and Alan, Charles, George, Ewan and Frances

Alan David
1887–1969
married
Catharine Hill

and Sheila, Isla, Jean and David

Catriona

William Alan
1926–
married
Sheila Brodie

Sheila

Anne
1963–

Alan
1965–2007

James
1972–

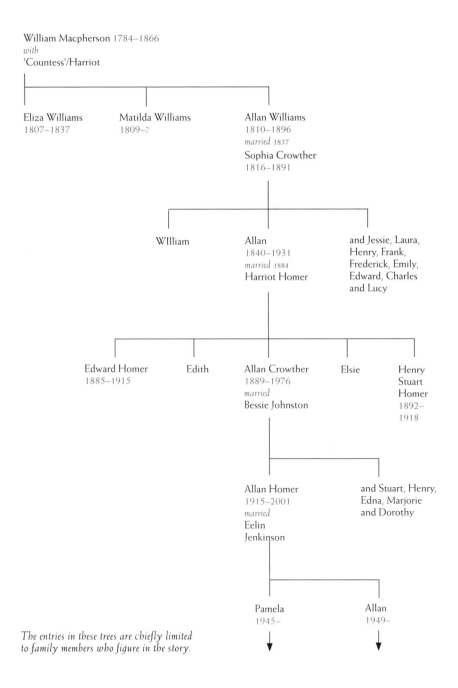

William Macpherson 1784–1866
with
'Countess'/Harriot

Eliza Williams
1807–1837

Matilda Williams
1809–?

Allan Williams
1810–1896
married 1837
Sophia Crowther
1816–1891

WIlliam

Allan
1840–1931
married 1884
Harriot Homer

and Jessie, Laura,
Henry, Frank,
Frederick, Emily,
Edward, Charles
and Lucy

Edward Homer
1885–1915

Edith

Allan Crowther
1889–1976
married
Bessie Johnston

Elsie

Henry
Stuart
Homer
1892–
1918

Allan Homer
1915–2001
married
Eelin
Jenkinson

and Stuart, Henry,
Edna, Marjorie
and Dorothy

Pamela
1945–

Allan
1949–

*The entries in these trees are chiefly limited
to family members who figure in the story.*

A NOTE ON CONVENTIONS

Quotations: Direct quotations in the text have been transcribed exactly from the original documents, except on rare occasions where I have inserted a punctuation mark where one is obviously required. I have not used *sic* to identify misspellings.

Place names: Place names follow common English usage at the appropriate time in the story: hence Calcutta for the modern Kolkata, Oudh for Awadh (now part of Uttar Pradesh), Guiana for Guyana, and so on.

Currency: Rather than attempting to convert specific sums of money—whether pounds, shillings and pence, rupees or guilders—to modern equivalents, I have provided a rough indication of their value during the relevant period in the story.

Measures: Likewise distances and areas are expressed using measures appropriate to place and time. One mile equals about 1.6 kilometres; a square mile about 2.6 square kilometres; and one acre about 0.4 hectares.

A NOTE ON SOURCES

Detailed references for this book, including notes on selected illustrations, are available through the National Library of Australia catalogue: go to http://nla.gov.au/nla.cat-vn4853958 or search the catalogue for 'A private empire'. The E Notes are fully searchable and printable. They are chiefly confined to sources, with occasional elaboration or explanation of points made in the text. The main source throughout the book, as explained in Chapter 1, is the Macpherson family collection, in the possession of Sir William Macpherson of Cluny. These have been surveyed by the National Register of Archives for Scotland (NRAS2614). Without the NRAS Guide my research would have been much more onerous. Many files from the late eighteenth and early nineteenth centuries have been copied by the Centre of South Asian Studies at Cambridge University.

I have also drawn on other private collections, mentioned in the Acknowledgements, and public repositories, especially the British Library, the National Archives of Scotland, the National Library of Scotland, the National Archives (UK) (copies in the National Library of Australia), the State Library of New South Wales and the State Records of New South Wales.

The E Notes include numerous references to secondary works on Scotland, India, the West Indies and Australia. I am also indebted to many writers on broad themes covered in the book, and apologise where I have not acknowledged their works by name.

ACKNOWLEDGEMENTS

I can date the beginnings of this book almost to the hour. In autumn 2003 I visited old friends Bruce Mitchell and Jillian Oppenheimer at their grand colonial homestead near Walcha, high on the New England Tableland in New South Wales. Several years previously they had visited Scotland, researching the history of Keera, the property that Jillian's ancestor, Donald Munro, had acquired after the Macphersons had left there in the late 1850s. Around their fireplace they related, with characteristic enthusiasm, the essence of the story you have read in this book. I saw at once that this was a story worth pursuing. They encouraged me to write to Sir William Macpherson in Scotland. During the next half dozen years they continued to assist me, with detailed comments on each chapter, based on their intimate knowledge of the Scots in Australia. Sadly, Bruce died before I had completed the Epilogue.

If Bruce and Jillian are, chronologically, my first debt, Sir William Macpherson is my largest. He welcomed me to his home in Blairgowrie and gave me complete access to the archive begun in the eighteenth century by his great-great-great-grandfather. He diligently read my draft chapters, correcting points of detail, helping me find information I had missed, commenting on style, but never attempting to influence what I had to say. No historian could hope for more congenial working conditions or a more generous host.

I warmly thank other members of the Macpherson family, especially Sir William's cousin Jean Ann Scott Miller, whose enthusiastic support helped me maintain momentum and whose sharp editorial eye saved me from occasional inaccuracies and solecisms. In France, Martin Blake and Elisabeth Espitalié showed me documents and illustrations relating to Emma Blake, who married Allan Macpherson in 1853, while in Iceland, Alistair Macintyre, descendant of General John Macintyre, offered wry and perceptive comments on every chapter, finding patterns in the story that I had failed to see.

Pam Webster in south-eastern Queensland and Allan Williams in central Queensland have been keen supporters. Pam showed me documents and photographs relating to the Williams family, shared her own knowledge of the family's past, introduced me to her uncle Henry and aunt Elaine Williams at Chinchilla, and accompanied me on a long drive to Allan Macpherson's old pastoral station at Roma.

In Scotland, Malcolm and Kathie Fraser of Reelig kindly allowed me to read relevant material in their family archive, which offered a valuable perspective on Berbice in the early nineteenth century. David Alston of Cromarty shared with me his detailed knowledge of Scots in the West Indies. In England, Canon George Burgon sent me church records relating to 'Uncle Allan' Macpherson in the 1850s. Suzanne Foster, Archivist at Winchester College, located photographs from Willie Macpherson's time there. In New South Wales, Hugh Munro lent me Emma Macpherson's watercolours for copying. Dariel Larkins shared with me her memories of Allan Macpherson's homestead at Bernera, where she lived for many years.

In addition to those I have already mentioned, many friends and colleagues have commented on the draft. Alan Atkinson, Bain Attwood, Eric Richards, Barry Smith and my daughter Lali Foster (who also helped with some research), commented on the whole typescript, at various stages, while my mother, Hazel Foster, no longer able to read, picked up ambiguities in my stumbling oral version. In Canada, Alan G. Macpherson, the Clan Historian, commented meticulously on the draft and explained to me the complexities of clan genealogies. Robin Jeffrey, Barry Higman and Isabel McBryde advised me on specific chapters. Michael McKernan offered astute comments and unwavering support from beginning to end. Ken Inglis, long before this project began, helped me try to see the past as contemporaries might have seen it; and later, in his inimitable way, suggested where one word would serve better than another, or better than my two. I hope readers who know his work see in this book some evidence of his influence.

Others have assisted my research and travels in various ways: John L. Macpherson of Mittagong, Ewen MacPherson of Talla-Shee, Allan Fletcher Macpherson of Belleville, Peter Keegan of Roma, Don and Pat Tite of Mount Abundance Station, Alvin Thompson in Barbados, Winston McGowan in Guyana and Ian Macpherson McCulloch in Canada. Patsy Grigg made my occasional visits to London feel like coming home.

I have drawn extensively on the resources of two outstanding libraries, the Australian National University Library and the National Library of Australia. I thank too the institutions that have allowed me to reproduce material in their collections. Peter Stanley referred me to Murdoch Books, where Diana Hill embraced the project, and the publishing team worked hard to realise my ambitions.

The book is affectionately dedicated to my wife, Mary Varghese, whose support has been essential to the project, in more ways than one.

Stephen Foster
Canberra, May 2010

Published in 2010 by Pier 9, an imprint of Murdoch Books Pty Limited

Murdoch Books Australia
Pier 8/9
23 Hickson Road
Millers Point NSW 2000
Phone: +61 (0) 2 8220 2000
Fax: +61 (0) 2 8220 2558
www.murdochbooks.com.au

Murdoch Books UK Limited
Erico House, 6th Floor
93–99 Upper Richmond Road
Putney, London SW15 2TG
Phone: +44 (0) 20 8785 5995
Fax: +44 (0) 20 8785 5985
www.murdochbooks.co.uk

Publisher: Diana Hill
Project Manager: Emma Hutchinson
Designer: Katy Wall

National Library of Australia Cataloguing-in-Publication entry
Author: Foster, S. G. (Stephen Glynn), 1948-.
Title: A private empire / Stephen Foster.
ISBN: 9781741965056 (pbk.)
Notes: Includes bibliographical references and index.
Subjects: Macpherson family.
            Great Britain–History.
            Great Britain–Colonies—History.
            Scotland–Genealogy.
            Scotland–History.
Dewey Number: 920.00929163

Catalogue entry can be accessed at: http://nla.gov.au/nla.cat-vn4853958

A catalogue record for this book is available from the British Library.
Printed in China by 1010 Printing International Limited.